DAVID BUSCH'S NIKON® V1

GUIDE TO DIGITAL MOVIE MAKING AND STILL PHOTOGRAPHY

David D. Busch

Good Luck w/ your Nikon V1.

Course Technology PTR

A part of Cengage Learning

COURSE TECHNOLOGY
CENGAGE Learning®

Australia, Brazil, Japan, Korea, Mexico, Singapore, Spain, United Kingdom, United States

COURSE TECHNOLOGY
CENGAGE Learning

David Busch's Nikon® V1 Guide to Digital Movie Making and Still Photography
David D. Busch

Publisher and General Manager, Course Technology PTR:
Stacy L. Hiquet

Associate Director of Marketing:
Sarah Panella

Manager of Editorial Services:
Heather Talbot

Senior Marketing Manager:
Mark Hughes

Executive Editor:
Kevin Harreld

Project Editor:
Jenny Davidson

Series Technical Editor:
Michael D. Sullivan

Interior Layout Tech:
Bill Hartman

Cover Designer:
Mike Tanamachi

Indexer:
Katherine Stimson

Proofreader:
Sara Gullion

Library of Congress Control Number: 2012930749

ISBN-13: 978-1-133-59591-5

ISBN-10: 1-133-59591-X

Course Technology, a part of Cengage Learning
20 Channel Center Street
Boston, MA 02210
USA

Cengage Learning is a leading provider of customized learning solutions with office locations around the globe, including Singapore, the United Kingdom, Australia, Mexico, Brazil, and Japan. Locate your local office at: **international.cengage.com/region**.

Cengage Learning products are represented in Canada by Nelson Education, Ltd.

For your lifelong learning solutions, visit **courseptr.com**.

Visit our corporate website at **cengage.com**.

Printed in the United States of America
1 2 3 4 5 6 7 14 13 12

For Cathy

Acknowledgments

Once again thanks to the folks at Course Technology PTR, who have pioneered publishing digital imaging books in full color at a price anyone can afford. Special thanks to executive editor Kevin Harreld, who always gives me the freedom to let my imagination run free with a topic, as well as my veteran production team including project editor Jenny Davidson and technical editor Mike Sullivan. Also thanks to Bill Hartman, layout; Katherine Stimson, indexing; Sara Gullion, proofreading; Mike Tanamachi, cover design; and my agent, Carole Jelen, who has the amazing ability to keep both publishers and authors happy.

Back cover photo by Nancy Balluck: http://www.nancyballuckphotography.com/

About the Author

With more than a 1.5 million books in print, **David D. Busch** is the world's #1 selling digital camera guide author, and the originator of popular series like *David Busch's Pro Secrets, David Busch's Compact Field Guides,* and *David Busch's Quick Snap Guides.* He has written dozens of hugely successful guidebooks for digital camera models, including the all-time #1 bestsellers for many Nikon models, additional user guides for other camera models, as well as many popular books devoted to digital cameras, including *Mastering Digital SLR Photography, Third Edition* and *Digital SLR Pro Secrets.* As a roving photojournalist for more than 20 years, he illustrated his books, magazine articles, and newspaper reports with award-winning images. He's operated his own commercial studio, suffocated in formal dress while shooting weddings-for-hire, and shot sports for a daily newspaper and upstate New York college. His articles and photographs have appeared in *Popular Photography & Imaging, The Rangefinder, The Professional Photographer,* and hundreds of other publications. He's also reviewed dozens of digital cameras for CNet and *Computer Shopper,* and his advice has been featured on NPR's *All Tech Considered.*

When About.com named its top five books on Beginning Digital Photography, debuting at the #1 and #2 slots were Busch's *Digital Photography All-In-One Desk Reference for Dummies* and *Mastering Digital SLR Photography.* During the past year, he's had as many as five of his books listed in the Top 20 of Amazon.com's Digital Photography Bestseller list—simultaneously! Busch's 150-plus other books published since 1983 include bestsellers like *David Busch's Quick Snap Guide to Using Digital SLR Lenses.*

Busch is a member of the Cleveland Photographic Society (www.clevelandphoto.org), which has operated continuously since 1887.

Visit his website at http://www.dslrguides.com./blog

Contents

Chapter 3
Nikon V1 Roadmap 39

PART II
BEYOND THE BASICS

Chapter 4
Shooting Stills and Movies 63

Chapter 5 Understanding Exposure 81

Chapter 6 Advanced Shooting 111

Chapter 7 Movie Making with Your Nikon V1 141

PART III
ADVANCED TOOLS

Chapter 8 The Playback, Shooting, and Setup Menus 173

Chapter 9 Working with Lenses 235

Chapter 10 Making Light Work for You 253

Preface

You don't want good pictures from your new Nikon V1—you demand *outstanding photos.* After all, the V1 is the first advanced interchangeable lens mirrorless camera in the Nikon 1 product line. It boasts 10 megapixels of resolution, blazing-fast automatic focus, and innovative features like Motion Snapshots, Smart Photo Selector (which shoots 20 pictures in a fraction of a second and chooses the best one for you), slow-motion video at 400 and 1200 frames per second, and *full resolution* still photographs at up to 60 frames per second.

But your gateway to pixel proficiency is dragged down by the slim little book included in the box as a manual. You know everything you need to know is in there, somewhere, but you don't know where to start. In addition, the camera manual doesn't offer much information on photography or digital photography. Nor are you interested in spending hours or days studying a comprehensive book on digital camera photography that doesn't necessarily apply directly to your V1.

What you need is a guide that explains the purpose and function of the V1's basic controls, how you should use them, and *why.* Ideally, there should be information about file formats, resolution, aperture/priority exposure, and special autofocus modes, but you'd prefer to read about those topics only after you've had the chance to go out and take a few hundred great pictures with your new camera. Why isn't there a book that summarizes the most important information in its first two or three chapters, with lots of illustrations showing what your results will look like when you use this setting or that?

Now there is such a book. If you want a quick introduction to the V1's focus controls, flash, how to use the focal lengths available with the various interchangeable lenses offered for this camera, or which exposure modes are best, this book is for you. If you can't decide on what basic settings to use with your camera because you can't figure out how changing ISO or white balance or focus defaults will affect your pictures, you need this guide.

Introduction

I love the new Nikon V1! When it was introduced, I purchased all four lenses available for it, plus the SB-N5 flash, and ordered the F-mount adapter that allows using all my Nikon lenses on this camera. With the tiny 10mm f/2.8 pancake lens, it's a perfect walk-around camera for those times when a fast moderate wide angle is all you need. The V1 is still compact with the 10-30mm zoom, and tolerably small when you swap in the 30-110mm lens. If you don't want to change lenses all the time, the 10-100mm zoom is the answer—but it's huge, easily larger than the other three lenses combined. But it makes the most sense if you're shooting movies with the V1, as its long range (the equivalent of 27-270mm), silent voice coil AF motor, and three-speed power zoom is perfect for video with the camera locked down on a tripod.

My assessment, after using the V1 extensively, is that Nikon has been daring in carving out a new niche. It's not simply a killer to compete with other mirrorless cameras. Yes, advanced photographers looking for a small alternative to their Nikon dSLRs will buy these, but these purchasers will be chiefly Nikon fans who want to remain loyal to their favorite vendor.

The true audience for the Nikon 1 cameras are part of a new niche. They are folks who are enthusiastic about photography, but, up until now, have not been enthusiastic about cameras. They want a small camera that's expandable, very easy to use, and with a selection of options. The Nikon 1 cameras provide flexibility and advanced features without the need to fuss as much with settings. Can you benefit from scene modes, with the camera making all the adjustments based on the type of subject you're shooting? The Nikon V1 has scene modes for Portrait, Landscape, and other typical subjects—but doesn't make you decide which scene mode you're shooting. In Still Image mode the camera defaults to Automatic Scene Selection. You can still choose Program, Shutter-priority, Aperture-priority, or Manual exposure modes if you've progressed to that point, but if you want scene modes, you don't have to choose which mode to use.

There's a Smart Photo Selector mode that will take a bunch of pictures for you, and choose the sharpest, best-composed image, plus four alternates. You can shoot HD video or slow-motion movies without bothering to learn the mechanics of how they work. Can't decide whether to shoot a still image or a video clip? The Motion Snapshot mode will give you a still image and a one-second slow-motion movie with each press of the shutter. If you think about the kind of user who might want features like these, you'll find it easier to understand the niche that Nikon is carving out. Best of all, the Nikon 1 cameras still offer the kind of control advanced photographers want—semi-automatic and manual exposure, manual focus, lens selection—so these models can serve the more traditional enthusiast niche as well as this new one. That's why I think the Nikon 1 cameras will be successful, even though they're not the cameras that Nikon users had expected. They're something better.

But once you've confirmed that you made a wise purchase decision, the question comes up, *how do I use this thing?* All those cool features can be mind numbing to learn, if all you have as a guide is the manual furnished with the camera. Help is on the way. I sincerely believe that this book is your best bet for learning how to use your new camera, and for learning how to use it well.

If you're a Nikon V1 owner who's looking to learn more about how to use this great camera, you've probably already explored your options. There are DVDs and online tutorials—but who can learn how to use a camera by sitting in front of a television or computer screen? Do you want to watch a movie or click on HTML links, or do you want to go out and take photos with your camera? Videos are fun, but not the best answer.

There's always the manual furnished with the V1. It is compact and filled with information, but there's really very little about *why* you should use particular settings or features, and its organization may make it difficult to find what you need. Multiple cross-references may send you flipping back and forth between two or three sections of the book to find what you want to know. The basic manual is also hobbled by black-and-white line drawings and tiny monochrome pictures that aren't very good examples of what you can do.

Also available are third-party guides to the V1, like this one. I haven't been happy with some of these guidebooks, which is why I wrote this one. The existing books range from skimpy and illustrated by black-and-white photos to lushly illustrated in full color but too generic to do much good. Photography instruction is useful, but it needs to be related directly to the Nikon V1 as much as possible.

I've tried to make *David Busch's Nikon V1 Guide to Digital Movie Making and Still Photography* different from your other V1 learn-up options. The roadmap sections use larger, color pictures to show you where all the buttons and dials are, and the explanations of what they do are longer and more comprehensive. I've tried to avoid overly general advice, including the two-page checklists on how to take a "sports picture" or a "portrait picture" or a "travel picture." Instead, you'll find tips and techniques for using all the features of your Nikon V1 to take *any kind of picture* you want. If you want to know where you should stand to take a picture of a quarterback dropping back to unleash a pass, there are plenty of books that will tell you that. This one concentrates on teaching you how to select the best autofocus mode, shutter speed, f/stop, or flash capability to take a great picture under any conditions.

This book is not a lame rewriting of the manual that came with the camera. Some folks spend five minutes with a book like this one, spot some information that also appears in the original manual, and decide "Rehash!" without really understanding the differences. Yes, you'll find information here that is also in the owner's manual, such as the parameters you can enter when changing your V1's operation in the various menus. Basic descriptions—before I dig in and start providing in-depth tips and information—may also be vaguely similar. There are only so many ways you can say, for example, "Hold the shutter release down halfway to lock in exposure." But if you need advice on when and how to use the most important functions, you'll find the information here.

David Busch's Nikon V1 Guide to Digital Movie Making and Still Photography is aimed at both Nikon and digital camera veterans as well as newcomers to digital photography and digital cameras. Both groups can be overwhelmed by the options the V1 offers, while underwhelmed by the explanations they receive in their user's manual. The manuals are great if you already know what you don't know, and you can find an answer somewhere in a booklet arranged by menu listings and written by a camera vendor employee who last threw together instructions on how to operate a camcorder.

Why the Nikon V1 Needs Special Coverage

There are many general digital photography books on the market. Why do I concentrate on books about specific digital cameras like the V1 ? One reason is that I feel digital photographers deserve books tailored to their equipment.

When I started writing some of the first digital photography books (ever) in 1995, digital cameras cost as much as $30,000 and few people other than certain professionals could justify the most advanced models. Most of my readers a dozen years ago were stuck using the point-and-shoot low-resolution digital cameras of the time—even if they were advanced photographers. I took tons of digital pictures with an early digital camera with 1024 × 768 (less than 1 megapixel!) resolution, and which cost $850.

Today, that same $850 buys you a sophisticated model like the Nikon V1. The digital camera is no longer the exclusive bailiwick of the professional, the wealthy, or the serious photography addict willing to scrimp and save to acquire a dream camera. Digital cameras have become the favored camera for anyone who wants to go beyond point-and-shoot capabilities. And Nikon cameras have enjoyed a dominating position among digital cameras because of Nikon's innovation in introducing affordable cameras with interesting features and outstanding performance (particularly in the area of high ISO image quality).

You've selected your camera of choice, and you belong in the Nikon camp if you fall into one of the following categories:

- Individuals who want to get better pictures, or perhaps transform their growing interest in photography into a full-fledged hobby or artistic outlet with a V1 and advanced techniques.
- Those who want to produce more professional-looking images for their personal or business website, and feel that the V1 will give them more control and capabilities than the typical fully automatic point-and-shoot camera.
- Small business owners with more advanced graphics capabilities who want to use the V1 to document or promote their business.
- Corporate workers who may or may not have photographic skills in their job descriptions, but who work regularly with graphics and need to learn how to use digital images taken with a Nikon V1 for reports, presentations, or other applications.
- Professional webmasters with strong skills in programming (including Java, JavaScript, HTML, Perl, etc.) but little background in photography, but who realize that the V1 can be used for sophisticated photography.
- Graphic artists and others who already may be adept in image editing with Photoshop or another program, and who may already be using a film camera (Nikon or otherwise), but who need to learn more about digital photography and the special capabilities of the V1 digital camera.

Who Am I?

After spending years as the world's most successful unknown author, I've become slightly less obscure in the past few years, thanks to a horde of camera guidebooks and other photographically oriented tomes. You may have seen my photography articles in *Popular Photography & Imaging* magazine. I've also written about 2,000 articles for magazines like *Petersen's PhotoGraphic* (which is now defunct through no fault of my own), plus *The Rangefinder*, *Professional Photographer*, and dozens of other photographic publications. You might have caught my advice on National Public Radio's *All Tech Considered*. But, first, and foremost, I'm a photojournalist and made my living in the field until I began devoting most of my time to writing books.

Although I love writing, I'm happiest when I'm out taking pictures, which is why I invariably spend several days each week photographing landscapes, people, close-up subjects, and other things. I spend a month or two each year traveling to events, such as Native American "powwows," Civil War re-enactments, county fairs, ballets, and sports (baseball, basketball, football, and soccer are favorites). I actually wrote several chapters of this very book—including these words—in a room in Salamanca, Spain, where I spent 14 days on a solo visit, armed with the V1 you see on the cover (and a "backup" Nikon D7000), shooting photographs of the people, landscapes, and monuments that I've grown to love. And in the months prior to starting on this book, I spent time in Puerto Rico's Old San Juan, and in Arizona, catching up on baseball Spring Training and natural wonders like the Sedona Red Rocks and the Grand Canyon. I can offer you my personal advice on how to take photos under a variety of conditions because I've had to meet those challenges myself on an ongoing basis.

Like all my digital photography books, this one was written by someone with an incurable photography bug. I bought my first Nikon camera back in the 1960s, and I've used a variety of newer models since then. I've worked as a sports photographer for an Ohio newspaper and for an upstate New York college. I've operated my own commercial studio and photo lab, cranking out product shots on demand and then printing a few hundred glossy 8 × 10s on a tight deadline for a press kit. I've served as a photo-posing instructor for a modeling agency. People have actually paid me to shoot their weddings and immortalize them with portraits. I even prepared press kits and articles on photography as a PR consultant for a large Rochester, N.Y., company, which shall remain nameless. My trials and travails with imaging and computer technology have made their way into print in book form an alarming number of times.

Like you, I love photography for its own merits, and I view technology as just another tool to help me get the images I see in my mind's eye. But, also like you, I had to master this technology before I could apply it to my work. This book is the result of what I've learned, and I hope it will help you master your V1 digital camera, too.

As I write this, I'm currently in the throes of upgrading my website and blog, which you can find at www.dslrguides.com/blog, adding tutorials and information about my other books. I'll be adding more tips and recommendations (including a list of equipment and accessories that I can't live without) in the next few months. I hope you'll stop by for a visit. You can send me e-mail from one page at that website, and there's another listing any typos that you sharp-eyed readers may report. Your input is the best tool I have.

Part I

Getting Started with Your Nikon V1

This first part of the book, consisting of just three short chapters, is designed to familiarize you with the basics of your Nikon V1 as quickly as possible, even though I have no doubt that you've already been out shooting a few hundred (or thousand) photographs with your pride and joy.

After all, inserting a memory card, mounting a lens, stuffing a charged battery into the base, and removing the lens cap to fire off a shot or two isn't rocket science. Even the rawest neophyte can rotate the mode dial (located at middle right of the camera back panel) to the Still Image Mode green camera icon. By default, the V1 will use Automatic Scene Selection, and will choose an appropriate exposure mode. Point the V1 at something interesting and press the shutter release. Presto! A pretty good picture will pop up on the color LCD on the back of the camera, or, if you're holding the camera to your eye, on the electronic display inside the viewfinder window. It's easy!

But in digital photography, there is such a thing as *too* easy. If you bought a V1 and this book, you certainly had no intention of using the camera as a point-and-shoot snapshooter. After all, although it can function as a snapshot camera, the V1 is also suitable for more advanced photographic pursuits, with an extensive array of customization possibilities. As such, you don't want the camera's operation to be brainless; you want *access* to the advanced features to be easy.

You get that easy access with the Nikon V1. However, you'll still need to take the time to learn how to use these features, and I'm going to provide everything you need to know in these first three chapters to begin shooting:

- **Chapter 1:** This is a "Meet Your V1" introduction, where you'll find information about what came in the box with your camera and, more importantly, what *didn't* come with the camera that you seriously should consider adding to your arsenal. I'll also cover some things you might not have known about charging the V1's battery, choosing a memory card, setting the time and date, and a few other preflight tasks. This is basic stuff, and if you're a veteran (point-and-shoot, dSLR, super-zoom, or other type of digital camera), you can skim over it quickly. A lot of this first chapter is intended for newbies, and even if you personally don't find it essential, you'll probably agree that there was some point during your photographic development (so to speak) that you wished this information was spelled out for you. There's no extra charge!
- **Chapter 2:** Here, you'll find a Quick Start aimed at those who may not be old hands with cameras having this level of sophistication. The V1 has some interesting new features, including one of the most advanced and speedy autofocus systems ever seen in a mirrorless camera body. But even with all the goodies to play with and learning curve still to climb, you'll find that Chapter 2 will get you shooting quickly with a minimum of fuss.

- **Chapter 3:** This is a Streetsmart Roadmap to the Nikon V1. Confused by the tiny little diagrams and multiple cross-references for each and every control that send you scurrying around looking for information you know is buried somewhere in the small and inadequate manual stuffed in the box? This chapter uses multiple large full-color pictures that show every dial, knob, and button, and explains the operation of each in clear, easy-to-understand language. I'll give you the basics up front, and, even if I have to send you deeper into the book for a full discussion of a complex topic, you'll have what you need to use a control right away.

Once you've finished (or skimmed through) these three chapters, you'll be ready for Part II, which explains how to use the most important basic features, such as the V1's exposure controls, nifty autofocus system, and the related tools that put advanced still shooting and movie making tools at your fingertips. Then, you can visit Part III, the advanced tools section, which explains all the dozens of setup options that can be used to modify the capabilities you've learned to use so far, how to choose and use lenses, and introduces the Nikon V1's add-on flash capabilities. I'll wind up this book with Part IV, which covers image software, printing, and transfer options and includes some troubleshooting that may help you when good cameras (or memory cards) go bad.

1

Nikon V1: Thinking Outside of the Box

Whether you subscribe to the "my camera is just a tool" theory, or belong to the "an exquisite camera adds new capabilities to my shooting arsenal" camp, picking up a new Nikon V1 is a special experience. Those who simply wield tools will find this camera as comforting as an old friend, a solid piece of fine machinery ready and able to do their bidding as part of the creative process.

Other photographers see the compact size, selection of interchangeable lenses, decent low-light capabilities (up to ISO 3200, plus the equivalent of ISO 6400 at the Hi 1 setting), and full HD movie-making capabilities, and gain a sense of empowerment. For those coming from less versatile models, *here* is a camera with fewer limitations and more capabilities for exercising renewed creative vision. In either case, using less mawkish terms, the V1 is one of the coolest cameras Nikon has ever offered. Whether you're upgrading from another brand, from another Nikon compact model (like the Nikon P7100), or (O brave one!) your V1 is your first digital camera and/or interchangeable lens camera, welcome to the club.

But, now that you've unwrapped and recharged the beast, mounted a lens, and fueled it with a memory card, what do you *do* with it? That's where this chapter—and the chapters that follow—should come in handy. Like many of you, I am a Nikon user of long standing. And, like other members of our club, I had to learn at least some aspects of my newest camera for the very first time at some point. Experienced shooter, or Nikon newbie, you bought this book because you wanted to get the most from a very powerful tool, and I'm here to help.

There's a lot to learn, but you don't have to master every detail all at once. Some of the other camera guides I've seen winnow this information down to about one-third as many pages. Indeed, I find it odd that those guidebooks use the same basic template for the advanced cameras as for a resolutely amateur-level point-and-shoot model. A camera like the V1 has a lot more depth than that, and deserves the in-depth coverage you'll find here.

Whether you've already taken a dozen or twelve hundred photos with your new camera, now that you've got that initial creative burst out of your system, you'll want to take a more considered approach to operating the camera. This chapter and the next are designed to get your camera fired up and ready for shooting as quickly as possible. After all, the V1 is not strictly a point-and-shoot camera, even though it does boast easy-to-use Automatic Scene Selection mode and other automated options.

So I'm going to provide a basic pre-flight checklist that you need to complete before you really spread your wings and take off. You won't find a lot of detail in these first two chapters. Indeed, I'm going to tell you just what you absolutely *must* understand, accompanied by some interesting tidbits that will help you become acclimated to your V1. I'll go into more depth and even repeat some of what I explain here in later chapters, so you don't have to memorize everything you see. Just relax, follow a few easy steps, and then go out and begin taking your best shots—ever.

Even if you're a long-time shooter, I hope you won't be tempted to skip this chapter or the next one. I realize that you probably didn't purchase this book the same day you bought your camera and that, even if you did, the urge to go out and take a few hundred—or thousand—photos with your new camera is enticing. As valuable as a book like this one is, nobody can suppress their excitement long enough to read the instructions before initiating play with a new toy.

No matter how extensive your experience level is, you don't need to fret about wading through a manual to find out what you must know to take those first few tentative snaps. I'm going to help you hit the ground running with this chapter, which will help you set up your camera and begin shooting in minutes. Because I realize that some of you may already have experience with cameras that have some features similar to those found in the V1, each of the major sections in this chapter will begin with a brief description of what is covered in that section, so you can easily jump ahead to the next if you are in a hurry to get started.

First Things First

> This section helps get you oriented with all the things that come in the box with your Nikon V1, including what they do. I'll also describe some optional equipment you might want to have. If you want to get started immediately, skim through this section and jump ahead to "Initial Setup" later in the chapter.

The Nikon V1 comes in an impressive white and gold box filled with stuff, including connecting cords, booklets, a CD, and lots of paperwork. The most important components are the camera and lens (if you purchased your V1 with a lens), battery, battery charger, and, if you're the nervous type, the neck strap. You'll also need a memory card or two, as one is not included. If you purchased your V1 from a camera shop, as I did, the store personnel probably attached the neck strap for you, ran through some basic operational advice that you've already forgotten, tried to sell you a memory card, and then, after they'd given you all the help you could absorb, sent you on your way with a handshake.

Perhaps you purchased your V1 from one of those mass merchandisers that also sell washing machines and vacuum cleaners. In that case, you might have been sent on your way with only the handshake, or, maybe, not even that if you resisted the efforts to sell you an extended warranty. You save a few bucks at the big box stores, but you don't get the personal service a professional photo retailer provides. It's your choice. There's a third alternative, of course. You might have purchased your camera from a mail order or Internet source, and your V1 arrived in a big brown (or purple/red) truck. Your only interaction when you took possession of your camera was to scrawl your signature on an electronic clipboard.

In all three cases, the first thing to do is to carefully unpack the camera and double-check the contents with the checklist on one end of the box, helpfully designated under a "This package includes" listing. While this level of setup detail may seem as superfluous as the instructions on a bottle of shampoo, checking the contents *first* is always a good idea. No matter who sells a camera, it's common to open boxes, use a particular camera for a demonstration, and then repack the box without replacing all the pieces and parts afterwards. Someone might actually have helpfully checked out your camera on your behalf—and then mispacked the box. It's better to know *now* that something is missing so you can seek redress immediately, rather than discover two months from now that the video cable you thought you'd never use (but now *must* have) was never in the box. I once purchased a brand new Nikon camera kit that was supposed to include a second focusing screen; it wasn't in the box, but because I discovered the deficiency right away, the dealer ordered a replacement for me post haste.

At a minimum, the box should have the following:

- **Nikon V1 digital camera.** It almost goes without saying that you should check out the camera immediately, making sure the back-panel LCD isn't scratched or cracked, the memory and battery doors open properly, and, when a charged battery is inserted and lens mounted, the camera powers up and reports for duty. Out-of-the-box defects like these are rare, but they can happen. It's probably more common that your dealer played with the camera or, perhaps, it was a customer return. That's why it's best to buy your V1 from a retailer you trust to supply a factory-fresh camera.

- **Rechargeable Li-ion battery EN-EL15.** You'll need to charge this 7.0V, 1900mAh (milliampere hour) battery before use, and then navigate immediately to the Setup menu's Battery Info entry to make sure the battery accepted the juice and is showing a 100% charge. You'll want a second EN-EL15 battery as a spare (trust me), so buy one as soon as possible. This is the exact same battery found in some other Nikon cameras, including the V1's big brother dSLR, the D7000. It includes a terminal cover to protect the electrical contacts on the battery (and prevent short circuits).
- **Quick charger MH-25.** This charger comes with a power cable to plug the charger directly into a wall outlet.
- **EG-CP14 audio/video cable.** Use this supplied cable to connect your V1 to a standard definition (analog) television through the set's yellow RCA video jack when you want to view the camera's output on a larger screen. Although the V1 can be connected to a high-definition television, you'll need to buy a high-definition multimedia interface (HDMI) cable to do that. No HDMI cable is included with the camera.
- **USB cable UC-E6.** You can use this cable to transfer photos from the camera to your computer, although I don't recommend that because direct transfer uses a lot of battery power.
- **AN-N1000 neck strap.** Nikon provides you with a neck strap emblazoned with your camera model. It's not very adjustable, and, while useful for showing off to your friends exactly which nifty new camera you bought, the Nikon strap also can serve to alert observant unsavory types that you're sporting a higher-end model that's worthy of their attention. I never attach the Nikon strap to my cameras (although once I put a D3x strap on a Nikon D40 as a jest), and instead opt for a more serviceable strap from Op-Tech (www.optechusa.com) or, best of all, an UPstrap (www.upstrap-pro.com). An UPstrap is shown in Figure 1.1, with its patented non-slip pad that keeps your V1 on your shoulder, and not crashing to the ground. If you order one of these, tell inventor-photographer Al Stegmeyer that I sent you.
- **BF-N1000 body cap.** The body cap keeps dust from infiltrating your camera when a lens is not mounted. Always carry a body cap (and rear lens cap) in your camera bag for those times when you need to have the camera bare of optics for more than a minute or two. (That usually happens when repacking a bag efficiently for transport, or when you are carrying an extra body or two for backup.) The body cap/lens cap nest together for compact storage.
- **BS-N1000 accessory shoe cover.** This little piece of plastic protects the electrical contacts of the accessory shoe on top of the V1. You can remove it when mounting an electronic flash, Nikon GP-N100 GPS device, or other accessory. Find a safe

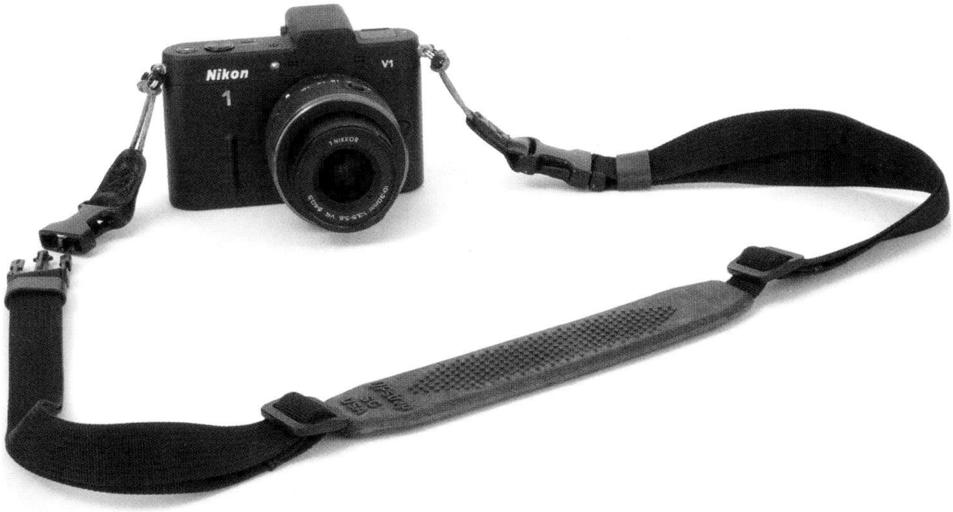

Figure 1.1 Third-party neck straps like this UPstrap model are often preferable to the Nikon-supplied strap.

place to keep it between uses, or purchase replacements for this easily mislaid item, as the accessory connector of the V1 is a bit more exposed and vulnerable than the typical hot shoe on other cameras.

- **User's manuals.** Even if you have this book, you'll probably want to check the user's guide that Nikon provides, if only to verify the actual nomenclature for some obscure accessory, or to double-check an error code. Google "Nikon V1 manual PDF" to find a downloadable, non-printable version that you can store on your laptop, a CD-ROM, or other media in case you want to access this reference when the paper version isn't handy. If you have an old memory card that's too small to be usable on a modern mirrorless camera (I still have some 128MB and 256MB cards), you can store the PDF on that. But an even better choice is to put the manual on a low-capacity USB "thumb" drive, which you can buy for less than $10. You'll then be able to access the reference anywhere you are, because you can always find someone with a computer that has a USB port and Adobe Acrobat Reader available. You might not be lucky enough to locate a computer with a memory reader.
- **Quick Start guide.** This little booklet tucked away in the camera's paperwork offers a reasonable summary of the Nikon V1's basic commands and settings, and can be stowed in your camera bag.
- **Software CD-ROM.** Here you'll find the Nikon ViewNX 2 software, a useful image management program, and the Short Movie Maker utility. I'll cover a variety of other software offerings later in Chapter 12 of this book.
- **Warranty and registration card.** Don't lose these! You can register your Nikon V1 by mail or online (in the USA, the URL is www.nikonusa.com/register), and you may need the information in this paperwork (plus the purchase receipt/invoice from your retailer) should you require Nikon service support.

Don't bother rooting around in the box for anything beyond what I've listed previously. There are a few things Nikon classifies as optional accessories, even though you (and I) might consider some of them essential. Here's a list of what you *don't* get in the box, but might want to think about as an impending purchase. I'll list them roughly in the order of importance:

- **Secure Digital card.** First-time digital camera buyers are sometimes shocked that their new tool doesn't come with a memory card. Why should it? The manufacturer doesn't have the slightest idea of what capacity or speed card you prefer, so why should they pack one in the box and charge you for it? That's especially true for the Nikon V1, which is likely to be purchased by avid photographers who have quite definite ideas about their ideal memory card. Perhaps you want to use tiny 4GB cards—and lots of them. I've met many paranoid wedding photographers who like to work with a horde of smaller cards (and then watch over them *very* protectively), on the theory that they are reducing their chances of losing a significant chunk of the event or reception at one time (of course, that's why you hire a second shooter as backup). Others, especially sports photographers, instead prefer a 16GB or 32GB card with room to spare. If you are shooting fast action, movies at full HD resolution and 60fps, or transfer lots of photos to your computer with a speedy card reader, you might opt for the speediest possible memory card. Buy one (or two, or three) of your own and have your flash memory ready when you unpack your V1.
- **Extra EN-EL15 battery.** I mentioned the need for an extra battery earlier, and I'll mention it here, again. Even though you might get 500 or more shots from a single battery, it's easy to exceed that figure in a few hours of shooting sports. Batteries can unexpectedly fail, too, or simply lose their charge from sitting around unused for a week or two. Buy an extra (I own four, in total), keep it charged, and free your mind from worry. This is the same battery used in cameras like the Nikon D7000, so if you own another Nikon that uses the same battery, you'll have a spare. Broad use of this unit also means you'll find a ready market for this battery should you later upgrade to a camera using a different power source.
- **Add-on speedlight.** Because the V1 has no built-in flash, you'll probably want to purchase the optional SB-N5 flash, a tiny unit that is a bit anemic, but which serves well as a fill flash indoors or in daylight.
- **ML-L3 infrared remote.** The V1 has an infrared sensor on the front and another on the rear that can receive signals from this optional remote control. So, you don't have to be located in front of the camera to use it, which is not the case with cameras that have only a front-facing IR receiver.
- **Nikon GP-N100 global positioning system (GPS) device.** This accessory attaches to the accessory shoe on top of the V1 and captures latitude, longitude, and altitude information, which is imprinted in a special data area of your image

files. The "geotagging" data can be plotted on a map in Nikon ViewNX or other software programs. I'll explain more about this feature in Chapter 11.

- **CB-N1000-series case.** Nikon offers leather "never-ready" cases in both black and white leather for those who feel their camera needs some extra protection at the cost of availability for grab shots. They consist of a camera sling that attaches to the V1's tripod socket, and a fold-over snap-off cover. The pros are that such a case does protect your camera from bumps, scratches, and the weather, and may be a good choice if you want to carry your V1 around with you everywhere, don't want to use a traditional shoulder bag, own only a single lens that happens to fit inside the case, and are spending most of your time doing something other than taking photos. However, if you're constantly bringing your camera to your eye to shoot something, and want to be able to swap lenses quickly, you'll find the V1 works quite well "naked" with only a sturdy neck strap, such as an UPstrap, to protect it.
- **EP-5b power connect/EH-5b AC adapter.** These optional components allow you to operate the V1 without a battery inserted. You might want to use this power source when shooting movies or stills for lengthy periods of time, longer than battery power is likely to last.

Initial Setup

This section helps you familiarize yourself with the three important controls most used to make adjustments: the multi selector and several other buttons. You'll also find information on charging the battery, setting the clock, mounting a lens, and making diopter vision adjustments. If you're comfortable with all these things, skim through and skip ahead to "Changing Default Settings" in the next section.

Once you've unpacked and inspected your camera, the initial setup of your Nikon V1 is fast and easy. Basically, you just need to charge the battery, attach a lens, and insert a memory card. I'll address each of these steps separately, but if you already are confident you can manage these setup tasks without further instructions, feel free to skip this section entirely. While many buyers of a V1 tend to be experienced photographers, I realize that some readers are ambitious, if inexperienced, and should, at the minimum, skim the contents of the next section, because I'm going to list a few options that you might not be aware of.

Mastering the Multi Selector

I'll be saving descriptions of most of the controls used with the Nikon V1 until Chapter 2, which provides a complete "roadmap" of the camera's buttons and dials and switches. However, you may need to perform a few tasks during this initial setup process, and most of them will require the MENU button and the multi selector pad. The MENU button is easy to find: it's located to the lower right of the LCD. It requires almost no explanation; when you want to access a menu, press it. To exit most menus, press it again.

The multi selector pad may remind you of the similar control found on many point-and-shoot cameras, and other digital SLRs. It consists of a thumbpad-sized button with labels at the North, South, East, and West positions, plus a button in the center. It can also be pushed in diagonal directions to give you Northeast, Southeast, Southwest, and Northwest orientations, and rotated to cycle among menu options. (See Figure 1.2.)

With the V1, the multi selector is used extensively for navigation—for example, to navigate among menus on the LCD or to choose one of the focus points, to advance or reverse display of a series of images during picture review. The center button is used to select a highlighted item from a menu. So, from time to time in this chapter (and throughout this book) I'll be referring to the multi selector and its left/right/up/down buttons, and center button.

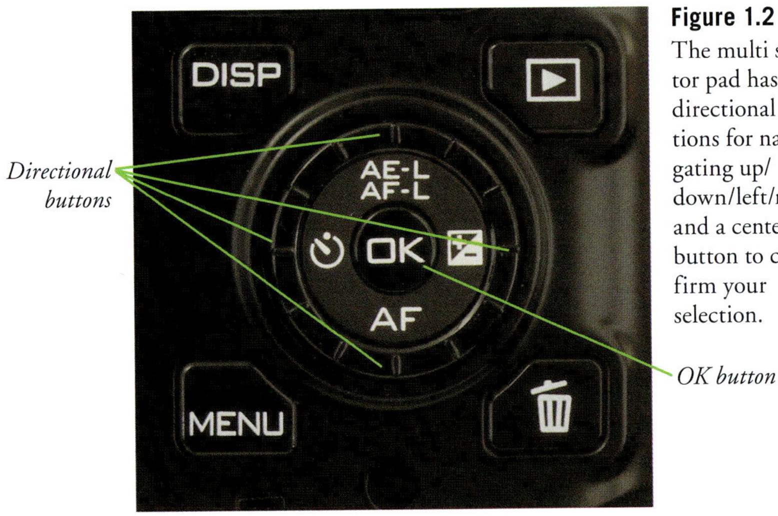

Figure 1.2
The multi selector pad has four directional positions for navigating up/down/left/right, and a center button to confirm your selection.

Each of those left/right/up/down positions also has secondary functions when you're not using the automatic Scene selection mode, which I'll detail in Chapters 2 and 3. They include exposure/focus lock (up button), focus modes (down button), exposure compensation (right button), and self-timer function (left button).

Setting the Clock

It's likely that your Nikon V1's internal clock hasn't been set to your local time, so you may need to do that first. You'll find complete instructions for setting the four options for the date/time (time zone, actual date and time, the date format, and whether you want the V1 to conform to Daylight Savings Time) in Chapter 8. However, if you think you can handle this step without instruction, press the MENU button, use the multi selector (that thumb-friendly button I just described, located to the immediate right of the back panel LCD) to scroll down to the Setup menu (represented by a yellow wrench icon), press the multi selector button to the right, and scroll down to Time Zone and Date choice, and press right again. The options will appear on the screen that appears next. Keep in mind that you'll need to reset your camera's internal clock from time to time, as it is not 100-percent accurate.

The first time you use your V1, you may be asked to choose a language. Use the up/down buttons on the multi selector pad to select a language and press the OK button to confirm.

Battery Included

Your Nikon V1 is a sophisticated hunk of machinery and electronics, but it needs a charged battery to function, so rejuvenating the EN-EL15 lithium-ion battery pack furnished with the camera should be your first step. A fully charged power source should be good for approximately 400 shots (350 if using the flash), based on standard tests defined by the Camera & Imaging Products Association (CIPA) document DC-002. You'll want to keep track of how many pictures *you* are able to take in your own typical circumstances, and use that figure as a guideline, instead.

All rechargeable batteries undergo some degree of self-discharge just sitting idle in the camera or in the original packaging. Lithium-ion power packs of this type typically lose a few percent of their charge every few days, even when the camera isn't turned on. Li-ion cells lose their power through a chemical reaction that continues when the camera is switched off. So, it's very likely that the battery purchased with your camera is at least partially pooped out, so you'll want to revive it before going out for some serious shooting.

A BATTERY AND A SPARE

I always recommend purchasing Nikon brand batteries (for about $50) over less expensive third-party packs, even though the $30 substitute batteries may offer more capacity at a lower price (some may even top the 1,900 mAh offered by the Nikon battery). My reasoning is that it doesn't make sense to save $20 on a component for a $900 camera, especially since batteries have been known to fail in potentially harmful ways. You need only look as far as Nikon's own recall of its earlier EN-EL3 batteries, which forced the company to ship out thousands of free replacement cells. You're unlikely to get the same support from a third-party battery supplier that sells under a half-dozen or more different product labels and brands, and may not even have an easy way to get the word out that a recall has been issued.

If your pictures are important to you, always have at least one spare battery available, and make sure it is an authentic Nikon product.

Charging the Battery

When the battery is inserted into the MH-25 charger properly (it's impossible to insert it incorrectly), a Charge light begins flashing, and remains flashing until the status lamp glows steadily indicating that charging is finished, in about 2.5 hours. You can use the supplied connector cable (at left in Figure 1.3) or attach a handy optional plug adapter that allows connecting the charger directly to a wall outlet (as shown at right in Figure 1.3). When the battery is charged, flip the lever on the bottom of the camera and slide the battery in, as shown in Figure 1.4. Check the Setup menu's Battery Info entry as I recommended earlier to make sure the battery is fully charged. If not, try putting it in the charger again. One of three things may be the culprit: a.) the actual charging cycle sometimes takes longer than you (or the charger) expected; b.) the battery is new and needs to be "seasoned" for a few charging cycles, after which it will accept a full charge and deliver more shots; c.) you've got a defective battery. The last

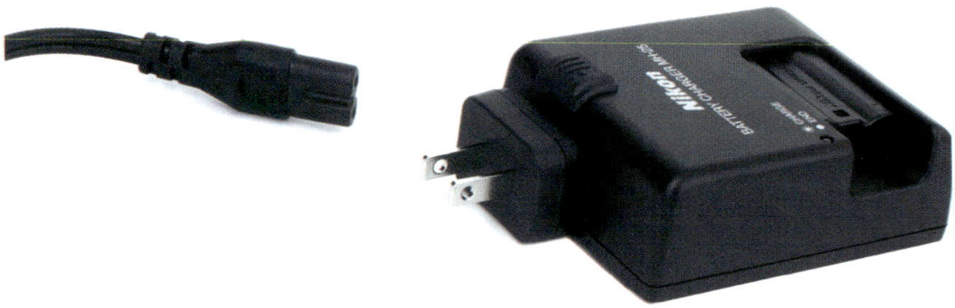

Figure 1.3
Charge the battery before use.

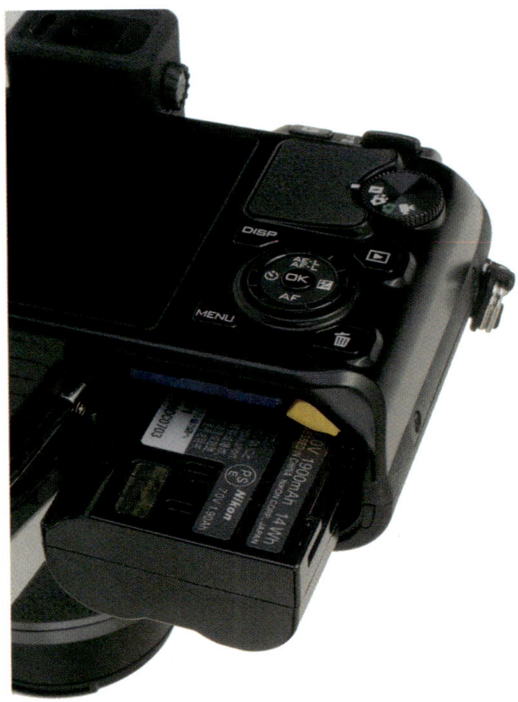

Figure 1.4
Insert the battery in the camera; it only fits one way.

is fairly rare, but before you start counting on getting a particular number of exposures from a battery, it's best to make sure it's fully charged, seasoned, and ready to deliver.

Final Steps

Your Nikon V1 is almost ready to fire up and shoot. You'll need to select and mount a lens, adjust the viewfinder for your vision, and insert a memory card. Each of these steps is easy, and if you've used any Nikon before, you already know exactly what to do. I'm going to provide a little extra detail for those of you who are new to the Nikon or SLR worlds.

Mounting the Lens

As you'll see, my recommended lens mounting procedure emphasizes protecting your equipment from accidental damage and minimizing the intrusion of dust. If your V1 has no lens attached, select the lens you want to use and loosen (but do not remove) the rear lens cap. I generally place the lens I am planning to mount vertically in a slot in my camera bag, where it's protected from mishaps, but ready to pick up quickly. By loosening the rear lens cap, you'll be able to lift it off the back of the lens at the last instant, so the rear element of the lens is covered until then.

After that, remove the body cap by rotating the cap towards the release button. You should always mount the body cap when there is no lens on the camera, because it helps keep dust out of the interior of the camera, where it can settle in the interior box, and potentially find its way onto the exposed sensor. (While the V1's sensor cleaning mechanism works fine, the less dust it has to contend with, the better.) The body cap also protects the vulnerable sensor from damage caused by intruding objects (including your fingers, if you're not cautious).

Once the body cap has been removed, remove the rear lens cap from the lens, set it aside, and then mount the lens on the camera by matching the alignment indicator on the lens barrel with the white dimple at the top of the lens mounting flange on the body. (See Figure 1.5.) Rotate the lens toward the shutter release until it seats securely.

If the lens hood is bayoneted on the lens in the reversed position, which may be the case for the N1 10-100mm and 30-110 Nikkor zooms (this makes the lens/hood combination more compact for transport), twist it off and remount with the front edge facing outward. (See Figure 1.6.) A lens hood protects the front of the lens from accidental bumps, and reduces flare caused by extraneous light arriving at the front element of the lens from outside the picture area.

Some lenses (specifically the 10-30mm and 30-110 zooms initially offered when the V1 was introduced; others may be offered after this book is published) can retract into themselves. When you power up the camera, you'll receive an on-screen reminder to extract the lens by pressing the large button on the lens barrel, and rotating the zoom ring to move the lens elements out to the shooting position.

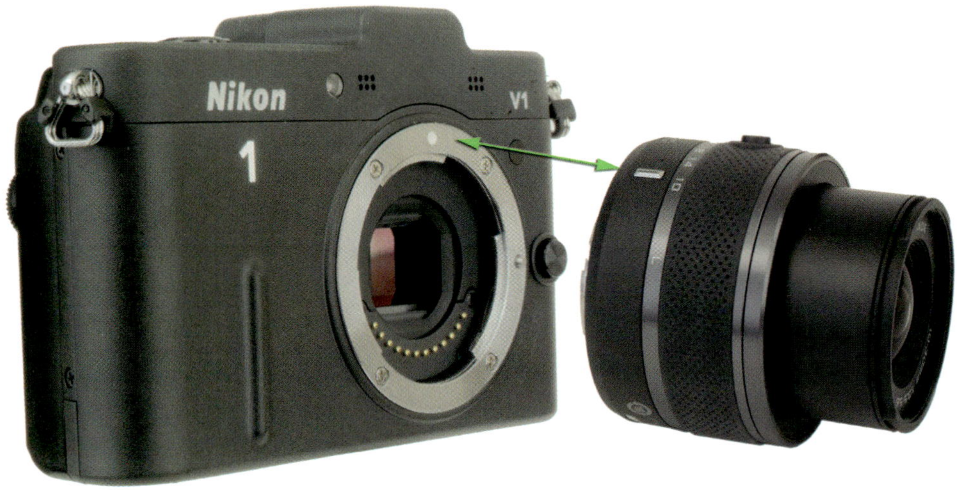

Figure 1.5
Match the indicator on the lens with the white dot on the camera mount to properly align the lens with the bayonet mount.

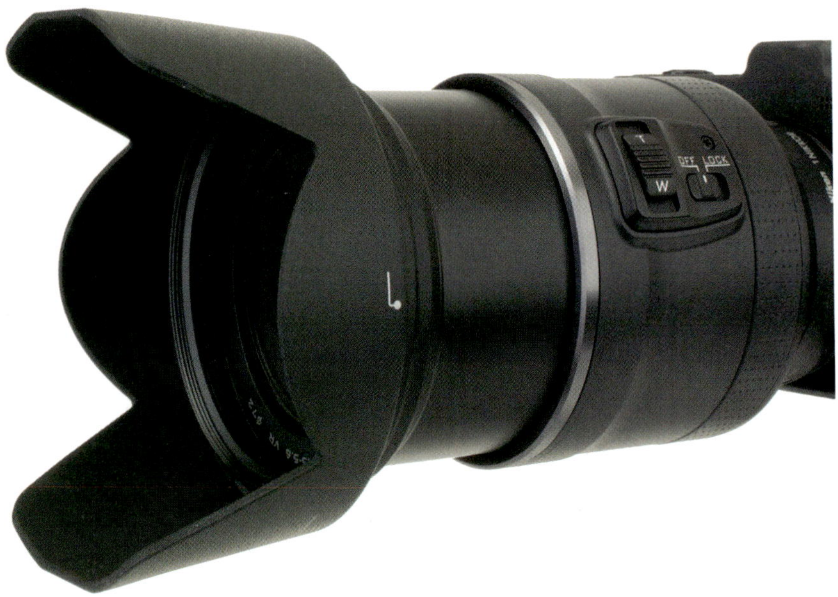

Figure 1.6
A lens hood protects the lens from extraneous light and accidental bumps.

Adjusting Diopter Correction

Those of us with less than perfect eyesight can often benefit from a little optical correction in the viewfinder. Your contact lenses or glasses may provide all the correction you need, but if you are a glasses wearer and want to use the V1 without your glasses, you can take advantage of the camera's built-in diopter adjustment, which can be varied from –3 to +1 correction. Press the shutter release halfway to illuminate the indicators in the viewfinder, then rotate the diopter adjustment dial next to the viewfinder (see Figure 1.7) while looking through the viewfinder until the indicators appear sharp.

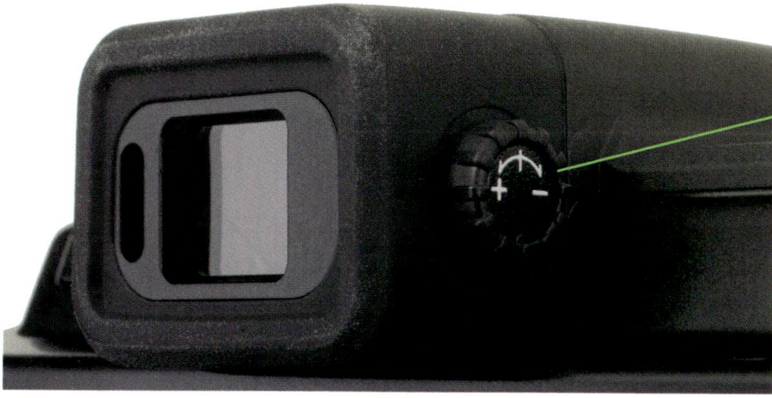

Figure 1.7
Viewfinder diopter correction from –3 to +1 can be dialed in.

If more than one person uses your V1, and each requires a different diopter setting on the camera itself, you can save a little time by noting the number of clicks and direction (clockwise to increase the diopter power; counterclockwise to decrease the diopter value) required to change from one user to the other.

Inserting a Secure Digital Memory Card

You've probably set up your V1 so you can't take photos without a memory card inserted. (There is a Slot Empty Release Lock in the Setup menu that enables/disables shutter release functions when a memory card is absent—learn about that in Chapter 7.) So, your final step will be to insert a memory card. Slide the lever on the access door on the bottom of the body (where the battery is inserted) towards the tripod socket to release the cover, and then open it. (You should only remove a memory card when the camera is switched off, or, at the very least, the yellow-green memory access light at the bottom right of the back panel that indicates the camera is writing to the card is not illuminated.)

Insert the memory card with the label facing the back of the camera oriented so the edge with the contacts (the metallic "fingers" with a Secure Digital card) goes into the slot first (see Figure 1.8). Close the door, and, if necessary, format the card. A Secure Digital card can be removed just by pressing it inward; it will pop out far enough that you can extract it.

Formatting a Memory Card

There are three ways to create a blank memory card for your V1, and two of them are wrong. Here are your options, both correct and incorrect:

- **Transfer (move) files to your computer.** When you transfer (rather than copy) all the image files to your computer from the memory card (either using a direct cable transfer or with a card reader, as described later in this chapter), the old image files are erased from the card, leaving the card blank. Theoretically. Unfortunately, this method does *not* remove files that you've labeled as Protected (using the Protect feature in the Setup menu, as described in Chapter 8) while viewing the image on the LCD, nor does it identify and lock out parts of your memory card that have become corrupted or unusable since the last time you formatted the card. Therefore, I recommend always formatting the card, rather than simply moving the image files, each time you want to make a blank card. The only exception is when you *want* to leave the protected/unerased images on the card for awhile longer, say, to share with friends, family, and colleagues.

- **(Don't) Format in your computer.** With the memory card inserted in a card reader or card slot in your computer, you can use Windows or Mac OS to reformat the memory card. Don't! The operating system won't necessarily install the correct file system. The only way to ensure that the card has been properly formatted for your camera is to perform the format in the camera itself. The only exception to this rule is when you have a seriously munged memory card that your camera refuses to format. Sometimes it is possible to revive such a corrupted card by allowing the operating system to reformat it first, then trying again in the camera.
- **Setup menu format.** To use one of the recommended methods to format a memory card, press the MENU button, use the up/down buttons of the multi selector (that thumb-pad-sized control to the right of the LCD) to choose the Setup menu (which is represented by a wrench icon), navigate to the Format Memory Card entry with the right button of the multi selector and select Yes from the screen that appears. Press OK to begin the format process.

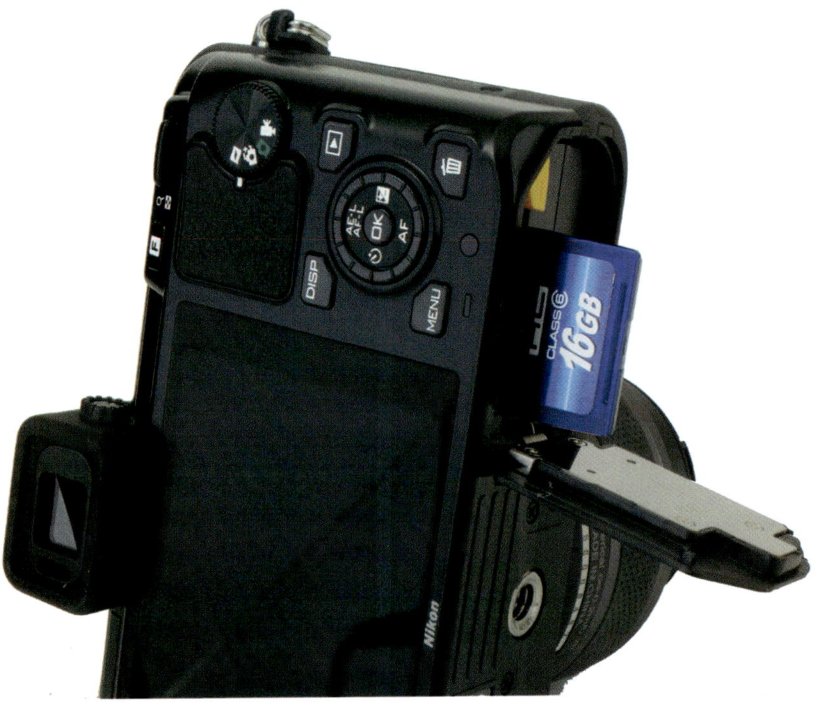

Figure 1.8
The memory card is always inserted with the label facing the back of the camera.

HOW MANY SHOTS?

The V1 provides a fairly accurate estimate of the number of shots remaining in the viewfinder, as well as at the lower-right edge of the viewfinder display when the display is active. (Tap the shutter release button to activate it.)

It is only an estimate, because the actual number will vary, depending on the capacity of your memory card, the file format(s) you've selected, and the content of the image itself. (Some photos may contain large areas that can be more efficiently compressed to a smaller size.)

For example, an 8GB card can hold about 1,150 JPEG Fine shots in full resolution (Large) format. When numbers exceed 1,000, the V1 displays a figure and decimal point, followed by a K superscript, so that 3,100 shots (or thereabouts) is represented by 3.1^K in the LCD and viewfinder. The V1 offers three different resolution settings that provide different numbers of exposures: Large (3872 × 2592; 10.1 megapixels), Medium (2896 × 1944; 5.6 megapixels), and Small (1936 × 1296; 2.5 megapixels).

Using RAW/NEF format (more on that later) reduces the number of shots. An 8GB card has enough room for about 460 RAW photos in Nikon's NEF format, or 330 pictures if you're shooting RAW+JPEG Fine pairs.

Table 1.1 shows the typical number of shots you can expect using an 8GB memory card, specified using the Image Quality and Image Size settings in the Shooting menu.

Table 1.1 File Capacity of 8GB Card

	Large	Medium	Small
JPEG Fine	1,150	1,800	3,100
JPEG Normal	2,250	3,550	5,950
JPEG Basic	4,450	6,950	11,400
RAW	461	N/A	N/A
RAW+JPEG Fine	330	353	402
RAW+JPEG Normal	115	227	262
RAW+JPEG Basic	129	136	142

2

Nikon V1 Quick Start

Now it's time to fire up your Nikon V1 and take some photos. The easy part is turning on the power—the Off/On button is on the top side, just southwest of the large shutter release button. Turn on the camera, and, if you mounted a lens and inserted a fresh battery and memory card—as I prompted you in the last chapter—you're ready to begin. Of course, if your lens is manually retractable, you'll need to press the release button on the lens and rotate it into the shooting position. A handy reminder on the display screen will alert you that this step is necessary. Unretracting the lens will also turn the camera on for you if it happens to be powered down. Then, you'll need to select a release mode, exposure mode, metering mode, focus mode, and, if need be, clip on the optional SB-N5 flash.

All Those Modes!

Your Nikon V1 has four distinctly different shooting modes: Motion Snapshot, Smart Photo Selector, Still Image mode, and Movie mode. Of course, as we move along, you'll discover that other settings are also described as modes, such as exposure modes, focus modes, and the like. But I intend to keep this Quick Start as simple as possible, so I'll have you use Still Image mode and Movie mode in this chapter, and save full descriptions of the other shooting modes for Chapter 4. For the incurably curious, I'll do nothing more than provide a quick description of each of these shooting modes, each of which can be selected by rotating the mode dial, shown in Figure 2.1:

- **Motion Snapshot.** This mode lets you record movie clippettes of about a second in length, played back in slow motion over about 2.5 seconds, along with a still photograph. This is a great feature for grabbing special moments. You can choose a background music "theme" from Beauty, Waves, Relaxation, and Tenderness motifs.

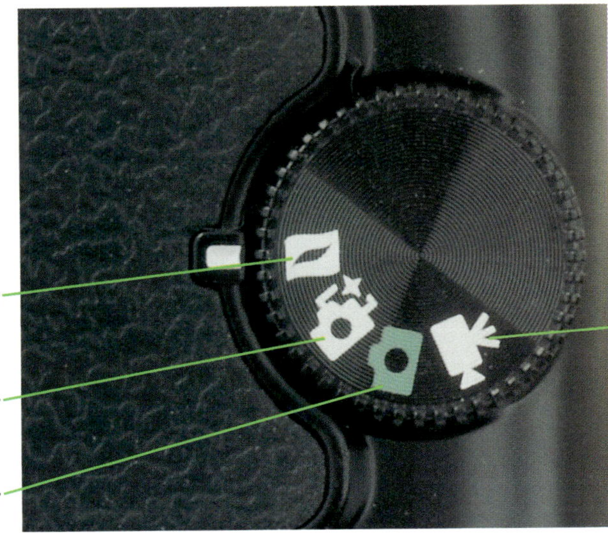

Figure 2.1
Mode dial.

- **Smart Photo Selector.** The V1 takes no fewer than 20 pictures, examines them, and uses its built-in smarts to choose the best composed and sharpest image, plus four additional candidates. Just press the shutter release down halfway to begin storing images temporarily in your camera's memory. The camera will refocus as necessary to follow a moving subject. Press the shutter button down all the way to end capture (the V1 will stop grabbing pictures all by itself after about 90 seconds). Ten pictures taken just before and just after you stop capture are retained. You will then be given the opportunity to choose your favorite from these, and the others can be deleted. I'll show you how to do this in Chapter 4.
- **Still Image mode.** This is the general purpose photography mode you'll use most of the time. The rest of this chapter (after the introduction to movies that follows this section) will be devoted to using Still Image mode to take your first pictures.
- **Movie mode.** Use this mode to take either high-definition (HD) movies or slow-motion movies (at 400 or 1200 frames per second, played back at about 7.5 percent of normal speed). Learn how to get started quickly shooting HD movies next.

Shooting Movies

If you'd like to shoot some movie clips right off the bat, nothing could be simpler. Your V1 can shoot regular movies or slow-motion movies, and I'll explain how to do both in more detail in Chapters 4 and 7. However, for conventional movies, just follow these steps:

1. **Select Movie mode.** Rotate the mode dial on the back right of the back panel to the white movie camera icon. The camera will examine the scene and choose an exposure mode automatically.

2. **Frame the shot.** Choose your subject using the viewfinder or LCD.
3. **Begin recording.** Press the red Movie recording button at the top-right edge of the camera. A red dot will appear in the viewfinder/LCD showing that video is being recorded, and the elapsed time appears in the lower-right corner.
4. **Take a still photograph (optional).** You can take a still photograph using the 16:9 HD TV proportions without interrupting your movie by pressing the shutter release button down all the way. The V1 will save a 2-megapixel image.
5. **Stop recording.** Press the red button a second time to stop recording the movie. You can shoot a movie up to 20 minutes in length or 4GB in size.

The rest of this chapter will deal with an introduction to shooting still images. For more guidance in shooting stills and movies and using the special modes, read Chapter 4.

Choosing a Still Image Release Mode

> This section shows you how to choose Single frame, Continuous mode, or Self-timer mode, and select other options, including mechanical or electronic shutter. Unless you have need of burst shooting or the self-timer, you can set your camera to Single frame mode and skip ahead to "Selecting an Exposure Mode."

The release mode determines when (and how often) the V1 makes an exposure. If you're coming to the mirrorless camera world from a point-and-shoot camera, you might have used a model that labels these options as drive modes, dating back to the film era when cameras could be set for single shot or "motor drive" (continuous) shooting modes. Your V1 has several release modes when using Still Image shooting: Single frame, Continuous, Self-timer, Remote control, Movies in Still Image mode, and Electronic high speed shooting, which captures still shots at 10, 30, or 60 frames per second. The available modes are as follows:

- **Single frame.** In Single frame mode, the V1 takes one picture each time you press the shutter release button down all the way. You can take as many photographs in this mode as you have room for on your memory card. To choose Single frame mode, just follow these steps:

1. Press the MENU button (see Figure 2.2) located at the lower-right edge of the V1.
2. When the menu screen pops up (see Figure 2.3, left), use the multi selector down button to scroll to Continuous, then press the multi selector right button to select the entry.
3. When the Continuous screen appears (see Figure 2.3, right), use the up/down buttons to select Single frame, and then press the OK button to confirm.

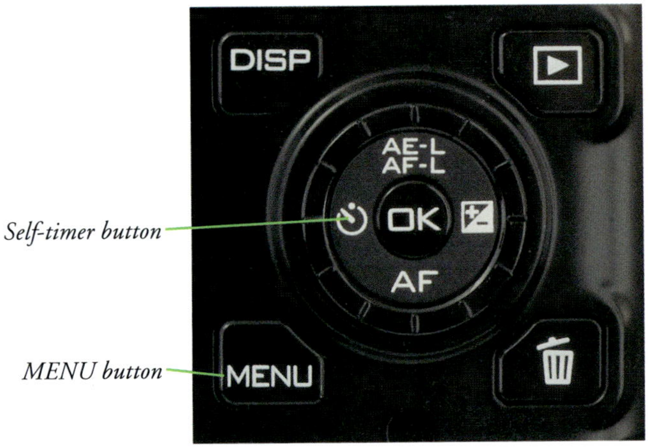

Figure 2.2
Press the MENU button to access the Shooting menu, or the Self-timer button to select the self-timer settings screen.

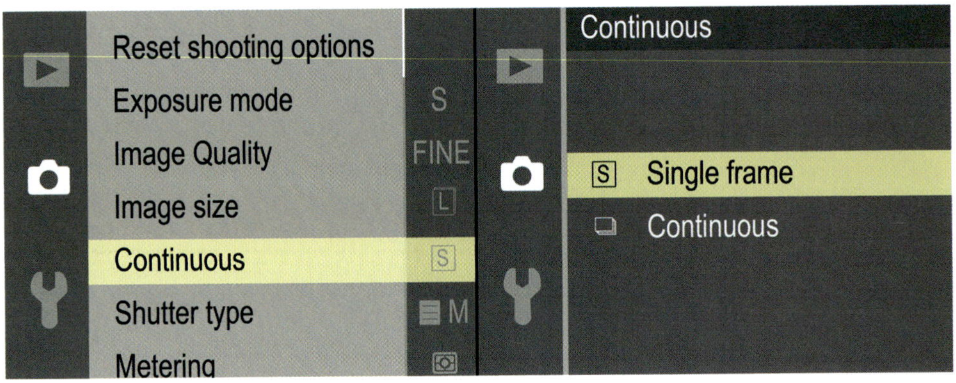

Figure 2.3
In the Shooting menu, choose Continuous to set Single frame or Continuous shooting modes (left), then select Single frame or Continuous.

- **Continuous.** This shooting mode can be set to produce bursts of up to 5 frames per second while the shutter release button is held down. You can take up to 100 pictures in a row in this mode if your memory card has sufficient storage space. Choose Continuous by following Steps 1-3 above.
- **Continuous—Electronic (Hi).** This is a special mode that's available when you choose the V1's Electronic (Hi) shutter mode. You can take still photographs at rates of 10, 30, or 60 frames per second. I'll explain how to use this specialized feature in Chapter 4, rather than in this Quick Start.
- **Self-timer.** You can use the self-timer as a replacement for a remote release, to reduce the effects of camera/user shake when the V1 is mounted on a tripod or, say, set on a firm surface, or when you want to get in the picture yourself. You can specify delays of 2, 5, or 10 seconds. To choose a Self-timer mode, just follow these steps:

1. Press the Self-timer button (shown earlier in Figure 2.2) located at the lower-right edge of the V1.

2. When the setting screen pops up (see Figure 2.4), use the multi selector down button to scroll to 10s, 5s, or 2s, depending on the delay you want.

3. Press OK to confirm your setting. To turn off the self-timer, use Steps 1-2 and select OFF.

- **Remote control.** The ML-L3 remote control can be used in two modes: Delayed Remote (shutter releases two seconds after you press the button on the ML-L3 IR remote); and Quick Response Remote (the shutter trips immediately when the button is pressed). To choose the Remote Control mode, use steps 1-3 above, and select the 2-second delayed remote, or quick response icons. In either mode, the camera will respond to signals from the remote control using either the front or back IR receivers, located for you in the roadmap sections of Chapter 3.

Note

If you plan to dash in front of the camera to join the scene when working with the self-timer, consider using manual focus so the V1 won't refocus on your fleeing form and produce unintended results. (Nikon really needs to offer an option to autofocus at the *end* of the self-timer cycle.) An alternative is to use the ML-L3 IR remote, because the camera focuses when you press the button (after you've ensconced yourself safely in the frame).

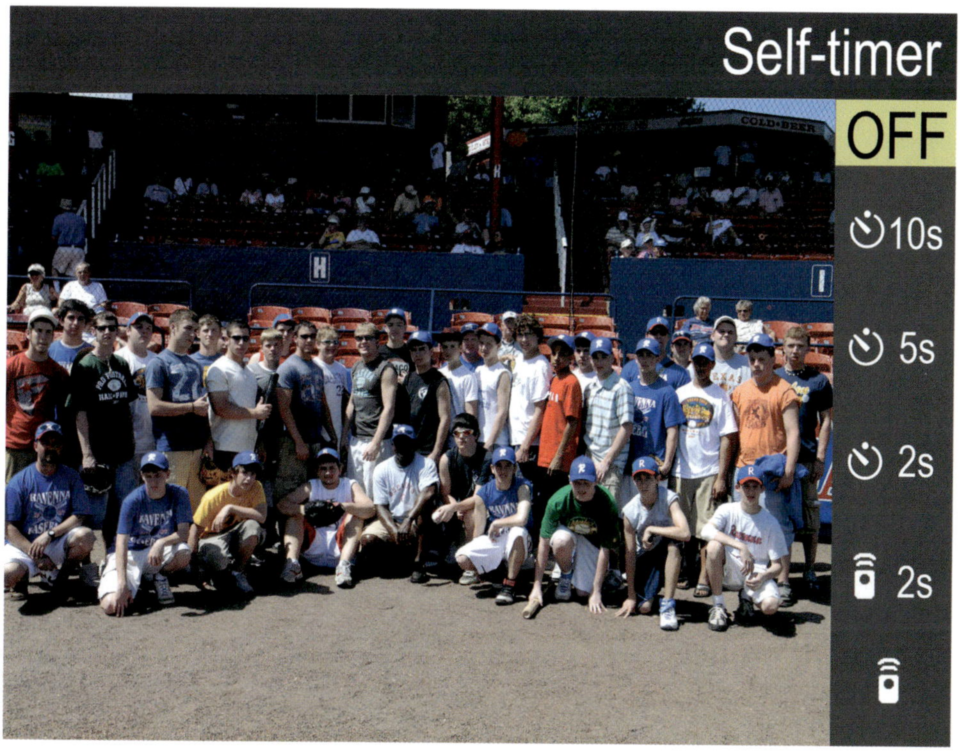

Figure 2.4 Choose a Self-timer or Remote control mode.

Selecting an Exposure Mode

> This section shows you how to choose an exposure mode. If you'd rather have the V1 make all of the decisions for you, just rotate the mode dial to the Still Image mode position with Scene Auto Selector active (described next), and jump to the section titled "Reviewing the Pictures You've Taken." If you'd rather choose one of the Scene modes, tailored to specific types of shooting situations, or try out the camera's semi-automatic modes, continue reading this section after the Scene Auto Selector instructions.

Choosing Scene Auto Selector

The Nikon V1 can select an exposure mode for you from among a modest selection of automatically chosen settings. The available Scene modes the camera will opt for include Portrait, Landscape, Night Portrait, Close-Up, and Auto (for other types of subjects). Unlike other cameras, you can't choose these Scene modes yourself. To shift into Scene Auto Selector mode (in case some other mode has been chosen), just follow these steps:

1. Rotate the mode dial to the green Still Image Mode icon.
2. Press the MENU button (shown earlier in Figure 2.1).
3. When the menu screen pops up, use the multi selector down button to scroll to Exposure Mode; then press the multi selector right button to select the entry.
4. When the Exposure Mode screen appears (see Figure 2.5), use the up/down buttons to select Scene Auto Selector, and then press the OK button to confirm.

The Scene modes chosen by the Scene Auto Selector take full control of the camera and make all the decisions for you. They are most useful while you're learning to use the camera, because you can just fire away. You'll end up with decent photos using appropriate settings, but your opportunities to use a little creativity (say, to overexpose an image to create a silhouette, or to deliberately use a slow shutter speed to add a little blur to an action shot) are minimal. I'll show you how to use exposure tools to add some creativity to your images in Chapters 5 and 6.

Choosing an Advanced Mode

Your V1 also has four semi-automatic and manual modes. These advanced modes include Programmed-auto (or Program mode), Shutter-priority auto, Aperture-priority auto, and Manual exposure mode. These are the modes you'll use most often after you've learned all your V1's features, because they allow you to specify how the camera chooses its settings when making an exposure, for greater creative control.

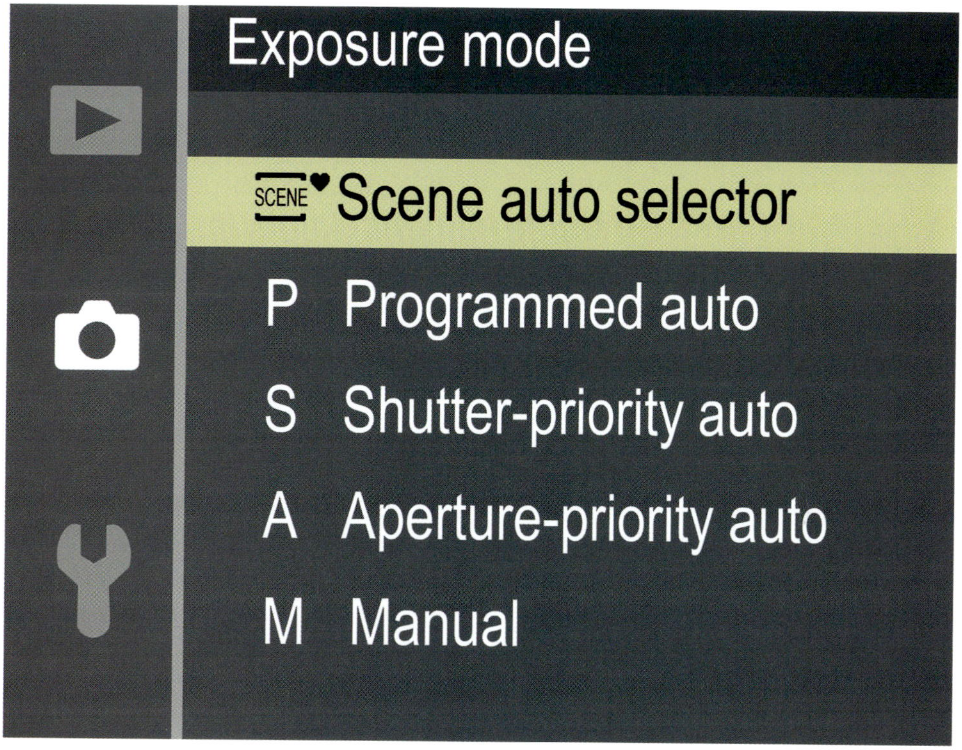

Figure 2.5 Choose an exposure mode.

If you're very new to digital photography, you might want to set the camera to P (Program mode) and start snapping away. That mode will make all the appropriate settings for you for many shooting situations. If you have more photographic experience, you might want to opt for one of the semi-automatic modes. To access these modes, just follow these steps:

1. Rotate the mode dial to the green Still Image mode icon.
2. Press the MENU button (shown earlier in Figure 2.1).
3. When the menu screen pops up, use the multi selector down button to scroll to Exposure Mode; then press the multi selector right button to select the entry.
4. When the Exposure Mode screen appears (see Figure 2.5), use the up/down buttons to select one of the four modes described next, and then press the OK button to confirm.

- **P (Program).** This mode allows the V1 to select the basic exposure settings, but you can still override the camera's choices to fine-tune your image, while maintaining metered exposure, as I'll explain in Chapter 4.
- **S (Shutter-priority).** This mode is useful when you want to use a particular shutter speed to stop action or produce creative blur effects. Choose your preferred shutter

speed by pressing the zoom bar to the right of the F button when the meter is active, and the V1 will select the appropriate f/stop for you.

- **A (Aperture-priority).** Choose when you want to use a particular lens opening, especially to control sharpness or how much of your image is in focus. Specify the f/stop you want using the zoom bar when the meter is "awake" (tap the shutter release to activate the meter, if necessary), and the V1 will select the appropriate shutter speed for you.
- **M (Manual).** Select when you want full control over the shutter speed and lens opening, either for creative effects or because you are using a studio flash or other flash unit not compatible with the V1's automatic flash metering. Press the zoom bar upwards to select a faster shutter speed/downwards to choose a slower shutter speed. Rotate the multi selector dial clockwise to choose smaller apertures, and counter-clockwise to select larger f/stops. (See Figure 2.6.)

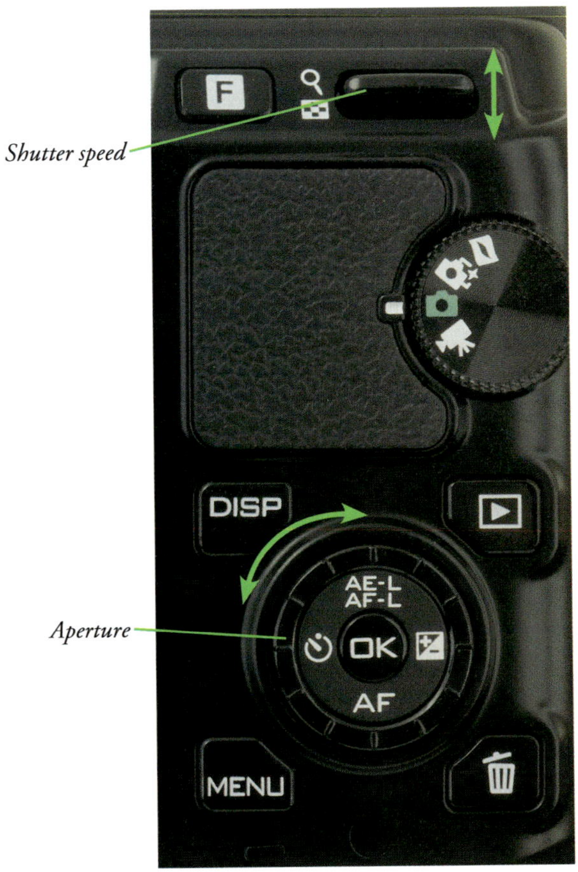

Figure 2.6
Press the zoom bar up/down to change shutter speed; rotate the multi selector dial to change aperture.

Choosing a Metering Mode

This section shows you how to choose the area the V1 will use to measure exposure: giving emphasis to the center of the frame; evaluating many different areas of the frame; or measuring light from a small spot in the center of the frame.

The metering mode you select determines how the V1 calculates exposure. The metering method is chosen for you when using Scene Auto Selector; the options described next are applied only when using PSAM exposure modes. You might want to select a particular metering mode for your first shots, although the default Matrix metering is probably the best choice as you get to know your camera. I'll explain when and how to use each of the three metering modes later. To change metering modes, just follow these steps:

1. Rotate the mode dial to the green Still Image mode icon.
2. Press the MENU button (shown earlier in Figure 2.1).
3. When the menu screen pops up, use the multi selector down button to scroll to Metering; then press the multi selector right button to select the entry.
4. When the Metering screen appears (see Figure 2.7), use the up/down buttons to select one of the three modes described next, and then press the OK button to confirm.

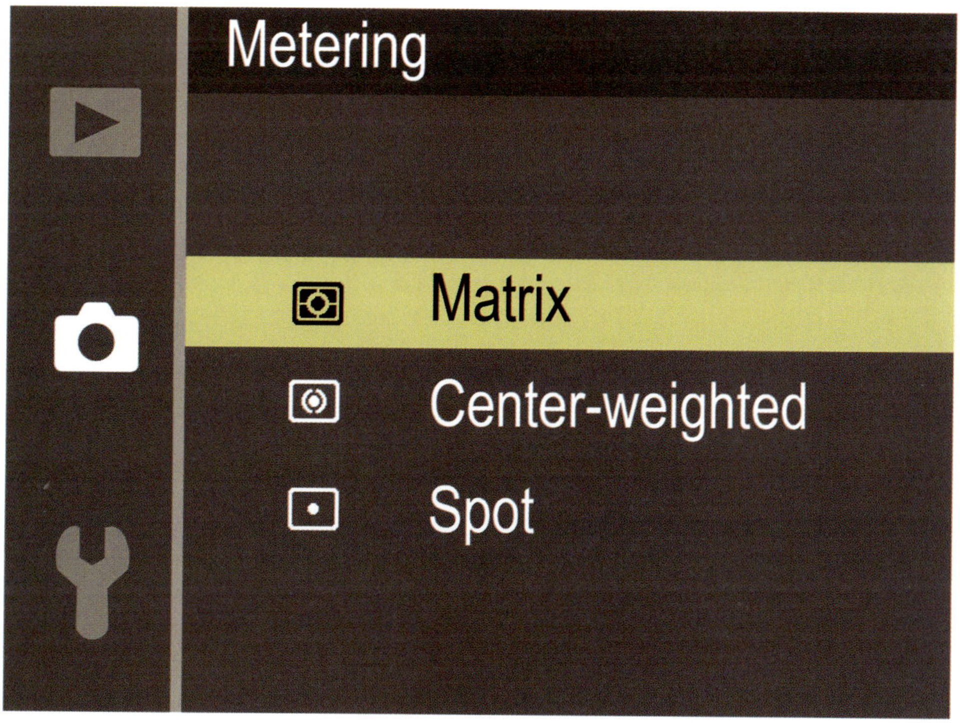

Figure 2.7
Metering modes are selected using the metering mode button and multi selector dial. The individual icons for the modes are shown on the left.

- **Matrix metering.** The standard metering mode; the V1 attempts to intelligently classify your image and choose the best exposure based on readings from a broad span of the sensor area, a database of thousands of patterns.
- **Center-weighted metering.** The V1 meters the entire scene, but gives the most emphasis to the central area of the frame, measuring about 4.5mm.
- **Spot metering.** Exposure is calculated from a smaller 3mm spot, about 2 percent of the image area, using the center focus area, except when working with Face-priority AF mode (discussed shortly), which meters from a focus area spot closest to the center of the selected face.

You'll find a detailed description of each of these modes in Chapter 4.

Choosing a Focus Mode

> This section shows you how to select *when* the V1 calculates focus: all the time (continuously), only once when you press a control like the shutter release button (single autofocus), or manually when you rotate a focus ring on the lens.

You can easily switch between automatic and manual focus modes using the menu system, as described several times previously in this chapter. You can select the autofocus mode (*when* the V1 measures and locks in focus) and autofocus pattern (*which* of the available autofocus points or zones are used to interpret correct focus). To specify when the V1 locks in focus when using PSAM exposure modes (focus modes cannot be chosen when using Scene Auto Selector), follow these steps:

1. Rotate the mode dial to the green Still Image mode icon.
2. Press the down multi selector button (shown earlier in Figure 2.1).
3. When the menu screen shown in Figure 2.8 pops up, use the multi selector up/down buttons to select one of the focus modes described next, and then press the OK button to confirm.

The five focus modes are described below. The first three are available when shooting stills; when shooting movies, only AF-F, AF-S, and MF can be selected:

- **(AF-C) Continuous-servo autofocus.** This mode, sometimes called *continuous autofocus*, sets focus when you partially depress the shutter button but continues to monitor the frame and refocuses if the camera or subject is moved. This is a useful mode for photographing sports and moving subjects. Note that in this mode, photos can be taken even if the camera has not quite locked in focus. The V1's hybrid focus system is very fast, so this won't happen very often.

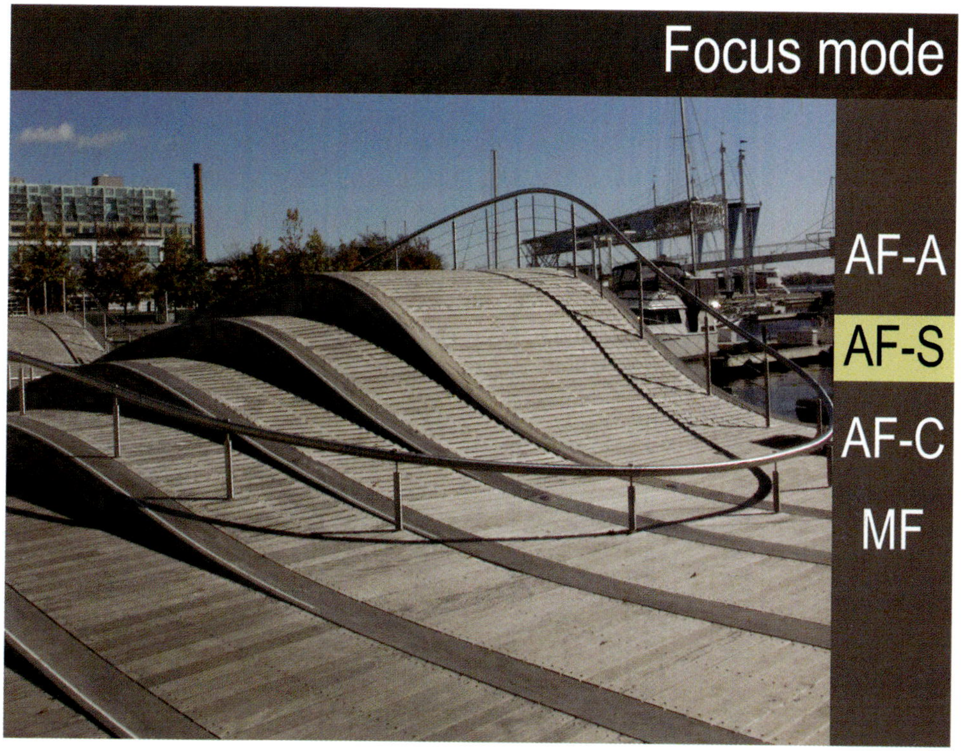

Figure 2.8
Choose an autofocus mode.

- **(AF-S) Single-servo autofocus.** This mode, sometimes called *single autofocus*, locks in a focus point when the shutter button is pressed down halfway. The focus will remain locked until you release the button or take the picture. This mode is best when your subject is relatively motionless.
- **(AF-A) Automatic autofocus.** In this mode, the V1 will select from AF-S or AF-C, depending on whether your subject is stationary or moving.
- **(AF-F) Full-time autofocus.** This mode is available only when shooting movies, and replaces the AF-C and AF-A options. (Only AF-S, AF-F, or Manual focus can be selected in Movie mode.) When using AF-F, the camera focus continuously, and images can be captured even if sharp focus is not quite locked in.
- **(M) Manual focus.** In this mode, you can adjust focus manually. I'll describe the procedure next.

Manual Focus

When you've set the camera to manual focus, you can adjust the zone of sharpness visually using the viewfinder or LCD, using a focus indicator bar.

Just follow these steps:

1. **Activate focus guides.** Press the multi selector OK button to produce an enlarged view of the center of the frame, as shown in Figure 2.9. A focus scale and navigation window appear at the right of the screen. The outer box represents the entire frame, and the yellow box within it shows the relative portion of the frame currently being magnified.
2. **Zoom in or out.** You can increase/decrease the amount of magnification by pressing the zoom bar in the upper-right corner of the back panel up or down. The size of the yellow box changes to indicate the zoom magnification. Up to 10X magnification can be achieved.
3. **Position magnified area.** Although you can adjust the framing of the camera to relocate the magnified area, if you've mounted the V1 on a tripod, you might want to "lock down" the setup. In that case, you can press the multi selector directional buttons to move the yellow box around in the navigation window, and, thus, the magnified area.
4. **Focus.** Rotate the multi selector dial to focus the image. The focus indicator bar at the right of the screen will show the approximate distance.
5. **Confirm focus.** Press the OK button to lock in focus when you're satisfied.

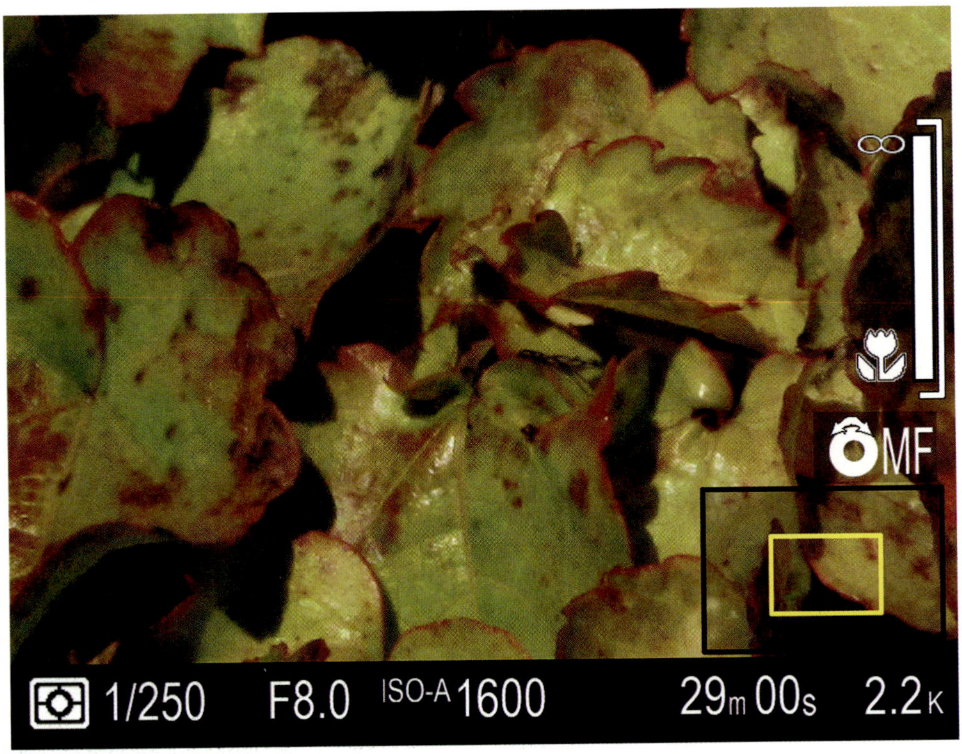

Figure 2.9
Manual focus using a zoomed-in view.

Choosing the Focus Area Mode

You can specify *where* automatic focus is applied by choosing a focus area mode. The Nikon V1 can detect the subject and select the area to focus, you can do that yourself, the camera can follow a subject as it moves, or it can be directed to look for human faces and focus on them. To choose a focus area mode (when the camera is not set to manual focus), follow these steps:

1. Rotate the mode dial to the green Still Image mode icon.
2. Press the MENU button.
3. Scroll down to AF-Area Mode and press the right button to produce the screen shown in Figure 2.10.
4. Use the multi selector up/down buttons to select one of the focus area modes described next, and then press the OK button to confirm.
5. If you want to activate Face Priority (a separate setting), return to the menu and scroll down one additional entry to Face Priority AF. Press the right multi selector button, select On, and press OK to confirm.

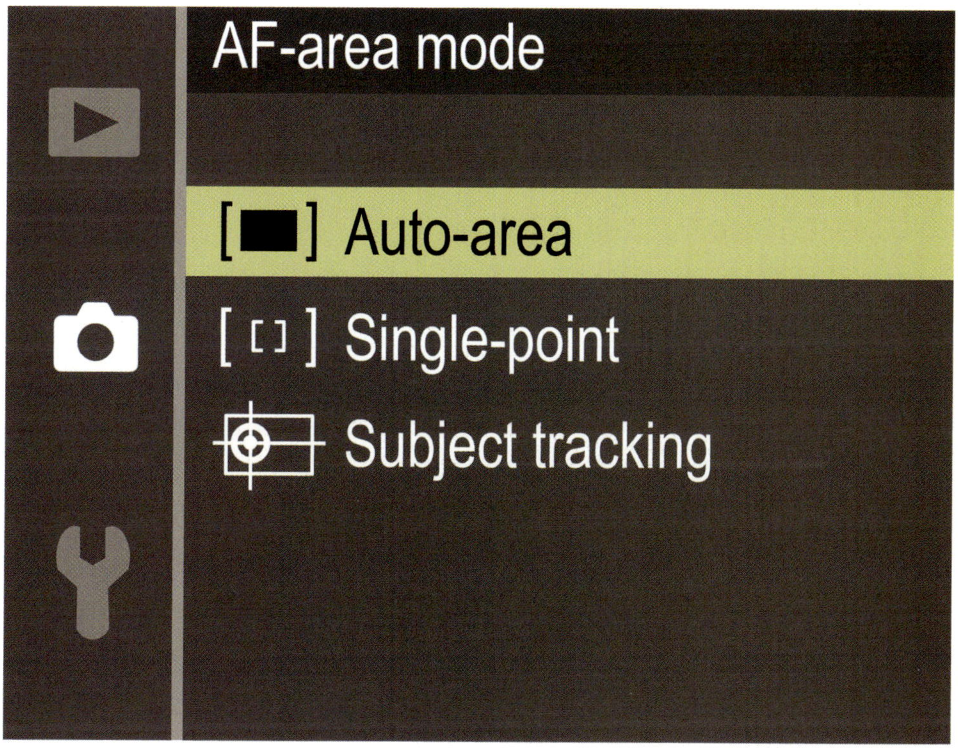

Figure 2.10 Select an auto-focus area mode.

The focus modes are described below.

- **Auto-area AF.** The V1 chooses a focus point. This setting is especially useful for grab shots, because the camera can usually select the subject and lock in focus for you very quickly.
- **Single-point.** The camera focuses on a point you select. This mode is best for subjects that aren't moving when you know exactly where you want to focus. Press the multi selector OK button to reveal the focus area selection display, then position the focus area over your subject with the directional buttons. Press OK to confirm focus. Press the AE-L/AF-L button (the up directional button) to lock focus even when the shutter button is released.
- **Subject tracking.** The camera focuses on a point you select, then follows your subject as it moves. Press the multi selector OK button to reveal the focus area selection display, then position the focus area over your subject with the directional buttons. Press OK to confirm your subject. The camera will follow the subject, and then lock in focus on that subject when you press the shutter release halfway. This mode is great for subjects that move erratically, especially children or pets. Press the AE-L/AF-L button (the up directional button) to lock focus even when the shutter button is released.
- **Face Priority.** When active, the V1 looks for human faces that are looking at the camera and places a double yellow border around the closest face. (Up to five faces may be detected.) Press the shutter release button down halfway to lock focus on that face.

Other Settings

This section describes some optional features you can select if you feel you need to choose the white balance or change the camera's sensitivity setting.

There are a few other settings you can make if you're feeling ambitious, but don't feel ashamed if you postpone using these features until you've racked up a little more experience with your V1.

Adjusting White Balance and ISO

If you like, you can custom-tailor your white balance (color balance) and ISO sensitivity settings. To start out, it's best to set white balance (WB) to Auto, and ISO to A400 Auto. Each can be specified using the menu system, in much the same way as described for other functions earlier in this chapter. Here's a recap of the steps:

1. Rotate the mode dial to the green Still Image mode icon.
2. Press the MENU button.

3. When the menu screen pops up, use the multi selector down button to select White Balance or ISO Sensitivity, then press the multi selector right button to select the entry of your choice.
4. From the White Balance and ISO Sensitivity screens, choose your setting:
   - For White Balance select Auto to let the V1 detect and set the white balance for you. Or, you can choose from Incandescent, Fluorescent, Direct Sunlight, Flash, Cloudy, Shade, or Preset. I'll explain how to use these and to fine-tune each of them in Chapter 4.
   - For ISO, choose A400 (settings from 100–400 will be selected automatically), A800 (for ISO 100–800), A3200 (for ISO 100–3200), or individual fixed values of 100, 200, 400, 800, 1600, 3200, or Hi 1 (ISO 6400 equivalent).
5. Press OK to confirm your choice.

Reviewing the Images You've Taken

Read this section when you're ready to take a closer look at the images you've taken, and want to know how to review pictures and zoom in.

The Nikon V1 has a broad range of playback and image review options, and I'll cover them in more detail in Chapter 3. For now, you'll want to learn just the basics. Here is all you really need to know at this time, as shown in Figure 2.11:

- **View image.** Press the Playback button (marked with a white right-pointing triangle) at the center of the right edge of the back panel to display the most recent image on the LCD.
- **View additional images.** Press the multi selector left or right buttons to review additional images. Press right to advance to the next image, or left to go back to a previous image.
- **Change information display.** Press the DISP button to change among overlays of basic image information or detailed shooting information. I'll show you the photo information screens in the next chapter.
- **Change magnification.** Press the zoom bar up or down to zoom in and out of an image. A thumbnail representation of the whole image appears in the lower-right corner with a yellow rectangle showing the relative level of zoom. At intermediate zoom positions, the yellow rectangle can be moved around within the frame using the multi selector directional buttons.

- **See thumbnail versions.** When viewing an image full screen, pressing the zoom bar down produces thumbnail views with 4, 9, or 72 images per screen, or a calendar view. (See Figure 2.12.) Pressing the zoom bar up again while in thumbnail view reduces the number of thumbnails until you reach the full screen display, where zooming begins again. While viewing thumbnail "contact sheets," you can use the multi selector directional buttons to move from one thumbnail to another. Press the OK button to view the selected image in full size. I'll explain more about using thumbnails and calendar view (retrieving all pictures taken on a certain date) in Chapter 3.
- **Rate your images.** Press the F button, located at the top of the back panel next to the AE-L/AF-L button, to apply one to four stars, or to mark an image for deletion. You can use these ratings to sort and search for images later.
- **Delete current image.** Press the Trash button to delete the currently displayed image.
- **Exit image review.** Press the Playback button again, or just tap the shutter release button to exit playback view.

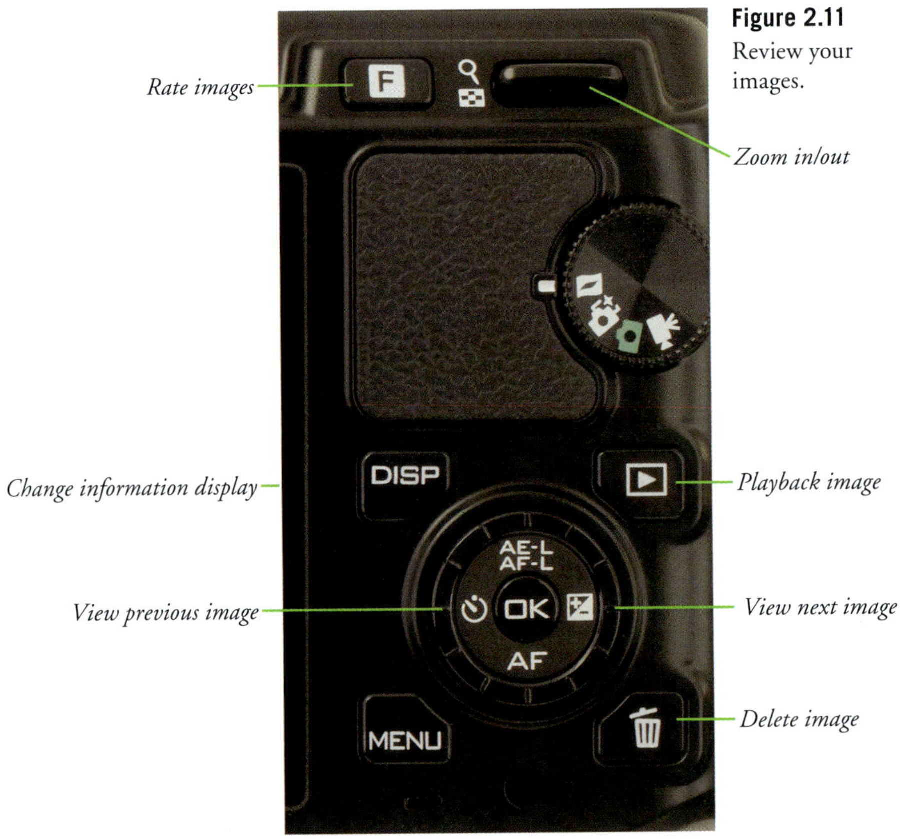

Figure 2.11
Review your images.

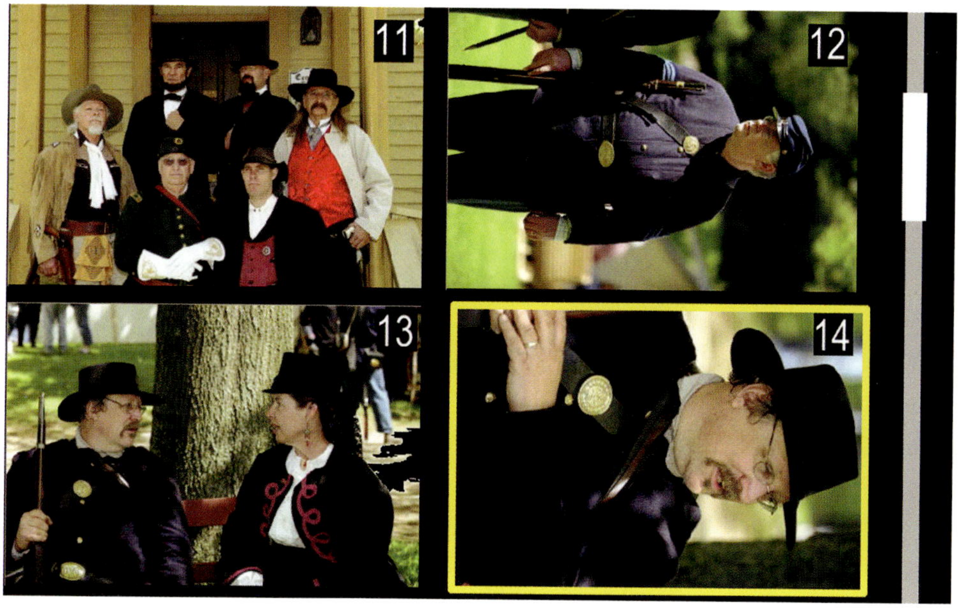

Figure 2.12 Viewing thumbnails.

Transferring Photos to Your Computer

The final step in your picture-taking session will be to transfer the photos you've taken to your computer for printing, further review, or image editing. Your V1 allows you to print directly to PictBridge-compatible printers and to create print orders right in the camera, plus you can select which images to transfer to your computer. I'll outline those options in Chapter 8.

I always recommend using a card reader attached to your computer to transfer files, because that process is generally a lot faster and doesn't drain the V1's battery. However, you can also use a cable for direct transfer, which may be your only option when you have the cable and a computer, but no card reader (perhaps you're using the computer of a friend or colleague, or at an Internet café).

To transfer images from the camera to a Mac or PC computer using the USB cable:

1. Turn off the camera.
2. Pry back the rubber cover that protects the V1's USB port, and plug the USB cable furnished with the camera into the USB port. (See Figure 2.13.)
3. Connect the other end of the USB cable to a USB port on your computer.
4. Turn on the camera. The operating system itself, or installed software such as Nikon Transfer or Adobe Photoshop Elements Transfer, usually detects the camera and offers to copy or move the pictures. Or, the camera appears on your desktop as a mass storage device, enabling you to drag and drop the files to your computer.

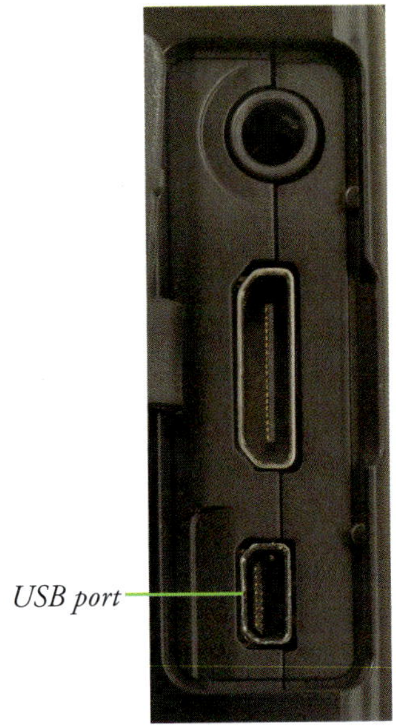

Figure 2.13
Images can be transferred to your computer using a USB cable connected to this port.

To transfer images from a memory card to the computer using a card reader, as shown in Figure 2.14:

1. Turn off the camera.
2. Open the memory card door and extract the Secure Digital card.
3. Insert the memory card into your memory card reader. Your installed software detects the files on the card and offers to transfer them. The card can also appear as a mass storage device on your desktop, which you can open and then drag and drop the files to your computer.

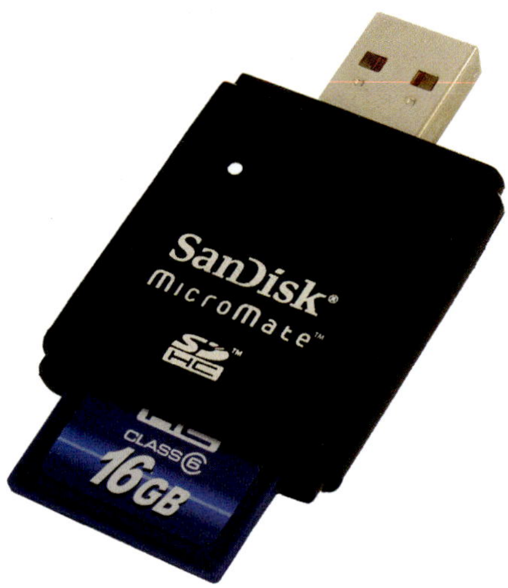

Figure 2.14
A card reader is the fastest way to transfer photos.

3

Nikon V1 Roadmap

Most of the Nikon V1's key functions and settings that are changed frequently can be accessed using either the menu system or the array of dials, buttons, and knobs that populate the camera's surface. While it might take some time to learn the position and function of each of these controls, once you've mastered them, the V1 camera is remarkably easy to use. That's because dedicated buttons with only one or two functions each are much faster to access than the alternative—a maze of menus that must be navigated every time you want to use a feature. The advantage of menu systems—dating back to early computer user interfaces of the 1980s—is that they are easy to *learn*. The ironic disadvantage of menus is that they are clumsy to *use*.

Imagine that you are familiar with digital cameras in general, but know virtually nothing about the Nikon V1. You've decided that you want to format the memory card. A-ha! There's a big ol' MENU button just to the lower right of the LCD on the back of the camera. Press it, and you'll see a series of different menu icons, which, when you scroll through them, have titles like Playback menu, Shooting menu, and Setup menu. You might guess that the Setup menu is the likely repository for a Format command, but even if you guess wrong, it takes only a minute or two to check out the other menus and discover the Format command tucked away within the Setup menu. A couple more button presses and you've successfully formatted your memory card.

You didn't really need instructions—the menu system itself led you to the right command. If you don't format another card for weeks and weeks, you can come back to the menus and discover how to perform the task all over again. The main cost to you was the time required to negotiate through all the menus to carry out the function; while menus are easy to learn, the multiple steps they call for can be cumbersome to use.

So, if you want to operate your V1 most efficiently, you'll need to learn the location, function, and application of all these menu entries and controls. What you really need is a street-level roadmap that shows where everything is, and how it's used. But what Nikon gives you in the user's manual is akin to a world globe with an overall view and many cross-references to the pages that will tell you what you really need to know. Check out the Parts of the Camera pages in Nikon's manual, which offers a handful of tiny black-and-white line drawings of the camera body that show front (see Figure 3.1), back, two sides, and the top and bottom of the V1. There are about six dozen callouts pointing to various buttons and dials. If you can find the control you want in this cramped layout, you'll still need to flip back and forth among multiple pages (individual buttons can have several different cross-references!) to locate the information.

Most other third-party books follow this format, featuring black-and-white photos or line drawings of front, back, and top views, and many labels. I originated the up-close-and-personal, full-color, street-level roadmap (rather than a satellite view) that I use in this book and my previous camera guidebooks. I provide you with many different views and lots of explanation accompanying each zone of the camera, so that by the time you finish this chapter, you'll have a basic understanding of every control and what it does. I'm not going to delve deeply into menu functions here—you'll find a more complete

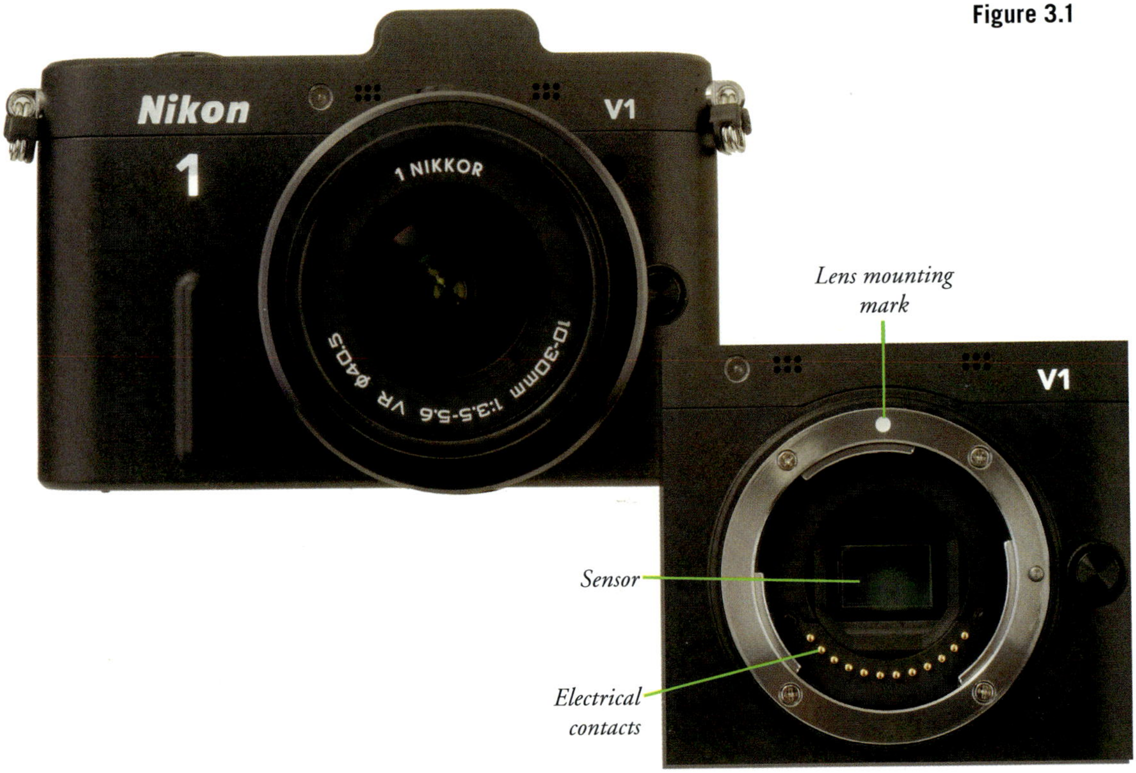

Figure 3.1

discussion of your Playback, Shooting, and Setup options in Chapter 8. Everything here is devoted to the button pusher and dial twirler in you.

You'll also find this "roadmap" chapter a good guide to the rest of the book, as well. I'll try to provide as much detail here about the use of the main controls as I can, but some topics (such as autofocus and exposure) are too complex to address in depth right away. So, I'll point you to the relevant chapters that discuss things like setup options, exposure, use of electronic flash, and working with lenses with the occasional cross-reference.

Nikon V1: Full Frontal

This is the side seen by your victims as you snap away. For the photographer, though, the front is the surface your fingers curl around as you hold the camera, and there are really only a few buttons to press, all within easy reach of the fingers of your left and right hands. There are additional controls on the lens itself. You'll need to look at several different views to see everything.

Figure 3.1 shows the front of the camera with the 10-30mm "kit" lens installed and, at lower right, removed. Figure 3.2 shows a view of the left side of the Nikon V1, as seen from the front.

Figure 3.2

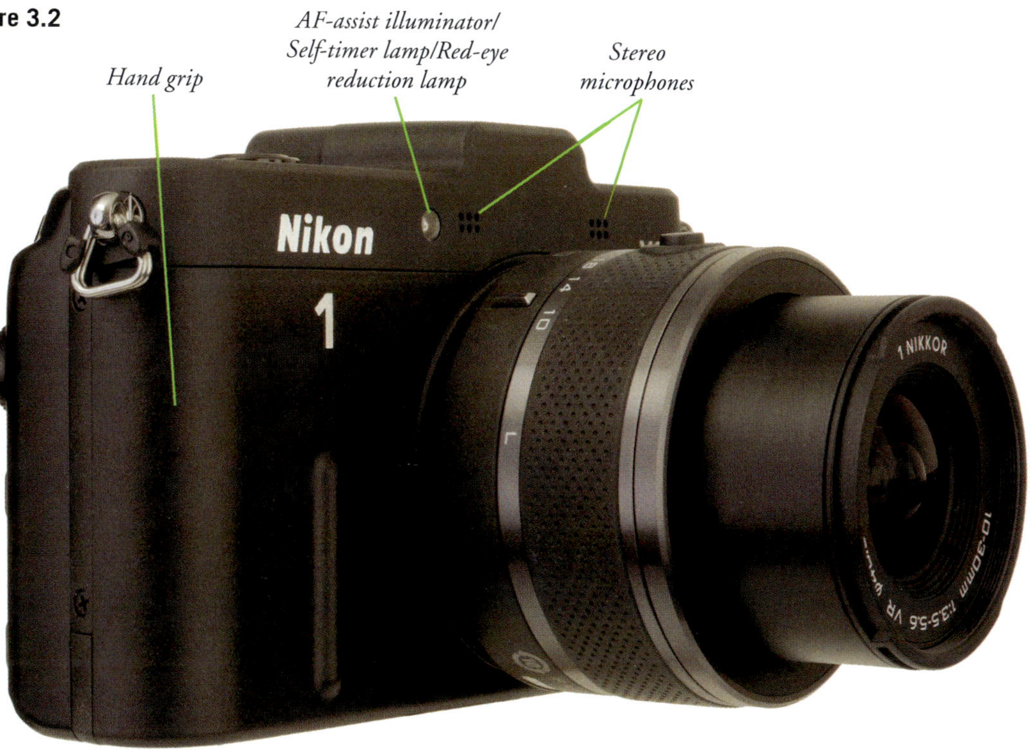

The main components shown in these two views that you need to know about are as follows:

- **Lens mounting mark.** Align this mark, shown in Figure 3.1, with the matching indicator on the lens to mount a lens on the camera.
- **Electrical contacts.** These mate with matching contacts on the lens and allow the camera and lens to communicate. The V1 controls the aperture and focus (all CX-mount lenses lack a focus ring) through these contacts.
- **Sensor.** Note that the sensor is exposed at all times (except when shooting a photo using the mechanical shutter), so you should be careful not to touch it when the lens is removed. If you must manually remove dust and artifacts from the sensor, non-contact methods such as a blower bulb are to be preferred over using brushes or swabs (the last resort, as described in Chapter 13).
- **AF-assist illuminator/Red-eye reduction/Self-timer lamp.** Figure 3.2 shows other components, such as this LED, which provides a blip of light shortly before a flash exposure to cause the subjects' pupils to close down, reducing the effect of red-eye reflections off their retinas. When using the self-timer, this lamp also flashes to mark the countdown until the photo is taken. It can also illuminate to provide assistance for the V1's autofocus mechanism at fairly close distances.
- **Hand grip.** This provides a comfortable hand hold, and also contains the V1's battery.
- **Stereo microphones.** These small microphones capture sound when shooting video, if you're not using an external mic.

You'll find more controls on the other side of the V1, shown in Figure 3.3. The main points of interest shown include:

- **Front infrared receiver.** This is one of two IR sensors located on the camera (the other is on the back). You'll use this one when triggering the camera with the Nikon ML-L3 infrared remote control while standing in front of the camera (say, when you want to get in the picture yourself).
- **Lens release button.** Press this button to unlock the lens, then rotate the lens away from the shutter release button to dismount your optics.
- **Neck strap eyelet.** It comes with a split-ring attached that can be used to fasten a neck strap to the V1.
- **Port cover.** This cover protects the USB, audiovisual, HDMI, and microphone ports when not in use.

Figure 3.3

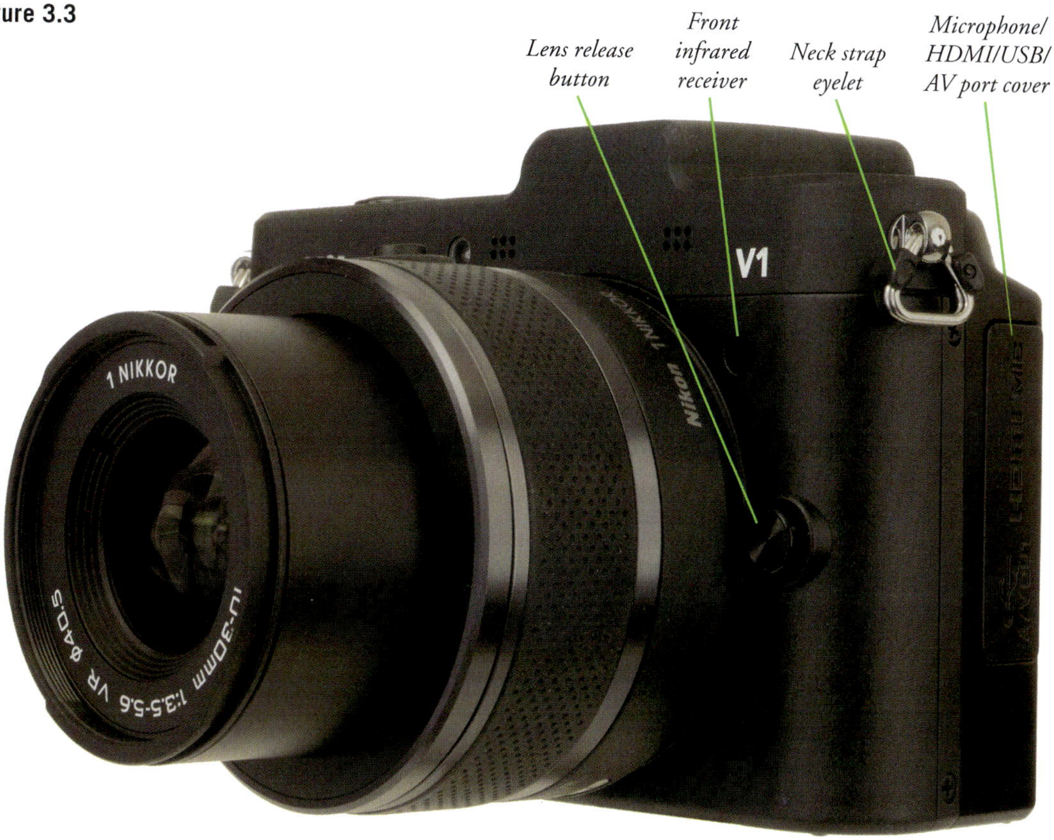

The V1's optional accessory electronic flash (also called a strobe or speedlight) is shown in Figure 3.4. These components include:

- **Attachable flash.** The flash is elevated from the top of the camera, theoretically reducing the chances of red-eye reflections, because the higher light source is less likely to reflect back from your subjects' eyes into the camera lens. In practice, the red-eye effect is still possible (and likely), and can be further minimized with the V1's red-eye reduction lamp, which flashes before the exposure, causing the subjects' pupils to contract. (Your image editor may also have anti-red-eye tools.)
- **Swivel.** The optional flash has a swivel point so you can use it for bouncing off ceilings or other surfaces (depending on whether you're shooting in vertical or horizontal orientations). Although theoretically the flash has a range of 2 feet to 66 feet, depending on the ISO sensitivity, bounce angle, and f/stop, in practice this tiny flash (powered by the V1's battery) is best for fill flash (to brighten shadows) and for shooting at distances no more than about a dozen feet. With direct flash, you'd need to shoot at f/5.6 at 10 feet and ISO 400 to produce a correct exposure. When bouncing or using other ISO settings, your results will vary. You'll find more about flash in Chapter 10.

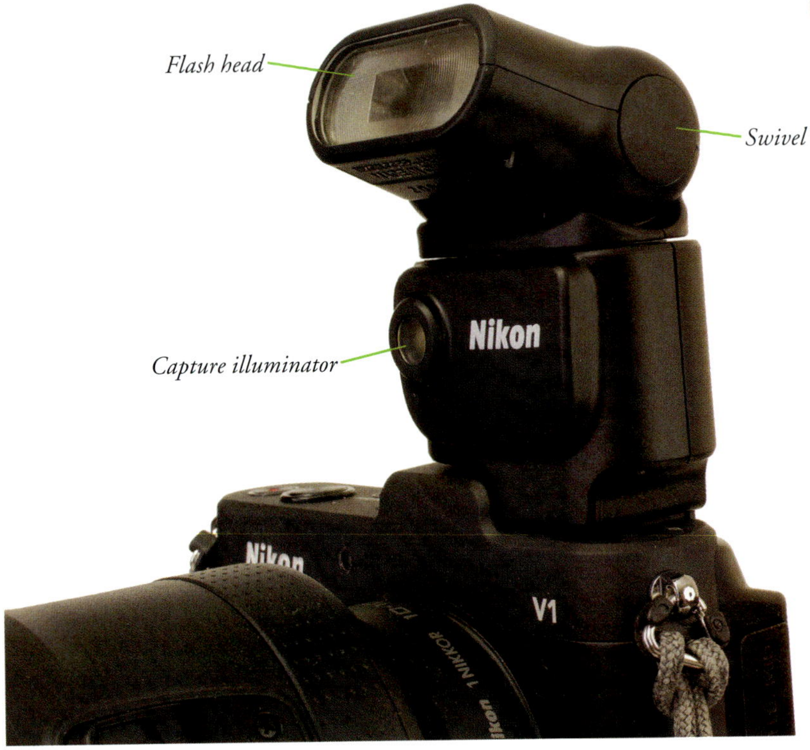

Figure 3.4

- **Capture illuminator.** This odd feature is an LED that provides a constant source that illuminates for about six seconds to deliver continuous light when using the Smart Photo Selector and Motion Snapshot modes (described in Chapter 4).

The main features on the side of the Nikon V1 are a pair of rubber covers that protect the three connector ports underneath from dust and moisture. The three connectors, shown in Figure 3.5, with the rubber covers removed, are as follows:

- **Stereo microphone connector.** Although the V1 has a pair of built-in microphones on the front, if you want better quality (and want to shield your video clip soundtracks from noises emanating from the camera, and/or your handling of it), you can plug in an accessory mic here.
- **HDMI port.** You need to buy an accessory cable to connect your V1 to an HDTV, as one to fit this port is not provided with the camera. If you have a high-resolution television, it's worth the expenditure to be able to view your camera's output in all its glory.
- **USB/Audio/Video port.** Plug in the USB cable furnished with your Nikon V1 and connect the other end to a USB port in your computer to transfer photos. You can also link this connector with a television to view your photos and movies on a large screen. Connect the red/white RCA plugs on the included cable to the audio input jacks of your monitor/TV, and the yellow plug to the video jack.

Figure 3.5

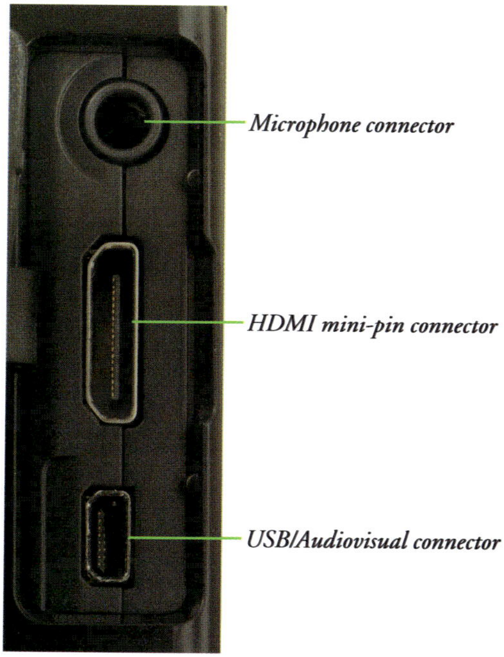

The Nikon V1's Business End

The back panel of the Nikon V1 (see Figure 3.6) bristles with more than a dozen different controls, buttons, and knobs. That might seem like a lot of controls to learn, but you'll find, as I noted earlier, that it's a lot easier to press a dedicated button and spin a dial than to jump to a menu every time you want to change a setting.

Figure 3.6

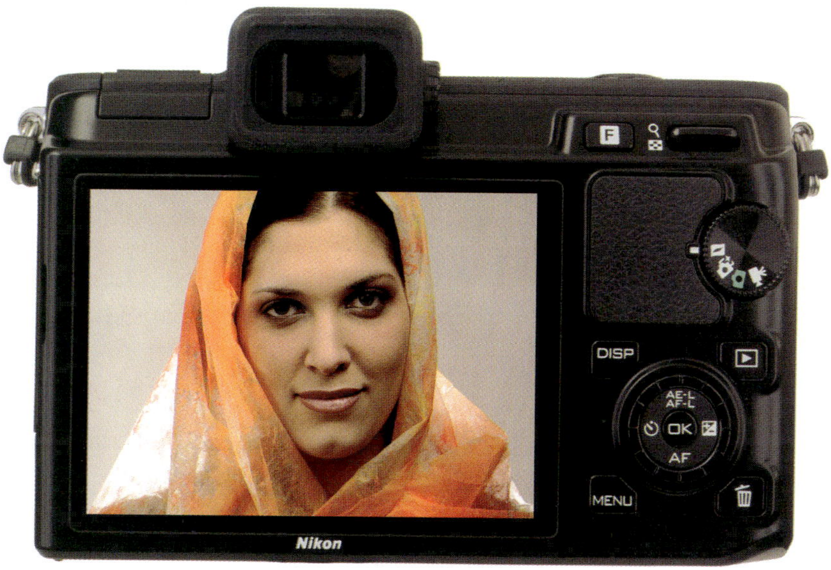

You can see the controls clustered along the top edge of the back panel in Figure 3.7. The key buttons and components and their functions are as follows:

- **Electronic viewfinder window.** You can frame your composition by peering into the viewfinder. It's surrounded by a soft rubber frame that seals out extraneous light when pressing your eye tightly up to the viewfinder, and it also protects your eyeglass lenses (if worn) from scratching.
- **Eye sensor.** The V1 can alternate between showing live views, playback display, or menus on either the back-panel LCD or the electronic viewfinder. Either display is activated by tapping the shutter release. Then, when you bring the camera to your eye, the sensor inside the eyepiece detects that orientation and switches the display from the LCD to the electronic viewfinder. If you prefer to use the electronic viewfinder only, press the DISP button northwest of the multi selector until the LCD screen goes blank.
- **Diopter adjustment dial.** Rotate this to adjust the diopter correction for your eyesight, as described in Chapter 1.
- **F (Feature) button.** This button performs different functions, depending on whether you're using Still Image, Movie, Motion Snapshot, or Playback camera modes:
  - **Still Image mode.** Press to produce a screen that allows you to choose Mechanical, Electronic, or Electronic (Hi) shutter operation. I'll explain the use of each of these in Chapter 4.
  - **Movie mode.** Press the F button to pop up a screen that lets you toggle between HD movie and Slow Motion movie modes, as described in Chapter 7.
  - **Motion Snapshot mode.** The F button produces a screen that allows you to choose from Beauty, Waves, Relaxation, and Tenderness themes.
  - **Playback mode.** When reviewing pictures, the F button pops up a scale that allows you to embed a star rating in an image's file, ranging from 0 stars to 5 stars, plus a "trash" (negative) star you can apply to mark an image for deletion.

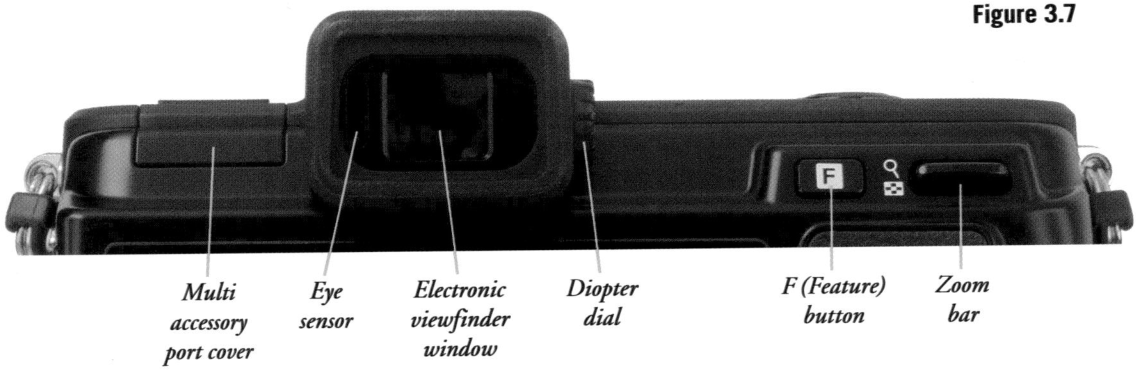

Figure 3.7

- **Multi accessory port cover.** This removable cover protects the accessory connector used to attach the optional flash and GPS units.
- **Zoom bar.** This bar can be pressed up or down to zoom in and out of an enlarged image, or to increase/decrease the number of thumbnail images shown on the screen during review.

You'll be using the buttons to the right of the LCD (shown in Figure 3.8) quite frequently, so learn their functions now.

- **Mode dial.** Changes from Motion Snapshot, Smart Photo Selector, Still Image, and Movie modes. I'll explain all these photo modes in Chapter 4, and describe how and when to use them.
- **MENU button.** Summons/exits the menu displayed on the rear LCD of the V1. When you're working with submenus, this button also serves to exit a submenu and return to the main menu.

Figure 3.8

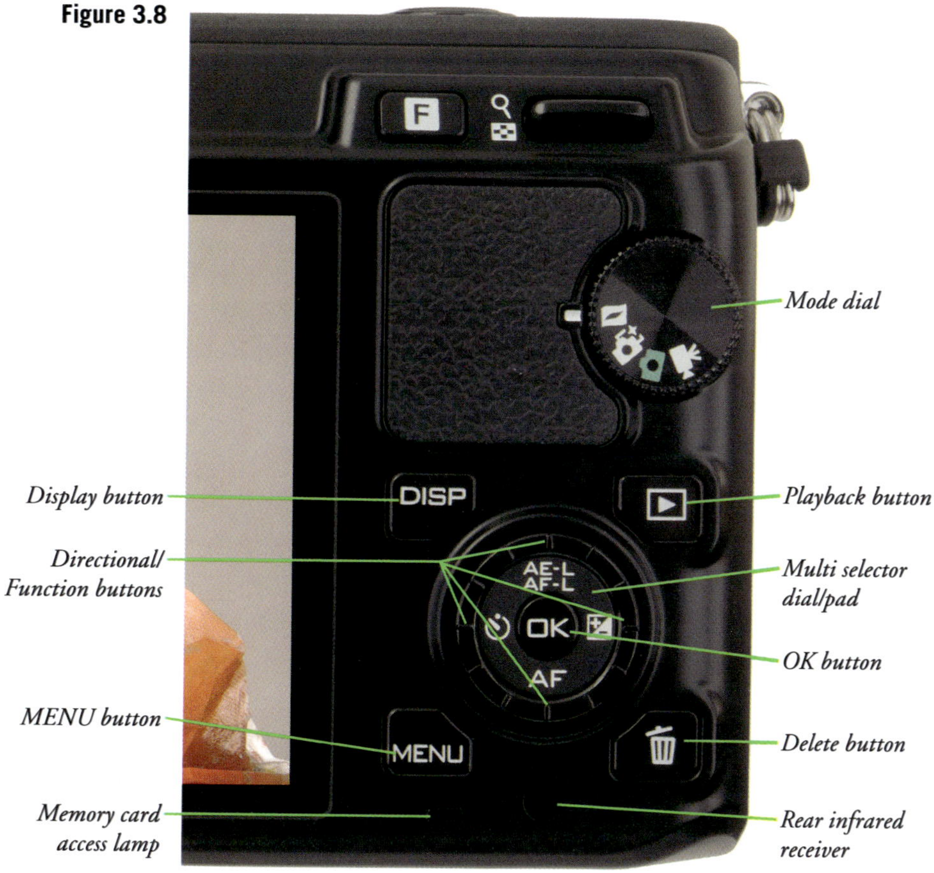

- **OK button.** The button in the center of the multi selector can be pressed to choose a highlighted selection in a menu and to confirm choices.
- **Display (DISP) button.** Use this button to change the amount and type of information shown on the screen in both Playback and Shooting modes. You can select a display mode for the LCD and electronic viewfinder separately. I'll show you how this data can be changed in the next section.
- **Multi selector.** This joypad-like button can be shifted up, down, side to side, and diagonally for a total of eight directions, or rotated. In navigational mode, it can be used for several functions, including AF-point selection, scrolling around a magnified image, trimming a photo, or setting white balance correction. Within menus, pressing the up/down arrows moves the on-screen cursor up or down; pressing towards the right selects the highlighted item and displays its options; pressing left cancels and returns to the previous menu.
- **Directional/Function buttons.** The N, S, E, and W positions on the multi selector each has secondary functions in shooting (non-Playback) mode. The up button can be used to lock focus/and or exposure; the right button produces an LCD pop-up that dials in exposure compensation when working in Program, Aperture-priority, or Shutter-priority modes (but not automatic scene selection or manual exposure). The down button lets you specify an autofocus mode (AF-S, AF-C, AF-A, or M). The left button is used to select a self-timer or remote control mode.
- **Rear infrared receiver.** This is one of two IR sensors on the camera; the other is located on the front. Both are active at the same time when the release mode is set to either instant or delayed remote. You'd use this receiver to trigger the camera using the ML-L3 infrared remote control when you want to release the shutter while standing behind the camera. For example, the V1 might be mounted on a tripod and you want to trip the shutter without shaking the camera or using the self-timer. You'll find that having both front and rear IR receivers is a vast improvement over earlier cameras that typically had only a receiver on the front.
- **Delete button.** In Playback mode, press once to delete the picture currently being reviewed. Press a second time to confirm the deletion, or the Playback button to chicken out and cancel.
- **Playback button.** Press this button to review images you've taken, using the controls and options I'll explain in the next section. To remove the displayed image, press the Playback button again, or simply tap the shutter release button.
- **Memory card access lamp.** Illuminates when the V1 is saving an image to the memory card.

What's on the Screen?

If you're accustomed to working with a digital SLR or a point-and-shoot digital camera, you'll find that the informational display on the Nikon V1 is probably a bit different from what you're used to. It has two complete electronic viewing systems, each used to show you everything you need to see to operate your camera, from a live view preview of your frame before you take the picture, to the menus used to make settings, to the picture review that displays your photos after they've been taken.

The two separate viewing systems (internal electronic viewfinder and back-panel LCD) can both be active at the same time, and the V1 will alternate between them, depending on whether the camera's eye sensors indicate that you have brought the camera to your eye, or are using it at arms' length. Both are always in the same mode simultaneously—shooting mode, playback mode, or menu mode—but the amount and type of information they display may be different. You can choose the data shown for each using the DISP button, as described next.

- **Shooting mode.** In shooting mode, there are three different displays for the back-panel LCD, and two for the internal electronic viewfinder. You can cycle among them by pressing the DISP on the back of the camera. It's important to note that the LCD and EVF can be showing different data displays. Each is set when you press the DISP button while using that particular viewing system (LCD or EVF).
  - **LCD.** When using the back-panel LCD, pressing the DISP button repeatedly cycles among a simplified display (see Figure 3.9), a detailed display (Figure 3.10), and LCD Off (nothing is shown on the LCD; you must use the internal EVF to preview your image).
  - **Internal EVF.** Pressing the DISP button cycles only between the simplified display and detailed display (they are identical to what you see in Figures 3.9 and 3.10). There is no option to turn the internal EVF off completely, except, of course, when you remove the V1 from your eye.

    As a result, you may find that the back-panel LCD is showing the detailed view while the internal EVF is displaying the simplified view. It's only mildly disconcerting, and, in fact, I use that mode nearly all of the time. I set the EVF to show only a minimal amount of information while I have the camera up to my eye and I'm composing the photo, while the back LCD provides the full display if I need it.
  - **Grid display.** An additional grid display option is available for any of the shooting mode views. The grid divides the frame into quarters horizontally and vertically with an overlay. It's not a "Rule of Thirds" layout, and so is of more use in checking the alignment of horizontal lines (such as the horizon) and vertical lines as you compose the image. Activate the grid in the Setup menu, using the Grid Display entry to turn it On or Off. (See Figure 3.11.)

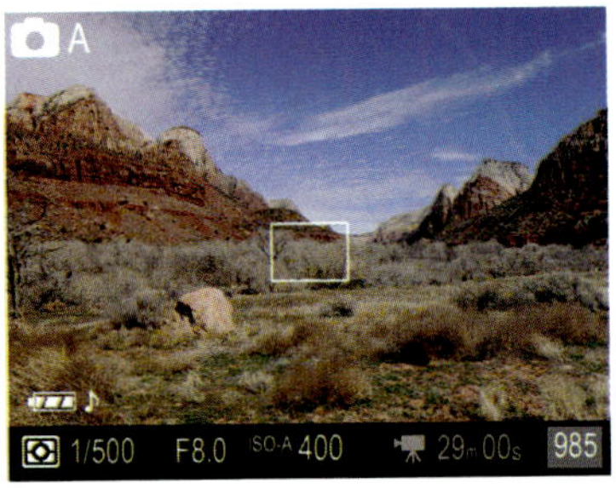

Figure 3.9 Simplified shooting mode display.

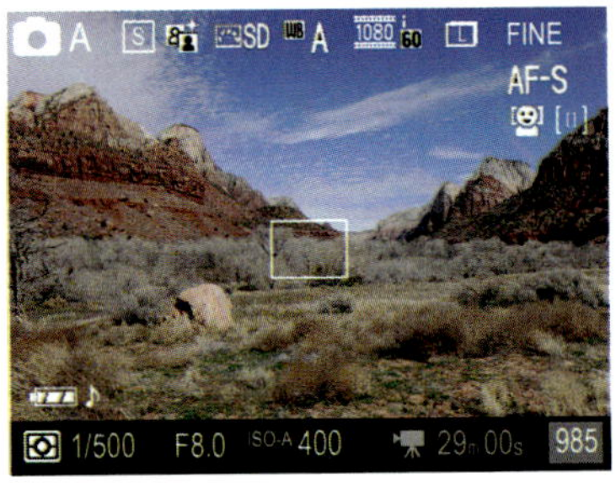

Figure 3.10 Detailed shooting mode display.

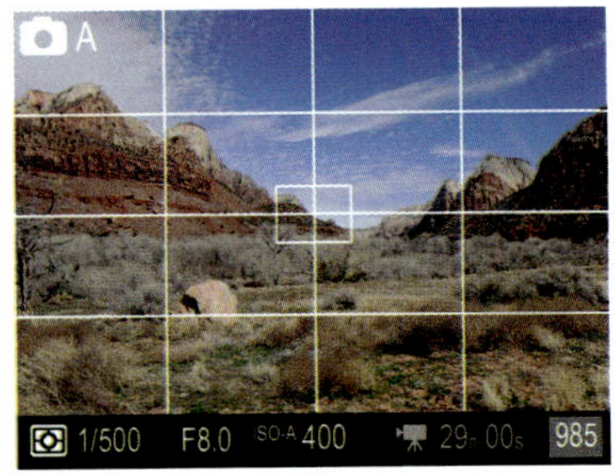

Figure 3.11 Optional grid display.

- **Picture Review/Playback mode.** When reviewing your images after they've been taken, the DISP button can be used to cycle among three different views: Picture only (just a "clean" image with no information overlay; this allows you to view your photo with no distractions) (see Figure 3.12); simple photo info (see Figure 3.13), with basic data arrayed along the bottom and upper left/right corners of the image; and detailed photo information (see Figure 3.14), which displays a reduced size thumbnail of your image along with complete shooting information, including a histogram display. I'll show you how to work with histograms in Chapter 5.

  As in shooting mode, you can have different playback displays in the EVF and back-panel LCD. I like to set the camera to show the plain-vanilla image in the EVF (which has a higher resolution and is less affected by ambient light), and the detailed photo info display on the LCD. In some ways, it's the best of two worlds.
- **Menu mode.** When viewing menus, the V1 shows the exact same image in the EVF and on the LCD, and the DISP button has no effect.

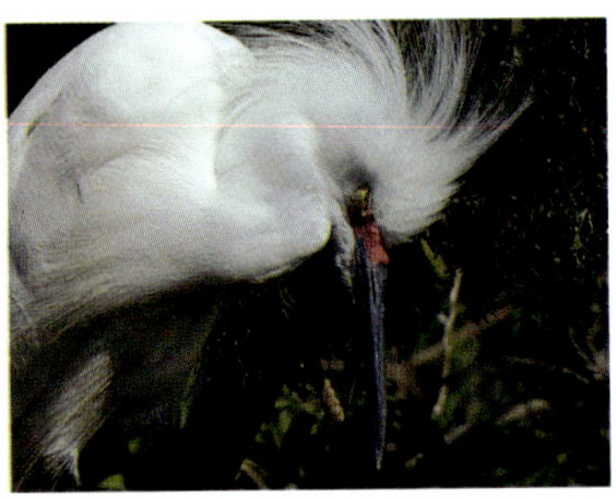

Figure 3.12 Image only photo playback.

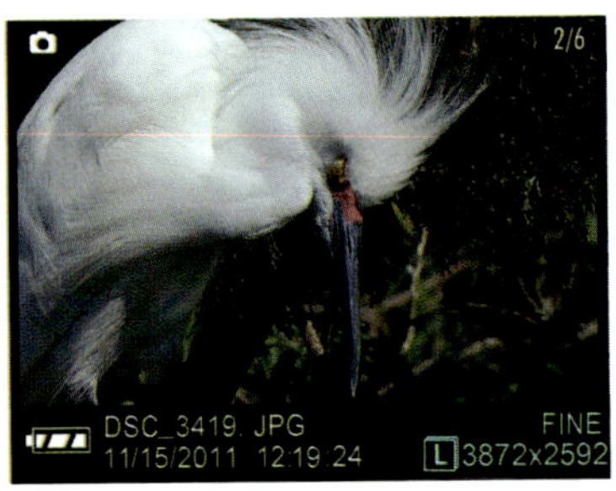

Figure 3.13 Simple photo info playback.

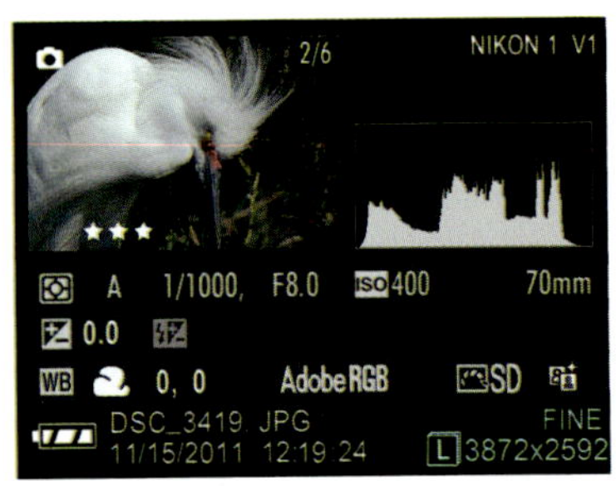

Figure 3.14 Detailed photo info playback.

Figure 3.15 provides a "roadmap" of the information shown in the shooting mode EVF/ LCD displays.

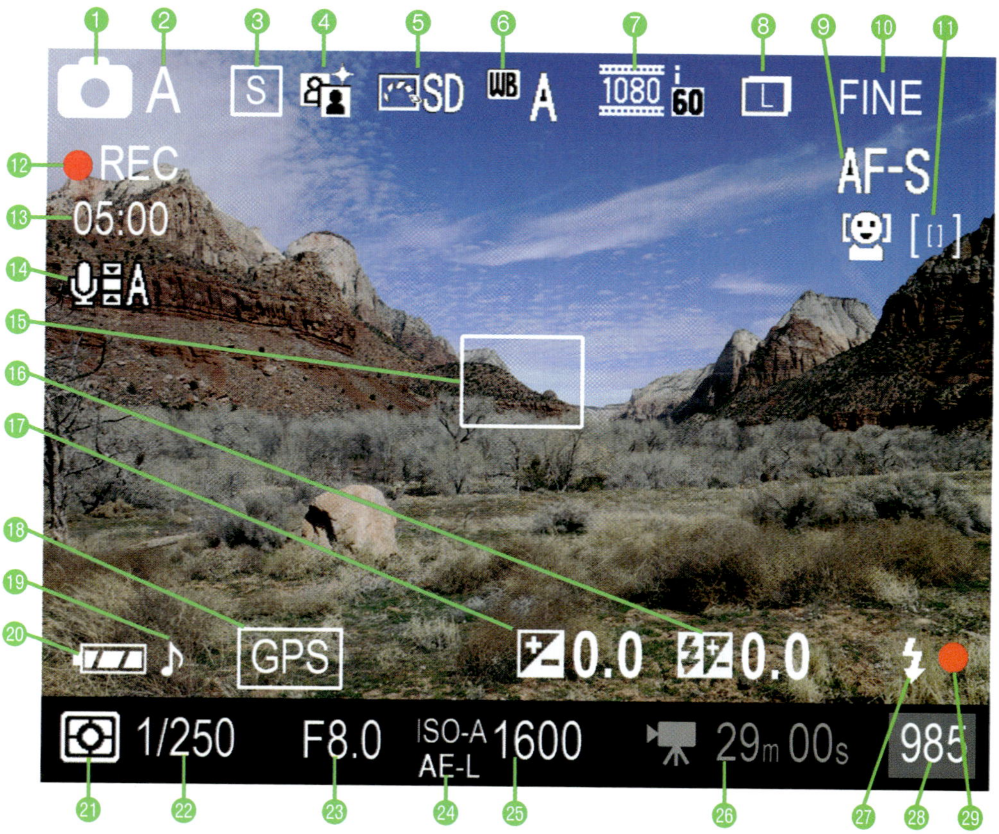

1 *Shooting mode*
2 *Exposure mode*
3 *Self-timer/Remote control/ Electronic (Hi) mode*
4 *Active D-Lighting*
5 *Picture Control*
6 *White balance*
7 *Movie settings*
8 *Image size*
9 *Focus mode*
10 *Image quality*
11 *AF-area mode*
12 *Recording indicator*
13 *Time elapsed*
14 *Microphone sensitivity*
15 *Focus area*
16 *Flash exposure compensation*
17 *Exposure compensation*
18 *GPS connection*
19 *Sound settings*
20 *Battery indicator*
21 *Metering mode*
22 *Shutter speed*
23 *Aperture*
24 *Autoexposure lock indicator*
25 *ISO setting*
26 *Movie Time available*
27 *Flash mode*
28 *Number of exposures remaining/Number of shots before buffer fills*
29 *Flash-ready indicator*

Figure 3.15 Detailed shooting mode display roadmap.

Playing Back Images

Reviewing images is a joy on the Nikon V1's big 921,000-dot three-inch LCD or the 1,440,000-dot internal electronic viewfinder. Both displays are big and bright, and there is abundant detail for interpreting your images.

Here are the basics involved in reviewing images on the EVF and LCD screen (or on a television/HDTV screen you have connected with a cable). You'll find more details about some of these functions later in this chapter, or, for more complex capabilities, in the chapters that I point you to. This section just lists the must-know information.

- **Start review.** To begin review, press the Playback button located northeast of the multi selector pad on the back of the V1. The most recently viewed image will appear on the LCD.
- **View thumbnail images.** To change the view from a single image to four, nine, or 72 thumbnails, or calendar view follow the instructions in the "Viewing Thumbnails" section that follows.
- **Zoom in and out.** To zoom in or out, press the zoom bar up (zoom in) or down (zoom out), following the instructions in the "Zooming the Nikon V1 Playback Display" in the next section. (It also shows you how to move the zoomed area around using the multi selector keypad.)
- **Move back and forth.** To advance to the next image, press the right edge of the multi selector pad; to go back to a previous shot, press the left edge. You can also rotate the multi selector dial clockwise (next image) or counterclockwise (previous image). When you reach the beginning/end of the photos in your folder, the display "wraps around" to the end/beginning of the available shots.
- **See different types of data.** To change the type of information about the displayed image that is shown, press the DISP button. To learn what data is available, read the "Using Shooting Data" section later in this chapter.
- **Remove images.** To delete an image that's currently on the screen, press the Trash button once, then press it again to confirm the deletion. To select and delete a group of images, use the Delete option in the Playback menu to specify particular photos to remove, as described in more detail in Chapter 8.
- **Cancel playback.** To cancel image review, press the Playback button again, or simply tap the shutter release button.

Zooming the Nikon V1 Playback Display

The Nikon V1 zooms in and out of preview images using the procedure that follows. Note that you can review images even when a lens is retracted.

1. When an image is displayed in any of the three playback modes (image only, simple photo information only, or detailed photo information only), press the zoom bar up to fill the screen with a slightly magnified version of the image.
2. A navigation window appears in the lower-right corner of the LCD showing the entire image. Keep pressing to continue zooming in to the maximum of approximately 25X enlargement (with a full resolution large image).
3. A yellow box in the navigation window shows the zoomed area within the full image. (See Figure 3.16.) The entire navigation window vanishes from the screen after a few seconds, leaving you with a full-screen view of the zoomed portion of the image.
4. Up to 5 faces will be detected by the V1, indicated by white borders in the navigation window. Rotate the multi selector dial to move highlighting to the individual faces.
5. Use the Zoom Out/Thumbnail button to zoom back out of the image.
6. Use the multi selector buttons to move the zoomed area around within the image. The navigation window will reappear for reference when zooming or scrolling around within the display.
7. To exit zoom in/zoom out display, tap the shutter release button halfway.

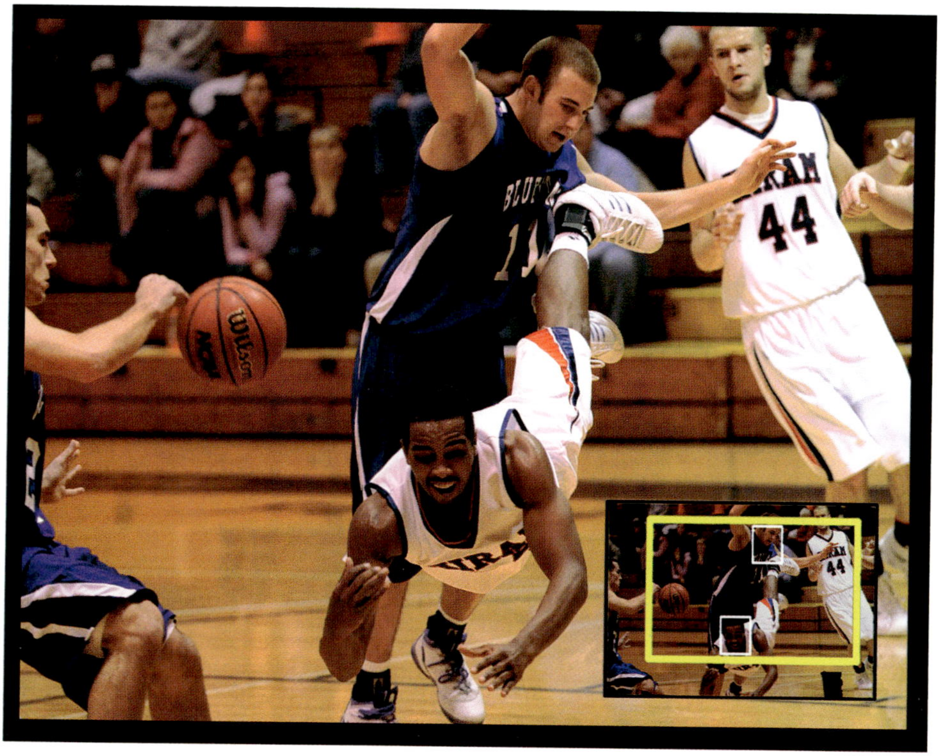

Figure 3.16 The Nikon V1 incorporates a small thumbnail image with a yellow box showing the current zoom area.

Viewing Thumbnails

The Nikon V1 provides other options for reviewing images in addition to zooming in and out. You can switch between single image view and four, nine, or 72 reduced-size thumbnail images on a single LCD screen. There's also a calendar view that shows images grouped by the date they were shot.

Pages of thumbnail images offer a quick way to scroll through a large number of pictures quickly to find the one you want to examine in more detail. The V1 lets you switch quickly from single- to four- to nine- to 72-image views, with a scroll bar displayed at the right side of the screen to show you the relative position of the displayed thumbnails within the full collection of images in the active folder on your memory card. Figure 3.17 offers a comparison between the three levels of thumbnail views. The zoom bar is used to move from one level of thumbnails to the next.

- **Add thumbnails.** To increase the number of thumbnails on the screen, press the zoom bar down. The V1 will switch from single image to four thumbnails to nine thumbnails to 72 thumbnails, and then on to calendar view, described next. (The display doesn't cycle back to single image again.)
- **Reduce number of thumbnails.** To decrease the number of thumbnails on the screen, press the zoom bar up to change from calendar view to 72 to nine thumbnails to four thumbnails, or from four to single-image display. Continuing to press the zoom bar up once you've returned to single-image display starts the zoom process described in the previous section.
- **Switch between thumbnails and full image.** When viewing thumbnails, you can quickly switch between thumbnail view and full image display by pressing the OK button in the center of the multi selector. If you want to return to thumbnail views instead, press the zoom bar up.
- **Change highlighted thumbnail area.** Use the multi selector to move the yellow highlight box around among the thumbnails.

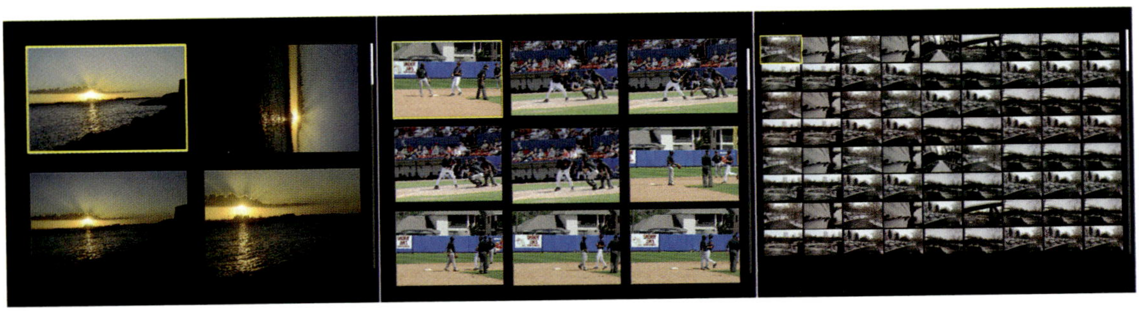

Figure 3.17 Switch between four thumbnails (left), nine thumbnails (center), or 72 thumbnails (right), by pressing the zoom bar.

- **Rate the highlighted image.** Press the F button, and then rotate the multi selector dial to assign one to five stars to the highlighted image, or mark it for deletion.
- **Delete images.** When viewing thumbnails or a single page image, press the Delete button to erase it. Press a second time to confirm deletion, or press the Playback button to cancel.
- **Exit image review.** Tap the shutter release button or press the Playback button to exit image review. If you've already extended a retracted lens, you don't have to worry about missing a shot because you were reviewing images; a half-press of shutter release automatically brings back the V1's exposure meters, the autofocus system, and, unless you've redefined your controls or are using manual focus, cancels image review.

Working with Calendar View

When you're in 72 thumbnail mode, pressing the zoom bar down one more time takes you to calendar view, where you can sort through images arranged by the date they were taken. This feature is especially useful when you're traveling and want to see only the pictures you took in, say, a particular city on a certain day.

- **View dates and images taken on that date.** A yellow highlight box appears around a selected date in the date list calendar, as shown in Figure 3.18.
- **Change dates.** Use the multi selector keys or rotate the multi selector dial to move through the date list.

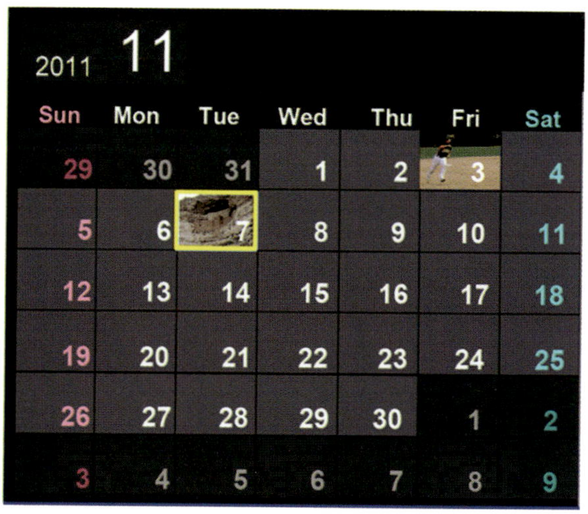

Figure 3.18
Calendar view allows you to browse through all images on your memory card taken on a certain date.

- **View a date's images.** Press the OK button to view the first picture taken on the selected date. You can then press the multi selector left/right buttons to advance or move back among the stored images starting from that image. Press the zoom bar up to return to the 72-image thumbnail display.
- **Other functions.** Once you begin viewing images starting with a particular calendar date, you can perform the other functions described in the viewing thumbnails section, including rating images, deleting images, or exiting image review.

Going Topside

The top surface of the Nikon V1 (see Figure 3.19) has its own set of frequently accessed components.

- **Multi accessory port.** Slide the SB-N5 electronic flash or GP-N100 GPS unit into this mount. When you need a more powerful speedlight, you can insert the AS-N1000 hot shoe adapter instead and use a dedicated flash unit, like the Nikon SB-400. There's more on using electronic flash in Chapter 10.
- **Focal plane indicator.** This indicator shows the *plane* of the sensor, for use in applications where exact measurement of the distance from the focal plane to the subject is necessary. (These are mostly scientific/close-up applications.)

Figure 3.19

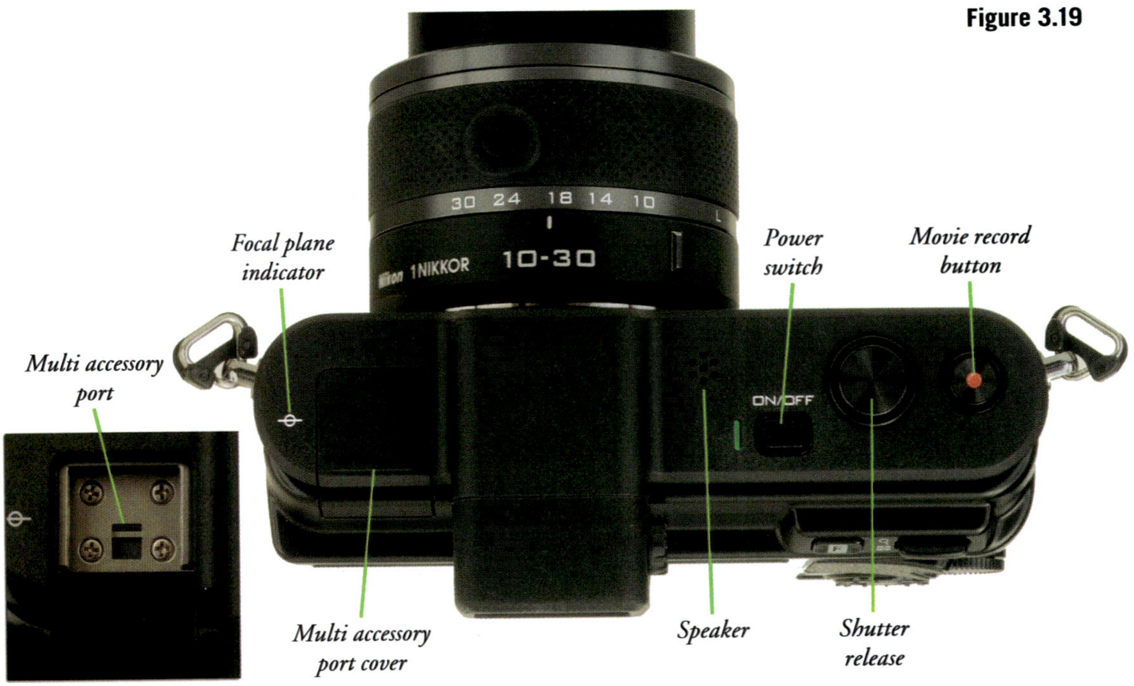

- **Speaker.** Your V1 emits sounds, such as your movie audio track during playback, through this device.
- **Shutter release button.** Partially depress this button to activate the exposure meter, lock in exposure, and focus. Press all the way to take the picture. Tapping the shutter release when the camera has turned off the autoexposure and autofocus mechanisms reactivates both. When a review image is displayed on the back-panel color LCD or in the EVF, tapping this button removes the image from the display and reactivates the autoexposure and autofocus mechanisms.
- **Power switch.** Press this button to turn the V1 on or off. The green LED to the left of the button will glow briefly as the camera powers up or down.
- **Movie Record button.** When the mode dial is set to Movie mode or Still Image mode, press once to begin recording a video clip; press again to stop recording. A recording indicator, elapsed time, and amount of time remaining appear on the display. You'll find more about movie making in Chapters 4 and 7.

Lens Components

As I write this, there are four lenses available for the Nikon 1 system, making it easy for me to purchase them all. I expect more lenses will be available during the life of this book, and any new lenses will probably contain some combination of the features shown in Figure 3.20. Pictured at left is the Nikkor 10-100mm zoom lens, and at right is the Nikkor 30-110mm zoom. The 10-100mm has some features not found in its smaller sibling, because it has been optimized for movie shooting. Conversely, the 30-110mm lens is a general purpose optic that has a few features you won't see on the larger lens. You'll find more about working with lenses in Chapter 9.

- **Lens hood.** The hood serves to shield the lens from extraneous light outside the picture area, and also protects the front glass element from knocks and dings. For that reason alone, I never shoot without a hood.
- **Lens hood alignment indicators.** A dot on the outer edge of the lens is lined up with a second dot on the lens hood, and the hood rotated to a third position where it locks in place.
- **Power zoom button.** The 10-100mm lens has a power zoom button, providing a smooth zoom that's especially useful while shooting movies. (Although zooming within a shot should be used carefully, or in moderation.) Press the T position on the lens barrel to zoom in, and the W to zoom back out. The harder you press, the faster the zoom. There are three zooming speeds available.

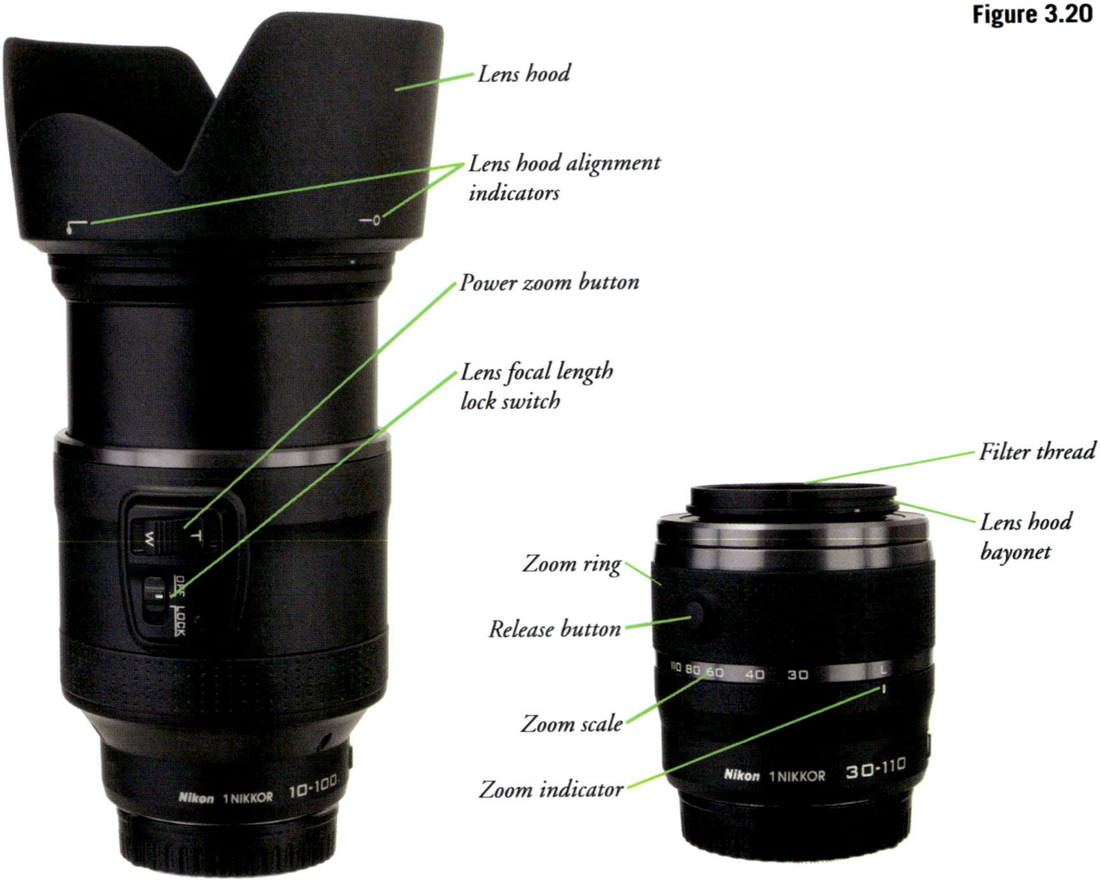

Figure 3.20

- **Lens focal length lock switch.** The 10-100 lens retracts automatically when the V1 camera is powered down, making the camera/lens more compact. If you want the lens to remain extended so you can begin shooting more quickly when the camera is powered back up, move this switch to the lock position.
- **Lens hood bayonet.** Lenses like the two shown use this bayonet to mount the lens hood. Such lenses generally will have a dot on the edge showing how to align the lens hood with the bayonet mount.
- **Filter thread.** Most lenses have a thread on the front for attaching filters and other add-ons, including non-bayoneting lens hoods.
- **Zoom ring.** Turn this ring to change the zoom setting. Lenses that use a power zoom lack this ring, and cannot be zoomed manually.
- **Zoom scale/zoom indicator.** These markings on manually zoomable lenses show the current focal length selected. Oddly enough, when using a power zoom lens, you never know the actual focal length, because the zoom setting is not shown on

either camera display. After you've taken the shot, the lens focal length is shown in the detailed picture display, however.

- **Release button.** Some lenses can be manually retracted and extended. Press this button to allow the zoom ring to be rotated to the retract/extend positions. Rotating the lens also turns the camera on if it happens to be powered down.

The back end of a lens intended for use on a Nikon 1 camera has other components that you seldom see (except when you swap lenses), shown in Figure 3.21, but still should know about:

- **Lens bayonet mount.** This is the mounting mechanism that attaches to a matching mount on the camera.
- **Electronic contacts.** These metal contacts pass information to matching contacts located in the camera body allowing a firm electrical connection so that exposure, distance, and other information can be exchanged between the camera and lens.
- **Lens mount alignment indicator.** Match this raised ridge on the lens barrel with the index dot on the camera body to mate the lens with the body when changing optics.

Figure 3.21

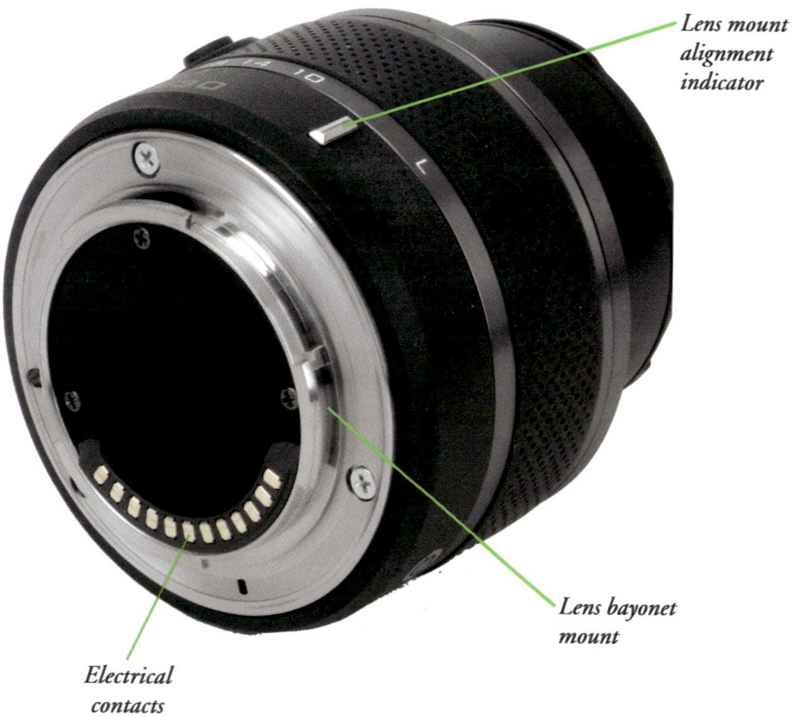

Underneath Your Nikon V1

There's not a lot going on with the bottom panel of your Nikon V1. You'll find the battery compartment access door, and a tripod socket, which secures the camera to a tripod. The socket accepts other accessories, such as quick release plates that allow rapid attaching and detaching the V1 from a matching platform affixed to your tripod. Figure 3.22 shows the underside view of the camera.

Figure 3.22

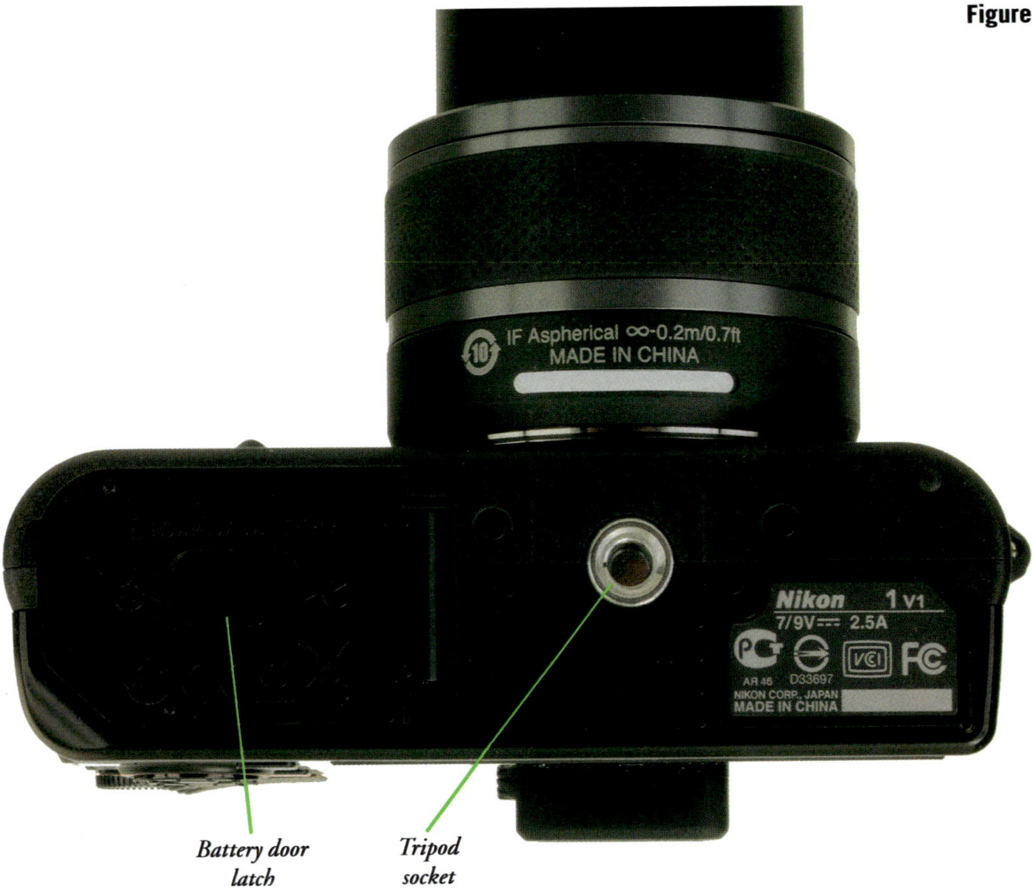

Part II

Beyond the Basics

So, why do you need the three chapters in Part II: Beyond the Basics? I think you'll find that even if you've mastered the fundamentals and controls of the V1 in Part I, there is lots of room to learn more and use the features of the camera to their fullest. Even if you're getting great exposures a high percentage of the time, you can fine-tune tonal values and use your shutter speed, aperture, and ISO controls creatively. Your camera's high performance autofocus system may zero in on your subject in most situations—but you still need to be able to tell the V1 *what* to focus on, and *when*. Other tools at your disposal let you freeze an instant of time, record a continuous series of instants as a movie, and improve your images in other imaginative ways. The chapters in this part will help you move your photography to the next level by understanding exposure, mastering the mysteries of autofocus, and using the Nikon V1's advanced features.

Chapter 4 provides a more thorough explanation of the Nikon V1's four shooting modes; Motion Snapshot; Smart Photo Selection; Still Image mode, and Movie mode. Chapter 5 explores techniques for getting the best exposure, and using techniques like high dynamic range (HDR) photography. Chapter 6 gives you the inside story on advanced shooting, including the mastery of autofocus and continuous shooting. In Chapter 7, you'll find tips for more advanced movie making techniques.

4

Shooting Stills and Movies

In many respects, the Nikon 1 cameras are a new type of tool, with some special features designed to appeal both to the point-and-shooter and to the veteran photographer who wants to explore new ways of capturing stills and movies. The Nikon V1, in particular, gives you the automated shooting you want in an easy-to-use camera, the full control over settings that allow adding a creative touch, and, as a bonus, some interesting new capabilities like motion snapshots and slow-motion movie shooting.

This chapter will introduce you to the full range of V1 shooting modes. I'm going to cover each of the four shooting modes in a bit of detail, but to avoid trying to cram everything about every topic in one humongous chapter, I'm going to save advanced shooting techniques in each mode for later in Part II. For example, you'll find exposure tips in Chapter 5, continuous shooting in Chapter 6, and movie making in Chapter 7.

Using Motion Snapshot Mode

Regardless of your level of expertise and experience, you've enjoyed taking still snapshots for as long as you've been using a camera. Snapshots are those grab shots you take to capture a moment and preserve a memory, usually with no artistic planning ahead of time, nor even an intent to be especially creative. Your camera is set on Automatic or Program mode, you switch it on, compose your shot, and click away. The captured image has its own charm simply because it's an unposed, unplanned snapshot.

The Nikon V1's Motion Snapshot mode brings the same concept to movie making, providing short, slow-motion glimpses of moments you capture in easy to digest bites.

If your "home movie" or "vacation movie" nights put everyone to sleep, your Nikon V1 motion snapshots should prove to be much more enjoyable and palatable.

What Are Motion Snapshots?

When you spin the mode dial to the Motion Snapshot position, the V1 is poised to capture a one-second clip whenever you specify. Here's a brief rundown of how it works:

1. **Start "buffering."** When you're almost ready to capture a motion snapshot, press the shutter release button down halfway. The V1 will begin capturing motion in your scene, *but will not store it to your memory card.* The video instead is temporarily stored in the camera's memory, or *buffer,* waiting until you decide to actually save a moment in time. This buffering process continues for about 90 seconds, or until you decide to take the motion snapshot.
2. **Capture the sequence.** When you choose to record a sequence, press the shutter release the rest of the way down. At that instant, about one second of the video currently in the buffer is saved, embracing the moments *just before* you press the button to *just after.* That is, you don't have to worry about "just missing" the decisive moment; the V1 will forgive your human "lag time" and grab the motion you were looking at when you chose to take the snapshot.
3. **Save to the memory card.** The motion snapshot, along with a still photo of the moment, is then saved to your memory card permanently for you to enjoy later.
4. **Review the snapshot.** The V1 next displays the motion snapshot you just shot in 2.5X slow motion, accompanied by theme music, and finishing with the still photograph of your scene.

You can view your motion snapshots individually, or as a montage/slide show. The next sections provide more details on how to shoot and display killer mini-videos.

Shooting Motion Snapshots

Follow these steps to record your own motion snapshots.

1. **Shift to Motion Snapshot mode.** Rotate the mode dial to the Motion Snapshot position, shown in Figure 4.1.
2. **Select a theme.** Press the F button to the left of the zoom bar. The screen shown in Figure 4.2 appears. Use the directional buttons to choose from Beauty, Waves, Relaxation, or Tenderness theme music. No audio preview is available. However, since there are only four themes, it's easy enough to shoot tests using each theme (just one time) and then evaluate them to decide which should be used in the future.

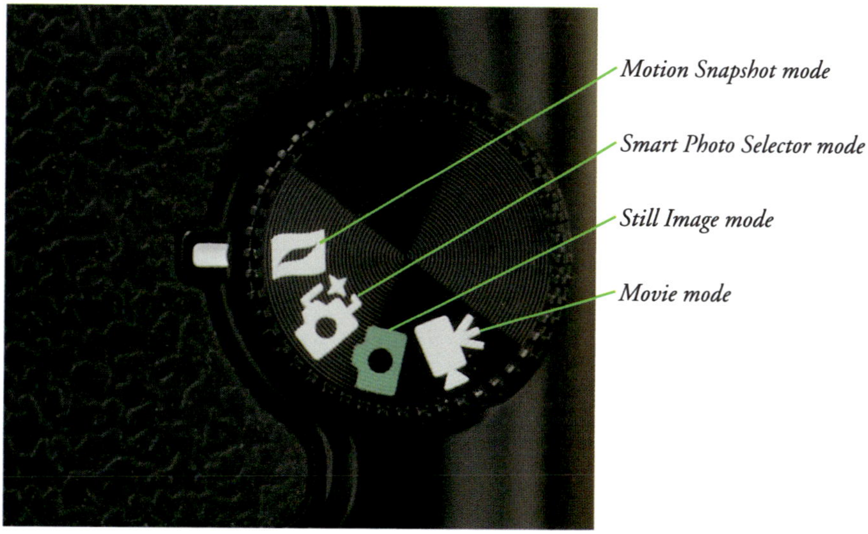

Figure 4.1
The mode dial with the four shooting modes.

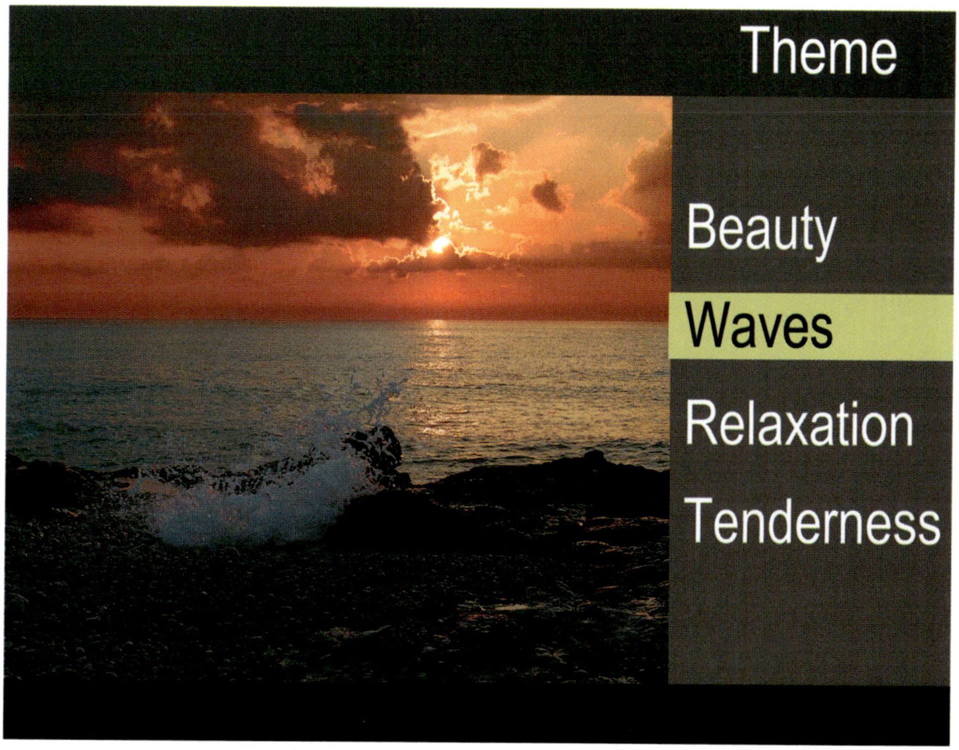

Figure 4.2
Select a musical theme for your motion snapshot.

3. **Choose settings.** When in Motion Snapshot mode, you can select from an array of adjustments, including exposure mode and metering modes, white balance, ISO sensitivity, Picture Controls, and autofocus options (see Figure 4.3), just as you can in Still, Smart Photo Selector, and Movie modes (although the choices available in each may vary slightly). I introduced many of those options in Chapter 2, and you'll find more details in the other chapters in Part II.
4. **Frame the photo.** You can use either the LCD or the EVF to compose your image.
5. **Begin buffering.** Press the shutter release halfway to begin capturing the scene to the V1's memory buffer. Note that the *shutter release* is used, and not the red movie button located to the right of the shutter button. The screen will look something like Figure 4.4 (depending on the display view and settings you've selected) to indicate that buffering is underway. The movie "time remaining" indicator at the bottom right of the screen shows that about 1 second of video will be captured. Buffering will continue for a maximum of about 90 seconds, or until you press the shutter button down to take the picture.

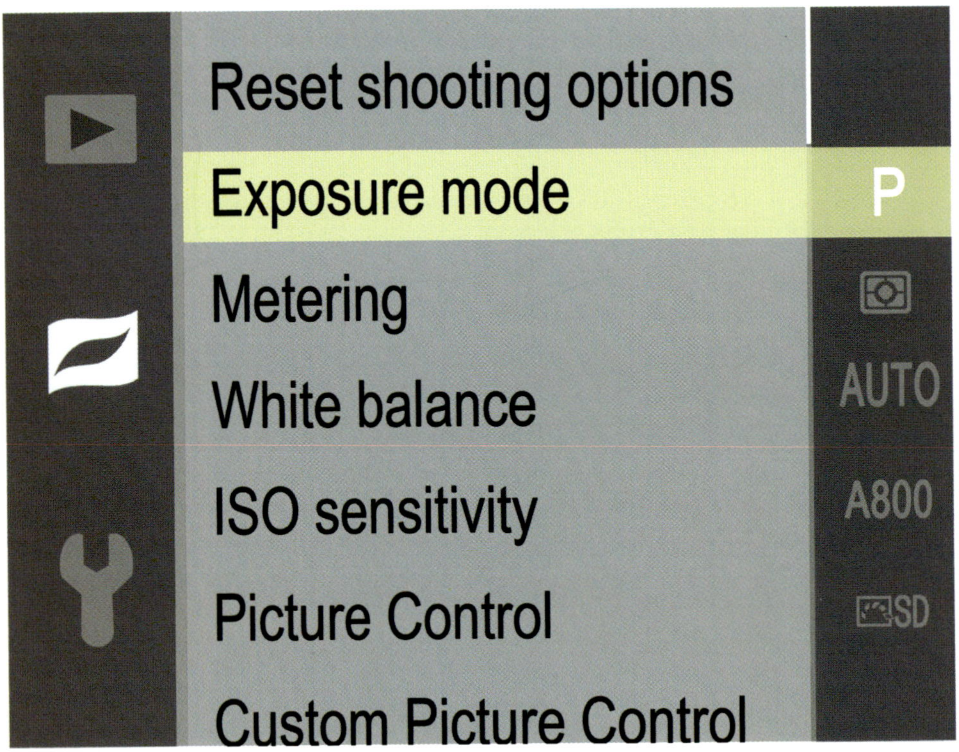

Figure 4.3
Choose settings for the motion snapshot.

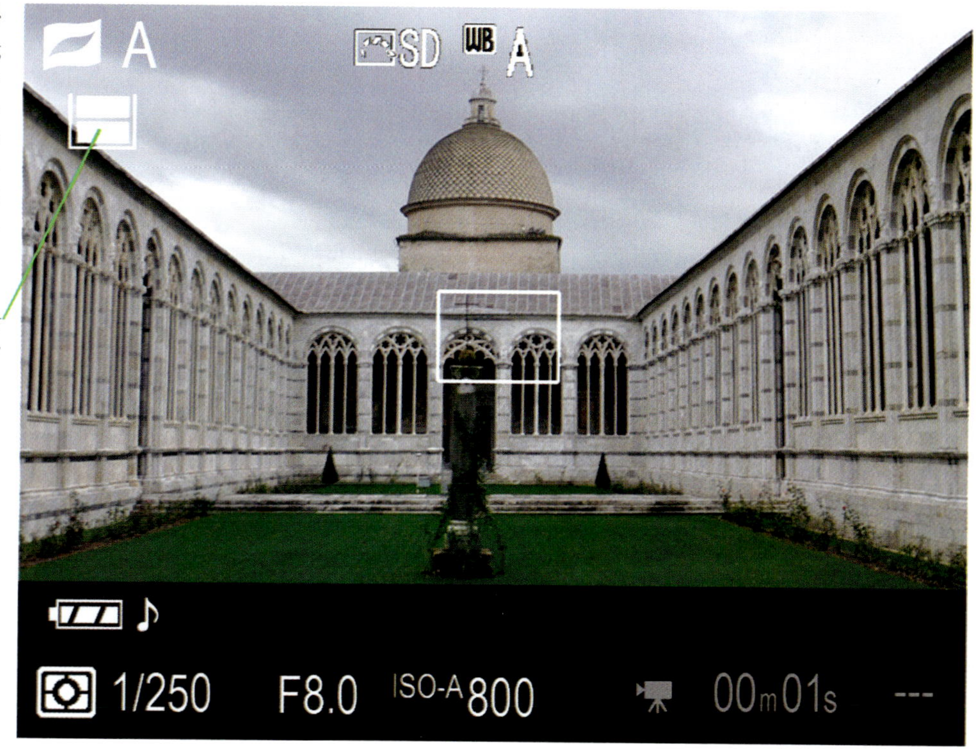

Figure 4.4
When buffering begins, an indicator is displayed in the upper-left corner of the monitor.

Buffering indicator

6. **Capture.** Gently press the shutter release down the rest of the way to capture the sequence. An animated sequence of rotating boxes will appear on the screen for a few seconds, indicating your motion snapshot is being saved to the memory card. Note that audio is not recorded; a motion snapshot captures only a video representation of the scene.
7. **Review.** The still snapshot will be displayed for a few seconds to allow you to confirm that you've captured the motion snapshot.

Shooting Motion Snapshots with Flash

If you have the optional SB-N5 flash unit, you've got an illuminator that will brighten your scene for a few seconds while shooting motion snapshots. Obviously, a series of flash bursts is not the best way to light a movie scene, but the SB-N5 provides the next best thing—a bright white LED on the front that can provide a bit of light for a period of up to six seconds. It's a perfect supplementary light source when you want to brighten indoor pictures or fill in shadows outdoors. Just follow these steps:

1. **Shift to Motion Snapshot mode and select a theme.** Rotate the mode dial to the Motion Snapshot position, and choose your musical theme, as described above.
2. **Mount the flash.** Slide the accessory shoe cover off and mount the SB-N5 flash, and rotate the switch on the back to the On position. (See Figure 4.5.)

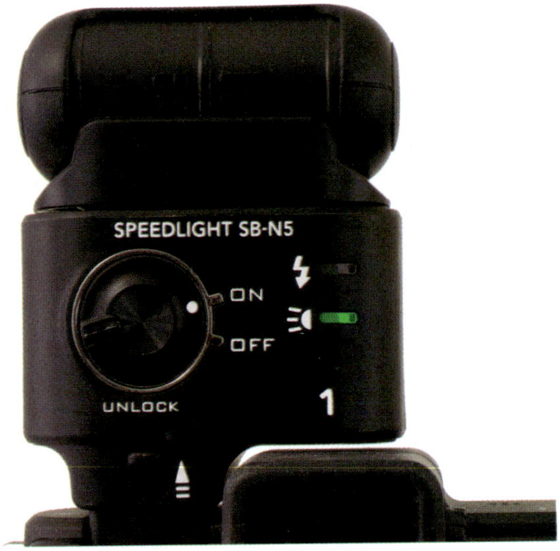

Figure 4.5 Mount the SB-N5 and turn it on.

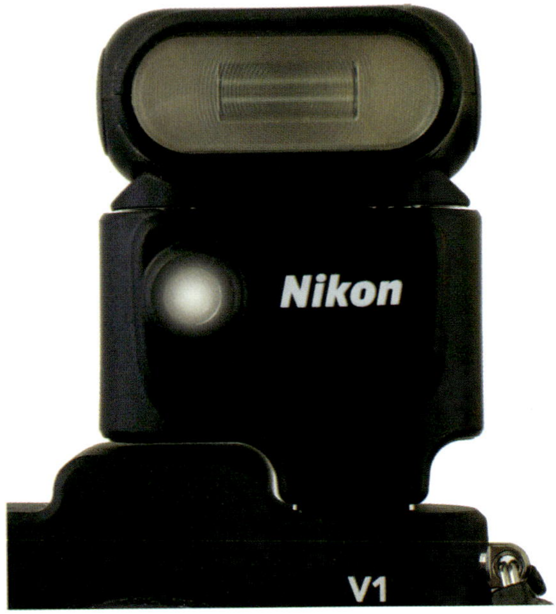

Figure 4.6 During buffering, the LED will illuminate.

3. **Choose settings and frame.** Choose your exposure, metering, and focus modes, and other settings as described earlier, and compose your photo.
4. **Buffer and shoot.** Press the shutter release halfway to begin capturing the scene to the V1's memory buffer. The white LED on the front of the SB-N5 will illuminate. (See Figure 4.6.) Buffering will continue for a maximum of about six seconds (because the LED does drain the battery), or until you press the shutter release down all the way, taking the picture. If buffering stops, lift your finger from the shutter release and press halfway again to resume.
5. **Review.** After you've taken your picture, the still snapshot will be displayed for a few seconds.

Viewing and Reviewing Your Motion Snapshots

Once you've recorded one or more motion snapshots, you can view them as a slide show, as explained in Chapter 8, or see them individually by following these steps:

1. **Press Playback.** The most recently shot image will appear on the screen.
2. **Select motion snapshot to view.** Use the left/right directional buttons to navigate to the sequence you want to view. The Motion Snapshot icon will appear in the upper-left corner of the screen in any playback mode but Image Only.
3. **Press OK to view.** In Simple Details mode, you'll be prompted to press the OK button to view the snapshot.

4. **Watch your motion snapshot.** The snapshot and its audio theme will be played back over a period of about 2.5 seconds, and then the on-screen image will fade to the still photo version, and the theme music will continue for about 10 seconds total. Note that if you've rotated the camera and recorded the snapshot in vertical orientation, it will *not* be rotated on the screen (unlike still shots), even if you've set Rotate On in the Playback menu.
5. **Adjust playback volume.** While the clip is playing, you can adjust the volume by pressing the zoom bar up or down.
6. **Delete (optional).** You can trash the motion snapshot by pressing the Delete button twice. Or, you can cancel and exit by pressing the Playback button or tapping the shutter release.

Using Smart Photo Selector Mode

The buffering used in the Motion Snapshot mode serves as one of the tools deployed by your V1 for its magic Smart Photo Selector mode. In use, the camera takes 20 exposures at a rate of 30 frames per second (in effect, a 2/3-second movie) and stores the images in its buffer for a short period of time. It then examines the pictures, rejecting the blurriest, and those that otherwise don't make the cut (say, your human subject has eyes closed), presenting you with the best shot and four additional candidates, which are all stored to the memory card. This is a fun feature, and easy to use. Just follow these steps:

1. **Shift to Smart Photo Selector mode.** Rotate the mode dial to the Smart Photo Selector position, shown earlier in Figure 4.1.
2. **Mount the flash (optional).** You can use the SB-N5 flash, as described under the Motion Snapshot description.
3. **Choose settings.** When in Smart Photo Selector mode, you can select from an array of adjustments, a different selection from the ones available in other modes. They include Image Quality, Image Size, Color Space, Noise Reduction, Vibration Reduction, and Built-in AF assist. I'll describe these in Chapter 8.

   Note that you can't choose an exposure or metering mode, nor focus modes—except that the V1 will automatically switch to close-up focusing if it detects that your main subject is located in the macro range. The camera will choose a scene mode for you, as described in Chapter 2.
4. **Frame the photo.** You can use either the LCD or the EVF to compose your image. For the "smarts" to work, your main subject should be in the center of the frame. The V1 will use this subject to gauge whether or not one of the buffered images is acceptable.

5. **Begin buffering.** Press the shutter release halfway to begin capturing the scene to the V1's memory buffer. The camera will adjust focus to accommodate subject movement closer or farther from the camera. AF area brackets that appear in the frame as soon as you switch to Smart Photo show the area of focus. Buffering will continue for a maximum of about 90 seconds, or until you press the shutter button down to take the picture.
6. **Capture.** Gently press the shutter release down the rest of the way to capture the sequence of pictures. Animated rotating boxes will appear on the screen for a few seconds, indicating your photos are being saved to the memory card.
7. **Review.** The image the V1 decides is best is displayed on the monitor, either the EVF or LCD, depending on which you were using when the capture was made.

Viewing and Reviewing Your Smart Snapshots

Viewing your Smart Photo Selector mode images is a bit counterintuitive, because the V1 stores them all to your memory card, but won't "allow" you to look at them all, except when you use the procedure I'll describe next. The process is simple, and easy to understand once you've tried it. Just follow these steps:

1. **Press Playback.** The most recently shot image will appear on the screen. The camera displays the series with a border, resembling a stack of prints with the selected best shot on top of the stack.
2. **Scroll through Smart Photos.** Use the left/right directional buttons to navigate to the "best shot" of the series you want to view. This is where things get a little interesting. The V1 will let you view *only* the best shot of the series in normal playback mode. For example, if you'd shot two Smart Photo sets on a blank memory card, the V1 would show that 10 pictures had been taken (five for each series), but might display only the fourth and seventh pictures, displaying them as 4/10 (four of ten) and 7/10 (seven of 10). The others are on your card, but are skipped over during normal playback, and you need to jump through a small hoop to see them.
3. **Choose the series to view.** When you see the "best" shot of the series you want to review, make sure the Simple Details screen is shown (press the DISP button if necessary to view it), and press the OK button. In Simple Details playback mode, you'll be prompted to press the OK button to view the snapshot and its runners-up.
4. **Examine the images.** Use the left/right directional buttons to scroll through the four candidates. (See Figure 4.7.) If you see one you prefer to the best shot selected by the V1, press the OK button to upgrade its status.

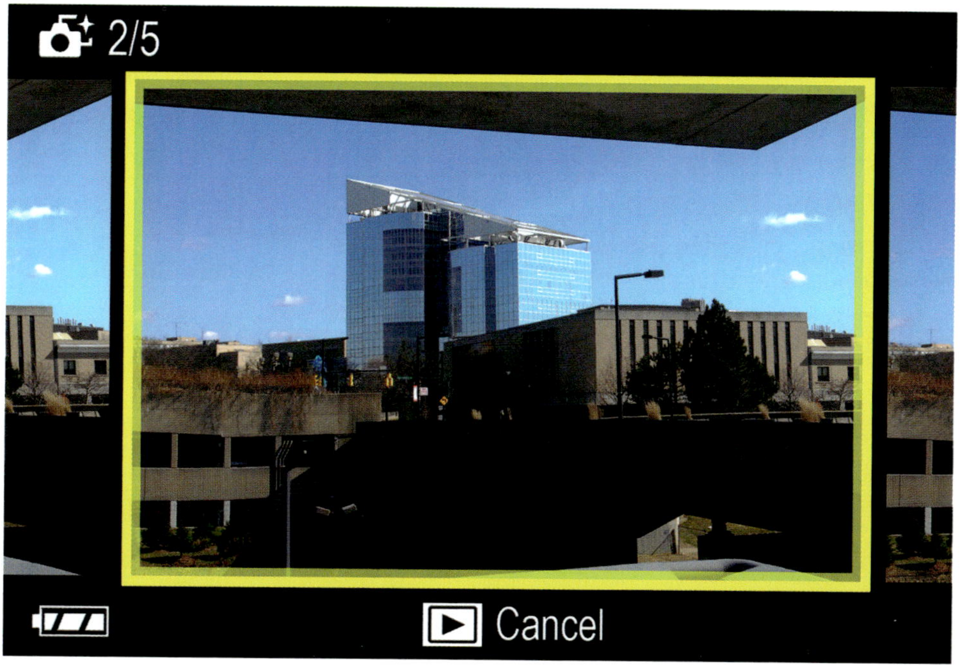

Figure 4.7
Review the best shot and runners-up.

5. **Delete (optional).** During best shot review, you can trash an individual image by pressing the Delete button. A screen appears with the options: This Image (to remove the current image) and All Except Best Shot (to delete the runner-up candidates). Press OK to confirm, and then select Yes from the next screen that appears to go ahead with trashing the selected image(s). Or, you can cancel and exit by pressing the Playback button.
6. **Return to normal playback.** Press the Playback button to exit best shot review.

Using Still Image Mode

Still Image mode is your all-purpose shooting mode used for most picture taking. Most of the rest of this book will deal with shooting in this mode. It features Automatic Scene Selection (in which the V1 chooses from among Portrait, Landscape, Night Portrait, Close-Up, and Auto Scene modes), and the usual selection of semi-automatic and manual modes (Program, Shutter-priority, Aperture-priority, and Manual; commonly referred to as PSAM modes). I introduced you to the use of Still Image mode in Chapter 2. I'll be recapping what you learned there and provide some extra details in Chapters 5 and 6.

To use Still Image mode in its most basic form, just follow these steps:

1. **Shift to Still Image mode.** Rotate the mode dial to the Still Image mode position, shown earlier in Figure 4.1.
2. **Mount the flash (optional).** You can use the SB-N5 flash, as described earlier under the Motion Snapshot description. I'll cover electronic flash in more detail in Chapter 10.
3. **Select exposure mode.** Press the MENU button, choose the Shooting menu, and scroll to Exposure Mode, press OK and select Scene Auto Selector, Programmed Auto, Shutter-Priority Auto, Aperture-Priority Auto, or Manual.
4. **Choose settings.** When in Still Image mode, you can select from a full array of adjustments, which I'll explain later in this chapter, in Chapter 5 (which deals with understanding exposure), and Chapter 8 (which explains how to choose and use all the menu settings of the V1).
5. **Frame the photo.** You can use either the LCD or the EVF to compose your image.
6. **Focus.** Press the shutter release halfway to focus the image. If the V1 is successful at locking in focus, the focus area will be highlighted in green; otherwise, the focus area will glow red. You'll find more focus options in Chapter 6.
7. **Shoot.** Gently press the shutter release down the rest of the way to capture the picture. The image you've just taken will be shown on the display for a few seconds.

Choosing a Shutter Type

The shutter is the component that exposes the sensor to light when the picture is taken. Of course, if you have peered inside the interior of your Nikon V1 when the lens is removed, you know that the sensor is generally exposed all the time (allowing the live view image with the EVF and LCD). It's "covered" only just prior to and after the actual exposure.

I put "covered" in quotes because the shutter in the Nikon 1 series of cameras isn't necessarily a physical shutter that shields the sensor from light. The Nikon V1 has a physical shutter at the focal plane that covers the sensor, and then opens during the exposure to capture the image. It also has an *electronic* shutter that performs the same function. In use, the camera darkens the shutter by dumping the current image from the sensor chip electronically, then activating the sensor to capture light *only* for the duration of the exposure. This process is very fast, and can operate much more quickly than the mechanical shutter, providing speeds as brief as 1/16,000th second. There are some advantages and disadvantages to each shutter type. This section will help you choose whether to use the mechanical or electronic shutter.

Using the Mechanical Shutter

You'll want to use the mechanical shutter for everyday use. Here are the most important considerations to take into account:

- **Shutter speed range.** The mechanical shutter offers shutter speeds from 30 seconds to 1/4000th second. Although the electronic shutter offers higher speeds, this range is sufficient for virtually every scene you might want to photograph.
- **Frame rates.** Because of its higher speeds, the electronic shutter can capture images at faster frame rates, which is why it is always used for shooting movies (at up to 60 frames per second) and for slow-motion video (at up to 1200 frames per second).
- **Flash synchronization.** The mechanical shutter allows using electronic flash, such as the SB-N5 at shutter speeds up to 1/250th second; the electronic shutter can sync at speeds of only 1/60th second or slower. As you'll learn in Chapter 10, faster shutter speeds reduce the chance of "ghost" images caused by a secondary exposure from the ambient light (which becomes more likely the slower the shutter speed is).
- **Less subject distortion.** When your subject is moving during the time the sensor is capturing the picture, the final image can suffer from several kinds of distortion. Parts of the image are exposed at different times, while the camera or subject move during exposure, producing a wobbly look ("jello" effect especially noticeable during video shooting), skew, or smear. The mechanical shutter minimizes these effects because the curtains that expose the sensor travel so quickly across the frame.
- **Better image quality.** Mechanical shutters reduce an effect called "blooming" that can appear around bright highlights when using an electronic shutter. Images taken with an electronic shutter also tend to have higher levels of noise, a grainy texture that appears during the processing of the image.
- **Audible noise.** Mechanical shutters do produce a clicking sound—there's no way around it—and electronic shutters can operate silently. So, if you must have absolutely silent operation, the electronic shutter is preferable.

As you can see, the mechanical shutter is superior in most aspects to the electronic shutter, except when higher shutter speeds, faster frame rates, or silent operation is required.

To set the Nikon V1 to use the mechanical shutter, just follow these steps (you can also select one of these options using the Shutter Type entry in the Shooting menu):

1. **Choose Still Image mode.** Rotate the mode dial to the Still Image mode position, shown in Figure 4.1 earlier in this chapter.
2. **Press the F button.** The screen shown in Figure 4.8 appears.

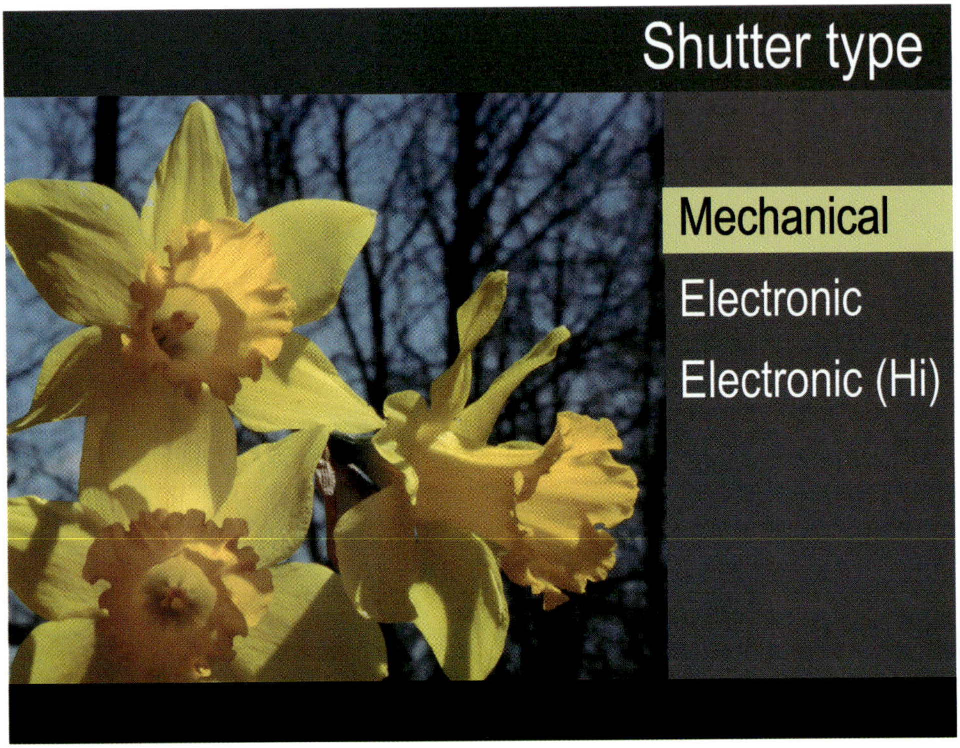

Figure 4.8
Choose shutter type from this screen.

3. **Choose mechanical shutter.** Use the multi selector directional buttons to select Mechanical Shutter.
4. **Confirm.** Press OK to confirm your choice.

Using the Electronic Shutter and Electronic Shutter (Hi)

You can specify the Electronic Shutter or Electronic Shutter (Hi) by following steps 1-4 in the previous section, but selecting Electronic Shutter or Electronic Shutter (Hi) instead. When either electronic shutter is activated, the following features are available:

- **High Shutter Speeds.** In either electronic shutter mode, you can select shutter speeds faster than 1/4000th second, specifically 1/5000th, 1/6400th, 1/8000th, 1/10,000th, 1/13,000th, and 1/16,000th second when using Manual or Shutter-priority modes. The V1 may select these faster shutter speeds, if required, in Program and Aperture-priority modes. In practice, however, speeds of 1/4000th second or slower are all that you really need.
- **Faster frame rates.** Continuous shooting is possible at about 5 frames per second when using the electronic shutter (the same as with the mechanical shutter). Switch

to Electronic Shutter (Hi), and the V1 defaults to 10 fps. You can also choose 30 fps or 60 fps. The Electronic Shutter (Hi) is also used for slow-motion movies at reduced resolutions, at 400 fps (640 × 240 pixels) or 1200 fps (320 × 120 pixels).

- **Silent shooting.** When using either electronic shutter mode, the V1 can shoot completely silently. This is a great option when capturing images in museums, at religious ceremonies, and at plays and other performances where shutter clicking might be obtrusive.

I'll explain more about advanced continuous shooting techniques in Chapter 6, and slow-motion movie making in Chapter 7.

Shooting Movies in Still Image Mode

When the Nikon V1 is set to Still Image mode, you can record non-high-definition movies, using an aspect ratio of 3:2 (the same proportions as the still image frame), with a resolution of 1072 × 720 pixels. That's a handy feature to have if you're shooting still photos and see something that would be better captured as a video clip. To shoot movies without exiting Still Image mode, just follow these steps:

1. **Start movie recording.** While shooting still photos, press the red movie record button. The V1 will immediately switch to movie mode and the recording indicator will appear at the upper left of the screen. Audio will be recorded along with the video.

2. **Stop movie recording.** To stop shooting video, press the movie record button a second time. You can also switch back to still photography by pressing the shutter release button down all the way. The video recording will stop and a still photograph will be taken.

Using Movie Mode

Although it's convenient to be able to shoot 1072 × 720-pixel movies in still mode, you'll get the best quality capturing full HD movies using the mode dial's Movie mode. The Nikon V1 captures full HD video with a 16:9 aspect ratio at 1080i/60 frames per second, 1080p/60 fps, and 720p/60 frames per second (1920 × 1080 and 1280 × 720 pixels). It can also grab slow-motion movies at an 8:3 aspect ratio at 400 fps, and play them back at 30 fps to slow the image down to a crawl.

This section will introduce you to the basics of using each of these modes, and how to shoot stills while recording movies. I'll provide more detail on working with each option, including making movie settings, trimming movies, and movie sound options in the advanced movie making discussion in Chapter 7.

Shooting Conventional HD Movies

Most of the time you'll want to record conventional HD movies for showing on your computer screen, HDTV, or other display, for editing, using Nikon's Short Movie Maker Software or other programs, including Adobe Premiere, Adobe Premiere Elements, or iMovie.

It's easy to get started shooting movies. Just follow these steps:

1. **Shift to Movie mode.** Rotate the mode dial to the Movie mode position, shown earlier in Figure 4.1.
2. **Select exposure mode.** Press the MENU button, choose the Shooting menu, and scroll to Exposure Mode, press OK and select Scene Auto Selector, Programmed Auto, Shutter-Priority Auto, Aperture-Priority Auto, or Manual.
3. **Choose settings.** When in Movie mode, you can select from an array of other adjustments, including metering mode, white balance, ISO sensitivity, Picture Controls, and various movie options, including movie sound options, movie resolution, and fade-in/fade-out features.
4. **Frame the movie.** You can use either the LCD or the EVF to compose your image.
5. **Focus.** Press the shutter release halfway to focus the image. The subject in the center of the frame is used to establish focus, and face detection is not used. If the V1 is successful at locking in focus, the focus area will be highlighted in green; otherwise, the focus area will glow red. You'll find more focus options in Chapter 8.
6. **Lock focus/exposure.** When using an exposure mode other than Scene Auto Selector, you can lock exposure and focus by pressing the AE-L/AF-L button (the multi selector up button).
7. **Shoot.** Gently press the red movie record button to begin shooting. The recording indicator will appear at the left of the frame; the time elapsed and the time still available will be displayed.
8. **End recording.** Press the movie record button a second time to halt recording. Movie making will also end automatically when the memory card is full, the maximum size of 4GB is reached, or the maximum time of 20 minutes is recorded.

Shooting Still Images in Movie Mode

When the Nikon V1 is set to Movie mode and you are not shooting slow-motion video, you can grab as many as 20 still images without interrupting your HD movie recording. However, the stills you capture will be 7.5MP in 1080i mode, 2MP in 1080p mode, and 1MP in 720p mode, all using the 16:9 aspect ratio. Just press the shutter release button while shooting, and the frame being captured at that moment will be stored as a still image. As you shoot still photos, the number of still photos left in a decreasing number count are shown at the right-hand edge of the display.

Shooting Slow-Motion Movies

Slow-motion movies are silent clips recorded at the reduced aspect ratio of 8:3 at the amazing speed of 400 or 1200 frames per second. Because they are played back at 30 fps, one second of 400 fps slow-motion footage requires more than 13 seconds to play out on the screen, and one second of 1200 fps footage takes 40 seconds, producing a pronounced slo-mo effect. You can use these movies to analyze your golf stroke, high diving technique, or for comic or dramatic effect in your more ambitious video productions. Of course, it's not easy to intercut 8:3 aspect ratio clips with 16:9 HD clips, so the editing techniques are going to take some work (and are beyond the scope of this book). The main roadblock is that at 400 fps, the frame size is pared down to 640 × 240 pixels, and at 1200 fps to a teensy 320 × 120 pixels. In either case, the maximum shooting length is five seconds, which plays back in 1 minute, 6 seconds from a clip shot at 400 fps to 3 minutes, 20 seconds for a clip recorded at 1200 fps.

It's easy to get started shooting slow-motion movies. Just follow these steps:

1. **Shift to Movie mode.** Rotate the mode dial to the Movie mode position, shown in Figure 4.1.
2. **Select Slow Motion mode.** Press the F button and use the multi selector directional buttons to choose Slow Motion. Press the OK button to confirm your choice.
3. **Select exposure mode.** Press the MENU button, choose the Shooting menu, and scroll to Exposure Mode, press OK and select Programmed Auto, Shutter-Priority Auto, Aperture-Priority Auto, or Manual. Scene Auto Selector is not available.
4. **Choose settings.** When in Slow Motion Movie mode, you can select from an array of other adjustments, including frame rate, white balance, ISO sensitivity, Picture Controls, and vibration reduction.
5. **Frame the movie.** You can use either the LCD or the EVF to compose your image. A wide mask showing the 8:3 slow-motion filming area appears on the screen.
6. **Shoot.** Gently press the red movie record button to begin shooting. The recording indicator will appear at the left of the frame; the time elapsed and the time still available will be displayed. The camera focuses on the subject in the center of the screen, and face detection or still image shooting is not available.
7. **End recording.** Press the movie record button a second time to halt recording. Movie making will also end when the maximum time of about 5 seconds is reached, when the memory card is full, the maximum size of 4GB is reached, or, if you're using a slow memory card, the buffer fills before the existing recording is saved to the card.

Viewing Movies

You can view your movies in Playback mode. Just follow these steps:

1. **Start Playback review.** Press the Playback button. You can review your movies when the camera is set to any shooting mode. You don't need to be using Movie mode to view them. When using full-frame playback (that is, when not in thumbnail or calendar view), movies are indicated by a movie camera icon in the upper-left corner. (See Figure 4.9.)
2. **Select a movie to review.** When the clip you want to watch is shown on the screen, press the OK button to start.
3. **Pause movie.** Stop playback at any time by pressing the multi selector down button.
4. **Single frame advance/rewind.** When the movie is paused, pressing the right directional button advances one frame; the left directional button rewinds one frame. Or, you can rotate the multi selector dial clockwise or counterclockwise.
5. **Resume play.** Press the OK button to resume playback of the movie.

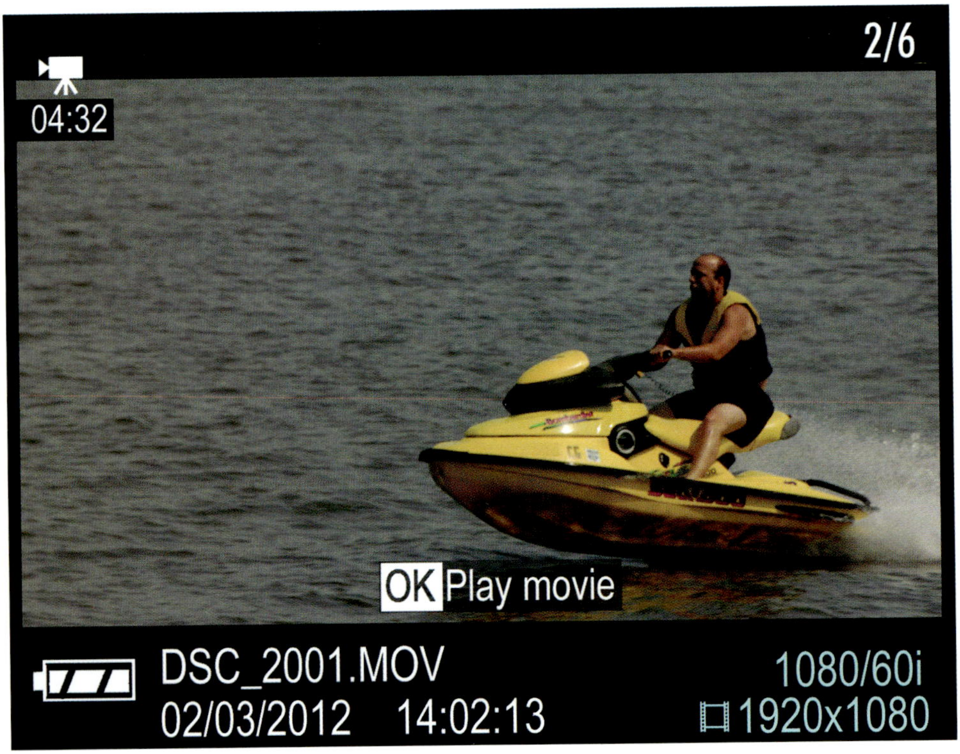

Figure 4.9
Select a movie to view in Playback mode.

6. **Fast forward/rewind.** Press the right directional button to advance, or the left directional button to rewind. A single press increases the speed from 1X to 2X. Keep pressing to accelerate playback to 5X, 10X, or 15X.
7. **Adjust volume.** The zoom bar can be pressed up or down to increase or decrease volume.
8. **Exit to Playback mode.** Press the up directional button to return to Playback mode to select a different still image or movie to resume.
9. **Return to shooting mode.** Tap the shutter release button halfway to return to shooting mode.

5

Understanding Exposure

When you bought your Nikon V1, you probably thought your days of worrying about getting the correct exposure were over. To paraphrase an old Kodak tagline dating back to the 19th Century—the goal is, "you press the button, and the camera does the rest." For the most part, that's a realistic objective. The V1 is one of the smartest cameras available when it comes to calculating the right exposure for most situations. You can generally choose Smart Photo Selector or switch to Program (P), Shutter-priority (S), or Aperture-priority (A) and shoot away.

For example, when you shoot with the main light source behind the subject, you end up with *backlighting*, which can result in an overexposed background and/or an underexposed subject. The Nikon V1 recognizes backlit situations nicely, and can properly base exposure on the main subject, producing a decent photo. Features like Active D-Lighting (discussed in Chapter 8) can fine-tune exposure as you take photos, to preserve detail in the highlights and shadows.

But what if you *want* to underexpose the subject, to produce a silhouette effect? Or, perhaps, you might want to use the V1's clip-on flash unit to fill in the shadows on your subject. The more you know about how to use your V1, the more you'll run into situations where you want to creatively tweak the exposure to provide a different look than you'd get with a straight shot.

This chapter shows you the fundamentals of exposure, so you'll be better equipped to override the Nikon V1's default settings when you want to, or need to. After all, correct exposure is one of the foundations of good photography, along with accurate focus and sharpness, appropriate color balance, freedom from unwanted noise and excessive contrast, as well as pleasing composition.

The Nikon V1 gives you a great deal of control over all of these, although composition is entirely up to you. You must still frame the photograph to create an interesting arrangement of subject matter, but all the other parameters are basic functions of the camera. You can let your V1 set them for you automatically, you can fine-tune how the camera applies its automatic settings, or you can make them yourself, manually. The amount of control you have over exposure, sensitivity (ISO settings), color balance, focus, and image parameters like sharpness and contrast make the V1 a versatile tool for creating images.

In the next few pages I'm going to give you a grounding in one of those foundations, and explain the basics of exposure, either as an introduction or as a refresher course, depending on your current level of expertise. When you finish this chapter, you'll understand most of what you need to know to take well-exposed photographs creatively in a broad range of situations.

Getting a Handle on Exposure

In the most basic sense, exposure is all about light. Exposure can make or break your photo. Correct exposure brings out the detail in the areas you want to picture, providing the range of tones and colors you need to create the desired image. Poor exposure can cloak important details in shadow, or wash them out in glare-filled featureless expanses of white. However, getting the perfect exposure requires some intelligence—either that built into the camera or the smarts in your head—because digital sensors can't capture all the tones we are able to see. If the range of tones in an image is extensive, embracing both inky black shadows and bright highlights, we often must settle for an exposure that renders most of those tones—but not all—in a way that best suits the photo we want to produce.

For example, look at two exposures presented in Figure 5.1. For the image at left, the highlights (chiefly the clouds at upper left and the top-left edge of the skyscraper) are well exposed, but everything else in the shot is seriously underexposed. The version on

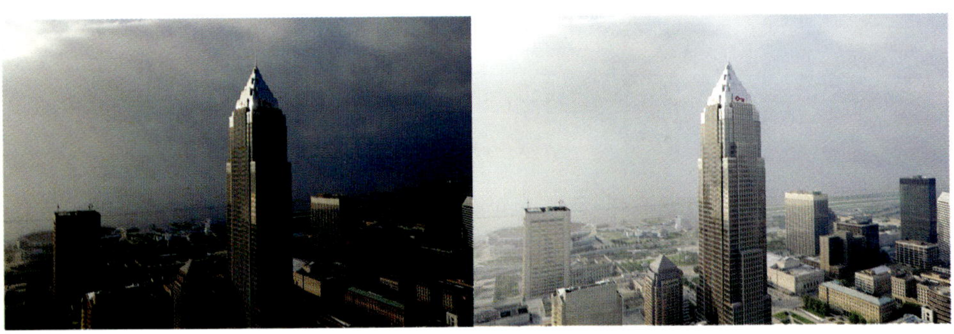

Figure 5.1
At left, the image is exposed for the highlights, losing shadow detail. At right, the exposure captures detail in the shadows, but the highlights are washed out.

the right, taken an instant later with the tripod-mounted camera, shows detail in the shadow areas of the buildings, but the highlights are completely washed out. The camera's sensor simply can't capture detail in both dark areas and bright areas in a single shot.

The solution, in this particular case, was to resort to a technique called High Dynamic Range (HDR) photography, in which the two exposures from Figure 5.1 were combined in an image editor such as Photoshop, or a specialized HDR tool like Photomatix (about $100 from www.hdrsoft.com). The resulting shot is shown in Figure 5.2. I'll explain more about HDR photography later in this chapter. For now, though, I'm going to concentrate on showing you how to get the best exposures possible without resorting to such tools, using only the features of your Nikon V1.

To understand exposure, you need to understand the six aspects of light that combine to produce an image. Start with a light source—the sun, an interior lamp, or the glow from a campfire—and trace its path to your camera, through the lens, and finally to the sensor that captures the illumination. Here's a brief review of the things within our control that affect exposure, listed in "chronological" order (that is, as the light moves from the subject to the sensor):

- **Light at its source.** Our eyes and our cameras—film or digital—are most sensitive to that portion of the electromagnetic spectrum we call *visible light.* That light has several important aspects that are relevant to photography, such as color, and harshness (which is determined primarily by the apparent size of the light source as it

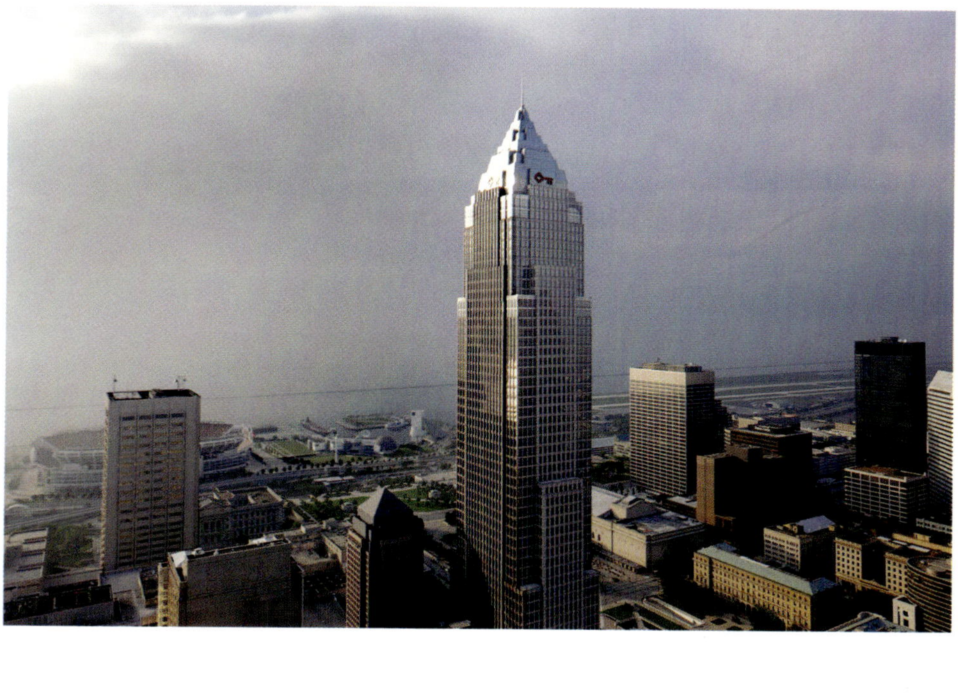

Figure 5.2 Combining the two exposures produces the best compromise image.

illuminates a subject). But, in terms of exposure, the important attribute of a light source is its *intensity.* We may have direct control over intensity, which might be the case with an interior light that can be brightened or dimmed. Or, we might have only indirect control over intensity, as with sunlight, which can be made to appear dimmer by introducing translucent light-absorbing or reflective materials in its path.

- **Light's duration.** We tend to think of most light sources as continuous. But, as you'll learn in Chapter 10, the duration of light can change quickly enough to modify the exposure, as when the main illumination in a photograph comes from an intermittent source, such as an electronic flash.
- **Light reflected, transmitted, or emitted.** Once light is produced by its source, either continuously or in a brief burst, we are able to see and photograph objects by the light that is reflected from our subjects towards the camera lens; transmitted (say, from translucent objects that are lit from behind); or emitted (by a candle or television screen). When more or less light reaches the lens from the subject, we need to adjust the exposure. This part of the equation is under our control to the extent we can increase the amount of light falling on or passing through the subject (by adding extra light sources or using reflectors), or by pumping up the light that's emitted (by increasing the brightness of the glowing object).
- **Light passed by the lens.** Not all the illumination that reaches the front of the lens makes it all the way through. Filters can remove some of the light before it enters the lens. Inside the lens barrel is a variable-sized diaphragm that produces an opening called an *aperture* that dilates and contracts to control the amount of light that enters the lens. You, or the V1's autoexposure system, can control exposure by varying the size of the aperture. The relative size of the aperture is called the *f/stop.* (See Figure 5.3.)
- **Light passing through the shutter.** Once light passes through the lens, the amount of time the sensor receives it is determined by the V1's shutter, which can remain open for as long as 30 seconds (or up to 120 seconds if you use the Bulb setting, available with the ML-L3 remote control) or as briefly as 1/4,000th second with the mechanical shutter, or 1/16,000th second with the electronic shutter.
- **Light captured by the sensor.** Not all the light falling onto the sensor is captured. If the number of photons reaching a particular photosite doesn't pass a set threshold, no information is recorded. Similarly, if too much light illuminates a pixel in the sensor, then the excess isn't recorded or, worse, spills over to contaminate adjacent pixels. We can modify the minimum and maximum number of pixels that contribute to image detail by adjusting the ISO setting. At higher ISOs, the incoming light is amplified to boost the effective sensitivity of the sensor.

These four factors—quantity of light, light passed by the lens, the amount of time the shutter is open, and the sensitivity of the sensor—all work proportionately and reciprocally to produce an exposure. That is, if you double the amount of light, increase the aperture by one stop, make the shutter speed twice as long, or boost the ISO setting 2X, you'll get twice as much exposure. Similarly, you can increase any of these factors while decreasing one of the others by a similar amount to keep the same exposure.

F/STOPS AND SHUTTER SPEEDS

If you're *really* new to more advanced cameras (and I realize that some ambitious amateurs do purchase the V1 as their first digital SLR), you might need to know that the lens aperture, or f/stop, is a ratio, much like a fraction, which is why f/2 is larger than f/4, just as 1/2 is larger than 1/4. However, f/2 is actually *four times* as large as f/4. (If you remember your high-school geometry, you'll know that to double the area of a circle, you multiply its diameter by the square root of two: 1.4.)

Lenses are usually marked with intermediate f/stops that represent a size that's twice as much/half as much as the previous aperture. So, a lens might be marked: f/2, f/2.8, f/4, f/5.6, f/8, f/11, f/16 with each larger number representing an aperture that admits half as much light as the one before, as shown in Figure 5.3.

Shutter speeds are actual fractions (of a second), but the numerator is omitted, so that 60, 125, 250, 500, 1,000, and so forth represent 1/60th, 1/125th, 1/250th, 1/500th, and 1/1,000th second. To avoid confusion, Nikon uses quotation marks to signify longer exposures: 2", 2"5, 4", and so forth representing 2.0, 2.5, and 4.0-second exposures, respectively.

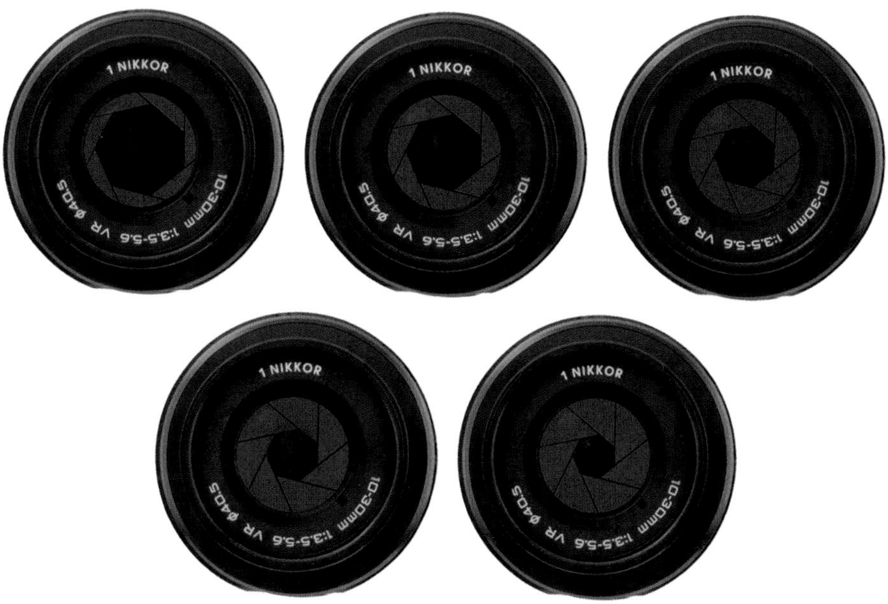

Figure 5.3
This graphic (which isn't an actual photograph of the interior of a lens) represents the relative size of typical apertures. Top row (left to right): f/4, f/5.6, f/8; bottom row: f/11, f/16.

Most commonly, exposure settings are made using the aperture and shutter speed, followed by adjusting the ISO sensitivity, if it's not possible to get the preferred exposure (that is, the one that uses the "best" f/stop or shutter speed for the depth-of-field or action stopping we want). Table 5.1 shows equivalent exposure settings using various shutter speeds and f/stops.

Table 5.1 Equivalent Exposures

Shutter speed	f/stop	Shutter speed	f/stop
1/60th second	f/16	1/500th second	f/5.6
1/125th second	f/11	1/1,000th second	f/4
1/250th second	f/8		

When the V1 is set for P mode, the metering system selects the correct exposure for you automatically, but you can change quickly to an equivalent exposure by pressing the zoom bar up or down until the desired equivalent exposure combination is displayed. You can use this Flexible Program feature more easily if you remember that you need to press the zoom bar down when you want to increase the amount of depth-of-field or use a slower shutter speed; or press up when you want to reduce the depth-of-field or use a faster shutter speed. The need for more/less DOF and slower/faster shutter speed are the primary reasons you'd want to use Flexible Program. This program shift mode does not work when you're using flash. An asterisk (*) is displayed next to the P on the monitor when this adjustment is in effect.

In Aperture-priority (A) and Shutter-priority (S) modes, you can also change to an equivalent exposure, but only by either adjusting the aperture (the camera chooses the shutter speed) or shutter speed (the camera selects the aperture). I'll cover all these exposure modes later in the chapter.

F/STOPS VERSUS STOPS

In photography parlance, *f/stop* always means the aperture or lens opening. However, for lack of a current commonly used word for one exposure increment, the term *stop* is often used. (In the past, EV served this purpose, but Exposure Value and its abbreviation have since been inextricably intertwined with its use in describing Exposure Compensation.) In this book, when I say "stop" by itself (no *f/*), I mean one whole unit of exposure, and am not necessarily referring to an actual f/stop or lens aperture. So, adjusting the exposure by "one stop" can mean both changing to the next shutter speed increment (say, from 1/125th second to 1/250th second) or the next aperture (such as f/4 to f/5.6). Similarly, 1/3 stop or 1/2 stop increments can mean either shutter speed or aperture changes, depending on the context. Be forewarned.

How the V1 Calculates Exposure

Your V1 calculates exposure by measuring the light that passes through the lens and reaches the sensor, based on the assumption that each area being measured reflects about the same amount of light as a neutral gray card that reflects a "middle" gray of about 12- to 18-percent reflectance. (The photographic "gray cards" you buy at a camera store have an 18-percent gray tone; your camera is calibrated to interpret a somewhat darker 12-percent gray; I'll explain more about this later.) That "average" 12- to 18-percent gray assumption is necessary, because different subjects reflect different amounts of light. In a photo containing, say, a white cat and a dark gray cat, the white cat might reflect five times as much light as the gray cat. An exposure based on the white cat will cause the gray cat to appear to be black, while an exposure based only on the gray cat will make the white cat washed out.

This is more easily understood if you look at some photos of subjects that are dark (they reflect little light), those that have predominantly middle tones, and subjects that are highly reflective. The next few figures show some images of actual cats (actually, the *same* cat rendered in black, gray, and white varieties through the magic of Photoshop), with each of the three strips exposed using a different cat for reference.

Correctly Exposed

The three pictures shown in Figure 5.4 represent how the black, gray, and white cats would appear if the exposure were calculated by measuring the light reflecting from the middle, gray cat, which, for the sake of illustration, we'll assume reflects approximately 12 to 18 percent of the light that strikes it. The exposure meter sees an object that it thinks is a middle gray, calculates an exposure based on that, and the feline in the center of the strip is rendered at its proper tonal value. Best of all, because the resulting exposure is correct, the black cat at left and white cat at right are rendered properly as well.

When you're shooting pictures with your V1, and the meter happens to base its exposure on a subject that averages that "ideal" middle gray, then you'll end up with similar (accurate) results. The camera's exposure algorithms are concocted to ensure this kind of result as often as possible, barring any unusual subjects (that is, those that are backlit,

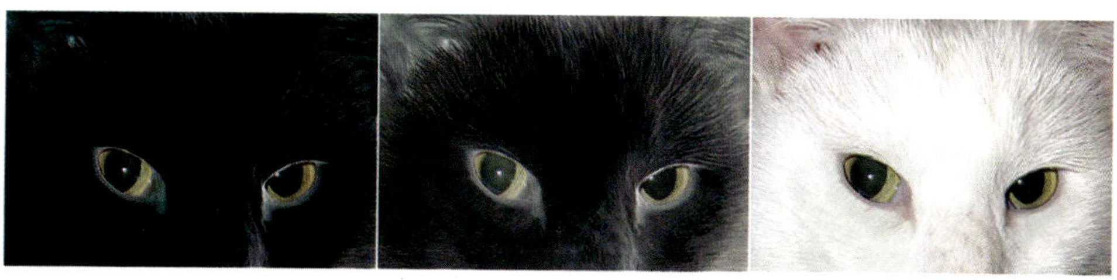

Figure 5.4 When exposure is calculated based on the middle-gray cat in the center, the black and white cats are rendered accurately, too.

or have uneven illumination). The V1 has three different metering modes (described next), plus Scene modes, each of which is equipped to handle certain types of unusual subjects, as I'll outline.

Overexposed

The strip of three images in Figure 5.5 shows what would happen if the exposure were calculated based on metering the leftmost, black cat. The light meter sees less light reflecting from the black cat than it would see from a gray middle-tone subject, and so figures, "Aha! I need to add exposure to brighten this subject up to a middle gray!" That lightens the black cat, so it now appears to be gray.

But now the cat in the middle that was *originally* middle gray is overexposed and becomes light gray. And the white cat at right is now seriously overexposed, and loses detail in the highlights, which have become a featureless white.

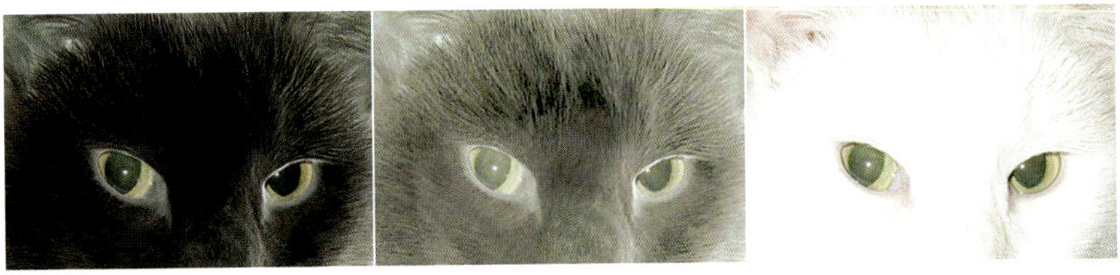

Figure 5.5
When exposure is calculated based on the black cat at the left, the black cat looks gray, the gray cat appears to be a light gray, and the white cat is seriously overexposed.

Underexposed

The third possibility in this simplified scenario is that the light meter might measure the illumination bouncing off the white cat, and try to render that feline as a middle gray. A lot of light is reflected by the white kitty, so the exposure is *reduced*, bringing that cat closer to a middle gray tone. The cats that were originally gray and black are now rendered too dark. Clearly, measuring the gray cat—or a substitute that reflects about the same amount of light—is the only way to ensure that the exposure is precisely correct. (See Figure 5.6.)

As you can see, the ideal way to measure exposure is to meter from a subject that reflects 12 to 18 percent of the light that reaches it. If you want the most precise exposure calculations, if you don't have a gray cat handy, the solution is to use a stand-in, such as

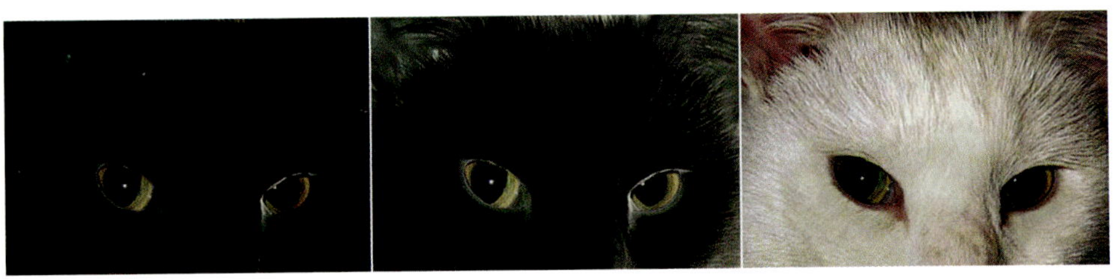

Figure 5.6
When exposure is calculated based on the white cat on the right, the other two cats are underexposed.

the evenly illuminated gray card I mentioned earlier. But, because the standard Kodak gray card reflects 18 percent of the light that reaches it and, as I said, your camera is calibrated for a somewhat darker 12-percent tone, you would need to add about one-half stop *more* exposure than the value metered from the card.

Another substitute for a gray card is the palm of a human hand (the backside of the hand is too variable). But a human palm, regardless of ethnic group, is even brighter than a standard gray card, so instead of one-half stop more exposure, you need to add one additional stop. That is, if your meter reading is 1/500th of a second at f/11, use 1/500th second at f/8 or 1/250th second at f/11 instead. (Both exposures are equivalent.)

If you actually wanted to use a gray card, place it in your frame near your main subject, facing the camera, and with the exact same even illumination falling on it that is falling on your subject. Then, use the Spot metering function (described in the next section) to calculate exposure. Of course, in most situations, it's not necessary to do this. Your camera's light meter will do a good job of calculating the right exposure, especially if you use the exposure tips in the next section. But, I felt that explaining exactly what is going on during exposure calculation would help you understand how your V1's metering system works.

WHY THE GRAY CARD CONFUSION?

Why are so many photographers under the impression that cameras and meters are calibrated to the 18-percent "standard," rather than the true value, which may be 12 to 14 percent, depending on the vendor? You'll find this misinformation in an alarming number of places. I've seen the 18-percent "myth" taught in camera classes; I've found it in books, and even been given this wrong information from the technical staff of camera vendors. (They should know better—the same vendors' engineers who design and calibrate the cameras have the right figure.)

The most common explanation is that during a revision of Kodak's instructions for its gray cards in the 1970s, the advice to open up an extra half stop was omitted, and a whole generation of shooters grew up thinking that a measurement off a gray card could be used as-is. The proviso returned to the instructions by 1987, it's said, but by then it was too late. Next to me is a (c)2006 version of the instructions for KODAK Gray Cards, Publication R-27Q, and the current directions read (with a bit of paraphrasing from me in italics):

- For subjects of normal reflectance increase the indicated exposure by 1/2 stop.
- For light subjects use the indicated exposure; for very light subjects, decrease the exposure by 1/2 stop. (*That is, you're measuring a cat that's lighter than middle gray.)*
- If the subject is dark to very dark, increase the indicated exposure by 1 to 1-1/2 stops. *(You're shooting a black cat.)*

To meter properly you'll want to choose both the *metering method* (how light is evaluated) and *exposure method* (how the appropriate shutter speeds and apertures are chosen). I'll describe both in the following sections.

> **MODES, MODES, AND MORE MODES**
>
> Call them modes or methods, the Nikon V1 seems to have a lot of different sets of options that are described using similar terms. Here's how to sort them out:
>
> - **Metering method.** These modes determine the *parts of the image* within the frame that are examined in order to calculate exposure. The V1 may look at many different points within the image, segregating them by zone (Matrix metering), examine the same number of points, but give greater weight to those located in the middle of the frame (Center-weighted metering), or evaluate only a limited number of points in a limited area (Spot metering).
> - **Exposure method.** These modes determine *which* settings are used to expose the image. The V1 may adjust the shutter speed, the aperture, or both, depending on the method you choose.

Choosing a Metering Method

The V1 has three different schemes for evaluating the light received by its exposure sensors: Matrix, Center-weighted, and Spot metering. You can select the mode you want to use when in Motion Snapshot or Still Image modes, or when using the mechanical shutter in Movie modes (you can't choose metering method in Smart Photo Selector mode at all, because the camera makes the choice). Press the MENU button, navigate to Metering, and choose one of the three options. (See Figure 5.7.) Here is what you need to know about each metering method:

Matrix Metering

For its various Matrix metering modes, the V1 examines many different areas of the frame. When Matrix metering is active, an icon appears in the bottom-left corner of the monitor. The V1 evaluates the differences between the zones, and compares them with a built-in database of several hundred thousand images to make an educated guess about what kind of picture you're taking. For example, if the top sections of a picture are much lighter than the bottom portions, the algorithm can assume that the scene is a landscape photo with lots of sky. An image that includes most of the lighter portions in the center area may be a portrait. A typical image suitable for Matrix metering is shown in Figure 5.8, with a representation of the icon in the upper-left corner. (The reference icon shown is not overlaid on the screen like this in the actual camera display.)

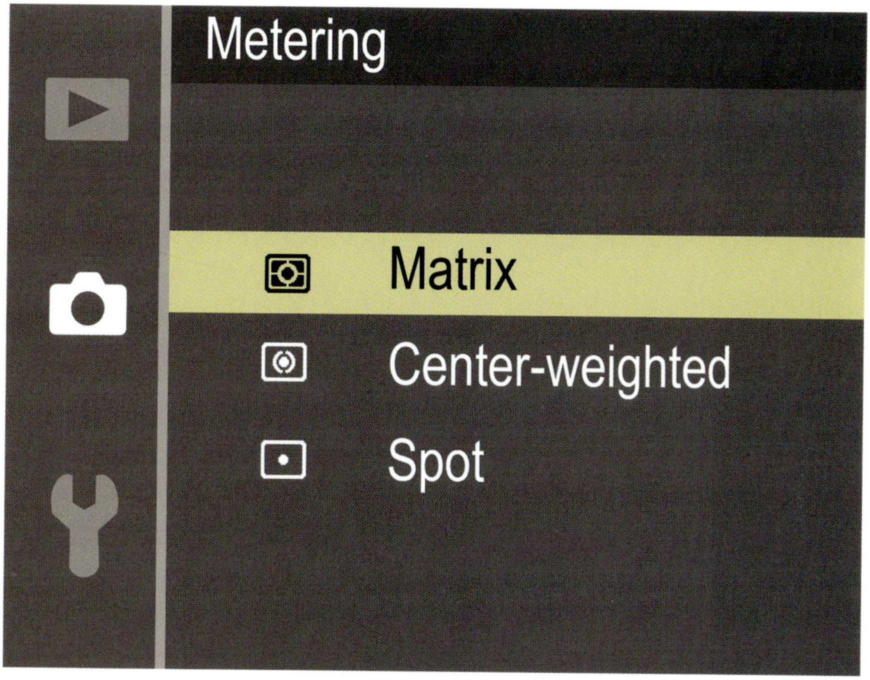

Figure 5.7 Select one of the three metering modes.

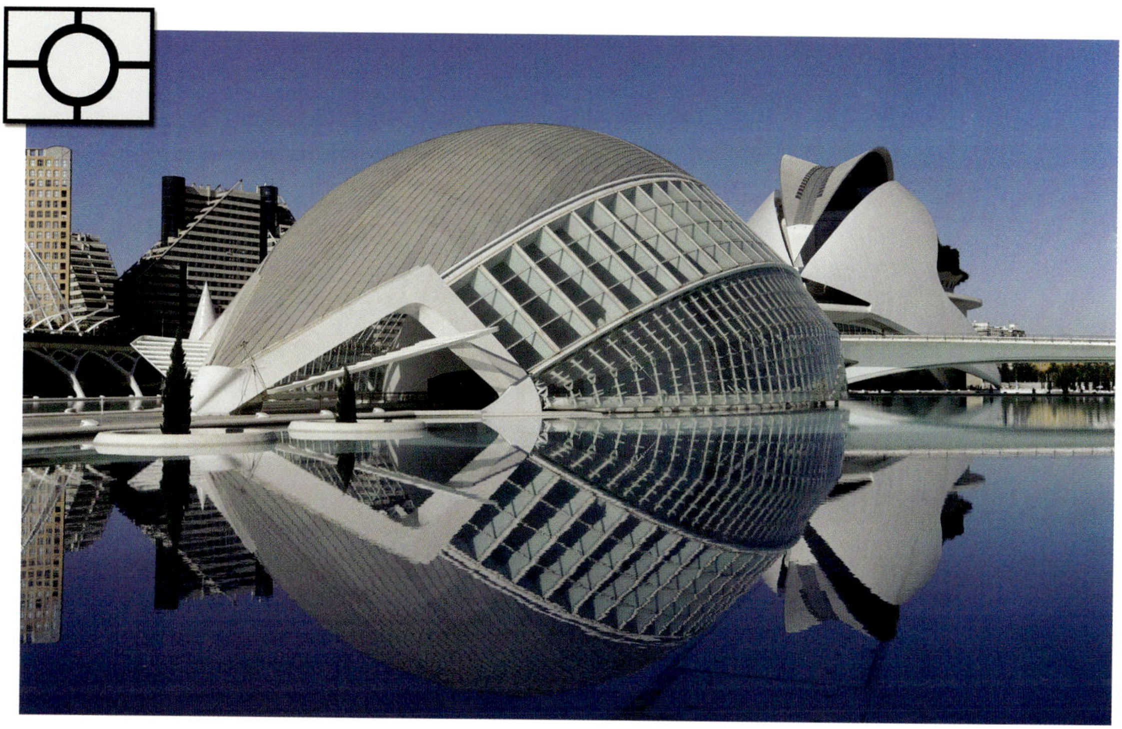

Figure 5.8 Complex scenes lend themselves to the exposure interpretation provided by Matrix metering.

Matrix metering is best for most general subjects, because it is able to intelligently analyze a scene and make an excellent guess of what kind of subject you're shooting a great deal of the time. The camera can tell the difference between low-contrast and high-contrast subjects by looking at the range of differences in brightness across the scene. Because the V1 has a fairly good idea about what kind of subject matter you are shooting, it can underexpose slightly when appropriate to preserve highlight detail when image contrast is high. (It's often possible to pull detail out of shadows that are too dark using an image editor, but once highlights are converted to white pixels, they are gone forever.)

CAUTION

If you're using a strong filter, including a polarizing filter, split-color filter, or neutral-density filter (particularly a graduated neutral-density filter), you should switch from Matrix metering to Center-weighted, because the filter can affect the relationships between the different areas of the frame used to calculate a Matrix exposure. For example, a polarizing filter produces a sky that is darker than usual, hindering the Matrix algorithm's recognition of a landscape photo.

Center-Weighted Metering

In this mode, the exposure meter emphasizes a 4.5mm zone in the center of the frame to calculate exposure. About 75 percent of the exposure is based on that central area, and the remaining exposure is based on the rest of the frame. The theory, here, is that, for most pictures, the main subject will be located in the center. So, if the V1 reads the center portion and determines that the exposure for that region should be f/8 at 1/250th second, while the outer area, which is a bit darker, calls for f/4 at 1/125th second, the camera will give the center portion the most weight and arrive at a final exposure of f/5.6 at 1/250th second.

Center-weighting works best for portraits, architectural photos, backlit subjects with extra bright backgrounds (such as snow or sand), and other pictures in which the most important subject is located in the middle of the frame, as in Figure 5.9. As the name suggests, the light reading is *weighted* towards the central portion, but information is also used from the rest of the frame. If your main subject is surrounded by very bright or very dark areas, the exposure might not be exactly right. However, this scheme works well in many situations if you don't want to use one of the other modes. This mode can be useful for close-ups of subjects like flowers, or for portraits.

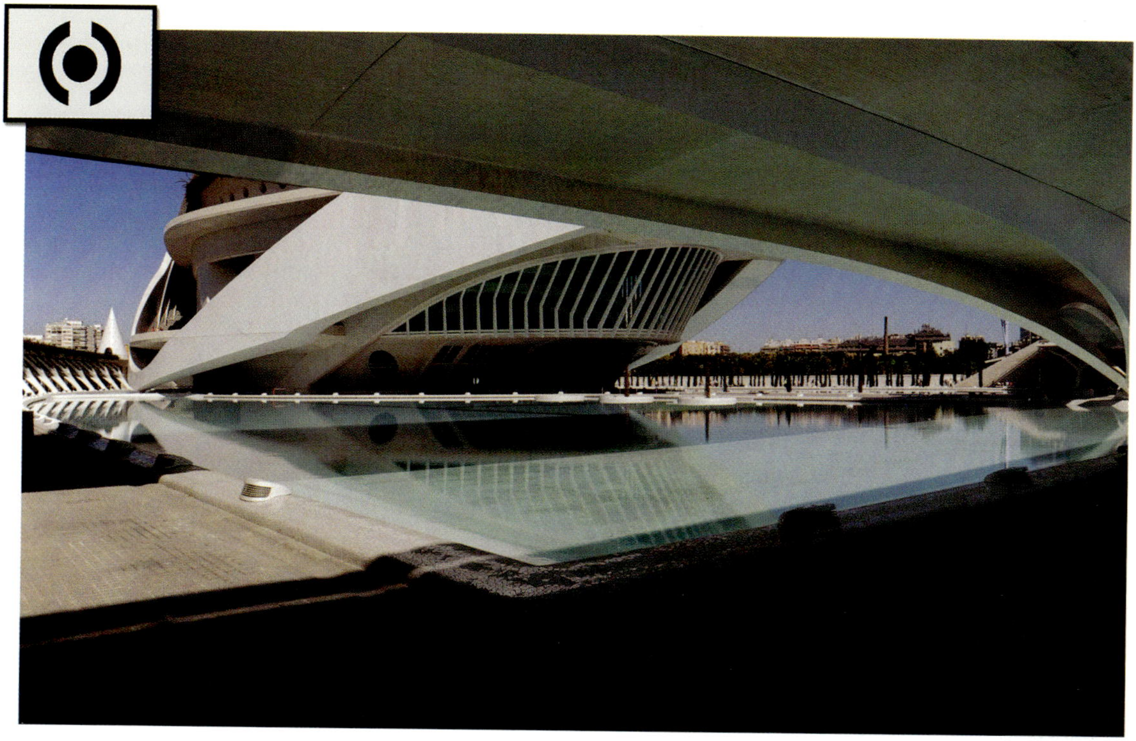

Figure 5.9 Center-weighted metering calculates exposure based on the full frame, but gives 75 percent of the weight to a 4.5mm area in the middle of the image. Scenes with the main subject in the center, surrounded by areas that are significantly darker or lighter, are perfect for Center-weighted metering.

Spot Metering

Spot metering is especially favored by old-timers who have used a hand-held light meter to measure exposure at various points (such as metering highlights and shadows separately), and digital photography veterans who want more precise metering. However, you can use Spot metering in any situation where you want to individually measure the light reflecting from light, midtone, or dark areas of your subject—or any combination of areas.

This mode confines the reading to a limited 2mm area in the viewfinder. The circle is centered on the *current focus point.* This is the only metering method you can use to tell the V1 exactly where to measure exposure. You'll find Spot metering useful when you want to base exposure on a small area in the frame. This mode is best for subjects where the background is significantly brighter or darker, as in Figure 5.10.

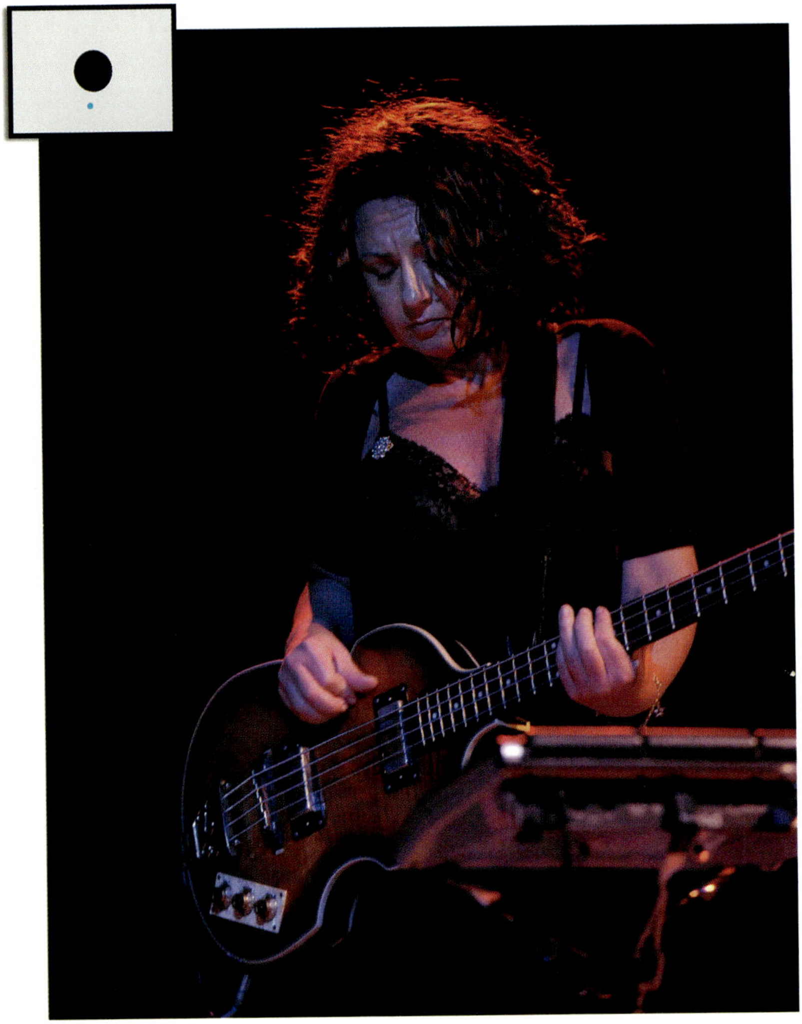

Figure 5.10
Spot metering calculates exposure based on a 2mm spot centered around the current focus point. It allowed measuring exposure from this performer's face.

Choosing an Exposure Method

You'll find four methods for choosing the appropriate shutter speed and aperture, when using the semi-automatic/manual modes. (When using Scene Auto Selector mode, the exposure method is chosen for you by the camera.) You can choose among Program, Shutter-priority, Aperture-priority, or Manual from the Shooting menu when using any of the shooting modes except Smart Photo Selector, or when using the Electronic (Hi) shutter mode. (See Figure 5.11.) Your choice of which is best for a given shooting situation will depend on things like your need for lots of (or less) depth-of-field, a desire to freeze action or allow motion blur, or how much noise you find acceptable in an image. Each of the V1's exposure methods emphasizes one aspect of image capture or another. This section introduces you to all four.

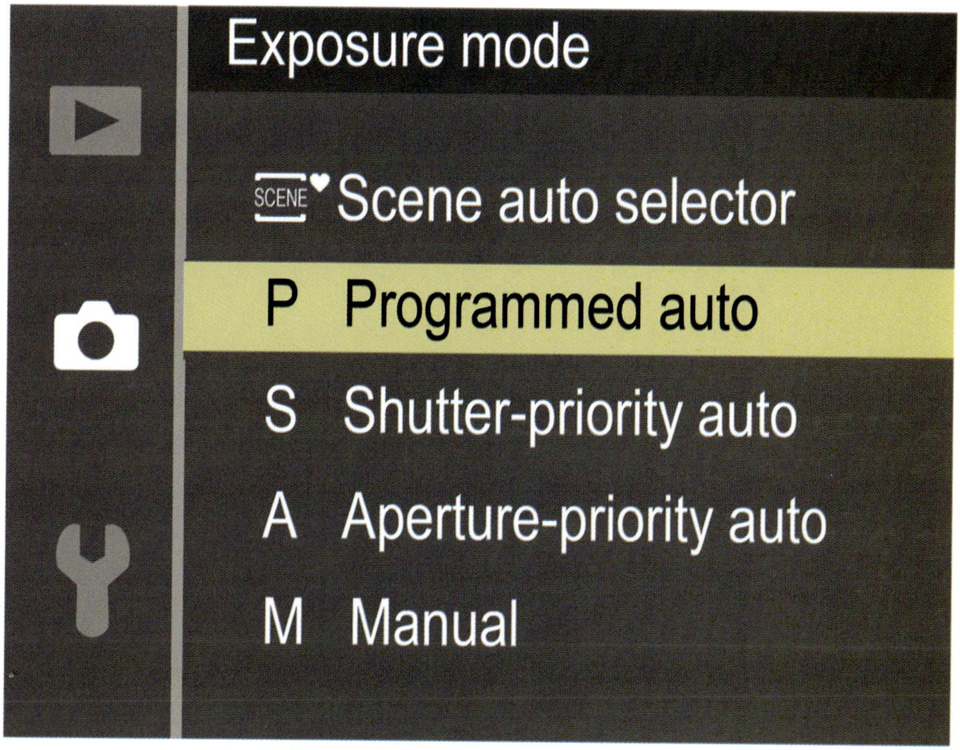

Figure 5.11 Select an exposure method.

Program Mode

Program mode (P) uses the V1's built-in smarts to select the correct f/stop and shutter speed using a database of picture information that tells it which combination of shutter speed and aperture will work best for a particular photo. If the correct exposure cannot be achieved at the current ISO setting or ISO range, the Lo or Hi indicator appears at the bottom of the monitor and a focus bracket flashes red in the center of the frame. You can then boost or reduce the ISO to increase or decrease sensitivity.

The V1's recommended exposure can be overridden if you want. Use the EV (exposure value) setting feature (described next, because it also applies to S and A modes) to add or subtract exposure from the metered value. And, as I mentioned earlier in this chapter, in Program mode you can press the zoom bar up or down to change from the recommended setting to an equivalent setting (as shown earlier in Table 6.1) that produces the same exposure, but using a different combination of f/stop and shutter speed.

This is called "Flexible Program" by Nikon. As I noted, you can press the zoom bar down to reduce the size of the aperture (going from, say, f/4 to f/5.6), so that the V1 will automatically use a slower shutter speed (going from, say, 1/250th second to 1/125th second). Press the zoom bar up to use a larger f/stop, while automatically producing a shorter shutter speed that provides the same equivalent exposure as metered in P mode. The asterisk appears next to the P in the monitor so you'll know you've overridden the V1's default program setting. Your adjustment remains in force until you press the zoom bar up or down until the * is no longer displayed, or you switch to another exposure mode, turn the camera off, or the V1 goes to sleep (enters standby mode).

MAKING EXPOSURE COMPENSATION CHANGES

Sometimes you'll want more or less exposure than indicated by the V1's metering system. Perhaps you want to underexpose to create a silhouette effect, or overexpose to produce a high-key look. It's easy to use the V1's exposure compensation system to override the exposure recommendations, in Program, Shutter-priority, and Aperture-priority modes. (It's not available when using Scene Auto Selector or Manual exposure, nor when using the Electronic (Hi) shutter mode.)

Press the right directional button on the multi selector to produce the EV scale shown in Figure 5.12. Then press the zoom bar up to add exposure, and down to subtract exposure, in the range plus or minus 3EV, in 1/3 stop increments. The EV change you've made remains for the exposures that follow, until you manually zero it out. It is not reset when the camera is powered down.

Exposure compensation works best when used with Center-weighted or Spot metering.

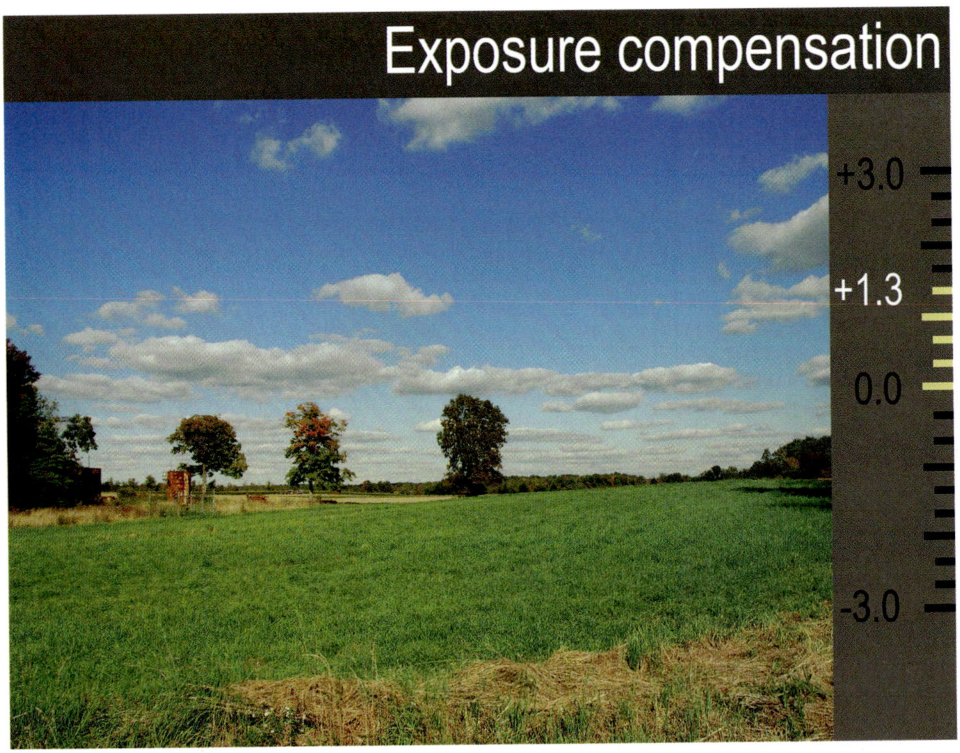

Figure 5.12
Press the right directional button, then use the zoom bar to adjust exposure compensation.

Shutter-Priority

Shutter-priority (S) is the inverse of Aperture-priority: you choose the shutter speed you'd like to use, and the camera's metering system selects the appropriate f/stop. Perhaps you're shooting action photos and you want to use the absolute fastest shutter speed available with your camera; in other cases, you might want to use a slow shutter speed to add some blur to a sports photo that would be mundane if the action were completely frozen. (See the ends of the hockey sticks in Figure 5.13.) Shutter-priority mode gives you some control over how much action-freezing capability your digital camera brings to bear in a particular situation.

You'll also encounter the same problem as with Aperture-priority when you select a shutter speed that's too long or too short for correct exposure under some conditions. I've shot outdoor soccer games on sunny Fall evenings and used Shutter-priority mode to lock in a 1/1,000th second shutter speed, and was unable to continue when the sun dipped behind some trees and there was no longer enough light to shoot at that speed, even with the lens wide open.

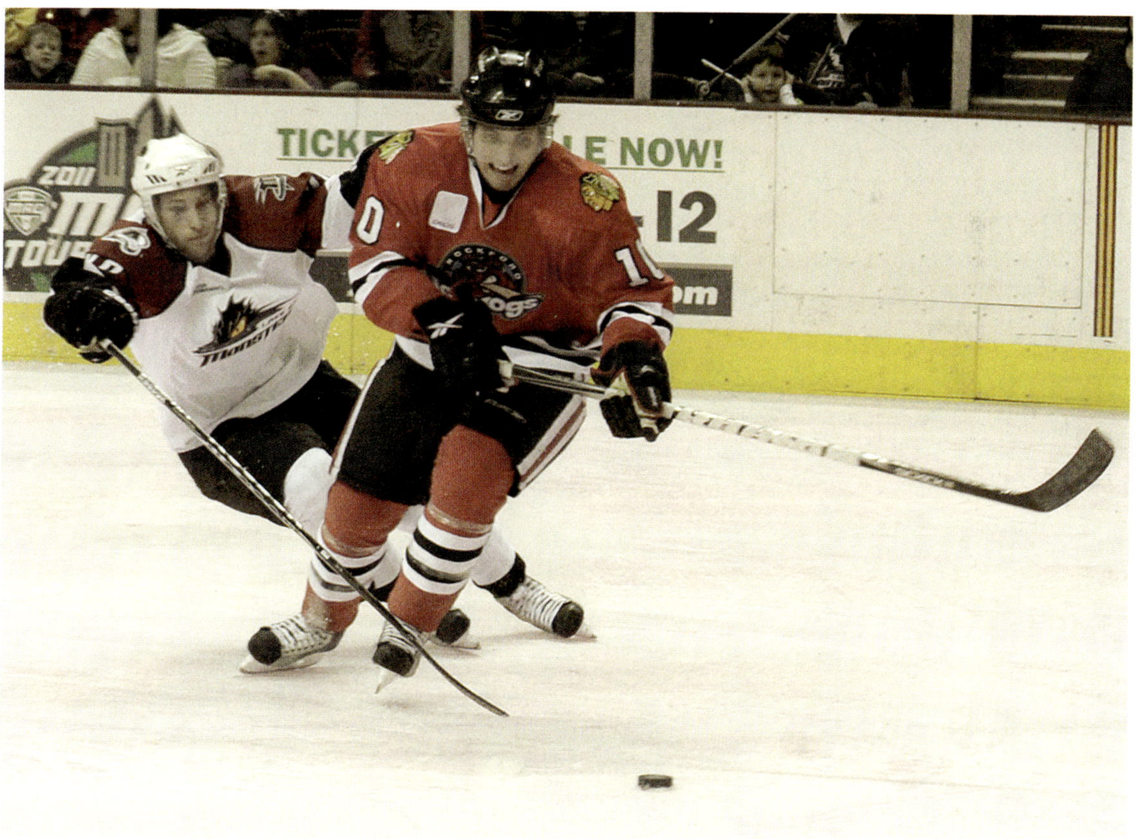

Figure 5.13 Lock the shutter at a specific speed to introduce blur into an action shot.

Aperture-Priority

In A mode, you specify the lens opening used, and the V1 selects the shutter speed. Aperture-priority is especially good when you want to use a particular lens opening to achieve a desired effect. Perhaps you'd like to use the smallest f/stop possible to maximize depth-of-field in a close-up picture. Or, you might want to use a large f/stop to throw everything except your main subject out of focus, as in Figure 5.14. Maybe you'd

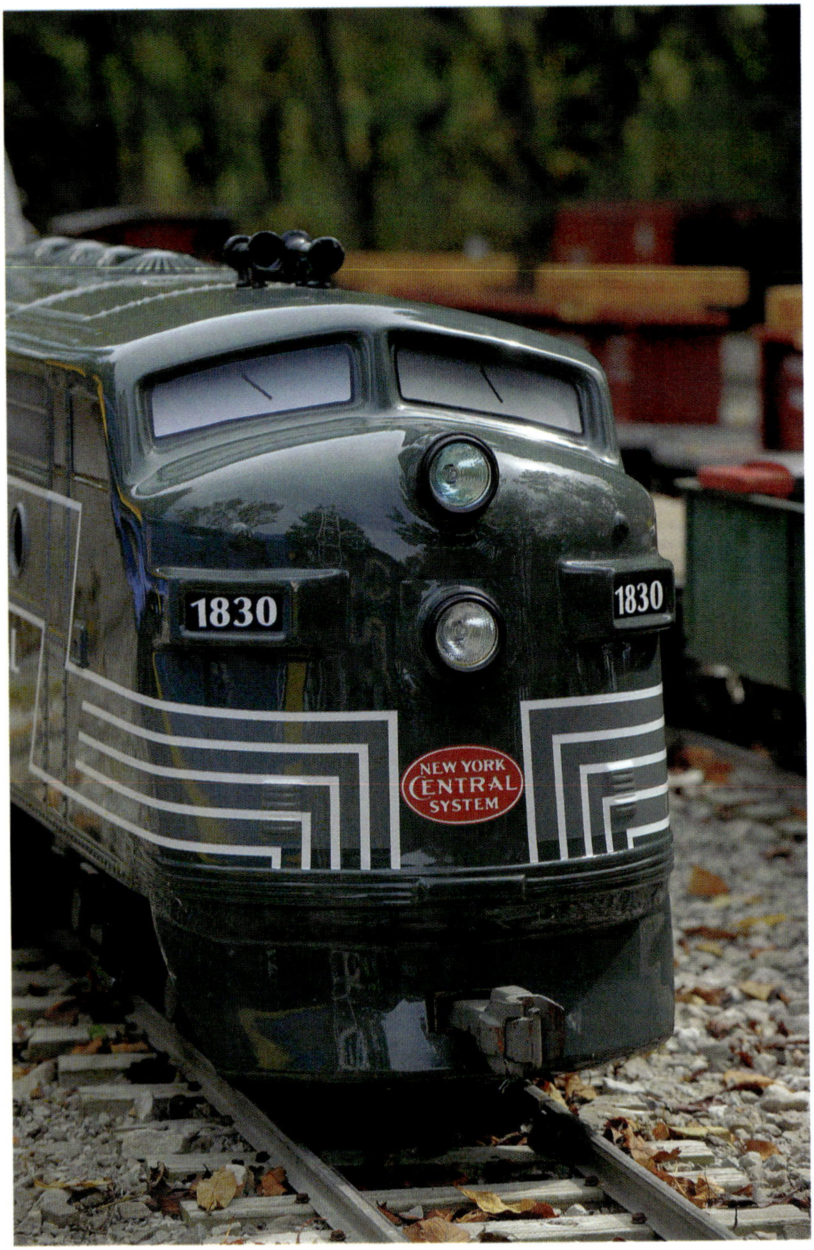

Figure 5.14
Use Aperture-priority to "lock in" a large f/stop when you want to blur the background.

just like to "lock in" a particular f/stop because it's the sharpest available aperture with that lens. Or, you might prefer to use, say, f/8 on a lens with a maximum aperture of f/3.5, because you want the best compromise between speed and sharpness.

Aperture-priority can even be used to specify a *range* of shutter speeds you want to use under varying lighting conditions, which seems almost contradictory. But think about it. You're shooting a soccer game outdoors with a telephoto lens and want a relatively high shutter speed, but you don't care if the speed changes a little should the sun duck behind a cloud. Set your V1 to A, and adjust the aperture until a shutter speed of, say, 1/1,000th second is selected at your current ISO setting. (In bright sunlight at ISO 400, that aperture is likely to be around f/11.) Then, go ahead and shoot, knowing that your V1 will maintain that f/11 aperture (for sufficient DOF as the soccer players move about the field), but will drop down to 1/750th or 1/500th second if necessary should the lighting change a little.

A Lo or Hi indicator in monitor indicates that the V1 is unable to select an appropriate shutter speed at the selected aperture and that over- and underexposure will occur at the current ISO setting. That's the major pitfall of using A: you might select an f/stop that is too small or too large to allow an optimal exposure with the available shutter speeds. For example, if you choose f/4 as your aperture and the illumination is quite bright (say, at the beach or in snow), even your camera's fastest mechanical shutter speed of 1/4,000th second might not be able to cut down the amount of light reaching the sensor to provide the right exposure. (In that case, you can switch to Electronic shutter and faster speeds will be used.)

Or, if you select f/8 in a dimly lit room, you might find yourself shooting with a very slow shutter speed that can cause blurring from subject movement or camera shake. Aperture-priority is best used by those with a bit of experience in choosing settings. Many seasoned photographers leave their V1 set on A all the time.

Manual Exposure

Part of being an experienced photographer comes from knowing when to rely on your V1's automation (with P mode), when to go semi-automatic (with S or A), and when to set exposure manually (using M). Some photographers actually prefer to set their exposure manually.

Manual exposure can come in handy in some situations. You might be taking a silhouette photo and find that none of the exposure modes or EV correction features give you exactly the effect you want. Set the exposure manually to use the exact shutter speed and f/stop you need.

Because, depending on your proclivities, you might not need to set exposure manually very often, you should still make sure you understand how it works. Fortunately, the V1 makes setting exposure manually very easy. Set Manual exposure in the Shooting menu, and then press the zoom bar up or down to set the shutter speed, and rotate the multi selector dial to adjust the aperture. Even though you're using Manual exposure mode, the V1's exposure meter is still operating; a scale at the bottom of the monitor screen shows you how far your chosen setting diverges from the metered exposure. (See Figure 5.15.)

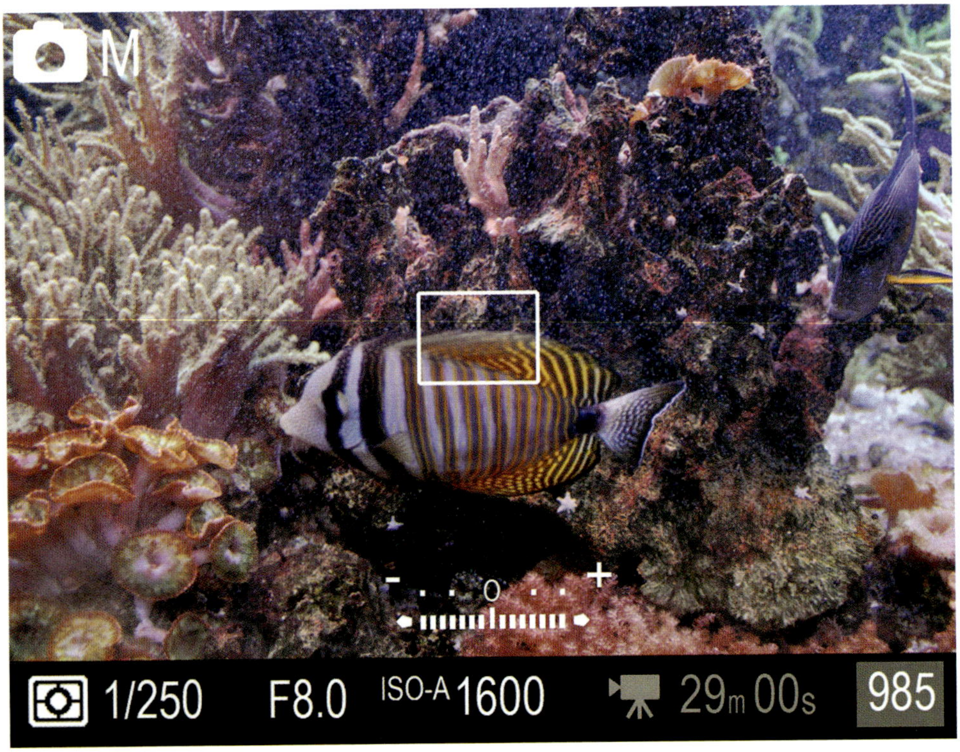

Figure 5.15
A scale shows relative exposure in Manual mode.

Adjusting Exposure with ISO Settings

Another way of adjusting exposures is by changing the ISO sensitivity setting. Sometimes photographers forget about this option, because the common practice is to set the ISO once for a particular shooting session, say, to the Auto 800 range to let the V1 select from a wide range of appropriate sensitivities. Or, you might choose a fixed setting of ISO 200 for bright sunlight outdoors, or ISO 800 when shooting indoors. ISOs higher than ISO 800 are sometimes seen as "bad" or "necessary evils." However, changing the ISO is a valid way of adjusting exposure settings, particularly with the Nikon V1, which produces good results at ISO settings that create grainy, unusable pictures with some other camera models.

Indeed, I find myself using ISO adjustment as a convenient alternate way of adding or subtracting EV when shooting in Manual mode, and as a quick way of choosing equivalent exposures when in Program or Shutter-priority or Aperture-priority modes. For example, I've selected a Manual exposure with both f/stop and shutter speed suitable for my image using, say, ISO 200. I can change the exposure in 1/3 stop increments by jumping to the Shooting menu and selecting ISO sensitivity. The difference in image quality/noise at ISO 200 is negligible if I dial in ISO 100 to reduce exposure a little, or change to ISO 400 to increase exposure. I keep my preferred f/stop and shutter speed, but still adjust the exposure.

Or, perhaps, I am using S mode and the metered exposure at ISO 200 is 1/500th second at f/11. If I decide on the spur of the moment I'd rather use 1/500th second at f/8, I can change the sensitivity to ISO 100. Of course, it's a good idea to monitor your ISO changes, so you don't end up at ISO 3200 outdoors when moving from an indoor location. An ISO indicator appears at the bottom of the monitor screen to remind you what sensitivity setting has been dialed in.

ISO settings can, of course, also be used to boost or reduce sensitivity in particular shooting situations. The V1 can use ISO settings from ISO 100 up to ISO 3200, plus Hi 1 (ISO 6400 equivalent). The camera can also adjust the ISO automatically as appropriate for various lighting conditions when you choose the A3200 Auto (ISO 100-3200), A800 Auto (ISO 100-800), or A400 (Auto ISO 100-400) options. When you choose one of these Auto ISO settings in the Shooting menu, the V1 adjusts the sensitivity dynamically to suit the subject matter, based on the minimum shutter speed limit you have prescribed. You should use Auto ISO cautiously if you don't want the V1 to use an ISO higher than you might otherwise have selected.

Dealing with Noise

Visual image noise is that random grainy effect that some like to use as a special effect, but which, most of the time, is objectionable because it robs your image of detail even as it adds that "interesting" texture. Noise is caused by two different phenomena: high ISO settings and long exposures. The potential for noise may be a special concern for digital photography veterans, because they know that the CX sensor, which is smaller relative to the larger DX and FX sensors found in Nikon's digital SLR cameras, are thought to produce excessive noise.

However, Nikon has taken several steps to keep the Nikon V1's noise at acceptable levels. The CX sensor was limited to a resolution of 10 megapixels, rather than some higher figure, such as 14 to 16 megapixels (and up) available with some other mirrorless models. At 10 megapixels, individual pixels are larger than those that would be required at higher resolutions, and thus more sensitive to light. Extra sensitivity means that the sensor signal doesn't have to be amplified as much to produce higher ISO settings, and the resulting noise is less. Nikon also limited the ISO range of the V1, establishing an upper ceiling of ISO 3200 (and ISO 6400 equivalent at the Hi 1 setting), where cameras with larger sensors often offer sensitivity settings of ISO 12800 or more. Finally, the individual photosites in the V1's sensor were designed to occupy as much of the sensor surface as possible, making them large enough to absorb light more efficiently.

High ISO noise commonly appears when you raise your camera's sensitivity setting above ISO 400. With the Nikon V1, noise may become fairly visible at ISO 1600, and is often quite noticeable at ISO 3200. At Hi 1, noise is usually quite bothersome. You can expect noise and increase in contrast in any pictures taken at these lofty ratings. High ISO noise appears as a result of the amplification needed to increase the sensitivity of the sensor. While higher ISOs do pull details out of dark areas, they also amplify non-signal information randomly, creating noise. You'll find a High ISO noise reduction choice in the Shooting menu, where you can turn it On or Off. Because noise reduction tends to soften the grainy look while robbing an image of detail, you may want to disable the feature if you're willing to accept a little noise in exchange for more details.

A similar noisy phenomenon occurs during long time exposures, which allow more photons to reach the sensor, increasing your ability to capture a picture under low light conditions. However, the longer exposures also increase the likelihood that some pixels will register random phantom photons, often because the longer an imager is "hot," the warmer it gets, and that heat can be mistaken for photons. There's also a special kind of noise that CMOS sensors like the one used in the V1 are potentially susceptible to. With a CCD, the entire signal is conveyed off the chip and funneled through a single amplifier and analog-to-digital conversion circuit. Any noise introduced there is, at least, consistent. CMOS imagers, on the other hand, contain millions of individual amplifiers and A/D converters, all working in unison. Because these circuits don't necessarily all process in precisely the same way all the time, they can introduce something called fixed-pattern noise into the image data.

You might want to apply the optional long exposure noise reduction that can be activated using Long Exp. NR in the Shooting menu, where the feature can be turned On or Off. This type of noise reduction involves the V1 taking a second, blank exposure, and comparing the random pixels in that image with the photograph you just took. Pixels that coincide in the two represent noise and can safely be suppressed. This noise reduction system, called *dark frame subtraction,* effectively doubles the amount of time required to take a picture, and is used only for exposures longer than one second. Noise reduction can reduce the amount of detail in your picture, as some image information may be removed along with the noise. So, you might want to use this feature with moderation.

You can also apply noise reduction to a lesser extent using Photoshop, and when converting RAW files to some other format, using your favorite RAW converter, or an industrial-strength product like Noise Ninja (www.picturecode.com) to wipe out noise after you've already taken the picture.

Bracketing and High Dynamic Range Photography

Bracketing is a method for shooting several consecutive exposures using different settings, as a way of improving the odds that one will be exactly right. Alternatively, bracketing can be used to create a series of photos with slightly different exposures in anticipation that one of the exposures will be "better" from a creative standpoint. For example, bracketing can supply you with a normal exposure of a backlit subject, one that's "underexposed," producing a silhouette effect, and a third that's "overexposed" to create still another look.

Before digital cameras took over the universe, it was common to bracket exposures, shooting, say, a series of three photos at 1/125th second, but varying the f/stop from f/8 to f/11 to f/16. In practice, smaller than whole-stop increments were used for greater precision, and lenses with apertures that were set manually commonly had half-stop detents on their aperture rings, or could easily be set to a mid-way position between whole f/stops. It was just as common to keep the same aperture and vary the shutter speed, although in the days before electronic shutters, film cameras often had only whole increment shutter speeds available.

Today, cameras like the V1 can bracket exposures much more precisely in 1/3 stop increments, although you must make the adjustments yourself, either using EV changes in P, S, or A modes, or by working in Manual exposure mode and setting the exposures yourself. The V1 does not have automatic exposure bracketing. However, manual exposure bracketing takes time, but the results can be worth it. Bracketing is especially useful when shooting *high dynamic range* (HDR) photos.

Bracketing and Merge to HDR

While my goal in this book is to show you how to take great photos *in the camera* rather than how to fix your errors in Photoshop, the Merge to HDR Pro (high dynamic range) feature in Adobe Photoshop and Photoshop Elements is too cool to ignore. The ability to have a bracketed set of exposures that are identical except for exposure is key to getting good results with this feature, which allows you to produce images with a full, rich dynamic range that includes a level of detail in the highlights and shadows that is almost impossible to achieve with digital cameras. In contrasty lighting situations, even the Nikon V1 has a tendency to blow out highlights when you expose solely for the shadows or midtones.

Suppose you wanted to photograph a dimly lit room that had a bright window showing an outdoors scene. Proper exposure for the room might be on the order of 1/60th second at f/2.8 at ISO 200, while the outdoors scene probably would require f/11 at 1/400th second. That's almost a 7 EV step difference (approximately 7 f/stops) and well beyond the dynamic range of any digital camera, including the Nikon V1.

When you're using Merge to HDR Pro, you'd take two to three pictures, one for the shadows, one for the highlights, and perhaps one for the midtones. (You could also take more than three pictures, but for this example, I'm going to assume you're working with just three.) Then, you'd use the Merge to HDR command to combine all of the images into one HDR image that integrates the well-exposed sections of each version. You can use the Nikon V1's bracketing feature to produce those images.

The images should be as identical as possible, except for exposure. So, it's a good idea to mount the V1 on a tripod, use a remote release like the ML-L3 infrared remote, and take all the exposures one after another. Just follow these steps:

1. **Set up the camera.** Mount the V1 on a tripod.
2. **Activate the remote control.** In Still Image mode, press the left multi selector button and choose either 2 Second Remote or Quick Release Remote. (See Figure 5.16.)
3. **Choose Manual exposure mode.** In Still Image mode, press the MENU button, navigate to Exposure mode, and choose Manual exposure.
4. **Choose RAW exposures.** In the Shooting menu, navigate to Image Quality and select NEF (RAW). You'll need RAW files to give you the 16-bit high dynamic range images that the Merge to HDR feature processes best.

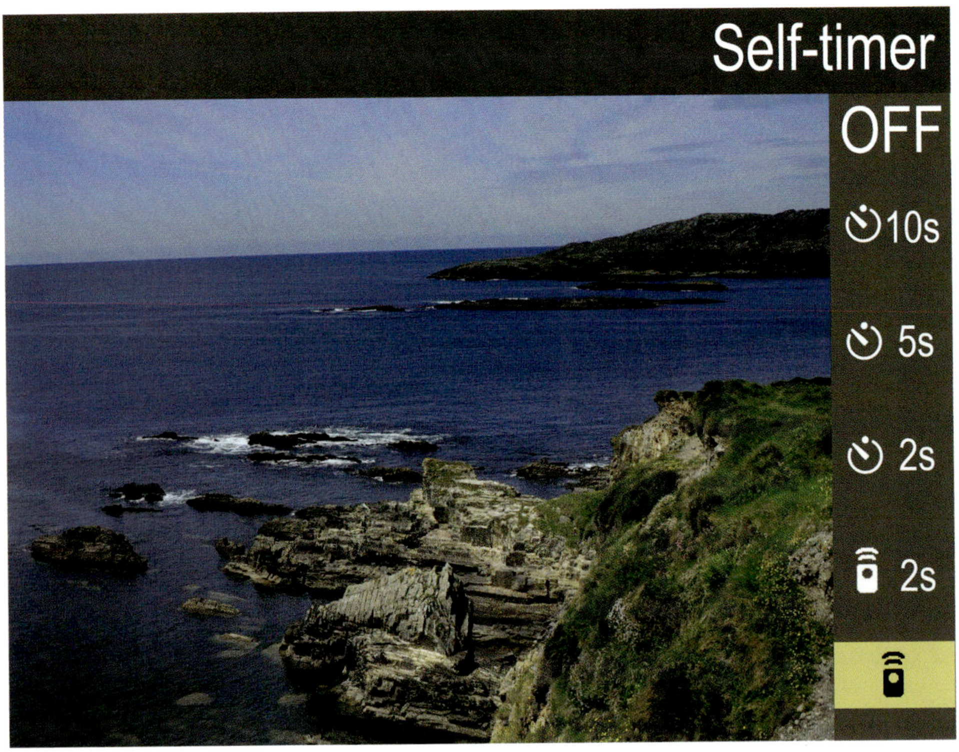

Figure 5.16
Choose Remote Control mode.

5. **Set the exposure.** Using the exposure scale at the bottom of the monitor, set the exposure so the image is one-stop underexposed. The scale will be biased towards the left.
6. **Set for manual focus.** Press the down directional button on the multi selector and choose MF.
7. **Focus the scene.** Press the OK button to produce the manual focus screen, and press the zoom bar up or down to focus. (See Figure 5.17.)
8. **Take the first shot.** Press the button on the ML-L3 remote and take the first exposure.
9. **Adjust shutter speed one stop.** Press the zoom bar up to adjust the shutter speed to one stop faster.
10. **Take the second shot.** Press the button on the ML-L3 remote and take the second exposure.
11. **Adjust shutter speed one more stop.** Press the zoom bar up to adjust the shutter speed to one stop faster.
12. **Take the third shot.** Press the button on the ML-L3 remote and take the final exposure. Continue with the Merge to HDR Pro steps listed next.

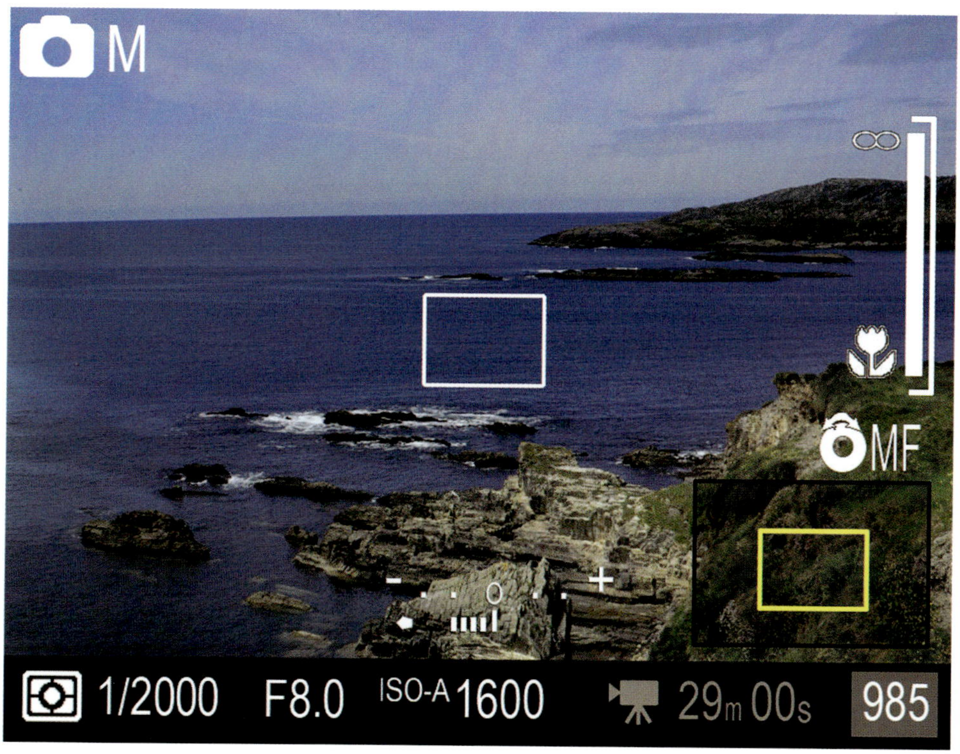

Figure 5.17
Manually focus the image.

The next steps show you how to combine the separate exposures into one merged high dynamic range image. The sample images in Figure 5.18 show the results you can get from a three-shot bracketed sequence.

1. **Copy your images to your computer.** If you use an application to transfer the files to your computer, make sure it does not make any adjustments to brightness, contrast, or exposure. You want the real raw information for Merge to HDR Pro to work with. If you do everything correctly, you'll end up with at least three photos like the ones shown in Figure 5.18.
2. **Activate Merge to HDR Pro.** Choose File > Automate > Merge to HDR Pro.
3. **Select the photos to be merged.** See Figure 5.19, where I have specified the three 16-bit NEF files. You'll note a checkbox that can be used to automatically align the images if they were not taken with the V1 mounted on a rock-steady support. This will adjust for any slight movement of the camera that might have occurred when you changed exposure settings.
4. **Click OK.** The merger begins.
5. **Save.** Once HDR merge has done its thing, you must save in PSD, PFM, TIFF, or EXR formats to retain the 16-bit file's floating-point data, in case you want to work with the HDR image later. Otherwise, you can convert to a normal 24-bit file and save in any compatible format.

If you do everything correctly, you'll end up with a photo like the one shown in Figure 5.20, which has the properly exposed foreground of the first shot, and the well-exposed

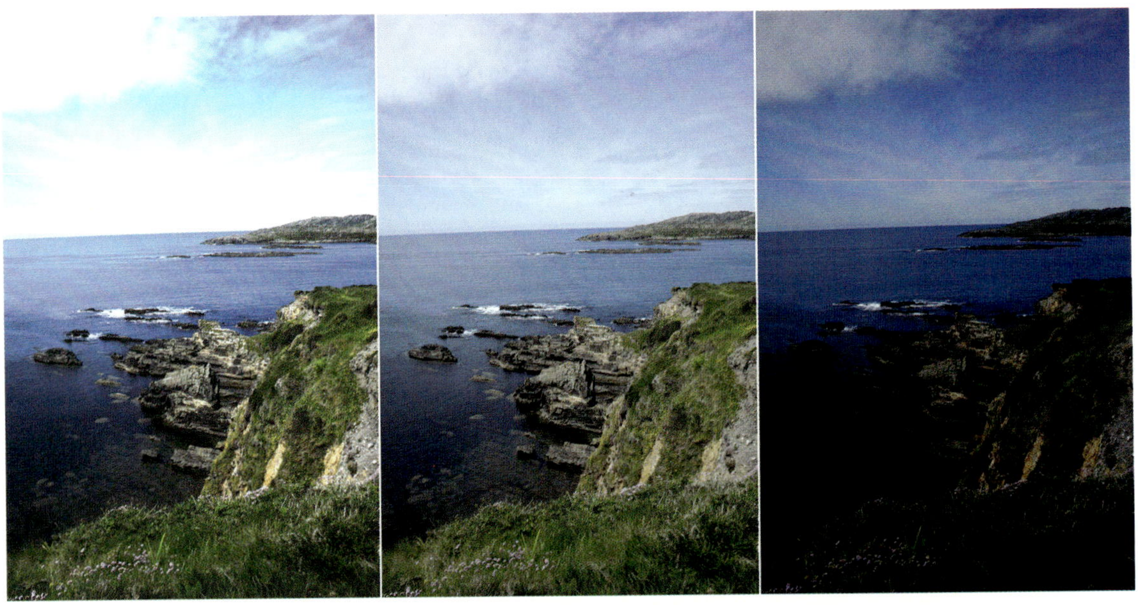

Figure 5.18 Make three exposures for the highlights, midtones, and shadow areas.

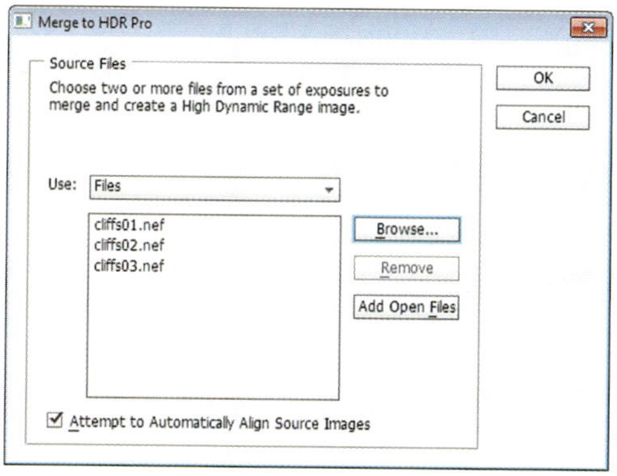

Figure 5.19
Use the Merge to HDR Pro command in Photoshop or Photoshop Elements to combine the two images.

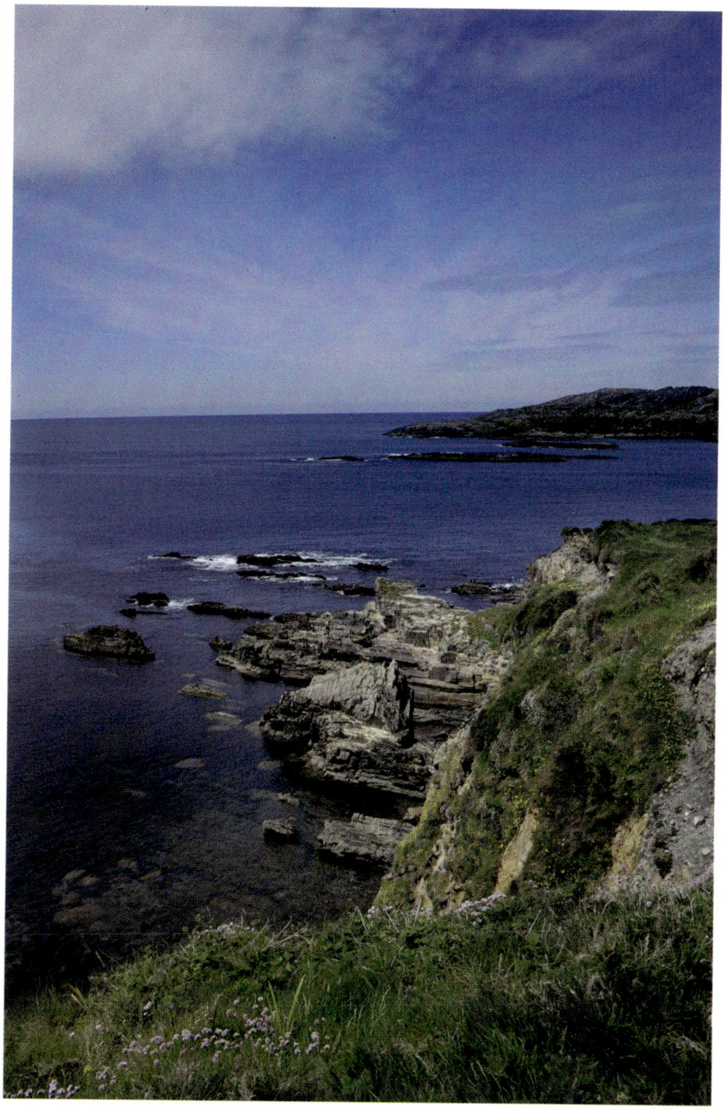

Figure 5.20
You'll end up with an extended dynamic range photo like this one.

rocks of the second and third images. Note that, ideally, nothing should move between shots. In the example pictures, the ocean waves are moving, but the exposures were made so close together that, after the merger, you can't really tell.

What if you don't have the opportunity, inclination, or skills to create several images at different exposures, as described? If you shoot in RAW format, you can still use Merge to HDR, working with a *single* original image file. What you do is import the image into Photoshop several times, using Adobe Camera Raw to create multiple copies of the file at different exposure levels.

For example, you'd create one copy that's too dark, so the shadows lose detail, but the highlights are preserved. Create another copy with the shadows intact and allow the highlights to wash out. Then, you can use Merge to HDR to combine the two and end up with a finished image that has the extended dynamic range you're looking for. (This concludes the image-editing portion of the chapter. We now return you to our alternate sponsor: photography.)

Fixing Exposures with Histograms

While you can often recover poorly exposed photos in your image editor, your best bet is to arrive at the correct exposure in the camera, minimizing the tweaks that you have to make in post-processing. However, you can't always judge exposure just by viewing the image on your V1's LCD after the shot is made. Nor can you get a 100 percent accurately exposed picture by using the V1's live viewing display. Ambient light may make the LCD difficult to see, and the brightness level you've set can affect the appearance of the playback image. Moreover the image you see on the internal EVF may not be 100 percent accurate.

Instead, you can use a histogram, which is a chart displayed on the V1's LCD that shows the number of tones being captured at each brightness level. You can use the information to provide correction for the next shot you take. The histogram is shown in the Detailed Display during picture review, as shown in Figure 5.21. This screen provides a small histogram at the right side that displays the distribution of luminance or brightness.

The luminance histogram is a chart that includes a representation of up to 256 vertical lines on a horizontal axis that show the number of pixels in the image at each brightness level, from 0 (black) on the left side to 255 (white) on the right. (The three-inch LCD and internal EVF don't have enough pixels to show each and every one of the 256 lines, but, instead provide a representation of the shape of the curve formed.) The more pixels at a given level, the taller the bar at that position. If no bar appears at a particular position on the scale from left to right, there are no pixels at that particular brightness level.

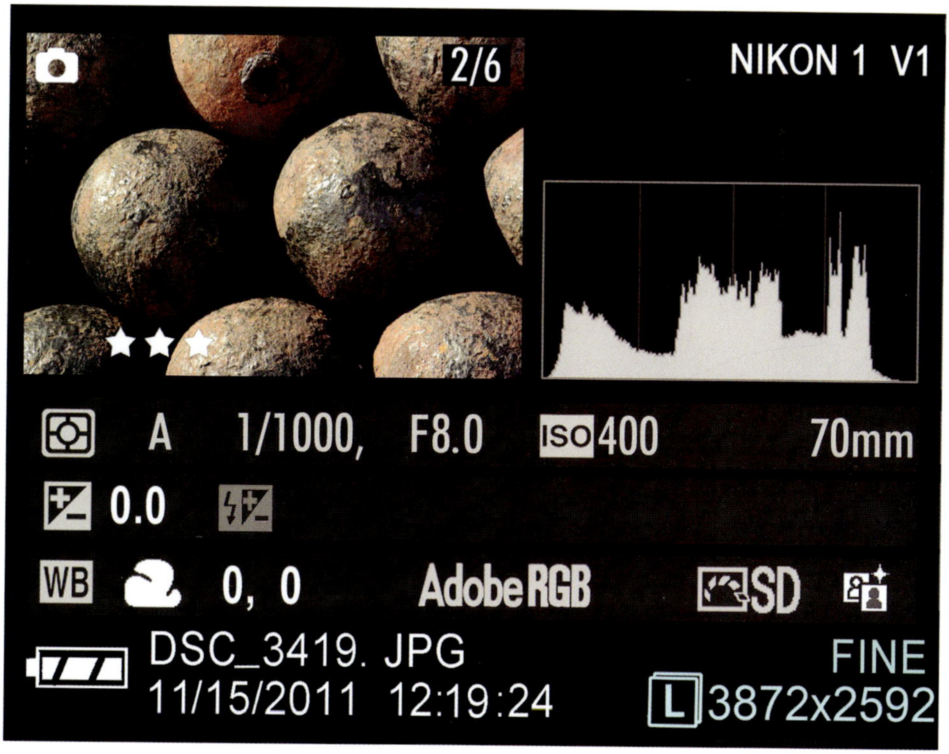

Figure 5.21 The V1's histogram screen shows luminance values.

As you can see, a typical histogram produces a mountain-like shape, with most of the pixels bunched in the middle tones, with fewer pixels at the dark and light ends of the scale. Ideally, though, there will be at least some pixels at either extreme, so that your image has both a true black and a true white representing some details. Learn to spot histograms that represent over- and underexposure, and add or subtract exposure using an EV modification to compensate.

For example, Figure 5.22 shows the histogram (in the inset) for an image that is badly underexposed. You can guess from the shape of the histogram that many of the dark tones to the left of the graph have been clipped off. There's plenty of room on the right side for additional pixels to reside without having them become overexposed. Or, a histogram might look like the insert in Figure 5.23, which is overexposed. In either case, you can increase or decrease the exposure (either by changing the f/stop or shutter speed in Manual mode or by adding or subtracting an EV value in A or S modes) to produce the corrected histogram shown inset in Figure 5.24, in which the tones "hug" the right side of the histogram to produce as many highlight details as possible. See "Making EV Changes," above for information on dialing in exposure compensation.

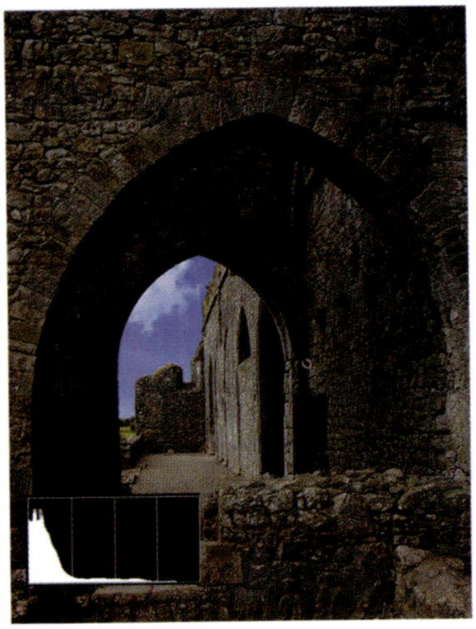

Figure 5.22 This histogram shows an underexposed image.

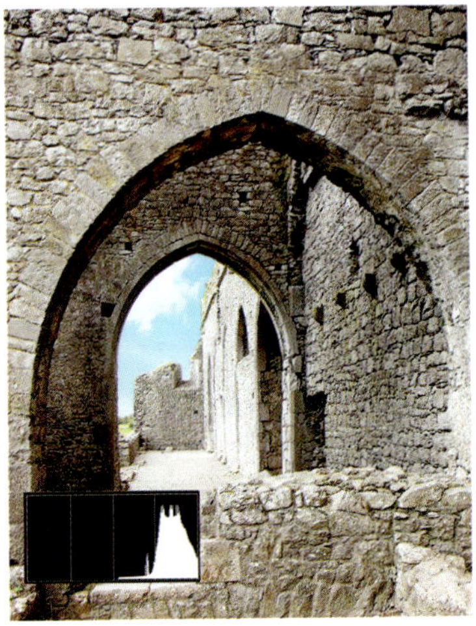

Figure 5.23 This histogram reveals that the image is overexposed.

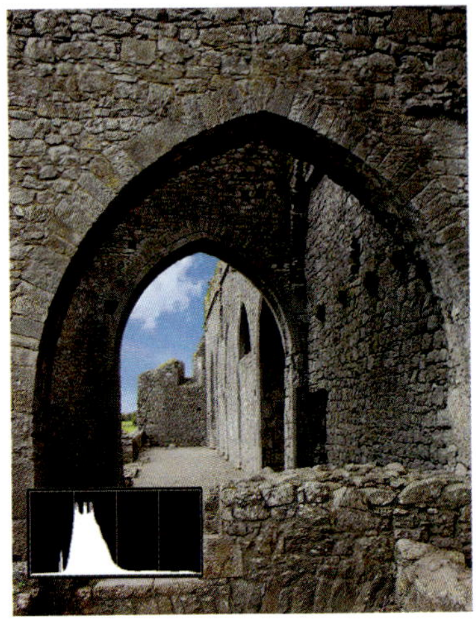

Figure 5.24 A histogram for a properly exposed image should look like this.

The histogram can also be used to aid in fixing the contrast of an image, although gauging incorrect contrast is more difficult. For example, if the histogram shows all the tones bunched up in one place in the image, the photo will be low in contrast. If the tones are spread out more or less evenly, the image is probably high in contrast. In either case, your best bet may be to switch to RAW (if you're not already using that format) so you can adjust contrast in post processing. However, you can also change to a Custom Picture Control with contrast set lower (+3 to –3) or higher (+1 to +3) as required. You'll find instructions for creating Picture Controls in Chapter 8.

6

Advanced Shooting

I've saved some advanced techniques for this chapter, which devotes a little extra space to some special features of the Nikon V1. This chapter covers autofocus, continuous shooting, high-speed photography, and long exposures.

Mastering the Mysteries of Autofocus

One of the most useful and powerful features of modern digital cameras is their ability to lock in sharp focus faster than the blink of an eye. Sometimes. Although autofocus has been with us for more than 20 years, it continues to be problematic. That's been especially true with mirrorless cameras prior to the introduction of the Nikon 1 series, because they generally used a slower form of autofocus, called *contrast detection,* rather than *phase detection.* (Don't worry, I'll explain both later in this chapter.) The Nikon V1 uses a hybrid system that combines the best features of both, giving you faster and more precise autofocus systems. This section will explain the mysteries of autofocus, and how to get sharp, well-focused images without fail.

Why is achieving good focus such a challenge? One key problem is that the camera doesn't really know, for certain, what subject you want to *be* in sharp focus. It may select an object and lock in focus with lightning speed—even though the subject is not the one that's the center of interest of your photograph. Or, the camera may lock focus too soon, or too late.

How Focus Works

Although Nikon added autofocus capabilities in the 1980s, back in the day of film cameras, prior to that focusing was always done manually. Honest. Even though the optical viewfinders that corresponded to the V1's electronic viewfinder and LCD were big and bright, special focusing screens, magnifiers, and other gadgets were often used to help the photographer achieve correct focus. Imagine what it must have been like to focus manually under demanding, fast-moving conditions such as sports photography.

Focusing was problematic because our eyes and brains have poor memory for correct focus, which is why your eye doctor must shift back and forth between sets of lenses and ask "Does that look sharper—or was it sharper before?" in determining your correct prescription. Similarly, manual focusing involves jogging the focus ring back and forth as you go from almost in focus, to sharp focus, to almost focused again. The little clockwise and counterclockwise arcs decrease in size until you've zeroed in on the point of correct focus. What you're looking for is the image with the most contrast between the edges of elements in the image.

The camera also looks for these contrast differences among pixels to determine relative sharpness. There are two ways that sharp focus is determined. One is *contrast detection,* used by all point-and-shoot cameras and most mirrorless models, and employed by the V1 in dim lighting conditions. The second method is called *phase detection,* a much faster system that the V1 uses in higher light levels (in other words, for everyday shooting).

Contrast Detection

This method is the easiest to understand, because it's the way we focus when using our naked eyes, focus binoculars, or sharpen an image when focusing manually while evaluating a scene with any kind of viewing system in a digital or film camera. It's a slower mode, suitable for static subjects, and used by the V1 in reduced light levels when the default phase detection system (described next) can't be applied. Contrast detection operates by visually or electronically examining the contrast between the edges of objects in an image, as you can see in Figure 6.1. At top in the figure, the transitions between the edges found in the image are soft and blurred because of the low contrast between them. The focus system looks only for contrast between edges, and those edges can run in any direction.

At the bottom of Figure 6.1, the image has been brought into sharp focus, and the edges have much more contrast; the transitions are sharp and clear. Although this example is a bit exaggerated so you can see the results on the printed page, it's easy to understand that when maximum contrast in a subject is achieved, it can be deemed to be in sharp focus. Achieving focus with contrast detection is generally slow, compared to phase detection (discussed next).

However, the V1 still does a good job with contrast detection. Like the human eye, the system evaluates the degree of focus, but, can remember the progression from blurry to sharp perfectly, so that autofocus can lock in much more quickly and, with an image that has sufficient contrast, more precisely.

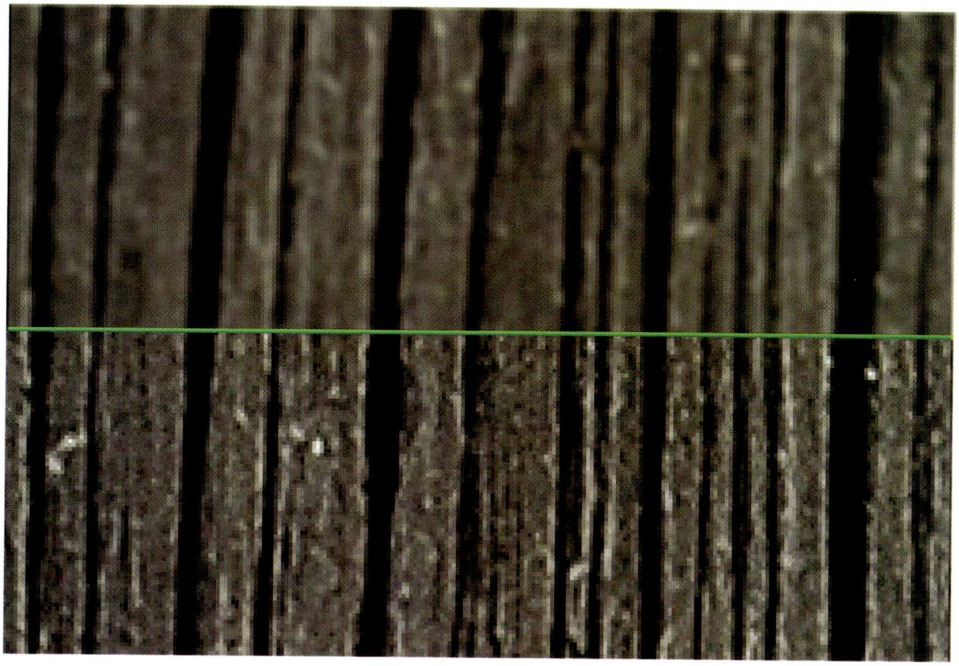

Figure 6.1 Focus in contrast detection mode evaluates the increase in contrast in the edges of subjects, starting with a blurry image (top) and producing a sharp, contrasty image (bottom).

Phase Detection

In phase detection mode, the Nikon V1 uses a different type of focusing system. Instead of evaluating the overall contrast of an image, the camera looks at certain autofocus zones within the frame using focus sensors built right into the imaging sensor, and splits each zone into two halves. The two parts of each zone are compared, much like (actually, *exactly* like) a two-window rangefinder used in surveying, weaponry—and non-SLR cameras like the venerable Leica M film models. The relative positions between the two images change as focus is moved in or out, until sharp focus is achieved when the images are "in phase," or lined up.

You can visualize how phase detection autofocus works if you look at Figures 6.2 and 6.3. (However, the action of your camera's actual autofocus sensors don't look *anything* like this; I'm providing a greatly simplified view just for illustration.) In Figure 6.2, a typical focus sensor is looking at a series of parallel vertical lines in a weathered piece of wood. The lines are broken into two halves by the camera's rangefinder algorithm, and you can see that they don't line up exactly; the image is slightly out of focus.

Fortunately, the rangefinder approach of phase detection tells the V1 exactly how out of focus the image is, and in which direction (focus is too near, or too far) thanks to the amount and direction of the displacement of the split image. The camera can quickly and precisely snap the image into sharp focus and line up the vertical lines, as shown in Figure 6.3. Of course, this scenario is ideal. When the same sensor is asked to measure focus for, in the worst case, subjects such as the sky (which may have neither

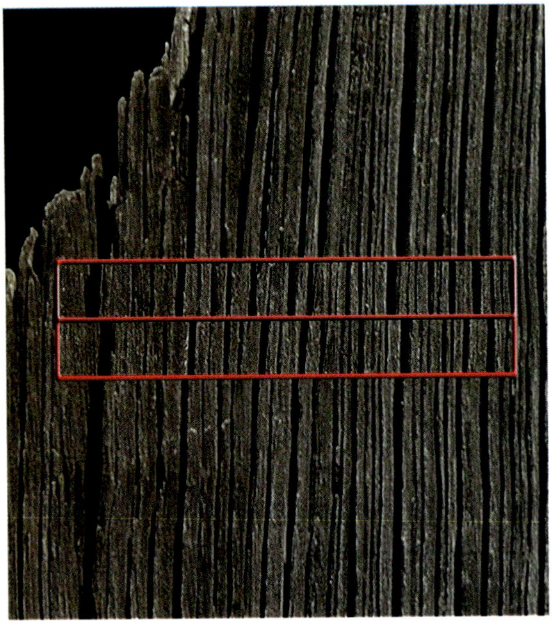

Figure 6.2 When an image is out of focus, the split lines don't align precisely.

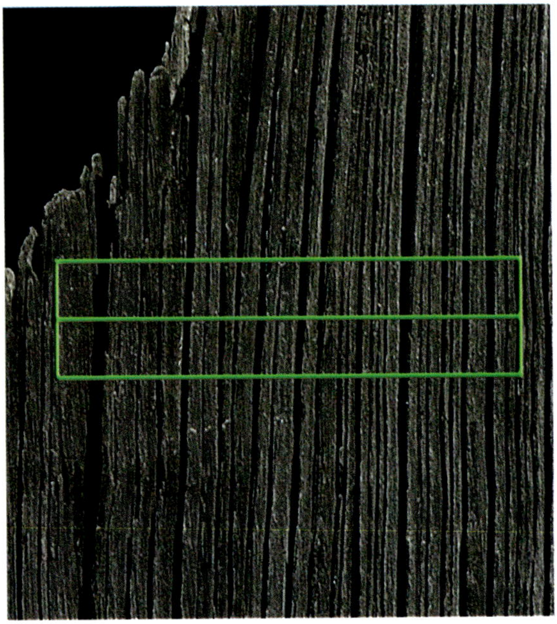

Figure 6.3 Using phase detection, the V1 is able to align the features of the image and achieve sharp focus quickly.

vertical nor horizontal lines), focus can slow down drastically, or even become impossible.

Phase detection uses 73 autofocus detectors embedded in the imaging sensor. The camera allocates the information from those sensors to 135 separate *autofocus zones* (I'll show you where they are in the AF-Area Selection section that follows), which are used to calculate focus in the V1's normal mode when light levels are sufficient. In lower light levels, the V1 switches to a contrast detection system, like the one described earlier. In addition, even when using phase detection, the V1 confirms its focus results by comparing the contrast of the image at the focus point. That makes the Nikon 1 autofocus system a true hybrid autofocus method.

If you're familiar with how phase detection works with a digital SLR camera, you can see that the Nikon V1's system is a bit different; dSLRs use a separate AF sensor located in the floor of the mirror box, and evaluate image information reflected downwards by the camera's partially silvered mirror. The V1 has no mirror, of course, so its phase detection system works with 73 special autofocus sensors embedded in the imaging sensor used to capture the image. The 73-element system allows many more focus zones: 135, compared with the 39 zones available with a camera like the Nikon D7000 digital SLR.

Unfortunately, while the V1's focus system finds it easy to measure degrees of apparent focus at each of the focus points in the viewfinder, it doesn't really know with any certainty *which* object should be in sharpest focus. Is it the closest object? The subject in the center? Something lurking *behind* the closest subject? A person standing over at the side of the picture? Many of the techniques for using autofocus effectively involve telling the Nikon V1 exactly what it should be focusing on, by choosing a focus zone or by allowing the camera to choose a focus zone for you. I'll address that topic shortly.

As the camera collects focus information from the sensors, it then evaluates it to determine whether the desired sharp focus has been achieved. The calculations may include whether the subject is moving, and whether the camera needs to "predict" where the subject will be when the shutter release button is fully depressed and the picture is taken. The speed with which the camera is able to evaluate focus and then move the lens elements into the proper position to achieve the sharpest focus determines how fast the autofocus mechanism is. Although your V1 will almost always focus more quickly than a human, there are types of shooting situations where that's not fast enough. For example, if you're having problems shooting sports because the V1's autofocus system manically follows each moving subject, a better choice might be to switch Autofocus modes or shift into Manual and prefocus on a spot where you anticipate the action will be, such as a goal line or soccer net.

Adding Circles of Confusion

But there are other factors in play, as well. You know that increased depth-of-field brings more of your subject into focus. But more depth-of-field also makes autofocusing (or manual focusing) more difficult in contrast detection mode because the contrast is lower between objects at different distances. So, autofocus with a 100mm focal length may be easier than at a 10mm focal length because the longer lens has less apparent depth-of-field. By the same token, a lens with a maximum aperture of f/3.5 (at its widest focal length) will be easier to autofocus (or manually focus) than one with an f/5.6 maximum aperture, because the f/5.6 lens has more depth-of-field *and* a dimmer view.

To make things even more complicated, many subjects aren't polite enough to remain still. They move around in the frame, so that even if the V1 is sharply focused on your main subject, it may change position and require refocusing. An intervening subject may pop into the frame and pass between you and the subject you meant to photograph. You (or the V1) have to decide whether to lock focus on this new subject, or remain focused on the original subject. Finally, there are some kinds of subjects that are difficult to bring into sharp focus because they lack enough contrast to allow the V1's AF system (or our eyes) to lock in. Blank walls, a clear blue sky, or problematic subjects such as birds in flight may make focusing difficult.

If you find all these focus factors confusing, you're on the right track. Focus is, in fact, measured using something called a *circle of confusion.* An ideal image consists of zillions of tiny little points, which, like all points, theoretically have no height or width. There is perfect contrast between the point and its surroundings. You can think of each point as a pinpoint of light in a darkened room. When a given point is out of focus, its

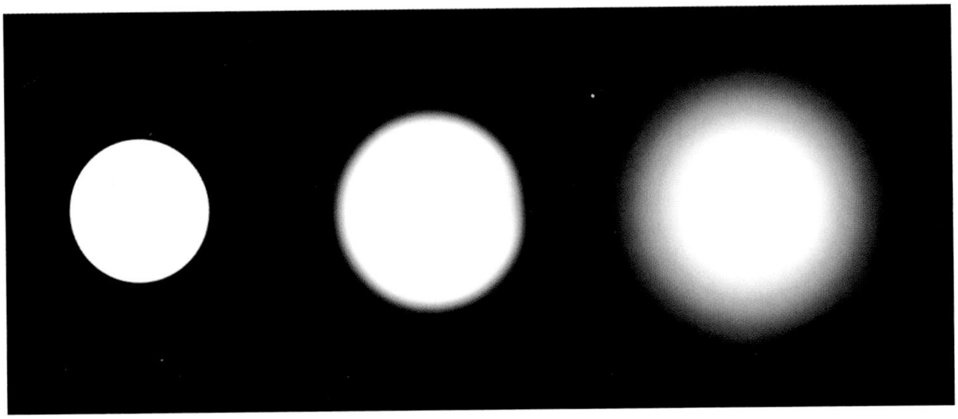

Figure 6.4
When a pinpoint of light (left) goes out of focus, its blurry edges form a circle of confusion (center and right).

edges decrease in contrast and it changes from a perfect point to a tiny disc with blurry edges (remember, blur is the lack of contrast between boundaries in an image). (See Figure 6.4.)

If this blurry disc—the circle of confusion—is small enough, our eye still perceives it as a point. It's only when the disc grows large enough that we can see it as a blur rather than a sharp point that a given point is viewed as out of focus. You can see, then, that enlarging an image, either by displaying it larger on your computer monitor or by making a large print, also enlarges the size of each circle of confusion. Moving closer to the image does the same thing. So, parts of an image that may look perfectly sharp in a 5 × 7-inch print viewed at arm's length, might appear blurry when blown up to 11 × 14 and examined at the same distance. Take a few steps back, however, and it may look sharp again.

To a lesser extent, the viewer also affects the apparent size of these circles of confusion. Some people see details better at a given distance and may perceive smaller circles of confusion than someone standing next to them. For the most part, however, such differences are small. Truly blurry images will look blurry to just about everyone under the same conditions.

Technically, there is just one plane within your picture area, parallel to the back of the camera (or sensor, in the case of a digital camera), that is in sharp focus. That's the plane in which the points of the image are rendered as precise points. At every other plane in front of or behind the focus plane, the points show up as discs that range from slightly blurry to extremely blurry (see Figure 6.5). In practice, the discs in many of these planes will still be so small that we see them as points, and that's where we get depth-of-field. Depth-of-field is just the range of planes that include discs that we perceive as points rather than blurred splotches. The size of this range increases as the aperture is reduced in size and is allocated roughly one-third in front of the plane of sharpest focus, and two-thirds behind it. The range of sharp focus is always greater behind your subject than in front of it.

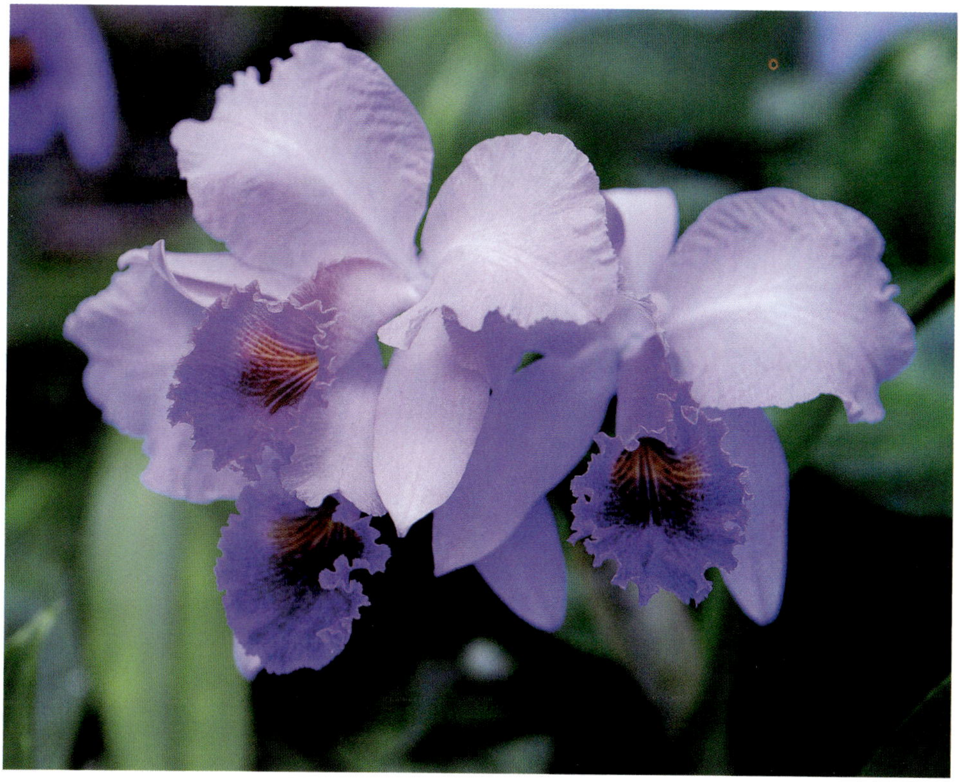

Figure 6.5
Only the blossoms in the foreground are in focus—the area behind them appears blurry because the depth-of-field is limited.

Using Autofocus with the Nikon V1

Autofocus can sometimes be frustrating for the new digital photographer, especially those coming from the point-and-shoot world. That's because correct focus plays a greater role among your creative options with a mirrorless camera, even when photographing the same subjects. Most point-and-shoot digital cameras have sensors that are even tinier than the CX-sized sensor in the V1. Those smaller sensors require shorter focal lengths, which have, effectively, more depth-of-field.

The bottom line is that with the average point-and-shoot camera, *everything* is in focus from about one foot to infinity and at virtually every f/stop. Unless you're shooting close-up photos a few inches from the camera, the depth-of-field is prodigious, and autofocus is almost a non-factor. The V1, on the other hand, uses longer focal length lenses to achieve the same field of view with its larger sensor, so there is less depth-of-field. (That's true even though the V1's sensor is smaller than those found in Nikon's DX and FX cameras—size is relative.) The depth-of-field available with the Nikon V1 cameras, which is more than found in the company's DX and FX models, is still less than with point-and-shoot cameras. That makes the correct use of autofocus more critical.

To maintain the most creative control, you have to choose three attributes:

- **How much is in focus.** Generally, by choosing the f/stop used, you'll determine the *range* of sharpness/amount of depth-of-field. The larger the DOF, the "easier" it is for the autofocus system's locked-in focus point to be appropriate (even though, strictly speaking, there is only one actual plane of sharp focus). With less depth-of-field, the accuracy of the focus point becomes more critical, because even a small error will result in an out-of-focus shot.
- **What subject is in focus.** The portion of your subject that is zeroed in for autofocus is determined by the autofocus zone that is active, and which is chosen either by you or by the Nikon V1 (as described next). For example, when shooting portraits, it's actually okay for part of the subject—or even part of the subject's face—to be slightly out of focus as long as the eyes (or even just the *nearest* eye) appear sharp.
- **When focus is applied.** For static shots of objects that aren't moving, *when* focus is applied doesn't matter much. But when you're shooting sports, or birds in flight, or children, the subject may move within the viewfinder as you're framing the image. Whether that movement is across the frame or headed right towards you, timing the instant when autofocus is applied can be important.

Autofocus Simplifies Our Lives... Doesn't It?

Manual focus is tricky, requires judgment, and fast reflexes, even with the V1's enlarged-view manual focus mode. So, we're all better off now that autofocus has become almost universal, right? On the one hand, AF does save time and allows us to capture subjects (particularly fast-moving sports) that are difficult to image sharply using manual focusing (unless you have training and know certain techniques). On the other hand, learning to apply the Nikon V1's autofocus system most effectively requires a bit of study and some practice. Then, once you're comfortable with autofocus, you'll know when it's appropriate to use the manual focus option, too.

The important thing to remember is that focus isn't absolute. For example, some things that look in sharp focus at a given viewing size and distance might not be in focus at a larger size and/or closer distance. In addition, the goal of optimum focus isn't always to make things look sharp. Not all of an image will be or should be sharp. Controlling exactly what is sharp and what is not is part of your creative palette. Use of depth-of-field characteristics to throw part of an image out of focus while other parts are sharply focused is one of the most valuable tools available to a photographer. But selective focus works only when the desired areas of an image are in focus properly. For the digital photographer, correct focus can be one of the trickiest parts of the technical and creative process.

There are three things to keep in mind when using autofocus:

- **Autofocus point selection.** This aspect controls how the V1 selects which areas of the frame are used to evaluate focus. Point selection allows the camera (or you) to specify a subject and lock focus in on that subject. Should the camera look for faces, and focus on the zones that contain them?
- **Autofocus mode.** This governs *when* during the framing and shooting process autofocus is achieved. Should the camera focus once when activated, or continue to monitor your subject and refocus should the subject move?
- **Autofocus activation.** When should the autofocus process begin, and when should it be locked? This aspect is related to the autofocus mode, but uses controls that you can specify to activate and/or lock the autofocus process.

Choosing an Autofocus Area Selection Mode

The V1 has three different focus area selection modes. I'm going to describe each of the three modes, and explain how to use them. You can set any of the three point selection modes:

1. Press the MENU button and scroll down to AF-Area Mode in the Shooting menu.
2. Move the cursor to the right and the screen shown in Figure 6.6 appears.

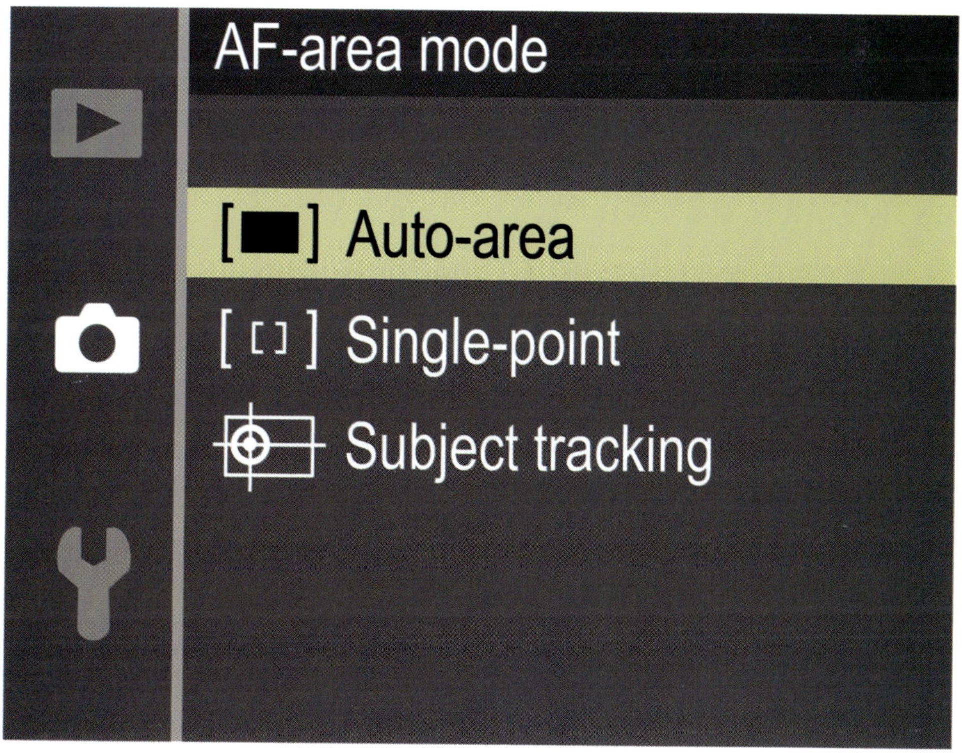

Figure 6.6 Select an autofocus-area mode.

3. Use the up/down directional keys to choose the AF-Area mode you want.
4. Press the OK button to confirm.
5. Tap the shutter release button or press MENU to exit the menu system.

Here's how each of the three modes work:

Auto-Area AF

In this mode, autofocus point selection is out of your hands; the V1 performs the task for you and selects which of the zones to use with its own intelligence, and may choose one or several zones, depending on your subject. Thanks to the communication between the Nikon 1 lenses and the camera, the V1 can even work with the supplied distance information to distinguish humans from their background, so a person standing at the side of the frame will be detected and used to evaluate focus, while the camera ignores the background area in the frame. In AF-S, AF-A, and AF-C modes, the active focus zones are highlighted in the viewfinder for about one second after focus is achieved. Zones are not used in manual focus mode (which uses your eyes' contrast detection capabilities), and thus not displayed. Figure 6.7 shows the approximate location of the focus zones used in this mode. In the figure, the green rectangles represent the zones selected by Auto-Area AF. I've also included a "ghost" image that shows the location of the other zones; these semi-transparent zones don't appear in the EVF or LCD—I show them just for illustrative purposes.

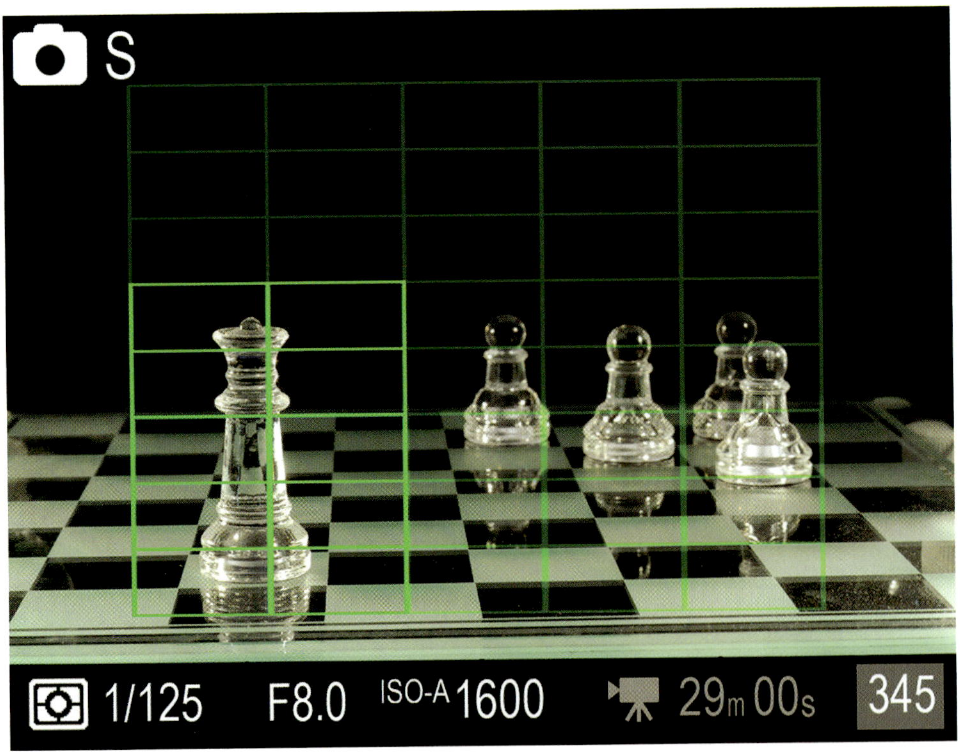

Figure 6.7
The focus zone you select can be moved around the screen.

Single-Point AF

In this mode, you always select the focus point manually. More zones are available than in Auto-Area AF, because the zones overlap. To move the point to any of the 135 zones just follow these steps:

1. **Access focus area selection.** While viewing your subject, press the OK button to activate the focus area selection display. A focus box will appear with four "compass" points that indicate its location can be moved.
2. **Move active zone around the screen.** Press the up/down/left right directional buttons to relocate the active zone. You can rotate the multi selector dial to move the focus zone left or right. The approximate area is highlighted in yellow in Figure 6.8. (The yellow highlighting does not appear on monitor.) The zones are arrayed 15 across horizontally and 9 vertically. Each zone overlaps the adjoining zone by about one-third, so each time you press the directional button, the zone will jump approximately two-thirds the width or height.
3. **Confirm choice.** Press the OK button to lock in the selected zone.
4. **Focus zone fixed.** Thereafter, the focus zone will be fixed at the zone you've selected, until you change it or switch to a different autofocus area mode.

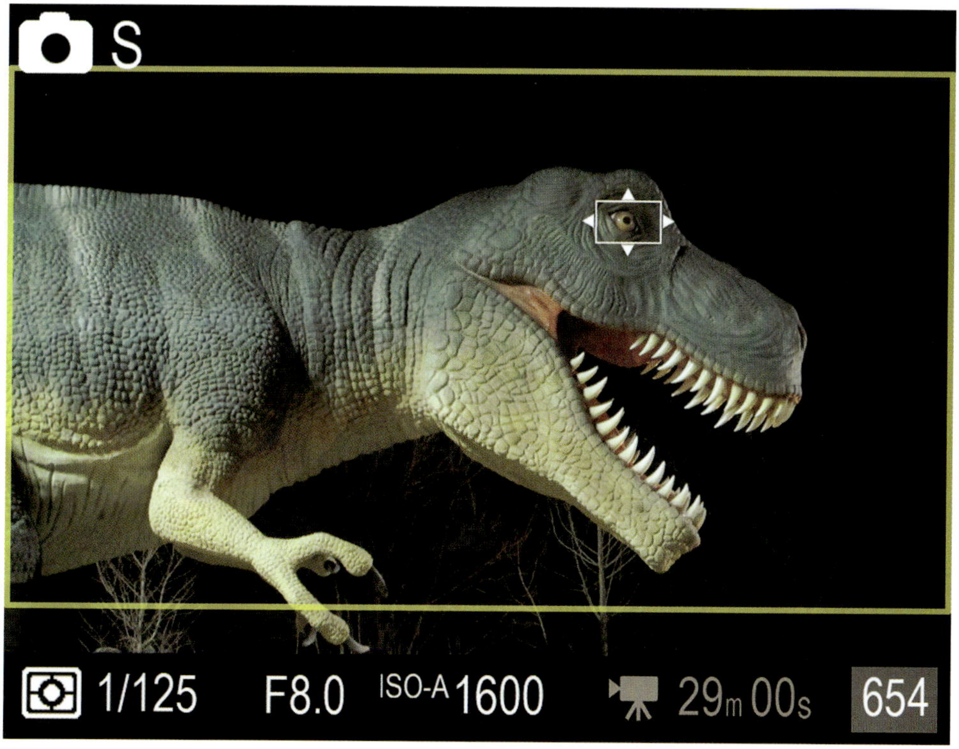

Figure 6.8
The focus zone you select can be moved around the screen.

Subject Tracking

As with Single-Point AF, you can select the focus zone used by the V1 to autofocus. However, once you've locked in the initial zone, the camera will relocate the active zone around the screen to track the movement of your subject. The system operates best with subjects moving toward or away from the camera, because focus changes dramatically with such movement. Side to side or diagonal movements are tracked a little less accurately, because the changes in focus are more subtle. To use subject tracking, just follow these steps:

1. **Access focus area selection.** While viewing your subject, press the OK button to activate the focus area selection display.
2. **Move the active zone to your subject.** Press the up/down/left right directional buttons to relocate the active zone on the subject you want to follow, as shown in Figure 6.9.
3. **Confirm choice.** Press the OK button to lock in the selected zone.
4. **Focus zone will track your subject.** Thereafter, the focus zone will move around the screen to track your subject, and when you press the shutter release halfway it will lock. The subject needs to remain in the area shown by the yellow highlighting in the figure (the highlighting does not appear on the monitor; it's just for illustrative purposes).

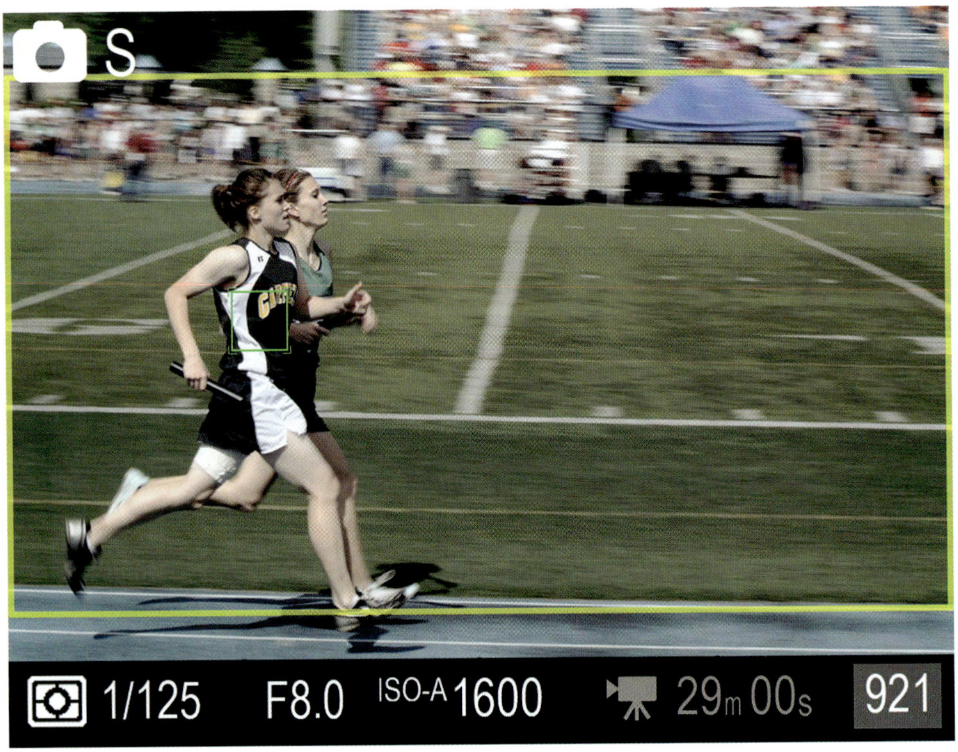

Figure 6.9
The V1 can track moving subjects.

Subject tracking works only so long as the Nikon V1 is able to recognize it as the same object. Here are some situations in which the camera can be "fooled."

- **Lack of differentiation.** A solid green ball rolling across the surface of a green pool table may be difficult to track: the V1 uses color as one of the aspects that differentiate your subject from its surroundings. Any subject that is too similar to its background may be problematic, as well as those that are extra large or small, bright, or dark.
- **Very rapid movement.** If your subject moves too quickly, the subject-tracking autofocus may lose it.
- **Leaving the frame.** If your subject moves out of the frame, the V1 will stop tracking it, and may not recognize it again if it returns.
- **Obscured by another subject.** Let's say you're shooting football and the referee suddenly stops between you and that tight end you were tracking; when the ref moves on, the camera probably won't be able to find the subject again.
- **Sudden change in size or color.** Although focus tracking works well with subjects that move relatively slowly toward or away from the camera, if your subject is running toward the camera and "grows" from a small element in the frame to one that fills the frame quickly, don't expect the Nikon V1 to be able to track it. A subject illuminated primarily by a red light that suddenly turns green may not be tracked, either. I've had this happen at concerts, when a performer bathed in a pure white light is unexpectedly highlighted by a red spot. The color change confuses the V1's tracking system.

Face-Priority AF

Although you don't select Face Priority AF in the AF-Area Selection menu, it's a form of autofocus that's closely related to the subject-tracking option I just described. The difference is that the Nikon V1 searches for faces and locks in on them. Unfortunately, you can't select which face the camera will give priority to, except by reframing the image. Just follow these steps to use Face Priority AF:

1. **Activate Face Priority AF.** Visit the Shooting menu, and navigate to Face Priority AF, which is one entry down from the AF-Area Mode listing. Press the right directional button to view the selection screen and choose On.
2. **Once activated, Face Priority AF operates in any AF-Area mode.** In Auto-Area, Single-Point, and Subject Tracking modes, the V1 will use Face Priority to choose the focus zone if one or more faces is detected facing the camera. Otherwise, each of these AF-area modes operate in its normal way, and if faces leave the frame (or turn away from the camera), Face Priority is abandoned.

3. **Up to five faces are located.** The yellow boxes appear around each face, with a double box around the face located closest to the camera. (See Figure 6.10.) You can't select a different frame, except by recomposing your image.

4. **Lock in focus.** Press the shutter release halfway, and focus will lock in on the selected face. The focus zone highlighting turns green.

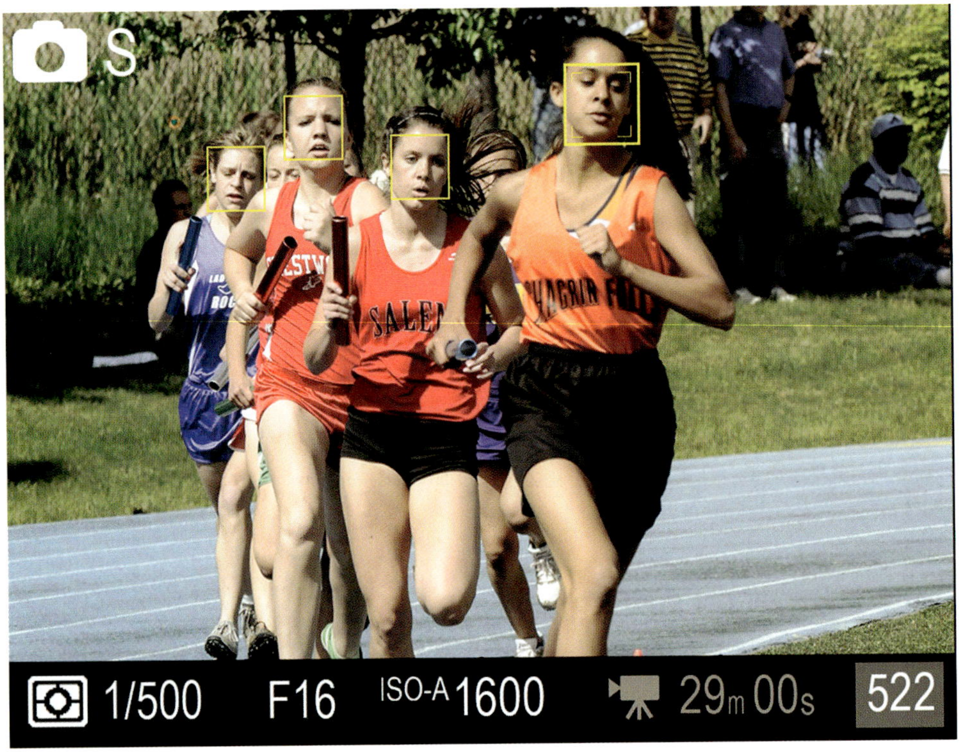

Figure 6.10
The closest face is selected automatically in Face Priority mode.

Autofocus Mode

Choosing the right autofocus mode is another key to focusing success. To save battery power, your V1 doesn't start to focus the lens until you partially depress the shutter release. But, autofocus isn't some mindless beast out there snapping your pictures in and out of focus with no feedback from you after you press that button. There are several settings you can modify that return at least a modicum of control to you.

Just press the down directional button and select from AF-S, AF-C, AF-A, or MF (manual focus) when using Still Image mode (see Figure 6.11), or AF-F, AF-S, or MF (manual focus) when using Movie mode. This choice determines *when* your V1 starts to autofocus, and what it does when focus is achieved. Automatic focus is not something that happens all the time when your camera is turned on. Your V1 activates autofocus when you either press the shutter release down halfway *or* press the AE-L/AF-L button (the up directional button). Here's a description of each of these modes:

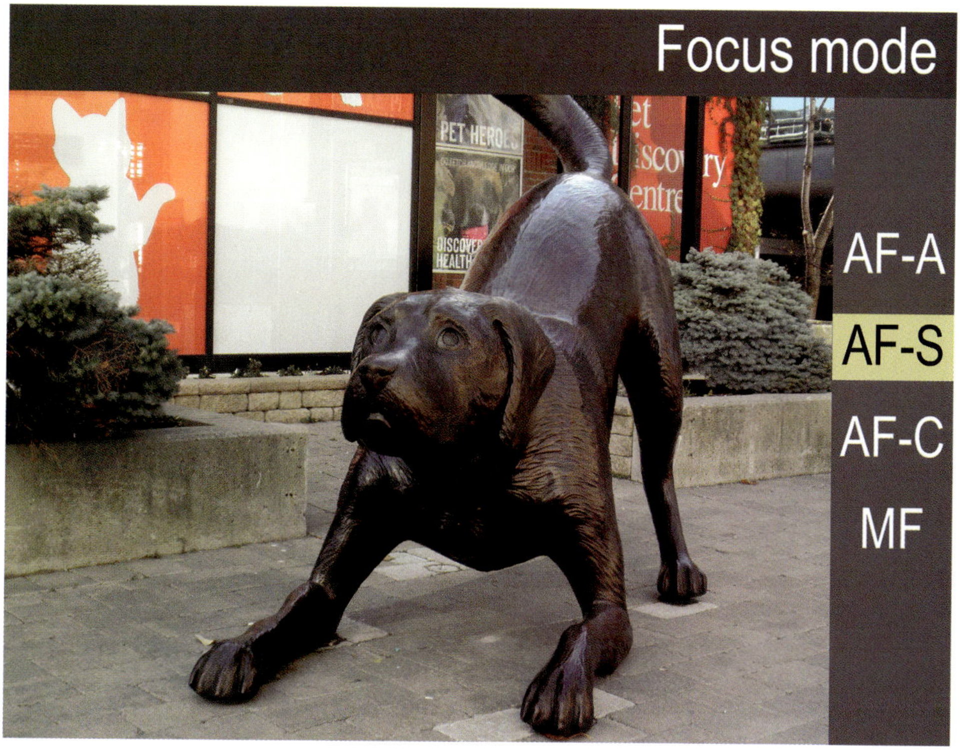

Figure 6.11
Choose an autofocus mode.

AF-S (Single-Servo Autofocus)

In this mode, generally just called *AF-S*, focus is set once and remains at that setting until the button is fully depressed, taking the picture, or until you release the shutter button without taking a shot. For non-action photography, this setting is usually your best choice, as it minimizes out-of-focus pictures (at the expense of spontaneity). It's available in both Still Image and Movie modes.

When sharp focus is achieved, the selected focus zone will flash green in the monitor. By keeping the shutter button depressed halfway, you'll find you can reframe the image while retaining the focus (and exposure) that's been set. You can also use the AE-L/AF-L button to lock focus. Because of the small delay while the camera zeroes in on correct focus, you might experience slightly more shutter lag. This mode uses less battery power.

AF-C (Continuous-Servo Autofocus)

This mode, also known as *AF-C,* is the mode to use for sports and other fast-moving subjects. In this mode, once the shutter release is partially depressed, the camera sets the focus but continues to monitor the subject, so that if it moves or you move, the lens will be refocused to suit. Focus and exposure aren't really locked until you press the shutter release down all the way to take the picture. You'll find that AF-C produces the least amount of shutter lag of any autofocus mode when set to release priority: press the button and the camera fires. It also uses the most battery power, because the autofocus system operates as long as the shutter release button is partially depressed. This mode works especially well with Subject Tracking autofocus zone selection. This mode is not available in Movie mode; use AF-F (described later), instead.

AF-A (Automatic Autofocus)

This setting, available only in Still Image mode, is actually a combination of the first two. When selected, the camera focuses using AF-S AF and locks in the focus setting. But, if the subject begins moving, it will switch automatically to AF-C and change the focus to keep the subject sharp. AF-A is a good choice when you're shooting a mixture of action pictures and less dynamic shots and want to use AF-S when possible. The camera will default to that mode, yet switch automatically to AF-C when it would be useful for subjects that might begin moving unexpectedly. However, as with AF-S, the shutter can be released only when the subject at the selected focus point is in focus.

AF-F Full-Time Autofocus

This setting, available only in Movie mode, replaces the AF-C and AF-A options. (Only AF-S, AF-F, or Manual focus can be selected in Movie mode.) When using AF-F, the camera focuses continuously, and images can be captured even if sharp focus is not quite locked in.

Manual Focus

When you've set the camera to manual focus, you can adjust the zone of sharpness visually using the viewfinder or LCD, as originally described in Chapter 2. To recap, just follow these steps:

1. **Activate focus guides.** Press the multi selector OK button to produce an enlarged view of the center of the frame, as shown in Figure 6.12. A focus scale and navigation window appear at the right of the screen. The outer box represents the entire frame, and the yellow box within it shows the relative portion of the frame currently being magnified.
2. **Zoom in or out.** You can increase/decrease the amount of magnification by pressing the zoom bar in the upper-right corner of the back panel up or down. The size of the yellow box changes to indicate the zoom magnification. Up to 10X magnification can be achieved.
3. **Position magnified area.** Although you can adjust the framing of the camera to relocate the magnified area, if you've mounted the V1 on a tripod, you might want to "lock down" the setup. In that case, you can press the multi selector directional buttons to move the yellow box around in the navigation window, and, thus, the magnified area.

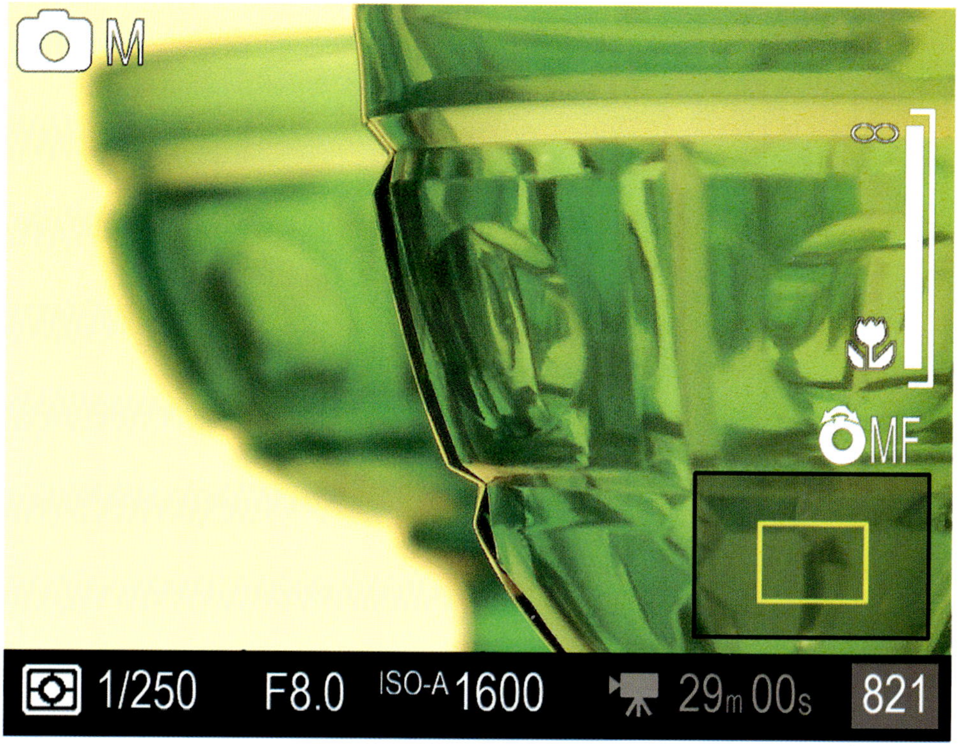

Figure 6.12
Manual focus is great for isolating subjects, such as this close-up of glassware, using selective focus.

4. **Focus.** Rotate the multi selector dial to focus the image. The focus indicator bar at the right of the screen will show the approximate distance.
5. **Confirm focus.** Press the OK button to lock in focus when you're satisfied.

Focus Stacking

If you are doing macro (close-up) photography of flowers, or other small objects at short distances, the depth-of-field often will be extremely narrow, even with a camera with a relatively small sensor like the Nikon V1. In some cases, it will be so narrow that it will be impossible to keep the entire subject in focus in one photograph. Although having part of the image out of focus can be a pleasing effect for a portrait of a person, it is likely to be a hindrance when you are trying to make an accurate photographic record of a flower, or small piece of precision equipment. One solution to this problem is focus stacking, a procedure that can be considered like HDR translated for the world of focus—taking multiple shots with different settings, and, using software as explained below, combining the best parts from each image in order to make a whole that is better than the sum of the parts. Focus stacking requires a non-moving object, so some subjects, such as flowers, are best photographed in a breezeless environment, such as indoors.

For example, see Figures 6.13 through 6.15, in which I took photographs of three colorful crayons using the V1's standard 10-30mm kit lens, which can focus down to about eight inches even at the 30mm telephoto setting. As you can see from these images, the depth-of-field was extremely narrow, and only a small part of the subject was in focus for each shot.

Now look at Figure 6.16, in which the entire subject is in reasonably sharp focus. This image is a composite, made up of the three shots above, as well as 10 others, each one focused on the same scene, but at very gradually increasing distances from the camera's lens. All 13 images were then combined in Adobe Photoshop CS5 using the focus stacking procedure. Here are the steps you can take to combine shots for the purpose of achieving sharp focus in this sort of situation:

1. **Set the camera firmly on a solid tripod.** A tripod or other equally firm support is absolutely essential for this procedure.
2. **Set the Nikon V1 for remote control.** Press the left directional button on the multi selector and choose either of the two remote control settings.
3. **Set the camera to manual focus mode.** Use the procedure described in the previous section to activate manual focus.
4. **Set the exposure, ISO, and white balance manually.** Use test shots if necessary to determine the best values. This step in the Shooting menu will help prevent visible variations from arising among the multiple shots that you'll be taking. You don't want the V1 to change the ISO setting or white balance between shots.
5. **Set the quality of the images to NEF (RAW) + JPEG FINE.** Use the Shooting menu to make this adjustment. Having both formats will give you flexibility when combining the images.
6. **Switch to Electronic shutter.** Press the F button and choose Electronic shutter. Disabling the mechanical shutter will eliminate one source of vibration.
7. **Turn off Image Stabilization.** Navigate to Vibration Reduction in the Shooting menu. You don't need it when the camera is securely mounted on a tripod, and disabling VR will keep the V1 from making any sort of image adjustment between exposures.
8. **Focus manually on the very closest point of the subject to the lens.** Rotate the multi selector dial to change the focus.
9. **Trip the shutter.** Use the ML-L3 infrared remote.
10. **Carefully refocus.** Gently rotate the multi selector dial to focus on a point slightly farther away from the lens and trip the shutter again.
11. **Continue taking photographs** in this way until you have covered the entire subject with in-focus shots.

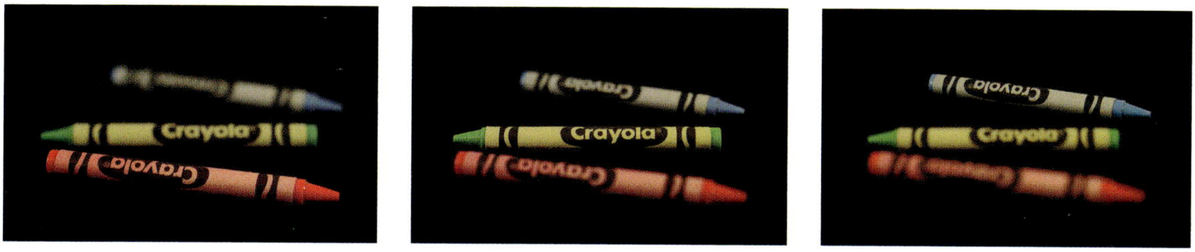

Figures 6.13 6.14 6.15 These three shots were all focused on different distances within the same scene. No single shot could bring the entire subject into sharp focus.

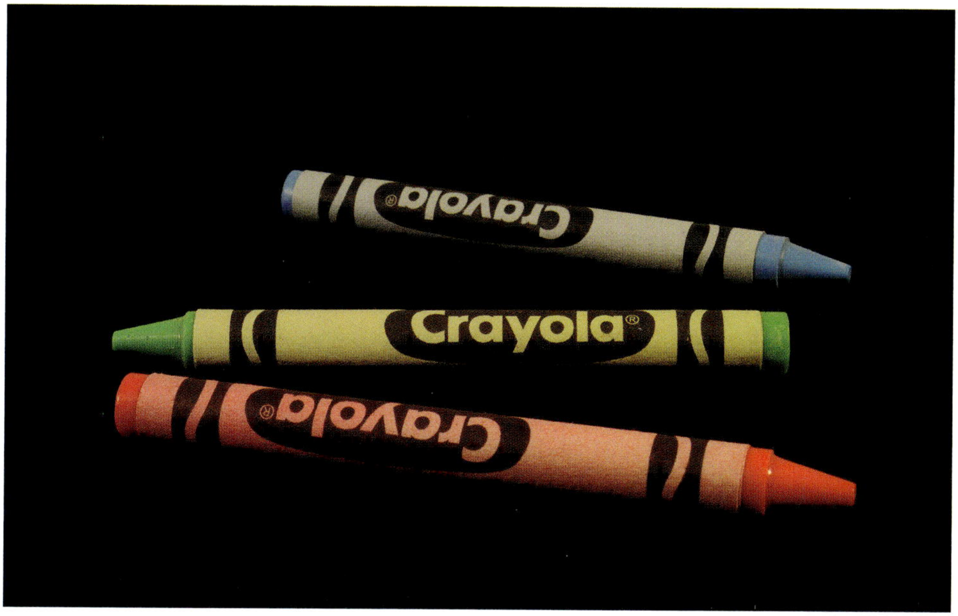

Figure 6.16 Three partially out-of-focus shots have been merged, along with ten others, through a focus stacking procedure in Adobe Photoshop CS5, to produce a single image with the entire subject in focus.

The next step is to process the images you've taken in Photoshop CS4 or CS5. Transfer the images to your computer, and then follow these steps:

1. In Photoshop, select File > Scripts > Load Files into Stack. In the dialog box that then appears, navigate on your computer to find the files for the photographs you have taken, and highlight them all.
2. At the bottom of the next dialog box that appears, check the box that says, "Attempt to Automatically Align Source Images," then click OK. The images will load; it may take several minutes for the program to load the images and attempt to arrange them into layers that are aligned based on their content.
3. Once the program has finished processing the images, go to the Layers panel and select all of the layers. You can do this by clicking on the top layer and then Shift-clicking on the bottom one.

4. While the layers are all selected, in Photoshop go to Edit > Auto-Blend Layers. In the dialog box that appears, select the two options, Stack Images and Seamless Tones and Colors, then click OK. The program will process the images, possibly for a considerable length of time.
5. If the procedure worked well, the result will be a single image made up of numerous layers that have been processed to produce a sharply focused rendering of your subject. If it did not work well, you may have to take additional images the next time, focusing very carefully on small slices of the subject as you move progressively farther away from the lens.

Although this procedure can work very well in Photoshop, you also may want to try it with programs that were developed more specifically for focus stacking and related procedures, such as Helicon Focus (www.heliconsoft.com), PhotoAcute (www.photo-acute.com), or CombineZM (www.hadleyweb.pwp.blueyonder.co.uk).

Continuous Shooting

The Nikon V1's continuous shooting modes remind me how far digital photography has brought us. The first accessory I purchased when I worked as a sports photographer some years ago was a motor drive for my film SLR. It enabled me to snap off a series of shots in rapid succession, which came in very handy when a fullback broke through the line and headed for the end zone. Even a seasoned action photographer can miss the decisive instant when a crucial block is made, or a baseball superstar's bat shatters and pieces of cork fly out. Continuous shooting simplifies taking a series of pictures, either to ensure that one has more or less the exact moment you want to capture or to capture a sequence that is interesting as a collection of successive images.

The V1's "motor drive" capabilities are, in many ways, much superior to what you get with a film camera. For one thing, a motor-driven film camera can eat up film at an incredible pace, which is why many of them are used with cassettes that hold hundreds of feet of film stock. At three frames per second (typical of film cameras), a short burst of a few seconds can burn up as much as half of an ordinary 36-exposure roll of film. Digital cameras, in contrast, have reusable "film," so if you waste a few dozen shots on non-decisive moments, you can erase them and shoot more. In addition, the V1 has much higher frame rates. In Continuous mode, you can snap off up to 5 frames per second (see Figure 6.17), and in Electronic shutter (Hi) mode, machine gun 10, 30, or an amazing 60 frames per second at full resolution. Of course, there are some restrictions. The next sections tell you what you need to know to use continuous shooting effectively.

Continuous Mode: 5 fps

To shoot continuously at a 5 fps clip in Still Image mode, you need to follow these guidelines:

- **Set Shooting defaults.** To get the maximum 5 fps, shooting defaults must be in force, with the exceptions noted below. In Still Image mode, press the MENU button, choose Reset Shooting Options from the Shooting menu, and choose Yes.
- **Choose either Mechanical or Electronic shutter.** In Still Image mode, press the F button and select Mechanical or Electronic shutter.
- **Select Continuous mode.** Press the MENU button and in the Shooting menu scroll to the Continuous menu entry, and choose Continuous shooting.
- **Choose Shutter-priority or Manual exposure mode.** Select either of these in the Shooting menu. These modes are required so you can ensure that a fast enough shutter speed is used. With Aperture-priority activated, the V1 may select a slower shutter speed, and that may reduce the maximum frame rate possible.
- **Set shutter speed to 1/250th second or faster.** A fast shutter speed is required to allow capturing images at 5 frames per second.
- **Fire away.** The V1's memory buffer can hold up to 100 photographs. However, the actual number you can shoot in one burst may vary, depending on the format you choose for your images. (See Figure 6.17.) The approximate number of images that can be captured using the current camera settings is displayed in the lower-right corner of the monitor when the shutter release is pressed halfway. Table 6.1 gives you a rough idea of the buffer's capacity when using the Mechanical shutter and full resolution.

To increase the numbers shown in Table 6.1, reduce the Image quality setting by switching to JPEG only (from JPEG+RAW), to a lower JPEG quality setting, such as JPEG Normal, or by reducing the V1's resolution from L to M or S. The reason the size

Table 6.1 Maximum Bursts in Continuous Mode

Image Quality	Buffer Capacity
NEF (RAW)	44
NEF (RAW)+JPEG FINE	42
JPEG FINE	58
JPEG Normal	74
JPEG Basic	99

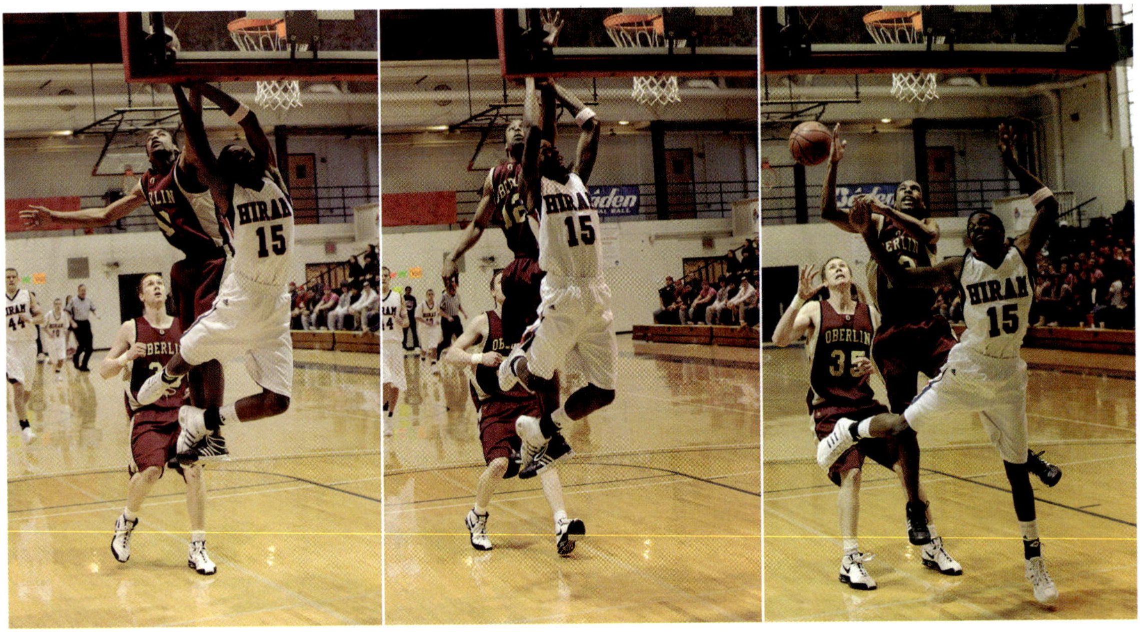

Figure 6.17 Continuous shooting allows you to capture an entire sequence of exciting moments as they unfold.

of your bursts is limited is that continuous images are first shuttled into the V1's internal memory buffer, then doled out to the Secure Digital card as quickly as they can be written to the card. Technically, the V1 takes the RAW data received from the digital image processor and converts it to the output format you've selected—either JPG or NEF (RAW)—and deposits it in the buffer ready to store on the card.

This internal "smart" buffer can suck up photos much more quickly than the SD card and, indeed, some memory cards are significantly faster or slower than others. When the buffer fills, you can't take any more continuous shots until the V1 has written some of them to the card, making more room in the buffer. You should keep in mind that faster SD cards write images more quickly, freeing up buffer space faster. Today, SD cards are speed-rated using a "Class" figure, with Class 4 (4 megabits per second transfer speed) being the slowest units commonly available. Most SD cards on the market are at least Class 6 (6 megabits per second), with the most common "speedy" cards rated as Class 10 (at least 10 megabits per second). We're starting to see SDXC memory cards given a Class 10 designation, but with read/write speeds that actually top out at 20 megabits per second. (Theoretically, SDXC cards could eventually have speeds that are 10 to 20 times faster.)

Continuous Mode: 10, 30, or 60 fps

To shoot continuously at these faster rates, you'll need to switch to the Nikon V1's Electronic (Hi) shutter setting. You don't need to have the camera set for Continuous shooting mode; bursts are the default (and only action possible) when using the Electronic shutter (Hi) setting. Just follow these steps:

1. **Switch to Electronic (Hi) shutter.** Although you can switch back and forth between Mechanical, Electronic, and Electronic (Hi) shutters using the F button when in Still Image mode, if you want to change the frame rate, visit the Shutter Type entry in the Shooting menu.
2. **Choose Electronic (Hi).** Scroll down to the Electronic (Hi) setting, then press the right directional button to reach the screen where you can specify frame rate. (See Figure 6.18.)
3. **Fire away.** Keep in mind that as you shoot bursts, the exposure for all the frames is fixed at the exposure values specified for the first frame in a burst. If you're shooting under variable lighting conditions, such as in a gymnasium that has non-incandescent three-phase lighting that "cycles," you may see some variation in exposures.

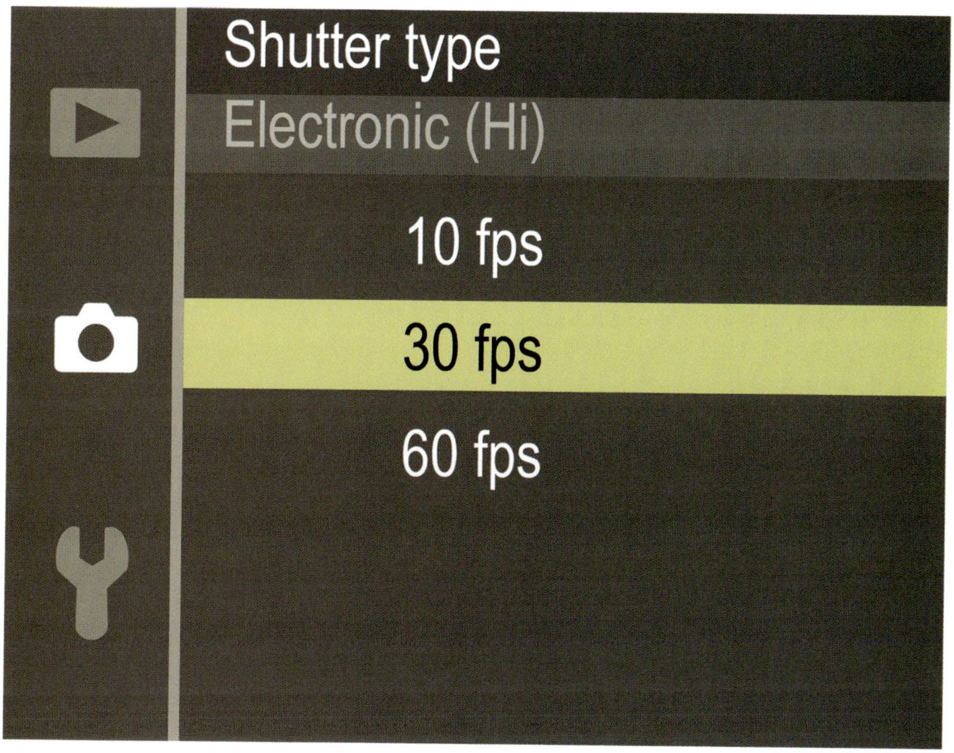

Figure 6.18
Select a frame rate for the electronic shutter.

A Tiny Slice of Time

Exposures that seem impossibly brief can reveal a world we didn't know existed. In the 1930s, Dr. Harold Edgerton, a professor of electrical engineering at MIT, pioneered high-speed photography using a repeating electronic flash unit he patented called the *stroboscope*. As the inventor of the electronic flash, he popularized its use to freeze objects in motion, and you've probably seen his photographs of bullets piercing balloons and drops of milk forming a coronet-shaped splash.

Electronic flash freezes action by virtue of its extremely short duration—as brief as 1/50,000th second or less. The V1's add-on SB-N5 flash unit can give you these ultra-quick glimpses of moving subjects. You can read more about using electronic flash to stop action in Chapter 10.

Of course, the V1 is fully capable of immobilizing all but the fastest movement using only its shutter speeds, which range all the way up to an astonishing 1/16,000th second with the electronic shutter (up to 1/4000th second with the mechanical shutter). Indeed, you'll rarely have need for such a brief shutter speed in ordinary shooting. But if you wanted to use an aperture of f/2.8 at ISO 200 outdoors in bright sunlight, for some reason, a shutter speed of 1/8,000th second would more than do the job. You'd need a faster shutter speed only if you moved the ISO setting to a higher sensitivity (but why would you do that?). Under less than full sunlight, 1/8,000th second is more than fast enough for any conditions you're likely to encounter.

Most sports action can be frozen at 1/2,000th second or slower, and for many sports a slower shutter speed is actually preferable—for example, to allow the wheels of a racing automobile or motorcycle, or the rotors on a helicopter to blur realistically, as shown in Figure 6.19. At top, a 1/1,000th second shutter speed effectively stopped the rotors of the helicopter, making it look like a crash was impending. At bottom, I used a slower 1/250th second shutter speed to allow enough blur to make this a true action picture.

But if you want to do some exotic action-freezing photography without resorting to electronic flash, the V1's top shutter speeds are at your disposal.

Working with Short Exposures

You can have a lot of fun exploring the kinds of pictures you can take using very brief exposure times, whether you decide to take advantage of the action-stopping capabilities of your SB-N5 electronic flash or work with the Nikon V1's faster shutter speeds. Here are a few ideas to get you started:

- **Take revealing images.** Fast shutter speeds can help you reveal the real subject behind the façade, by freezing constant motion to capture an enlightening moment in time. Legendary fashion/portrait photographer Philippe Halsman used leaping photos of famous people, such as the Duke and Duchess of Windsor, Richard Nixon, and Salvador Dali, to illuminate their real selves. Halsman said, "*When you*

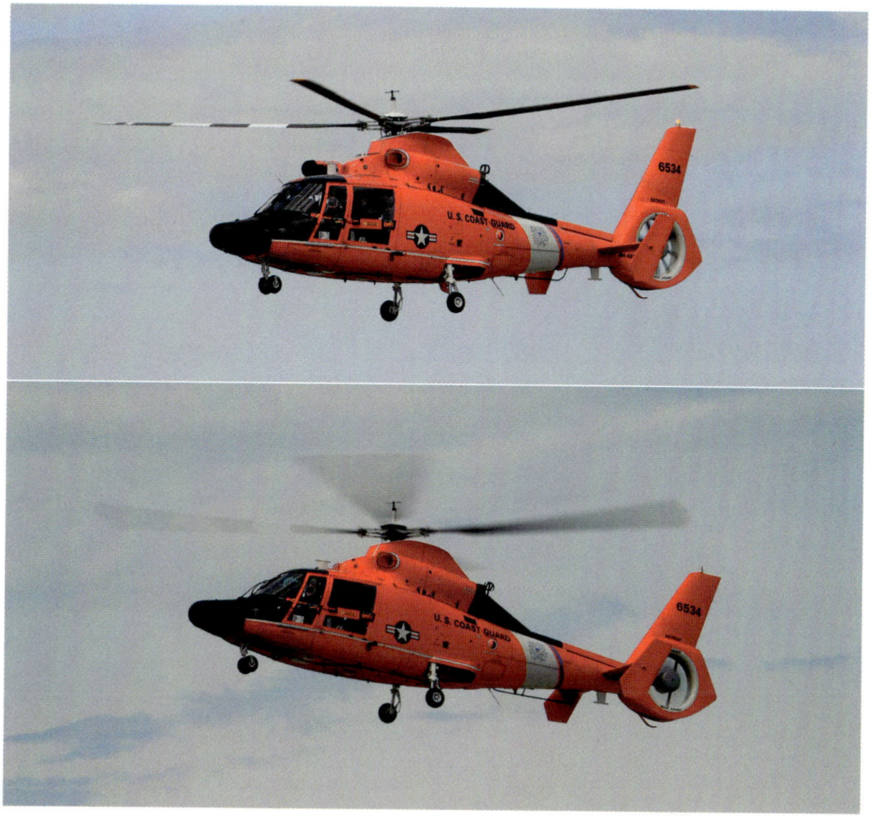

Figure 6.19
A little blur can be a good thing, as these shots of a helicopter at 1/1000th second (top) and 1/250th second (bottom) show.

ask a person to jump, his attention is mostly directed toward the act of jumping and the mask falls so that the real person appears." Try some high-speed portraits of people you know in motion to see how they appear when concentrating on something other than the portrait.

- **Create unreal images.** High-speed photography can also produce photographs that show your subjects in ways that are quite unreal. A motocross cyclist leaping over a ramp, but with all motion stopped so that the rider and machine look as if they were frozen in mid-air, make for an unusual picture. When we're accustomed to seeing subjects in motion, seeing them stopped in time can verge on the surreal.
- **Capture unseen perspectives.** Some things are *never* seen in real life, except when viewed in a stop-action photograph. Edgerton's balloon bursts were only a starting point. Freeze a hummingbird in flight for a view of wings that never seem to stop. Or, capture the splashes as liquid falls into a bowl, as shown in Figure 6.20. No electronic flash was required for this image (and wouldn't have illuminated the water in the bowl as evenly). Instead, a clutch of high intensity lamps and an ISO setting of 1600 allowed the V1 to capture this image at 1/4,000th second.

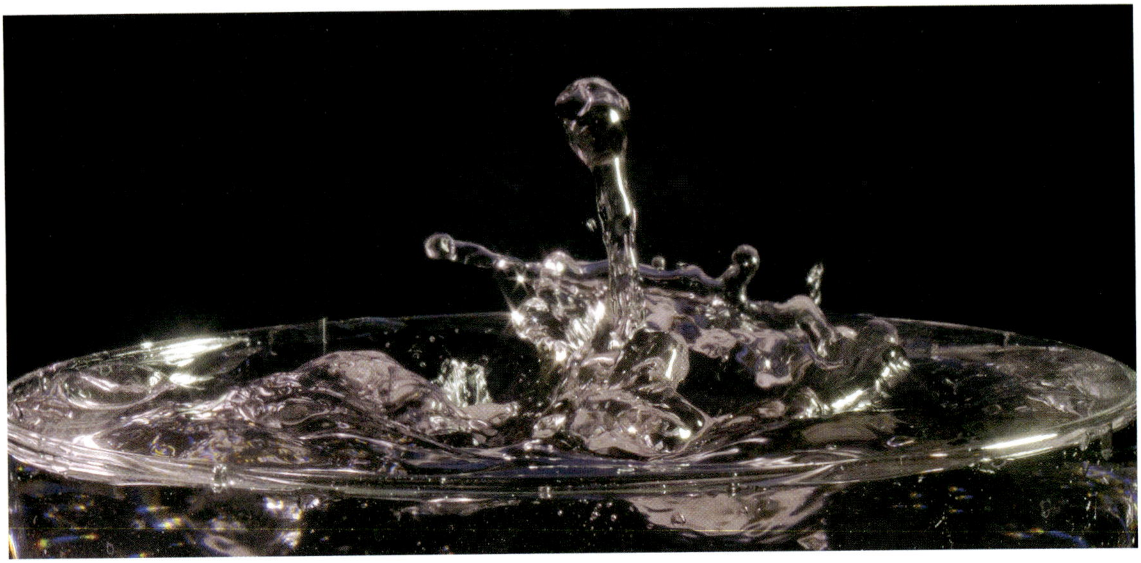

Figure 6.20 A large amount of artificial illumination and an ISO 1600 sensitivity setting allowed capturing this shot at 1/4,000th second without use of an electronic flash.

- **Vanquish camera shake and gain new angles.** Here's an idea that's so obvious it isn't always explored to its fullest extent. A high enough shutter speed is even better at correcting for camera movement than the V1's built-in Vibration Reduction feature. It can free you from the tyranny of a tripod in light levels too low for even VR to counter camera shake, making it easier to capture new angles, or to shoot quickly while moving around, especially with longer lenses. I tend to use a monopod or tripod for almost everything when I'm not using vibration reduction, and I end up missing some shots because of a reluctance to adjust my camera support to get a higher, lower, or different angle. If you have enough light and can use an f/stop wide enough to permit a high shutter speed, you'll find a new freedom to choose your shots.

Long Exposures

Longer exposures are a doorway into another world, showing us how even familiar scenes can look much different when photographed over periods measured in seconds. At night, long exposures produce streaks of light from moving, illuminated subjects like automobiles or amusement park rides. Extra long exposures of seemingly pitch-dark subjects can reveal interesting views using light levels barely bright enough to see by. At any time of day, including daytime (in which case you'll often need the help of neutral-density filters to make the long exposure practical), long exposures can cause moving objects to vanish entirely, because they don't remain stationary long enough to register in a photograph.

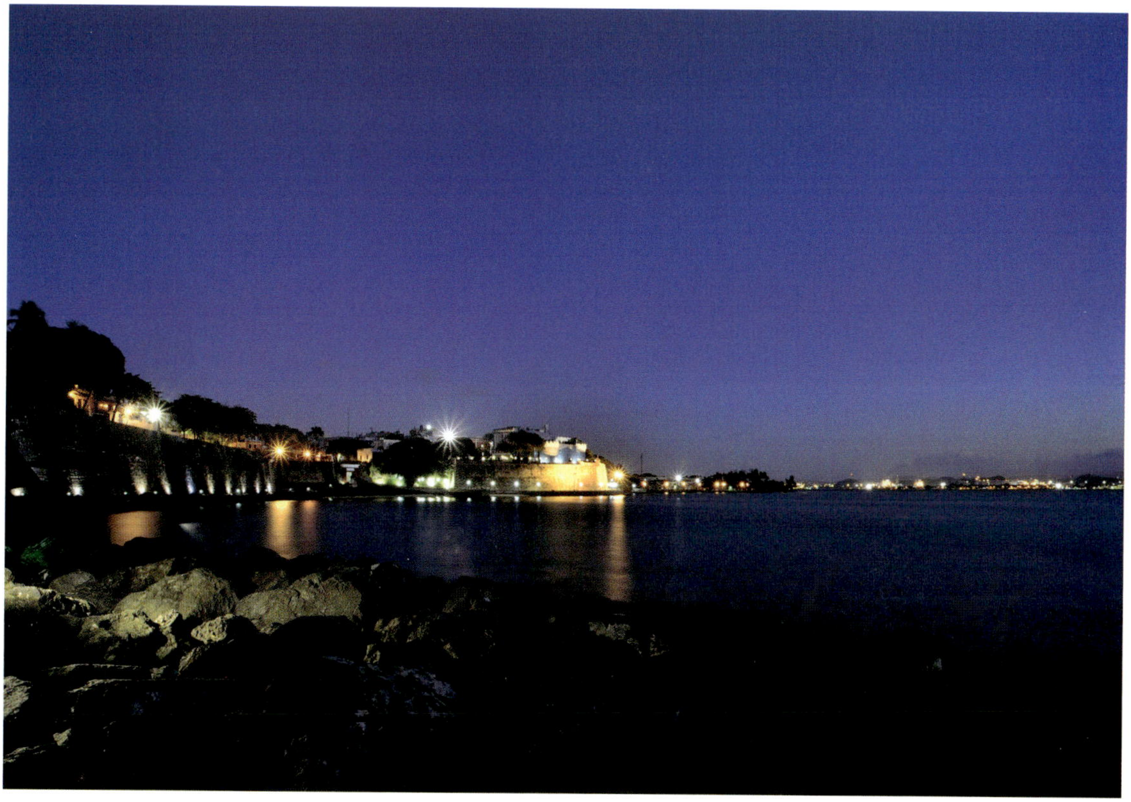

Figure 6.21 The ML-L3 remote control allows you to take longer exposures, such as this 60-second shot in San Juan, Puerto Rico.

The Nikon V1 allows you to take timed exposures of up to 30 seconds using the built-in mechanical or electronic shutters. You can take longer exposures using a "bulb"-type setting, which is available when you use Manual exposure mode and the ML-L3 infrared remote control. This type of exposure is so-called because in the olden days the photographer squeezed and held an air bulb attached to a tube that provided the force necessary to keep the shutter open. Traditionally, a bulb exposure is one that lasts as long as the shutter release button is pressed; when you release the button, the exposure ends. (See Figure 6.21.)

Working with Long Exposures

Because the V1 produces such good images at longer exposures, and there are so many creative things you can do with long exposure techniques, you'll want to do some experimenting. Get yourself a tripod or another firm support and take some test shots with long exposure noise reduction both enabled and disabled (to see whether you prefer low noise or high detail) and get started.

Here are some things to try:

- **Make people invisible.** One very cool thing about long exposures is that objects that move rapidly enough won't register at all in a photograph, while the subjects that remain stationary are portrayed in the normal way. That makes it easy to produce people-free landscape photos and architectural photos at night or, even, in full daylight if you use a neutral-density filter (or two) (or three) to allow an exposure of at least a few seconds. At ISO 100, f/16, and a pair of 8X (three-stop) neutral-density filters, you can use exposures of nearly two seconds; overcast days and/or even more neutral-density filtration would work even better if daylight people-vanishing is your goal. They'll have to be walking *very* briskly and across the field of view (rather than directly toward the camera) for this to work. At night, it's much easier to achieve this effect with the 20- to 30-second exposures that are possible, as you can see in Figure 6.22.
- **Create streaks.** If you aren't shooting for total invisibility, long exposures with the camera on a tripod can produce some interesting streaky effects. Even a single 8X ND filter will let you shoot at f/16 and 1/12th second in daylight.

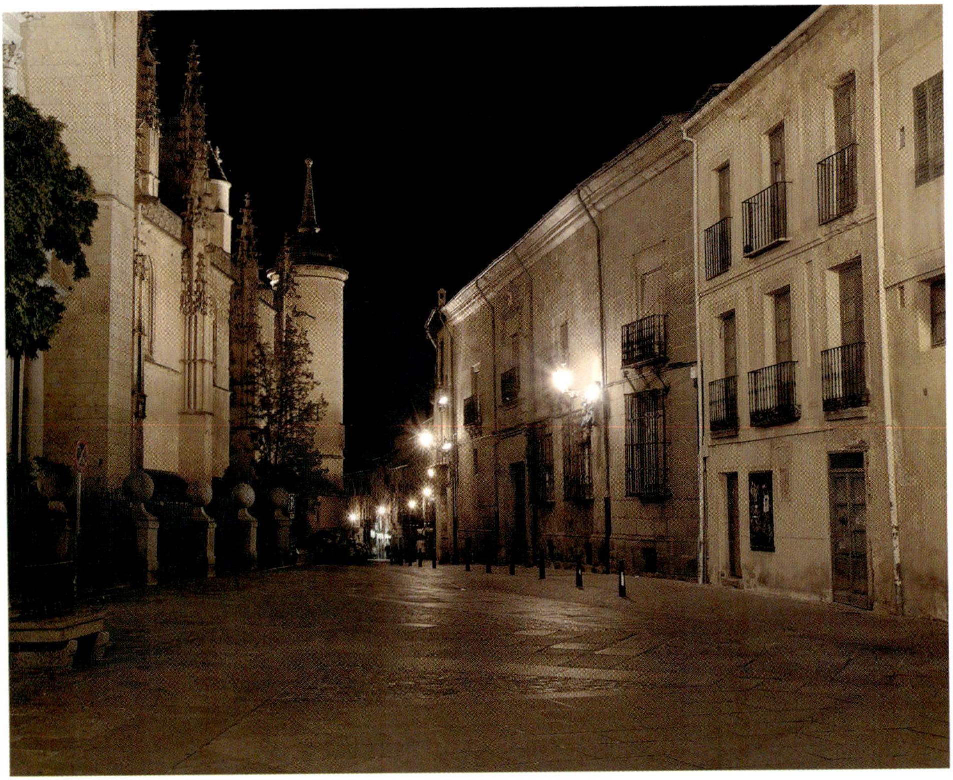

Figure 6.22
This European alleyway is thronged with people, but with the camera on a tripod, a 30-second exposure rendered the passersby almost invisible.

- **Produce light trails.** At night, car headlights and taillights and other moving sources of illumination can generate interesting light trails, as shown in Figure 6.23. Your camera doesn't even need to be mounted on a tripod; hand-holding the V1 for longer exposures adds movement and patterns to your streaky trails. If you're shooting fireworks, a longer exposure may allow you to combine several bursts into one picture.

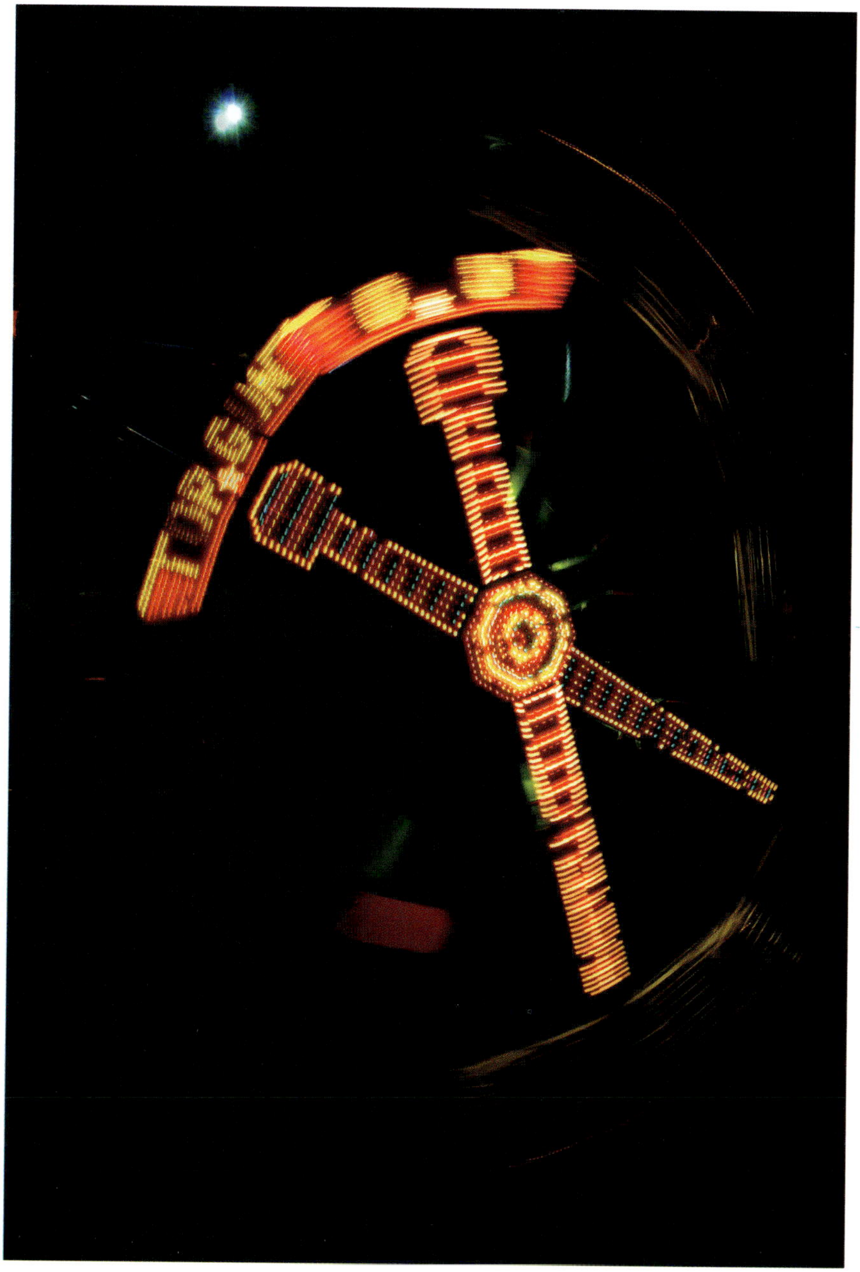

Figure 6.23
Long exposures can capture light trails from amusement park rides.

- **Blur waterfalls, etc.** You'll find that waterfalls and other sources of moving liquid produce a special type of long-exposure blur, because the water merges into a fantasy-like veil that looks different at different exposure times, and with different waterfalls. Cascades with turbulent flow produce a rougher look at a given longer exposure than falls that flow smoothly. Although blurred waterfalls have become almost a cliché, there are still plenty of variations for a creative photographer to explore. (See Figure 6.24.)
- **Show total darkness in new ways.** Even on the darkest, moonless nights, there is enough starlight or glow from distant illumination sources to see by, and, if you use a long exposure, there is enough light to take a picture, too.

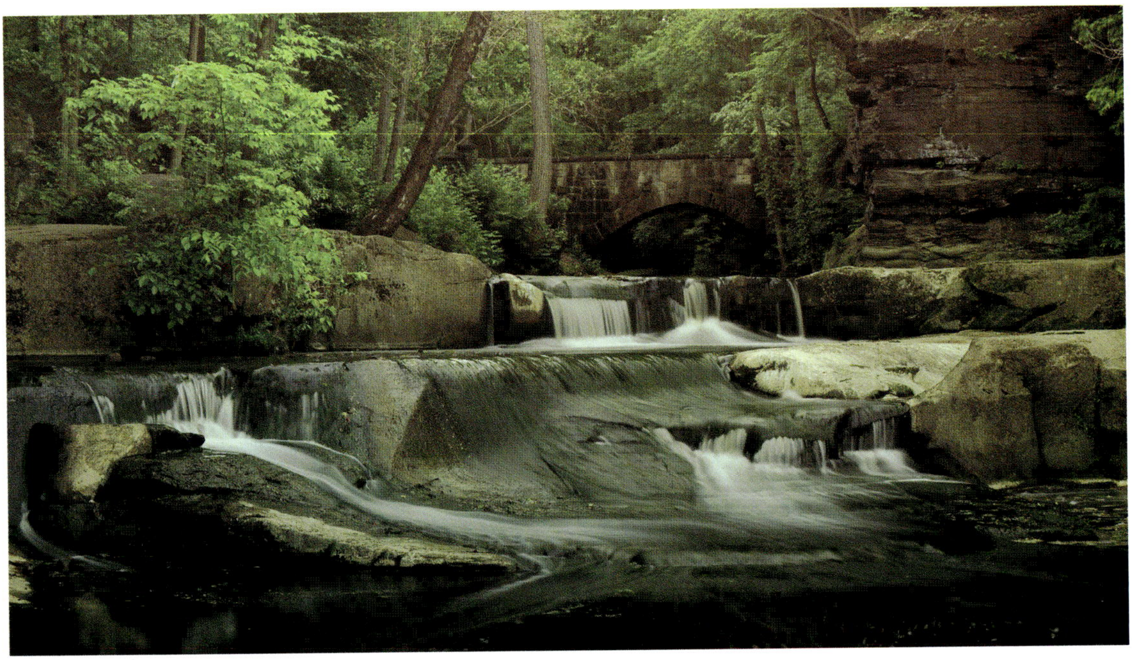

Figure 6.24 A three-second exposure blurred this cascade of flowing water.

7

Movie Making with Your Nikon V1

The Nikon V1 is a serious movie-making machine, capable of full-resolution HD movies with an aspect ratio (proportions) of 16:9, as well as reduced-resolution slow-motion video at 400 or 1200 frames per second. Whether you're looking to record informal clips of the family on vacation, the latest viral video for YouTube, or a clip that will be painstakingly crafted into a cinematic masterpiece using editing software, you'll find the basics quite easy. While I've covered basic movie shooting earlier in this book, this chapter is your opportunity to dig deep and learn more about the video capabilities of your V1, as well as some techniques you can use to shoot better movies.

Optimizing Your Movie Settings

If you want to capture video quickly, with no fuss, you don't have to devote a lot of time to making various settings. The default values of your Nikon V1 will do a good job. Just rotate the mode dial to the Movie icon, press the red Movie button, located to the right of the shutter release, and the camera will begin capturing HD video with stereo sound at whatever resolution you've previously set (either 1080i/1080p or 720p). Press the Movie button again to stop recording. That's all there is to it.

If a video opportunity pops up unexpectedly while you're shooting in Still Image mode, you don't even have to visit the mode dial. Move your trigger finger from the shutter release button to the Movie button and press down. The V1 will immediately begin recording non-HD movies with stereo sound at a resolution of 1072 × 720 pixels at the non-wide-screen aspect ratio (proportions) of 3:2 (the same as the still image). Press the

Movie button a second time to stop, or, if you see a still photo you want to take, press the shutter release button down all the way. Video recording will stop automatically as you take a still photo.

I'll show you how to optimize your settings before you start shooting video, but here are some considerations to be aware of as you get started. Many of these points will be covered in more detail later in this chapter:

- **Use the right card.** You'll want to use an SD or SDHC card with Class 6 or higher speed; if you use a slower card, like a Class 4 or especially Class 2, the recording may stop after a minute or two. Choose a memory card with at least 4GB capacity; 8GB or 16GB are even better. If you're going to be recording a lot of HD video, that could be a good reason to take advantage of the ability to use SDXC cards of 64GB capacity. Just make sure your memory card reader is SDXC compatible and your computer can read the files from that type of card. I've standardized on fast Class 6 or Class 10 16GB SDHC cards when I'm shooting movies; one of these cards will hold at least three hours of video. However, the camera cannot shoot a continuous movie scene for more than 29 minutes. You can start shooting the next clip right away, though, missing only about 30 seconds of the action. Of course that assumes there's enough space on your memory card and adequate battery power.
- **Add an external mic.** For the best sound quality, and to avoid picking up the sound of the autofocus or zoom motor, get an external stereo mic like the Nikon ME-1, which can be mounted on the optional AS-N1000 multi accessory port adapter, or on a flash bracket secured to the V1's tripod socket. If you're using an external mic, plugged into the port under the door on the camera's left side, you can also take advantage of two menu items: External Mic Sensitivity (at Auto or at a High level to pick up softer sounds) in the Setup menu and the Wind Noise Reduction (to muffle the sound of the wind, but also muffling the audio in general to some extent) in the Movie menu. I'll have more advice about capturing sound later in this chapter.
- **Minimize zooming.** While it's great to be able to use the zoom for filling the frame with a distant subject, think twice before zooming. Unless you are using an external mic, the sound of the zoom motor will be picked up and it will be audible when you play a movie. Any more than the occasional minor zoom will be very distracting to friends who watch your videos. And digital zoom will definitely degrade image quality. Don't use the digital zoom if quality is more important than recording a specific subject such as a famous movie star far from a distance.
- **Use a fully charged battery.** A fresh battery will allow about one hour of filming at normal (non-Winter) temperatures, but that can be shorter if AF-F is used and there are many focus adjustments. Individual clips can be no longer than 29 minutes, however.

- **Keep it cool.** Video quality can suffer terribly when the imaging sensor gets hot so keep the camera in a cool place. When shooting on hot days especially, the sensor can get hot more quickly than usual; when there's a risk of overheating, the camera will stop recording and it will shut down about five seconds later. Give it time to cool down before using it again.
- **Press the Movie button.** You don't have to hold it down. Press it again when you're done to stop recording.

If you've absorbed this basic information, you're ready to go. You'll want to optimize your movie settings to get the exact results you want. The next sections will show you how to select the right settings to use. First, here's a reminder of the type of settings you can make when shooting HD movies. I provided an initial overview in Chapter 4.

- **Select an exposure mode.** You can use any of the exposure modes when shooting HD movies. In the Shooting menu choose Exposure Mode, and opt for Scene Auto Selector, Programmed Auto, Shutter-Priority Auto, Aperture-Priority Auto, or Manual.
- **Select metering mode, white balance, and ISO sensitivity.** When in Movie mode, you can select in the Shooting menu from the standard choices for metering mode (Matrix, Center-weighted, or Spot); white balance (any of the fixed options, plus your own custom presets and a color temperature in degrees Kelvin); and ISO sensitivity (any available fixed ISO setting, plus the A400, A800, and A1600 auto range choices).
- **Choose other Shooting menu settings.** Picture Controls, Custom Picture Controls, High ISO noise reduction, and vibration reduction can be specified. I'll explain these in more detail in Chapter 8, which deals with setting up all the menu options of your Nikon V1. You cannot select AF-area mode or Face Priority mode.
- **Select frame rate.** When shooting slow-motion movies (only), you can choose a frame rate of 400 or 1200 fps.
- **Choose HD resolution and frame rate.** The Movie Settings entry in the Shooting menu lets you choose from 1080i/60 fps, 1080p/30 fps, or 720p/60 fps. I'll explain when and why you should choose each of these later in the chapter. These settings also determine the resolution of any still pictures you take while shooting movies: at 1080i, still frame captures are 3840 × 2160 pixels (7.5 megapixels); at 1080p and 720p, stills are captured at lower 2MP and 1MP resolutions, respectively.
- **Select other movie-specific settings.** In the Shooting menu you can choose movie settings such as fade in/fade out between clips, and movie sound options. I'll describe these later in this chapter.
- **Select a focus mode.** While you can't specify what focus zones are used when shooting movies, you can press the down directional button and choose from AF-S, AF-F, or MF (Manual) focus. I explained these focus modes in Chapter 6.

Once you've made the settings you want, you can shoot video. I've outlined the procedure earlier in this book, but here's a quick recap for those who hate jumping around:

1. **Frame the movie.** You can use either the LCD or the EVF to compose your image.
2. **Focus.** Press the shutter release halfway to focus the image. The subject in the center of the frame is used to establish focus, and face detection is not used. If the V1 is successful at locking in focus, the focus area will be highlighted in green; otherwise, the focus area will glow red.
3. **Lock focus/exposure.** When using an exposure mode other than Scene Auto Selector, you can lock exposure and focus by pressing the AE-L/AF-L button (the multi selector up button). You can use exposure compensation, as described in Chapter 5, by pressing the right directional button and dialing in EV adjustments with the zoom bar. Plus or minus 3EV can be specified by pressing the bar up or down.
4. **Begin capture.** Gently press the red movie record button to begin shooting. The recording indicator will appear at the left of the frame; the time elapsed, and the time still available will be displayed.
5. **Shoot stills (optional).** While shooting movies, you can capture up to 20 still images without interrupting the video by pressing the shutter release down all the way. Your still frame captures will be 7.5MP (in 1080i mode), 2MP (in 1080p mode), or 1MP (in 720p mode).
6. **End recording.** Press the movie record button a second time to halt recording. Movie making will also end automatically when the memory card is full, the maximum size of 4GB is reached, or the maximum time of 20 minutes is recorded.

NOT MUCH OF A LIMITATION

Unless you are shooting an entire performance from a fixed position, such as a stage play, the 20-minute limitation on HDTV movie duration of a single "take" or clip won't put much of a crimp in your style. Good motion picture practice calls for each production to consist of a series of relatively *short* clips, with 10 to 20 seconds a good average. You can assemble and edit your V1 movies into one long, finished production using one of the many movie-editing software packages available. Andy Warhol might have been successful with his 1963 five-hour epic *Sleep*, but the rest of us will do better with short sequences of the type produced by the Nikon V1. Your entire movie can run as long as 2 hours and 10 minutes at 720/60p.

Choosing Resolution and Frame Rate

Beginners (and a few old hands) are sometimes confused by the range of resolutions and frame rates available in the Movie Settings entry in the Shooting menu. This section will clear up the confusion. Both will help determine the "look" of your movie.

Selecting a Resolution and Frame Rate

The Nikon V1 offers two different resolutions for HD shooting using a 16:9 aspect ratio in Movie mode, and a third non-HD mode with 3:2 proportions, available only when shooting movies while in Still Image mode. A description of each follows. If you simply want to know the basic information needed to choose among the Movie Settings options, this list has what you need, and you can skip over the more technical sections that follow. I'll describe how to make all relevant movie settings shortly.

- **1080i/60, 1080p/30 (1920 × 1080 pixels).** This resolution is so-called "full HD" and conforms to the 16:9 proportions and resolution of most modern-day monitors. It theoretically provides the best image for static scenes that lack a lot of motion. This resolution consumes the most space on your memory card. Note that Nikon includes the *i* and *p* after the scan/frame rate (60i, 30p) in the V1 manual, but I'm conforming to the more common practice of including it as part of the label for resolution (1080i, 1080p).
- **720p/60 (1280 × 720 pixels).** This 16:9 format is called "standard HD" and is, on first glance, lower in resolution than either of the 1080i/1080p formats. But there's a fly in the ointment, as I'll explain shortly. For some types of scenes, those with fast movement, for example, 720p can produce a sharper, smoother picture. Moreover, 720p produces smaller files that require less storage space on your memory card. Figure 7.1 compares the 16:9 proportions of the HD format with the non-HD format described next.

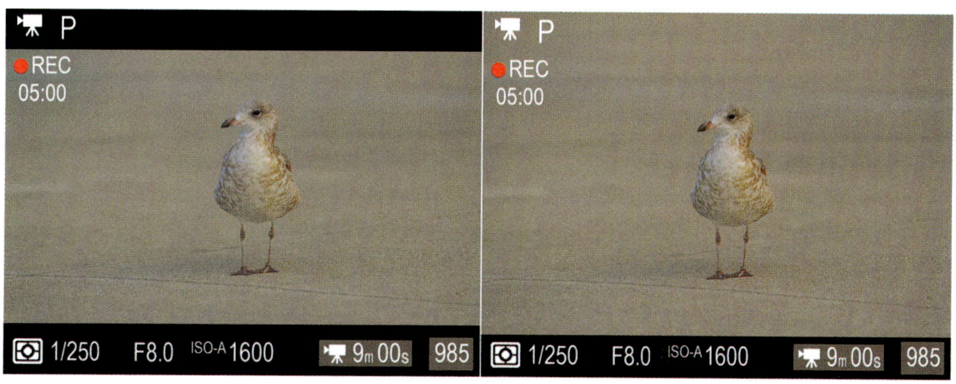

Figure 7.1 Full HD and Standard HD conform to the proportions of a 16:9 aspect ratio (left); the non-HD mode produced when shooting video in Still Image mode uses a 3:2 aspect ratio (right).

- **Non-HD/60 (1072 × 720 pixels).** In Still Image mode, you can press the Movie record button and shoot non-HD movies in this odd-ball format, which conforms to the 3:2 aspect ratio of the still photographic image. You can use this format when you don't require high definition output, and want to conserve storage space on your memory card.

Understanding Interlacing and Progressive Scan

TECH ALERT

The Nikon V1 is aimed at both point-and-shooters who are upgrading their equipment and goals, and at more advanced photographers who want to shoot stills and video with a more compact camera without making too many compromises feature-wise. That's why the V1 offers the resolution and frame rate options it has. This next section is aimed at more advanced movie makers who want to understand some of the nuts and bolts behind their choices. To understand which resolution and frame rate you might want to use, it's necessary to understand the difference between interlaced and progressive scans. I'll make the explanation as painless as possible. Those of you who just want to shoot movies can opt to choose 720p/60 in the Movie Settings section of the Shooting menu, and jump to the next section.

As you probably know, video images as you see them on your TV or monitor consist of a series of lines which are displayed, or *scanned* at a fixed rate. When captured by your Nikon V1, the images are also grabbed, using what is called a *rolling shutter,* which simply means that the image is grabbed one line at a time at the same fixed rate that will be used during playback. (There is a more expensive option, not used in the V1, called a *global shutter* that captures all the lines at one time.)

Line-by-line scanning during capture and playback can be done in one of two ways. With *interlaced scanning,* odd-numbered lines (lines 1, 3, 5, 7... and so forth) are captured with one pass, and then the even-numbered lines (2, 4, 6, 8...and so forth) are grabbed. With the 1080/60i format, roughly 60 pairs of odd/even line scans, or 60 *fields* are captured each second. (The actual number is 59.94 fields per second.) Interlaced scanning was developed for and works best with analog display systems such as older television sets. It was originally created as a way to reduce the amount of bandwidth required to transmit television pictures over the air. Modern LCD, LED, and plasma-based HDTV displays must de-interlace a 1080i image to display it. (See Figure 7.2.)

Newer displays work better with a second method, called *progressive scanning* or *sequential scanning.* Instead of two interlaced fields, the entire image is scanned as consecutive lines (lines 1, 2, 3, 4...and so forth). This happens at a rate of 30 frames per second (not

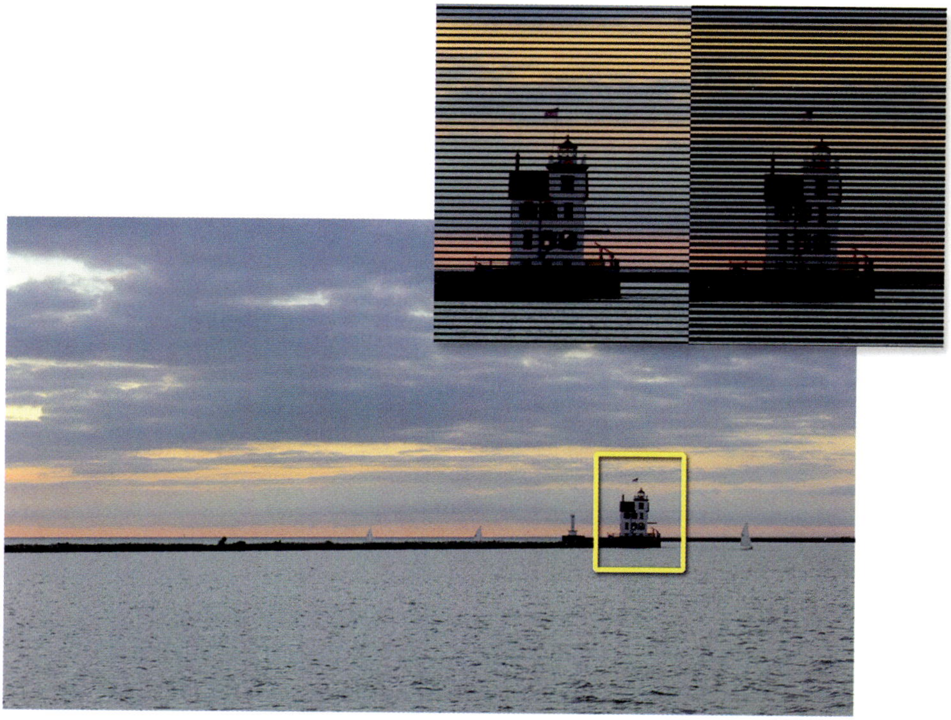

Figure 7.2
The inset shows how lines of the image alternate between odd and even in an interlaced video capture.

fields), or, more precisely, 29.97 frames per second. (All these numbers apply to the NTSC television system used in the United States, Canada, Japan, and some other countries; other places use systems like PAL, where the nominal scanning figures are 50/25 rather than 60/30.)

One problem with interlaced scanning appears when capturing video of moving subjects. Half of the image (one set of interlaced lines) will change to keep up with the movement of the subject while the other interlaced half retains the "old" image as it waits to be refreshed. Flicker or *interline twitter* results. That makes your progressive scan options 1080p/30 or 720p/60 a better choice for action photography.

DIFFERENT FLICKER

The Nikon V1's Flicker Reduction option, found in the Setup menu, does not affect interline twitter; it's used to reduce flicker and banding that can occur when shooting under fluorescent or mercury-vapor lighting, which "cycles" imperceptibly. Choose 60Hz in most cases to correspond with the frequency of your local power system. An alternate setting of 50Hz (cycles per second) is available if that's used in your area.

Which to Choose?

If you're shooting a relatively static image, choose 1080p/30 for the best combination of resolution and image quality. Use 1080i/60 only if you know you'll be mixing your video with existing 1080i/60 footage, or if you happen to be shooting for NBC, CBS, or The CW. (Ha!) For action shooting, choose 720p/60 to get the smoothest looking image, one that's more film-like (since the *true* "filmy" look of 720p/24 isn't available with the Nikon V1). Fox, ABC, and ESPN use 720p, for example.

You don't lose as much resolution as you might think in switching to 720p. With 1080i, each of the interlaced fields is actually 1920 × 540 pixels (about one million total pixels), with each field refreshed 30 times per second. In contrast, 720p captures 1280 × 720 pixels, but refreshes 60 times per second and also captures very close to one million pixels. In effect, 720p has more vertical resolution, giving almost exactly the same pixels captured per "frame," but twice as many frames per second. With moving images, that makes all the difference. Both 1080i/60 and 1080p/30 deliver roughly the same number of "pixels per second" as 720p/60. (Technoids call this *temporal resolution.*)

Shooting Slow-Motion Movies

Slow-motion movies are silent clips recorded at the reduced aspect ratio of 8:3 at the amazing speed of 400 or 1200 frames per second. Because they are played back at 30 fps, one second of 400 fps slow-motion footage requires more than 13 seconds to play out on the screen, and one second of 1200 fps footage takes 40 seconds, producing a pronounced slo-mo effect. You can use these movies to analyze your golf stroke, high diving technique, or for comic or dramatic effect in your more ambitious video productions. Of course, it's not easy to intercut 8:3 aspect ratio clips with 16:9 HD clips, so the editing techniques are going to take some work (and are beyond the scope of this book). The main roadblock is that at 400 fps, the frame size is pared down to 640 × 240 pixels, and at 1200 fps to a teensy 320 × 120 pixels. In either case, the maximum shooting length is five seconds, which plays back in 1 minute, 6 seconds from a clip shot at 400 fps to 3 minutes, 20 seconds for a clip recorded at 1200 fps.

It's easy to get started shooting slow-motion movies. Just follow these steps:

1. **Shift to Movie mode.** Rotate the mode dial to the Movie mode position.
2. **Select Slow Motion Mode.** Press the F button and use the multi selector directional buttons to choose Slow Motion. Press the OK button to confirm your choice.
3. **Select exposure mode.** Press the MENU button, choose the Shooting menu, and scroll to Exposure Mode, press OK and select Programmed Auto, Shutter-Priority Auto, Aperture Auto, or Manual. Scene Auto Selector is not available.
4. **Choose settings.** When in Slow Motion Movie mode, you can select from an array of other adjustments, including frame rate, white balance, ISO sensitivity, Picture Controls, and vibration reduction.

5. **Frame the movie.** You can use either the LCD or the EVF to compose your image. A wide mask showing the 8:3 slow motion filming area appears on the screen.
6. **Shoot.** Gently press the red movie record button to begin shooting. The recording indicator will appear at the left of the frame; the time elapsed, and the time still available will be displayed. The camera focuses on the subject in the center of the screen, and face detection is not available.
7. **End recording.** Press the movie record button a second time to halt recording. Movie making will also end when the maximum time of about 5 seconds is reached, when the memory card is full, the maximum size of 4GB is reached, or, if you're using a slow memory card, the buffer fills before the existing recording is saved to the card.

Viewing Movies

You can view your movies in Playback mode. Just follow these steps:

1. **Start Playback review.** Press the Playback button. You can review your movies when the camera is set to any shooting mode. You don't need to be using Movie mode to view them. When using full frame playback (that is, when not in thumbnail or calendar view), movies are indicated by a movie camera icon in the upper-left corner. (See Figure 7.3.)

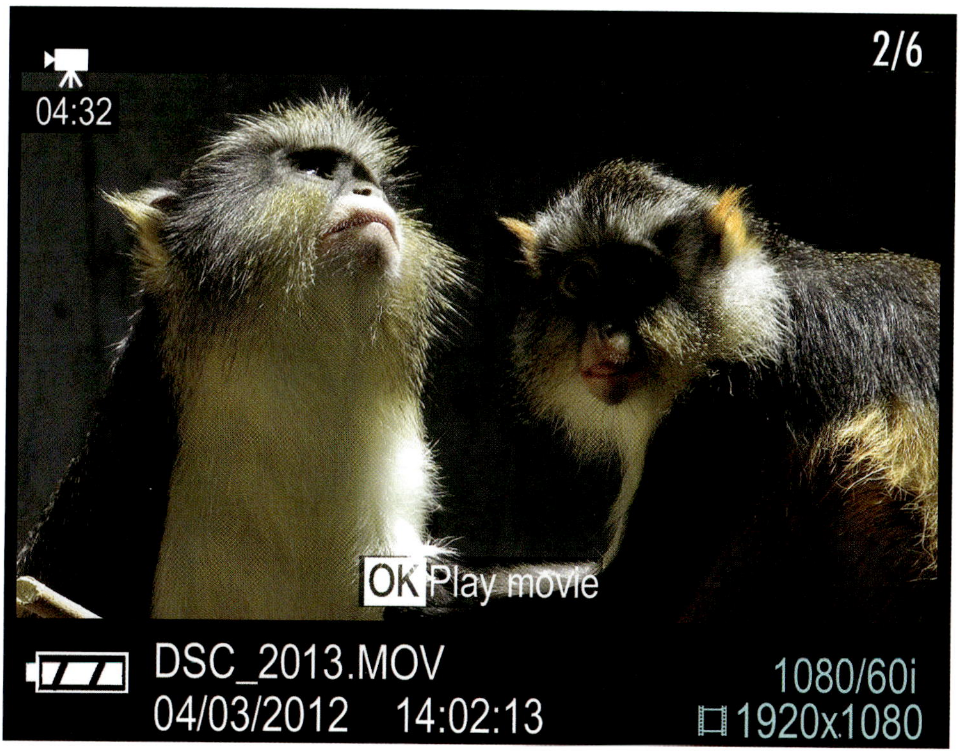

Figure 7.3 Select a movie to view in Playback mode.

2. **Select a movie to review.** When the clip you want to watch is shown on the screen, press the OK button to start.
3. **Pause movie.** Stop playback at any time by pressing the multi selector down button.
4. **Single frame advance/rewind.** When the movie is paused, pressing the right directional button advances one frame; the left directional button rewinds one frame. Or, you can rotate the multi selector dial clockwise or counter-clockwise.
5. **Resume play.** Press the OK button to resume playback of the movie.
6. **Fast forward/rewind.** Press the right directional button to advance, or the left directional button to rewind. A single press increases the speed from 1X to 2X. Keep pressing to accelerate playback to 5X, 10X, or 15X.
7. **Adjust volume.** The zoom bar can be pressed up or down to increase or decrease volume.
8. **Exit to Playback mode.** Press the up directional button to return to Playback mode to select a different still image or movie to resume.
9. **Return to shooting mode.** Tap the shutter release button halfway to return to shooting mode.

Fine-Tuning Movie Settings

Here's a summary of the various movie-related settings you can make:

- **Movie options.** When the mode dial is set to Movie, you can press the MENU button, navigate to the Shooting menu's Movie Settings entry, and choose 1080/60i, 1080/30p, or 720/60p (Nikon's terminology), as discussed previously in this chapter.
- **Fade in/Fade out.** This setting includes W (white) and B Fade (black), as well as OFF. When you choose W or B, each scene will fade to white or black, respectively, when you stop capturing. When you resume, the image will start in the faded position (either white or black) and fade into the full scene.
- **Movie Sound options.** This Shooting menu entry has two adjustments to make: Microphone and Wind Noise Reduction. Choose to turn the microphone Off if you want to shoot silently (particularly if you are going to add music, voice-over, or other sound later in your movie-editing software), or a sensitivity setting from Automatic, High, Medium, or Low. This is essentially a volume control for your internal microphones, or any external mic you attach. Wind Noise Reduction can be switched On or Off, to reduce the effects of air rushing past your microphone.

- **Vibration reduction.** Although VR also applies to still photography, it's especially important when shooting movie clips, to minimize the shakiness of a hand-held camera. Unless you want your viewers to be sea-sick, or you've mounted the V1 on a tripod, you'll probably want to choose Normal, or Active (for difficult situations, as when shooting from a moving vehicle), rather than Off.
- **Flicker reduction.** When shooting under fluorescent or mercury-vapor lighting, the flickering produced can be especially visible for movie clips. Choose the frequency of your local power supply (generally 60Hz in the US) to minimize this flicker.
- **White balance.** Like exposure, metering mode, and several other settings, white balance applies to both still and movie shooting. However, if you're shooting in an environment where the color balance can change abruptly (such as a concert), you might want to avoid the Auto setting and choose a fixed WB value instead. That will reduce the chances of the V1 trying to adjust white balance in the middle of a shot or between shots. At a concert, for example, you'll probably *want* the vivid changing colors to be captured exactly as they occur, rather than let the camera try to compensate.

Editing Your Movies

In-camera editing is limited to trimming the beginning or end from a clip, and the clip must be at least two seconds long. For more advanced editing, you'll need an application capable of editing AVI movie clips. Short Movie Creator is included with your V1, and you can use that to create movies combined from still photos or Smart Photo Selector, along with Motion Snapshots, other movies, and music. Macs are furnished with the free iMovie editor, while PCs can use the free Windows Live Essentials, which includes a movie editor. You can also Google "AVI Editor" to locate any of the hundreds of other free video editors available. Or, you can use a commercial product like Corel Video Studio, Adobe Premiere Elements, or Pinnacle Studio. These will let you combine several clips into one movie, add titles, special effects, and transitions between scenes.

To do in-camera editing/trimming, follow these steps:

1. **Select movie clip.** Press the MENU button and choose Playback. Use the directional buttons of the multi selector to navigate to Edit Movie and select it. A screen like the one shown in Figure 7.4 appears.
2. **Highlight Choose a Start Point.** Press the right directional button to produce a screen showing a scrolling list of the available movie clips on your memory card. (See Figure 7.5.)
3. **Choose movie clip.** Use the directional buttons or rotate the multi selector to choose a clip and press OK to select it. The screen shown in Figure 7.6 appears. You must select a clip at least two seconds long.

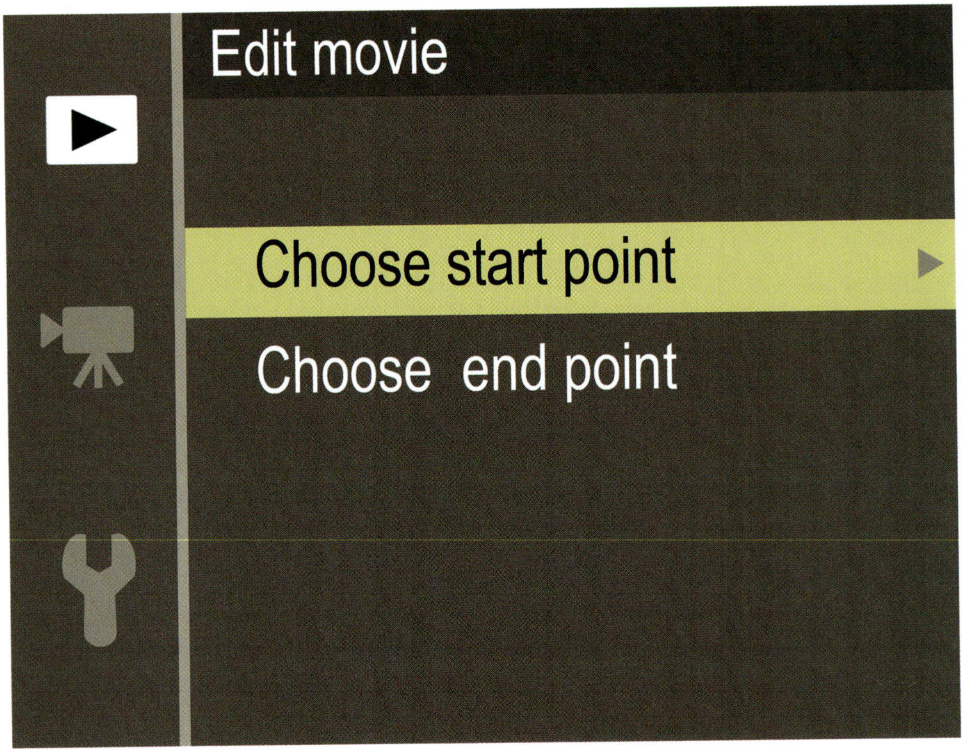

Figure 7.4
Choose to select start point or end point.

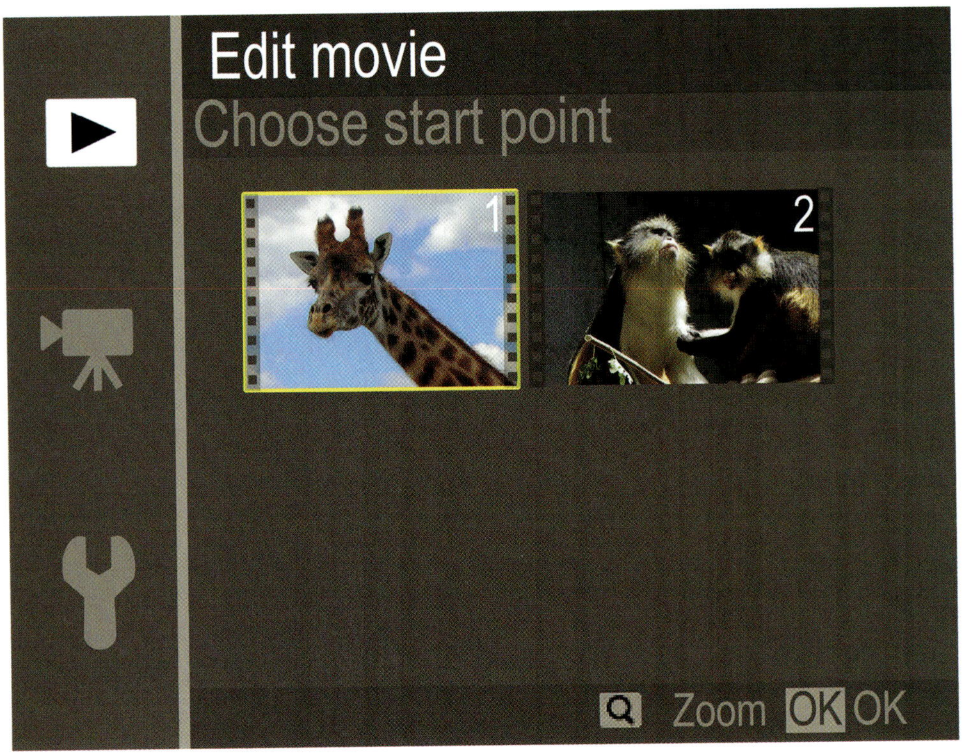

Figure 7.5
Select the movie to edit.

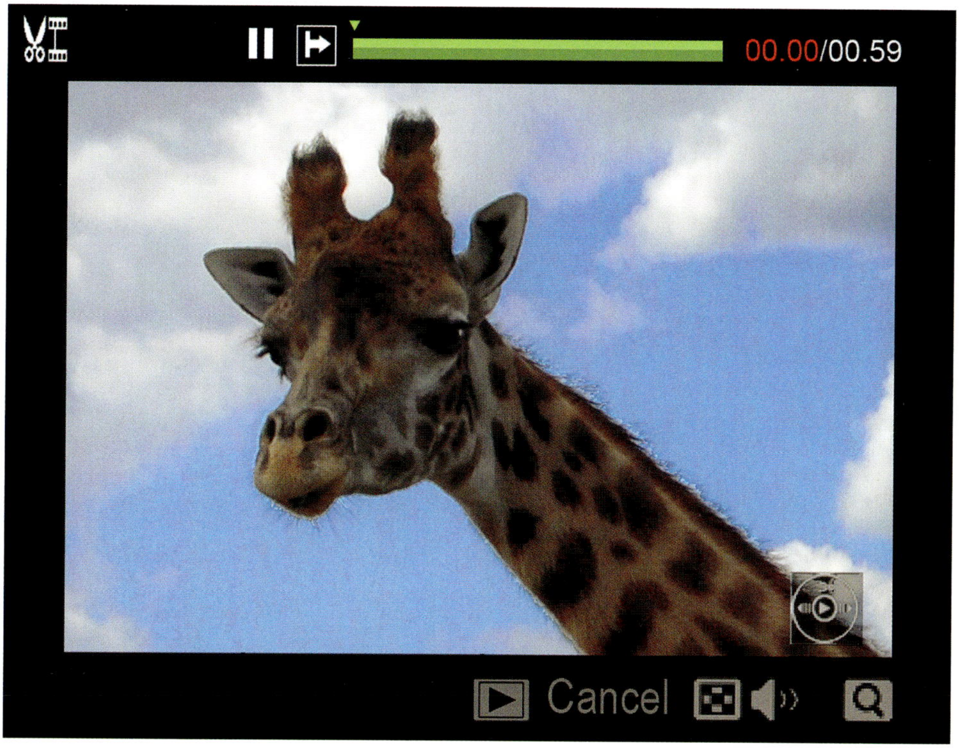

Figure 7.6
Play back movie and pause at the point where you want to trim.

4. **View the clip.** Press the OK button to begin playback. The down directional button will pause at any point in the clip. OK will resume playback. Pause when you reach the first frame you want to keep, and then press the down button to pause.
5. **Delete preceding frames.** Press the up directional button to delete all the frames that appear before the frame where you paused. An Edit Movie? dialog appears. Choose Yes to confirm, or No to cancel. The V1 will store a copy of the movie on your memory card.
6. **Trim from the end.** To trim video from the end of a clip, watch the movie until you reach the last frame you want to keep and then press the down button to pause. Then press the up button to trim. Confirm when the Edit Movie? dialog appears.
7. **Save movie.** You'll see a Saving Movie message and an icon as the V1 stores the trimmed clip to your memory card. Storage takes some time, and you don't want to interrupt it to avoid losing your saved clip. So, make sure your camera has a fully charged battery before you start to edit a clip.

Tips for Shooting Better Video

Once upon a time, the ability to shoot video with a digital still camera was one of those "Gee whiz" gimmicks camera makers seemed to include just to have a reason to get you to buy a new camera. That hasn't been true for a couple of years now, as the video quality of many digital still cameras has gotten quite good. The Nikon V1 is a stellar example. It's capable of HD-quality video and is actually able to outperform typical modestly priced digital video camcorders, especially when you consider the range of lenses and other helpful accessories available for it.

Producing good quality video is more complicated than just buying good equipment. There are techniques that make for gripping storytelling and a visual language the average person is very used to, but also pretty unaware of. While this book can't make you a professional videographer in half a chapter, there is some advice I can give you that will help you improve your results with the camera.

Producing high-quality videos can be a real challenge for amateur photographers. After all, by comparison we're used to watching the best productions that television, video, and motion pictures can offer. Whether it's fair or not, our efforts are compared to what we're used to seeing produced by experts. While this chapter can't make you into a pro videographer, it can help you improve your efforts.

There are a number of different things to consider when planning a video shoot, and when possible, a shooting script and storyboard can help you produce a higher quality video.

Keep Things Stable and on the Level

Camera shake's enough of a problem with still photography, but it becomes even more of a nuisance when you're shooting video. While the Nikon V1's image-stabilization feature can help minimize this, it can't work miracles. Placing your camera on a tripod will work much better than trying to hand-hold it while shooting. One bit of really good news is that compared to pro dSLRs the Nikon V1 can work very effectively on a lighter tripod.

Shooting Script

A shooting script is nothing more than a coordinated plan that covers both audio and video and provides order and structure for your video. A detailed script will cover what types of shots you're going after, what dialogue you're going to use, audio effects, transitions, and graphics.

Storyboards

A storyboard is a series of panels providing visuals of what each scene should look like. While the storyboards produced by Hollywood are generally of very high quality, there's nothing that says drawing skills are important for this step. Stick figures work just fine if that's the best you can do. The storyboard just helps you visualize locations, placement of actors/actresses, props and furniture, and also helps everyone involved get an idea of what you're trying to show. It also helps show how you want to frame or compose a shot. You can even shoot a series of still photos and transform them into a "storyboard" if you want, as in Figure 7.7.

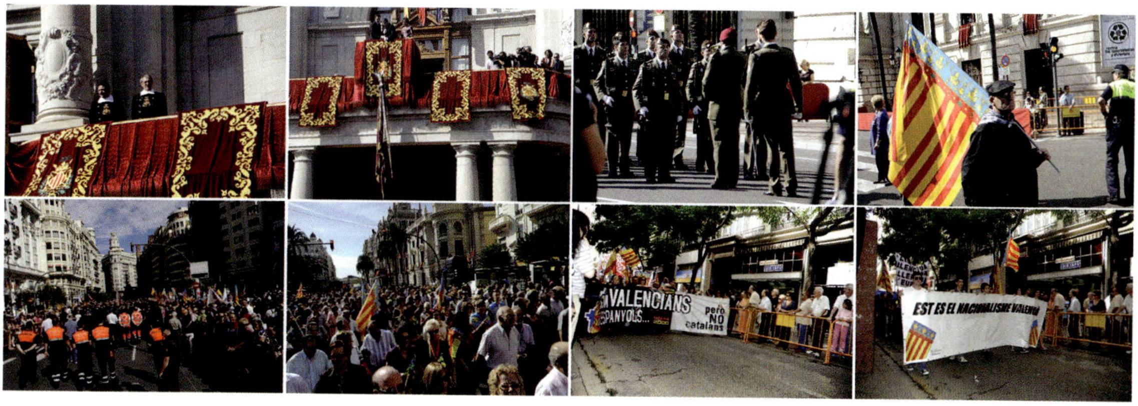

Figure 7.7 A storyboard is a series of simple sketches or photos to help visualize a segment of video.

Storytelling in Video

Today's audience is used to fast-paced, short-scene storytelling. In order to produce interesting video for such viewers, it's important to view video storytelling as a kind of shorthand code for the more leisurely efforts print media offers. Audio and video should always be advancing the story. While it's okay to let the camera linger from time to time, it should only be for a compelling reason and only briefly.

It only takes a second or two for an establishing shot to impart the necessary information. For example, many of the scenes for a video documenting a model being photographed in a Rock and Roll music setting might be close-ups and talking heads, but an establishing shot showing the studio where the video was captured helps set the scene. (See Figure 7.8.)

Provide variety too. Change camera angles and perspectives often and never leave a static scene on the screen for a long period of time. (You can record a static scene for a reasonably long period and then edit in other shots that cut away and back to the longer scene with close-ups that show each person talking.)

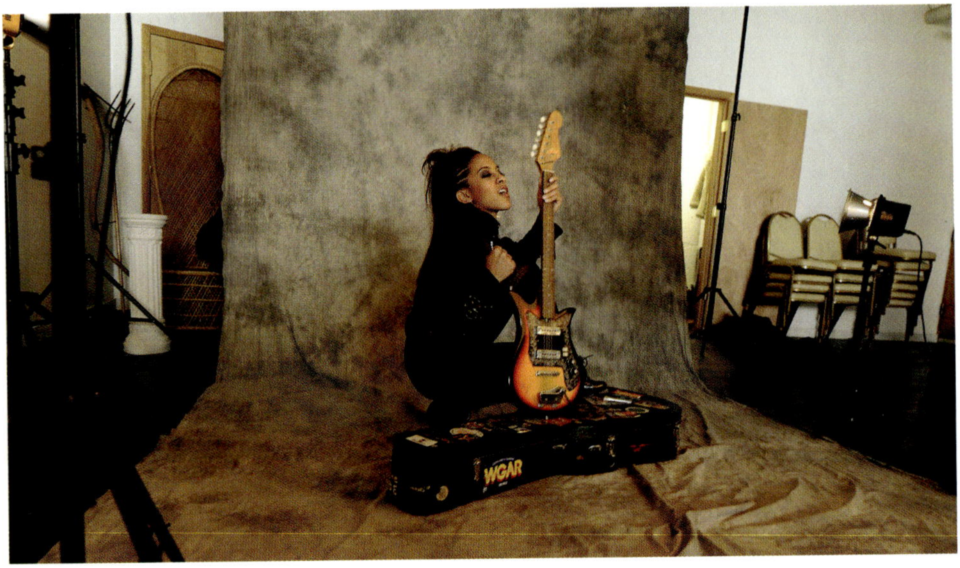

Figure 7.8
An establishing shot from a distance sets the stage for closer views.

When editing, keep transitions basic! I can't stress this one enough. Watch a television program or movie. The action "jumps" from one scene or person to the next. Fancy transitions that involve exotic "wipes," dissolves, or cross fades take too long for the average viewer and make your video ponderous.

Composition

In movie shooting, several factors restrict your composition, and impose requirements you just don't always have in still photography (although other rules of good composition do apply). Here are some of the key differences to keep in mind when composing movie frames:

- **Horizontal compositions only.** Some subjects, such as basketball players and tall buildings, just lend themselves to vertical compositions. But movies are shown in horizontal format only. So if you're interviewing a local basketball star, you can end up with a worst-case situation like the one shown in Figure 7.9. If you want to show how tall your subject is, it's often impractical to move back far enough to show him full-length. You really can't capture a vertical composition. Tricks like getting down on the floor and shooting up at your subject can exaggerate the perspective, but aren't a perfect solution.
- **Wasted space at the sides.** Moving in to frame the basketball player as outlined by the yellow box in Figure 7.9 means that you're still forced to leave a lot of empty space on either side. (Of course, you can fill that space with other people and/or interesting stuff, but that defeats your intent of concentrating on your main subject.) So when faced with some types of subjects in a horizontal frame, you can be

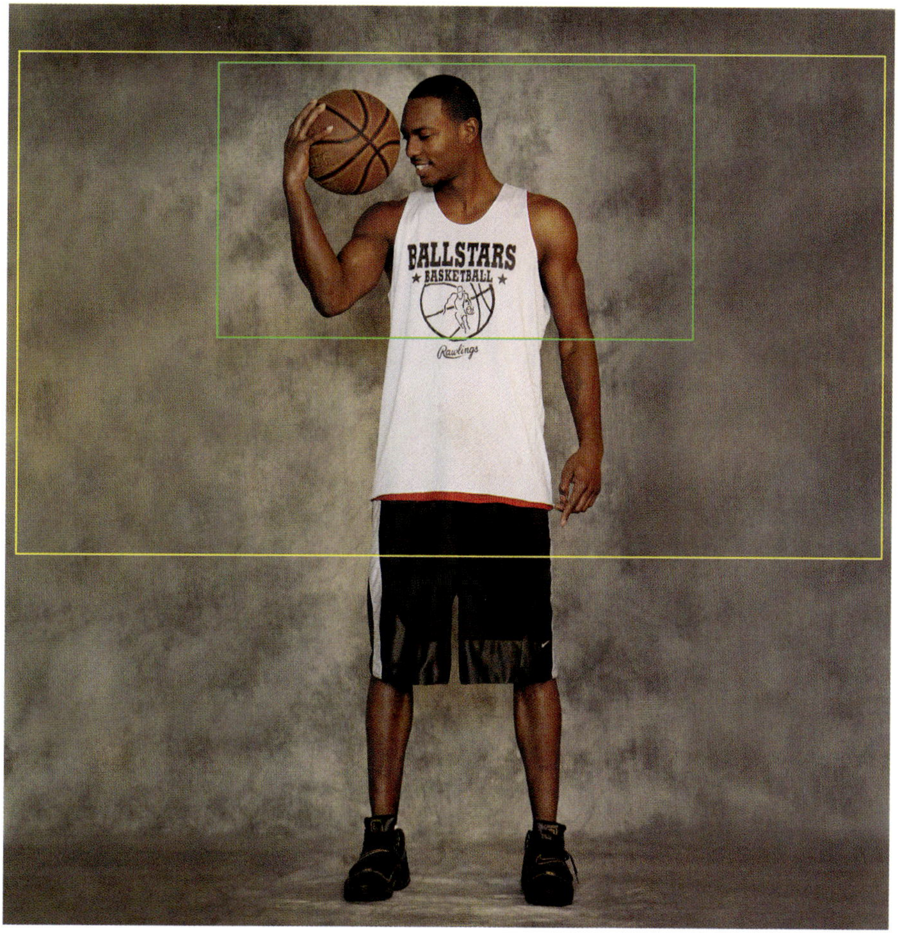

Figure 7.9
Movie shooting requires you to fit all your subjects into a horizontally oriented frame.

creative, or move in *really* tight. For example, if I was willing to give up the "height" aspect of my composition, I could have framed the shot as shown by the green box in the figure, and wasted less of the image area at either side.

- **Seamless (or seamed) transitions.** Unless you're telling a picture story with a photo essay, still pictures often stand alone. But with movies, each of your compositions must relate to the shot that preceded it, and the one that follows. It can be jarring to jump from a long shot to a tight close-up unless the director—you—–is very creative. Another common error is the "jump cut" in which successive shots vary only slightly in camera angle, making it appear that the main subject has "jumped" from one place to another. (Although everyone from French New Wave director Jean-Luc Goddard to Guy Ritchie—–Madonna's ex—–have used jump cuts effectively in their films.) The rule of thumb is to vary the camera angle by at least 30 degrees between shots to make it appear to be seamless. Unless you prefer that your images flaunt convention and appear to be "seamy."

- **The time dimension.** Unlike still photography, with motion pictures there's a lot more emphasis on using a series of images to build on each other to tell a story. Static shots where the camera is mounted on a tripod and everything is shot from the same distance are a recipe for dull videos. Watch a television program sometime and notice how often camera shots change distances and directions. Viewers are used to this variety and have come to expect it. Professional video productions are often done with multiple cameras shooting from different angles and positions. But many professional productions are shot with just one camera and careful planning, and you can do just fine with your Nikon V1.

Here's a look at the different types of commonly used compositional tools:

- **Establishing shot.** Much like it sounds, this type of composition, as shown earlier in Figure 7.8, establishes the scene and tells the viewer where the action is taking place. Let's say you're shooting a video of your offspring's move to college; the establishing shot could be a wide shot of the campus with a sign welcoming you to the school in the foreground. Another example would be for a child's birthday party; the establishing shot could be the front of the house decorated with birthday signs and streamers or a shot of the dining room table decked out with party favors and a candle-covered birthday cake. Or, in Figure 7.8, I wanted to show the studio where the video was shot.
- **Medium shot.** This shot is composed from about waist to head room (some space above the subject's head). It's useful for providing variety from a series of close-ups and also makes for a useful first look at a speaker. (See Figure 7.10.)
- **Close-up.** The close-up, usually described as "from shirt pocket to head room," provides a good composition for someone talking directly to the camera. Although it's common to have your talking head centered in the shot, that's not a

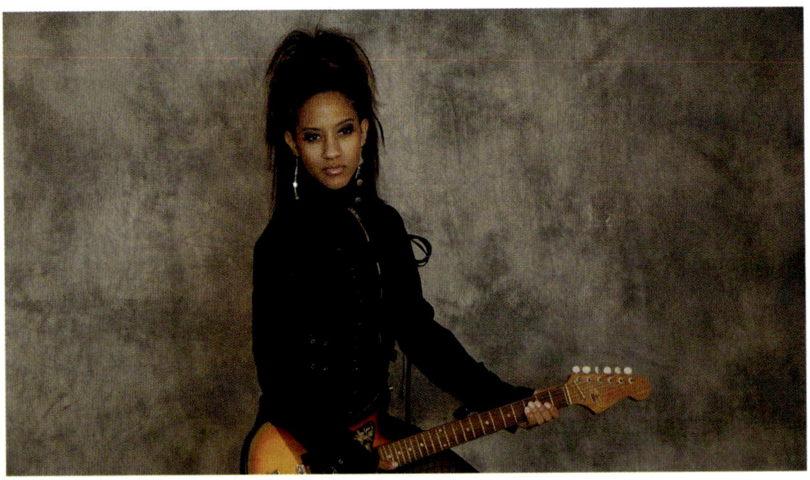

Figure 7.10
A medium shot is used to bring the viewer into a scene without shocking them. It can be used to introduce a character and provide context via their surroundings.

requirement. In Figure 7.11 the subject was offset to the right. This would allow other images, especially graphics or titles, to be superimposed in the frame in a "real" (professional) production. But the compositional technique can be used with Nikon V1 videos, too, even if special effects are not going to be added.

- **Extreme close-up.** When I went through broadcast training back in the '70s, this shot was described as the "big talking face" shot and we were actively discouraged from employing it. Styles and tastes change over the years and now the big talking face is much more commonly used (maybe people are better looking these days?) and so this view may be appropriate. Just remember, the Nikon V1 is capable of shooting in high-definition video and you may be playing the video on a high-def TV; be careful that you use this composition on a face that can stand up to high definition. (See Figure 7.12.)

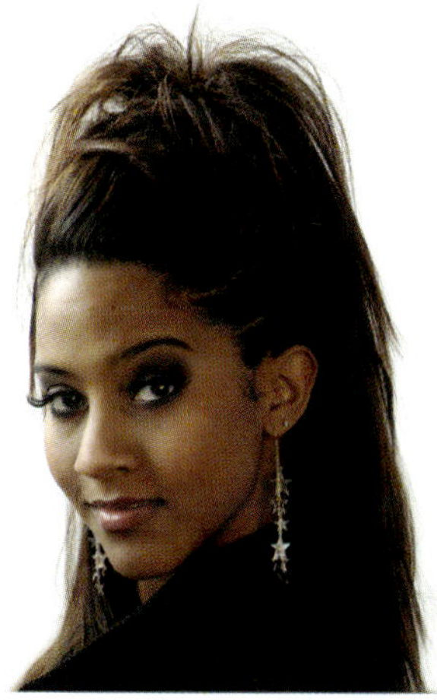

Figure 7.11
A close up generally shows the full face with a little head room at the top and down to the shoulders at the bottom of the frame.

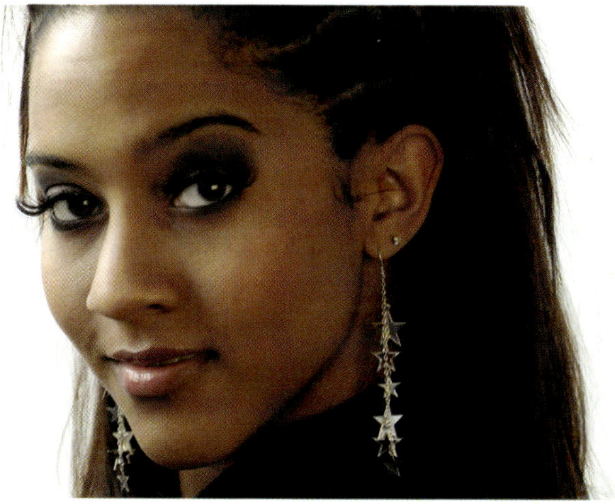

Figure 7.12
An extreme close-up is a very tight shot that cuts off everything above the top of the head and below the chin (or even closer!). Be careful using this shot since many of us look better from a distance!

- **"Two" shot.** A two shot shows a pair of subjects in one frame. They can be side by side or one in the foreground and one in the background. (See Figure 7.13.) This does not have to be a head to ground composition. Subjects can be standing or seated. A "three shot" is the same principle except that three people are in the frame.
- **Over the shoulder shot.** Long a composition of interview programs, the "Over the shoulder shot" uses the rear of one person's head and shoulder to serve as a frame for the other person. This puts the viewer's perspective as that of the person facing away from the camera. (See Figure 7.14.)

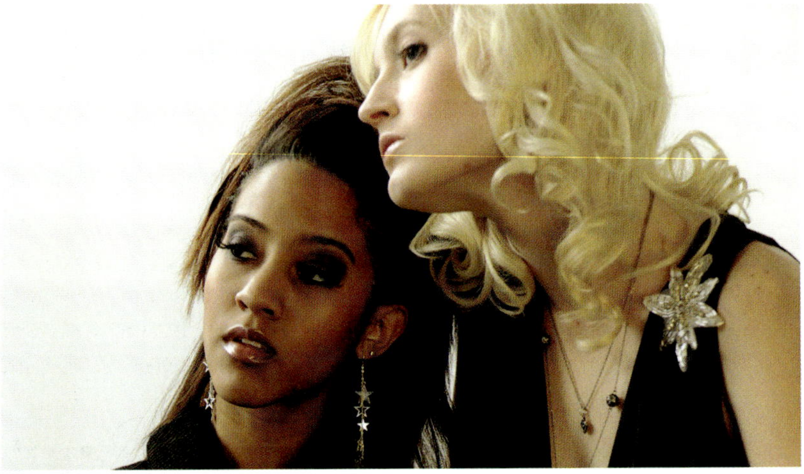

Figure 7.13
A "two shot" features two people in the frame. This version can be framed at various distances such as medium or close up.

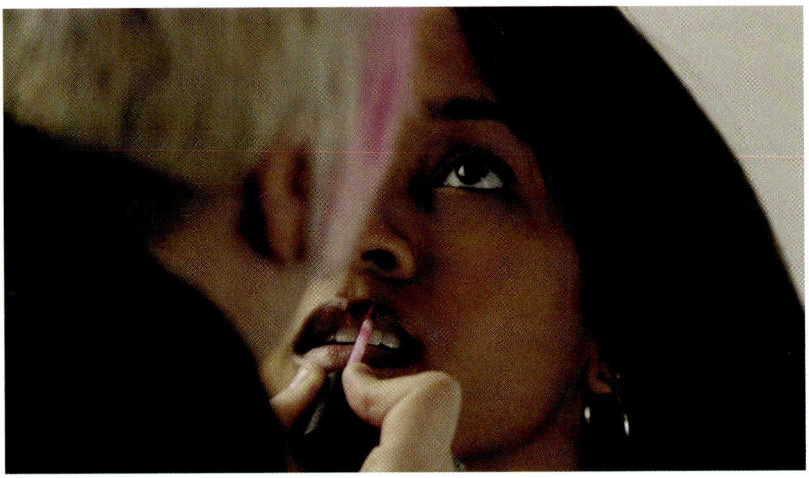

Figure 7.14
An "over-the-shoulder" shot is a popular shot for interview programs. This point of view helps make the viewers feel like they're the one asking the questions.

Lighting for Video

Much like in still photography, how you handle light pretty much can make or break your videography. Lighting for video can be more complicated than lighting for still photography, since both subject and camera movement is often part of the process.

Lighting for video presents several concerns. First off, you want enough illumination to create a useable video. Beyond that, you want to use light to help tell your story or increase drama. Let's take a better look at both.

Illumination

You can significantly improve the quality of your video by increasing the light falling in the scene. This is true indoors or out, by the way. While it may seem like sunlight is more than enough, it depends on how much contrast you're dealing with. If your subject is in shadow (which can help them from squinting) or wearing a ball cap, a video light can help make them look a lot better.

Lighting choices for amateur videographers are a lot better these days than they were a decade or two ago. An inexpensive incandescent video light, which will easily fit in a camera bag, can be found for $15 or $20. You can even get a good quality LED video light for less than $100. Work lights sold at many home improvement stores can also serve as video lights since you can set the camera's white balance to correct for any color casts. You'll need to mount these lights on a tripod or other support, or, perhaps, to a bracket that fastens to the tripod socket on the bottom of the camera.

Much of the challenge depends upon whether you're just trying to add some fill-light on your subject versus trying to boost the light on an entire scene. A small video light, or even the few seconds of light offered by the Capture Illuminator of the optional SB-N5 will do just fine for the former. Neither will handle the latter. Fortunately, the versatility of the Nikon V1 comes in quite handy here. Since the camera shoots video in Auto ISO mode, it can compensate for lower lighting levels and still produce a decent image. For best results though, better lighting is necessary.

Creative Lighting

While ramping up the light intensity will produce better technical quality in your video, it won't necessarily improve the artistic quality of it. Whether we're outdoors or indoors, we're used to seeing light come from above. Videographers need to consider how they position their lights to provide even illumination while up high enough to angle shadows down low and out of sight of the camera.

When considering lighting for video, there are several factors. One is the quality of the light. It can either be hard (direct) light or soft (diffused). Hard light is good for showing detail, but can also be very harsh and unforgiving. "Softening" the light, but diffusing it somehow, can reduce the intensity of the light but make for a kinder, gentler light as well.

While mixing light sources isn't always a good idea, one approach is to combine window light with supplemental lighting. Position your subject with the window to one side and bring in either a supplemental light or a reflector to the other side for reasonably even lighting.

Lighting Styles

Some lighting styles are more heavily used than others. Some forms are used for special effects, while others are designed to be invisible. At its most basic, lighting just illuminates the scene, but when used properly it can also create drama. Let's look at some types of lighting styles:

- **Three-point lighting.** This is a basic lighting setup for one person. A main light illuminates the strong side of a person's face, while a fill light lights up the other side. A third light is then positioned above and behind the subject to light the back of the head and shoulders. (See Figure 7.15.)
- **Flat lighting.** Use this type of lighting to provide illumination and nothing more. It calls for a variety of lights and diffusers set to raise the light level in a space enough for good video reproduction, but not to create a particular mood or emphasize a particular scene or individual. With flat lighting, you're trying to create even lighting levels throughout the video space and minimize any shadows. Generally, the lights are placed up high and angled downward (or possibly pointed straight up to bounce off of a white ceiling). (See Figure 7.16.)

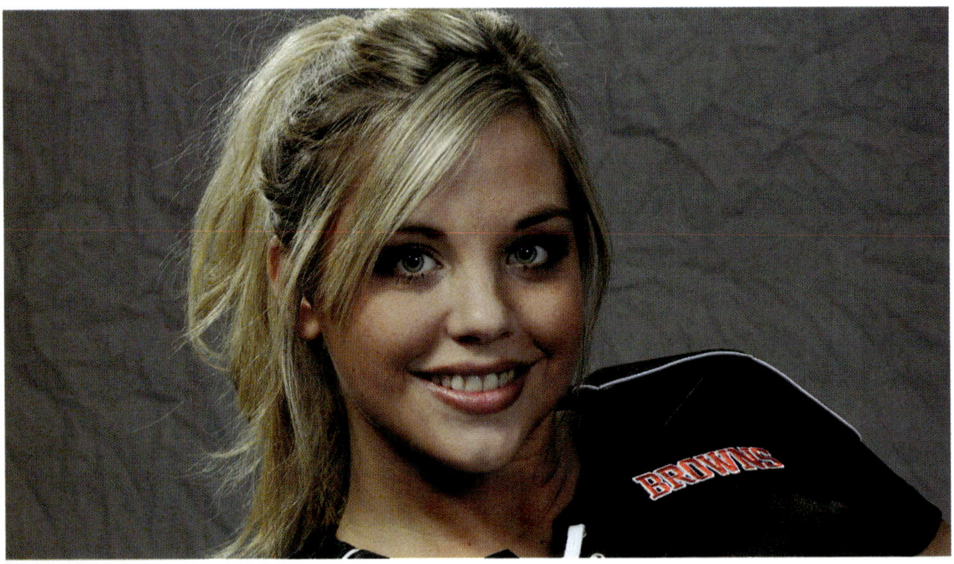

Figure 7.15
With three-point lighting, two lights are placed in front and to the side of the subject (45-degree angles are ideal) and positioned about a foot higher than the subject's head. Another light is directed on the background in order to separate the subject and the background.

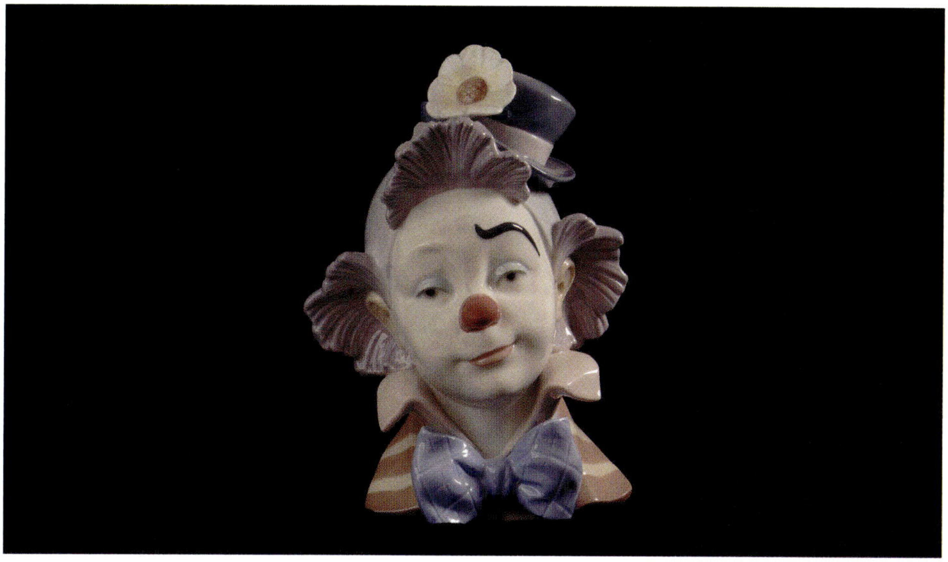

Figure 7.16
Flat lighting is another approach for creating even illumination. Here the lights can be bounced off of a white ceiling and walls to fill in shadows as much as possible. It is a flexible lighting approach since the subject can change positions without needing a change in light direction.

- **"Ghoul lighting."** This is the style of lighting used for old horror movies. The idea is to position the light down low, pointed upwards. It's such an unnatural style of lighting that it makes its targets seem weird and ghoulish.
- **Outdoor lighting.** While shooting outdoors may seem easier because the sun provides more light, it also presents its own problems. As a general rule of thumb, keep the sun behind you when you're shooting video outdoors, except when shooting faces (anything from a medium shot and closer) since the viewer won't want to see a squinting subject. When shooting another human this way, put the sun behind her and use a video light to balance light levels between the foreground and background. If the sun is simply too bright, position the subject in the shade and use the video light for your main illumination. Using reflectors (white board panels or aluminum foil covered cardboard panels are cheap options) can also help balance light effectively.

Audio

When it comes to making a successful video, audio quality is one of those things that separates the professionals from the amateurs. We're used to watching top-quality productions on television and in the movies, yet the average person has no idea how much effort goes in to producing what seems to be "natural" sound. Much of the sound you hear in such productions is actually recorded on carefully controlled sound stages and "sweetened" with a variety of sound effects and other recordings of "natural" sound.

Tips for Better Audio

Since recording high-quality audio is such a challenge, it's a good idea to do everything possible to maximize recording quality. Here are some ideas for improving the quality of the audio your camera records:

- **Get the camera and its microphone close to the subject.** The farther the microphone is from the audio source, the less effective it will be in picking up that sound. While having to position the camera and microphone closer to the subject affects your lens choices and lens perspective options, it will make the most of your audio source. Of course, if you're using a very wide-angle lens, getting too close to your subject can have unflattering results, so don't take this advice too far.
- **Use an external microphone.** Plug a stereo or monaural mic, like the Nikon ME-1, into the jack on the side of the V1, and you'll immediately enjoy better sound, because you won't be recording noises including autofocus motors or your own breathing.
- **Turn off any sound makers you can.** Little things like fans and air handling units aren't obvious to the human ear, but will be picked up by the microphone. Turn off any machinery or devices that you can plus make sure cell phones are set to silent mode. Also, do what you can to minimize sounds such as wind, radio, television, or people talking in the background.
- **Make sure to record some "natural" sound.** If you're shooting video at an event of some kind, make sure you get some background sound that you can add to your audio as desired in postproduction.
- **Consider recording audio separately.** Lip-syncing is probably beyond most of the people you're going to be shooting, but there's nothing that says you can't record narration separately and add it later. It's relatively easy if you learn how to use simple software video-editing programs like iMovie (for the Macintosh) or Windows Movie Maker (for Windows PCs). Any time the speaker is off-camera, you can work with separately recorded narration rather than recording the speaker on-camera. This can produce much cleaner sound.

External Microphones

The single most important thing you can do to improve your audio quality is to use an external microphone. The V1's internal stereo microphones mounted on the front of the camera will do a decent job, but have some significant drawbacks, partially spelled out in the previous section:

- **Camera noise.** The V1's electronic shutter may be silent, but there are plenty of other noise sources emanating from the camera, including your own breathing and rustling around as the camera shifts in your hand. Manual zooming with the

10-30mm and 30-110mm lenses (as well as with any other optics you may mount on your camera) is bound to affect your sound, and your fingers will fall directly in front of the built-in mics as you change focal lengths. An external microphone isolates the sound recording from camera noise.

- **Distance.** Anytime your V1 is located more than 6-8 feet from your subjects or sound source, the audio will suffer. An external unit allows you to place the mic right next to your subject.
- **Improved quality.** Obviously, Nikon isn't going to install a super-high quality microphone on a non-professional camera.
- **Directionality.** The V1's internal microphone generally records only sounds directly in front of it. An external microphone can be either of the directional type or omnidirectional, depending on whether you want to "shotgun" your sound or record more ambient sound.

You can choose from several different types of microphones, each of which has its own advantages and disadvantages. If you're serious about movie making with your V1, you might want to own more than one. Common configurations include:

- **Shotgun microphones.** These can be mounted directly on your Nikon V1, although, if the mic uses an accessory shoe mount, you'll need the optional AS-N1000 adapter to convert the camera's accessory port to a standard hot shoe. I prefer to use a bracket like the one shown in Figure 7.17, which further isolates the microphone from any camera noise. The Nikon ME-1 microphone (see Figure 7.17) is of this type, and a good choice. It's inexpensive. (I paid less than $140 for mine.) Intended to pick up sound from the general direction in which it's pointed, such a microphone will provide decent pickup of ambient sound in its environment.
- **Lapel microphones.** Also called *lavalieres*, these microphones attach to the subject's clothing and picks up their voice with the best quality. You'll need a long enough cord or a wireless mic (described later). These are especially good for video interviews, so whether you're producing a documentary or grilling relatives for a family history, you'll want one of these.
- **Hand-held microphones.** If you're capturing a singer crooning a tune, or want your subject to mimic famed faux newscaster Wally Ballou, a hand-held mic may be your best choice. They serve much the same purpose as a lapel microphone, and they're more intrusive—but that may be the point. A hand-held microphone can make a great prop for your fake newscast! The speaker can talk right into the microphone, point it at another person, or use it to record ambient sound. If your narrator is not going to appear on-camera, one of these can be an inexpensive way to improve sound.

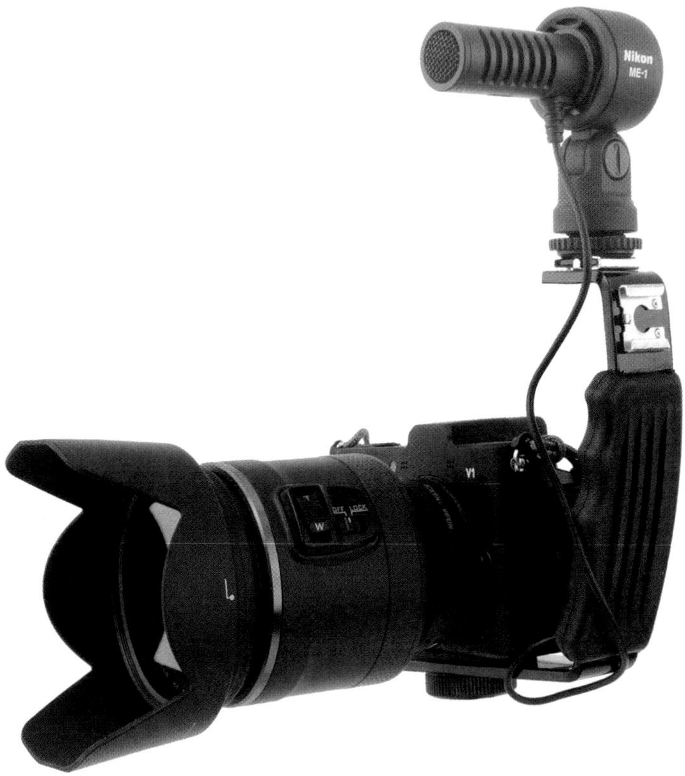

Figure 7.17
The Nikon ME-1 external microphone, with wind screen removed. When using the 10-100mm power zoom lens and a bracket like the one shown, your V1 movie kit will no longer be compact—but you'll get some great video.

- **Wired and wireless external microphones.** This option is the most expensive, but you get a receiver and a transmitter (both battery-powered, so you'll need to make sure you have enough batteries). The transmitter is connected to the microphone, and the receiver is connected to your Nikon V1. In addition to being less klutzy and enabling you to avoid having wires on view in your scene, wireless mics let you record sounds that are physically located some distance from your camera. Of course you need to keep in mind the range of your device, and be aware of possible signal interference from other electronic components in the vicinity.

WIND NOISE REDUCTION

Always use the wind screen with an external microphone to reduce the effect of noise produced by even light breezes blowing over the microphone. Both the camera and many mics include a low-cut filter to further reduce wind noise. However, these can also affect other sounds. You can disable the low-cut filters for the V1's internal microphones by choosing Off for Wind Noise Reduction in the Movie Sound Options menu when the mode dial is set to Movie mode. If you're using the Nikon ME-1 mic, set the unit's low-cut filter switch on the back of the microphone to Flat.

Lens Craft

I'll cover the use of lenses with the Nikon V1 in more detail in Chapter 9, but a discussion of lens selection when shooting movies may be useful at this point. In the video world, not all lenses are created equal. The two most important considerations are depth-of-field, or the beneficial lack thereof, and zooming. I'll address each of these separately.

Depth-of-Field and Video

Have you wondered why professional videographers have gone nuts over still cameras that can also shoot video? The producers of Saturday Night Live could afford to have Alex Buono, their director of photography, use the niftiest, most expensive high-resolution video cameras to shoot the opening sequences of the program. Instead, Buono opted for a pair of digital SLR cameras. One thing that makes digital still cameras so attractive for video is that they have relatively large sensors, which provides improved low-light performance and results in the oddly attractive reduced depth-of-field, compared with most professional video cameras.

Figure 7.18 provides a comparison of the relative size of sensors. The typical size of a professional video camera sensor is shown at lower left. The Nikon 1 sensor used in the V1 is shown just northwest of it. You can see that it is much larger, especially when compared with the sensor found in the Nikon P7100 compact camera. Of course, the DX sensor shown at upper left, and a full-frame FX sensor (not shown) are even larger.

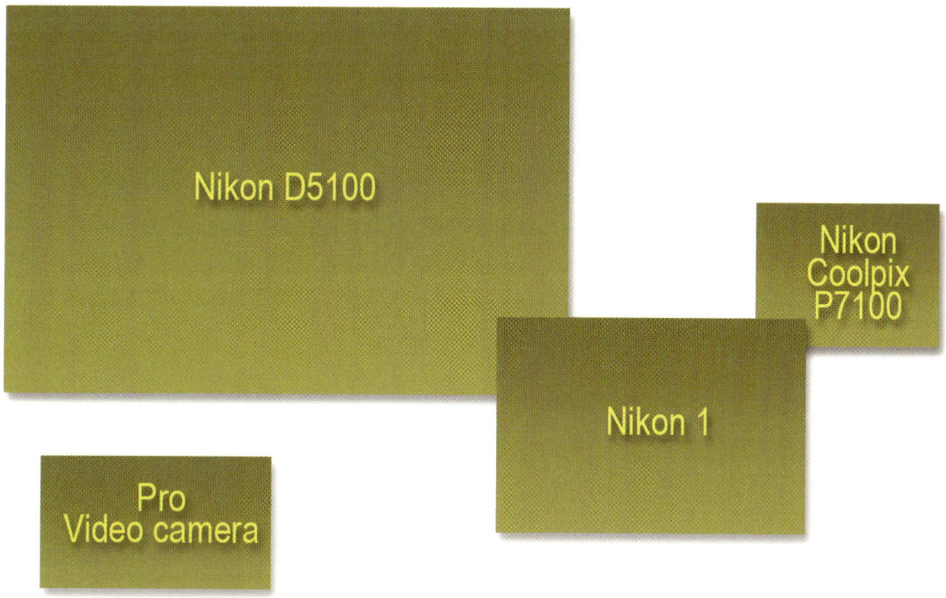

Figure 7.18
Sensor size comparison.

But, compared with the sensors used in many pro video cameras and the even smaller sensors found in the typical computer camcorder, the Nikon 1's image-grabber is larger.

As you'll learn in Chapter 9, a larger sensor calls for the use of longer focal lengths to produce the same field of view, so, in effect, a larger sensor has reduced depth-of-field. And *that's* what makes cameras like the Nikon V1 or larger models like the Nikon D5100 attractive from a creative standpoint. Less depth-of-field means greater control over the range of what's in focus. Your V1, with its larger sensor, has a distinct advantage over consumer camcorders in this regard, and even does a slightly better job than professional video cameras.

Zooming and Video

When shooting still photos, a zoom is a zoom is a zoom. The key considerations for a zoom lens used only for still photography are the maximum aperture available at each focal length ("How *fast* is this lens?), the zoom range ("How far can I zoom in or out?"), and its sharpness at any given f/stop. ("Do I lose sharpness when I shoot wide open?")

When shooting video, the priorities may change, and there are two additional parameters to consider. The first two I listed, lens speed and zoom range, have roughly the same importance in both still and video photography. Zoom range gains a bit of importance in videography, because you can always/usually move closer to shoot a still photograph, but when you're zooming during a shot most of us don't have that option (or the funds to buy/rent a dolly to smoothly move the camera during capture). But, oddly enough, overall sharpness may have slightly less importance under certain conditions when shooting video. That's because the image changes in some way many times per second (30–60 times per second with the Nikon V1), so any given frame doesn't hang around long enough for our eyes to pick out every single detail. You want a sharp image, of course, but your standards don't need to be quite as high when shooting video.

Here are the remaining considerations, and the two new ones:

- **Zoom lens maximum aperture.** The speed of the lens matters in several ways. A zoom with a relatively large maximum aperture lets you shoot in lower light levels, and a big f/stop allows you to minimize depth-of-field for selective focus. Keep in mind that the maximum aperture may change during zooming. The 10-30mm kit lens is an f/3.5 lens at the 10mm focal length, but provides only f/5.6 worth of light at 30mm.
- **Zoom range.** Use of zoom during actual capture should not be an everyday thing, unless you're shooting a kung-fu movie. However, there are effective uses for a zoom shot, particularly if it's a "long" one from extreme wide angle to extreme close-up (or vice versa). The Nikon 1 10-100mm zoom, or even the Nikon 1 30-110mm zoom can be used in this way. Most of the time, you'll use the zoom range to adjust the perspective of the camera *between* shots, and a longer zoom

range can mean less trotting back and forth to adjust the field of view. Zoom range also comes into play when you're working with selective focus (longer focal lengths have less depth-of-field), or want to expand or compress the apparent distance between foreground and background subjects. A longer range gives you more flexibility.

- **Power zoom.** The Nikon 1 10-100mm zoom is a humongous optic, but it has something going for it besides a 10X zoom range. Its power zoom is optimized for video shooting. Manual zooming with other lenses during capture can produce jerky images, even with vibration reduction turned on. The 10-100mm power zoom gives you smooth zooming, and you can change the speed of the zoom easily as you press the button on the lens.
- **Linearity.** Interchangeable lenses may have some drawbacks, as many photographers who have been using the video features of their digital SLRs have discovered. That's because, unless a lens is optimized for video shooting (as the Nikon 1 10-100mm lens is), zooming with a particular lens may not necessarily be linear. Rotating the zoom collar manually at a constant speed doesn't always produce a smooth zoom. There may be "jumps" as the elements of the lens shift around during the zoom. Keep that in mind if you plan to zoom during a shot, and are using a non-linear lens (say an F-mount lens you've attached using an adapter, like the one discussed in Chapter 9).

Part III

Advanced Tools

The next three chapters are devoted to helping you dig deeper into the capabilities of your Nikon V1, so you can exploit all those cool features that your previous camera lacked. Chapters 8 list every setting and option found in the Playback, Shooting, and Setup menus. I'll not only tell you what each menu item does, I'll explain exactly when and why you should use every option. Then, in Chapter 9, I'll show you how to select the best lenses for the kinds of photography you want to do, with my recommendations for starter lenses as well as more advanced optics for specialized applications.

Chapter 10 is devoted to the magic of light—your fundamental tool in creating any photograph. There are entire books devoted to working with electronic flash, but I hope to get you started with plenty of coverage of the Nikon V1's capabilities. I'll show you how to avoid that "built-in flash" look when using the optional SB-N5 flash unit. By the time you finish these essential chapters, you'll be well on the way to mastering your Nikon V1.

8

The Playback, Shooting, and Setup Menus

The Nikon V1 offers an amazing degree of adjustments for a camera in its price range. This versatility has made the V1 popular among advanced amateurs. You can enjoy this flexibility, too. If your camera doesn't behave in exactly the way you'd like, chances are you can make a small change in the Playback, Shooting, and Setup menus that will tailor the V1 to your needs.

This chapter will help you sort out the settings for these menus. As I've mentioned before, this book isn't intended to replace the manual you received with your V1, nor have I any interest in rehashing its contents. There is, however, some unavoidable duplication between the Nikon manual and the content of this chapter, because I'm going to explain all the key menu choices and the options you may have in using them. You should find, though, that I will give you the information you need in a much more helpful format, with plenty of detail on why you should make some settings that are particularly cryptic.

Anatomy of the Nikon V1's Menus

If you used any Nikon digital camera before you purchased your Nikon V1, you're probably already familiar with the basic menu system. The menus consist of a series of screens with entries, as shown in Figure 8.1.

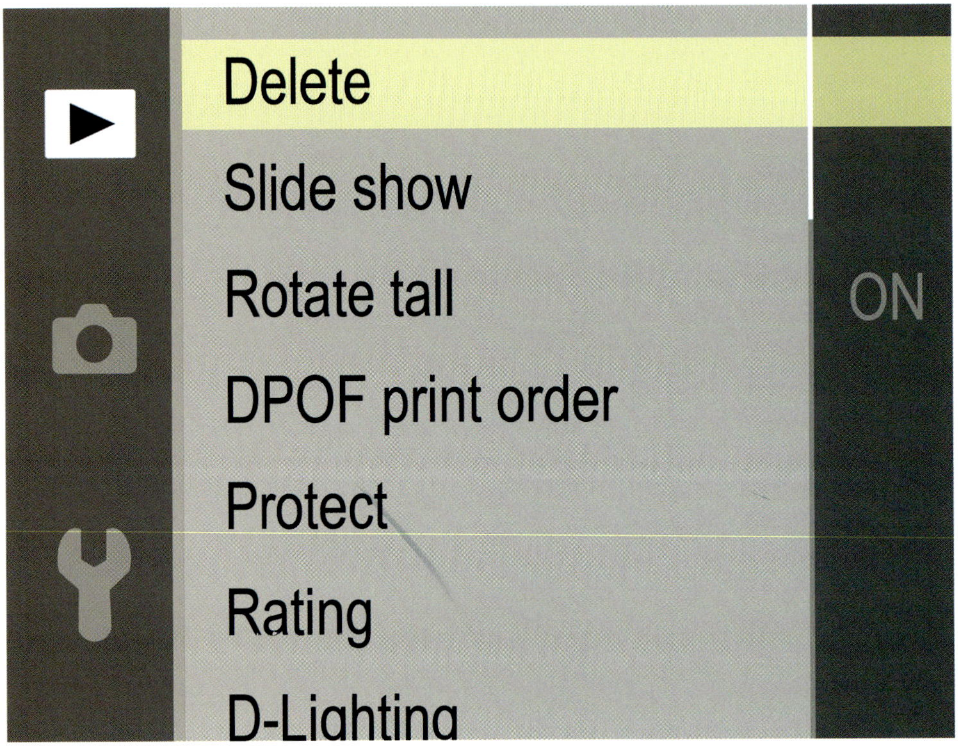

Figure 8.1
The multi selector's navigational buttons are used to move among the various menu entries.

Navigating among the various menus is easy and follows a consistent set of rules:

- Press the MENU button to display the main menu screens.
- Use the multi selector's left/right/up/down buttons to navigate among the menu entries to highlight your choice. Moving the highlighting to the left column lets you scroll up and down among the three top-level menus. From the top in Figure 8.1, they are Playback, Shooting, and Setup.
- A highlighted top-level menu's icon will change from gray and white to yellow highlighting. Use the multi selector's right button to move into the column containing that menu's choices, and the up/down buttons to scroll among the entries. If more than one screen full of choices is available, a scroll bar appears at the far right of the screen, with a position slider showing the relative position of the currently highlighted entry.
- To work with a highlighted menu entry, press the OK button in the center of the multi selector, or just press the right button on the multi selector. Any additional screens of choices will appear. You can move among them using the same multi selector movements.
- You can confirm a selection by pressing the OK button or, frequently, by pressing the right button on the multi selector once again.

- Pressing the multi selector left button usually backs you out of the current screen, and pressing the MENU button again usually does the same thing. You can exit the menu system at any time by tapping the shutter release button.
- The Nikon V1 "remembers" the top-level menu and specific menu entry you were using (but not any submenus) the last time the menu system was accessed, so pressing the MENU button brings you back to where you left off.

Playback Menu

The Playback menu has ten entries where you select options related to the display, review, editing, and printing of the photos you've taken. The choices you'll find include the following entries (the last three, Resize, Crop, and Edit Movie are not pictured in Figure 8.1, and don't appear until you scroll the listing to the bottom). None of these are available if you're using a blank card; they are activated only when you have one or more images taken:

- Delete
- Slide Show
- Rotate Tall
- DPOF Print Order
- Protect
- Rating
- D-Lighting
- Resize
- Crop
- Edit Movie

Delete

Choose this menu entry and you'll be given three choices: Delete Selected Images, Select Images By Date, Delete All Images, and Discard. (See Figure 8.2.) To delete only some pictures, choose Delete Selected Images and you'll see an image selection screen like the one shown in Figure 8.3. Then, follow these instructions:

1. **View images.** Use the multi selector left/right cursor keys or the dial to scroll among the available images. (See Figure 8.3.)
2. **See movies and still pictures.** Movie clips will have graphics representing sprocket holes displayed on either side of their thumbnails. Movie clips you have trimmed will have a scissors icon shown at the upper-left corner of the thumbnail.
3. **Mark images for deletion.** When you highlight an image or movie you think you might like to delete, press the up button to mark (with a trash can icon) or the down button to unmark.
4. **Zoom in to examine image.** Press and hold the zoom bar up to temporarily see the highlighted image in a larger size.

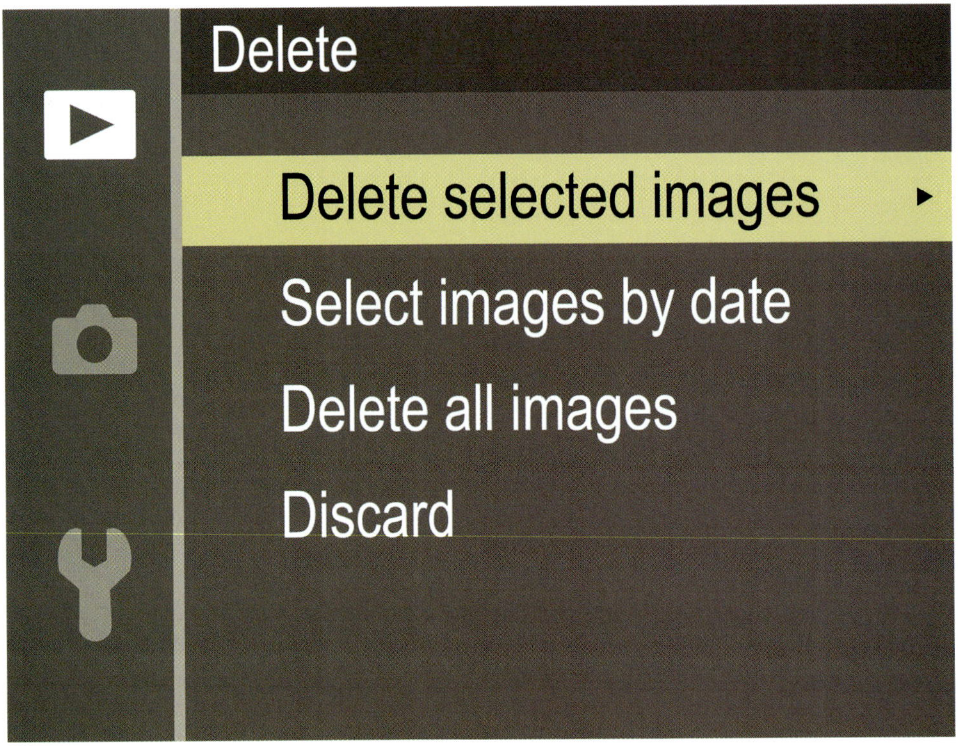

Figure 8.2
Choose which images to remove.

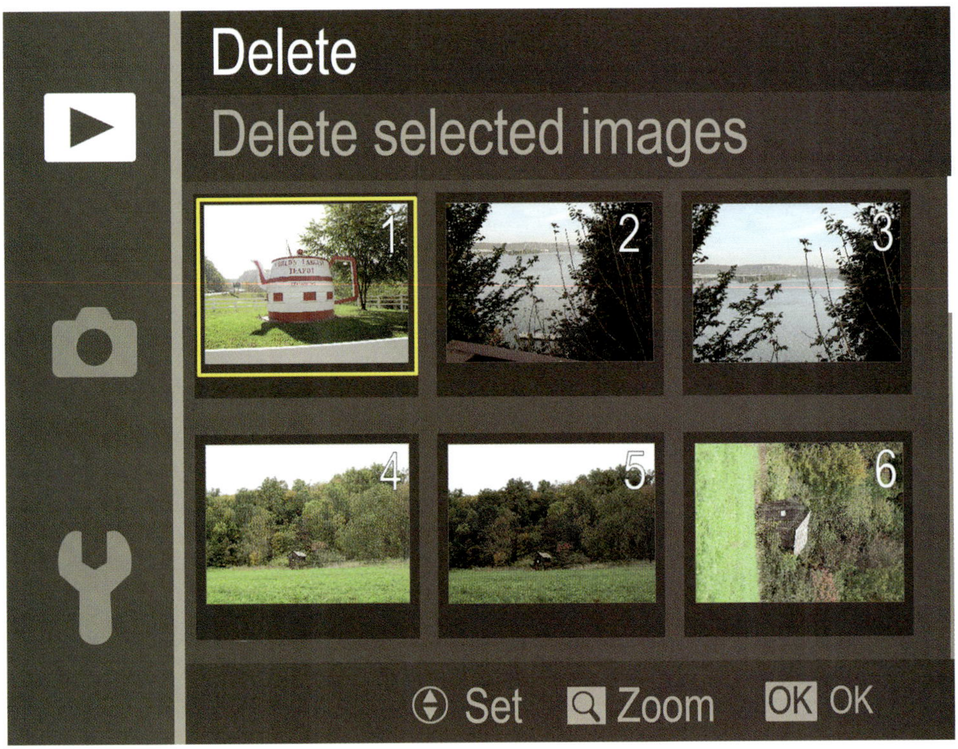

Figure 8.3
Delete specific selected images.

5. **Delete and Confirm.** When you've finished marking images to delete, press OK. A final screen will appear asking you to confirm the removal of the image(s). Choose Yes to delete the image(s) or No to cancel deletion, and then press OK. If you selected Yes, then you'll return to the Playback menu; if you chose No, you'll be taken back to the selection screen to mark/unmark images.
6. **Exit.** To back out of the selection screen, press the MENU button or tap the shutter release button.

In the main Delete screen you can also choose Select Images by Date. Just follow these steps:

1. **See available dates.** The Select Images by Date screen will show you a thumbnail of the first movie/still captured on a particular date. (See Figure 8.4.)
2. **See images for that date.** While you can mark a date and all its images for deletion from this screen, if you like you can press the zoom bar down to view all the images taken on that date in a scrollable list.
3. **Zoom in to examine image.** From the screen that appears, press and hold the zoom bar up to temporarily see a highlighted image for that date in a larger size.

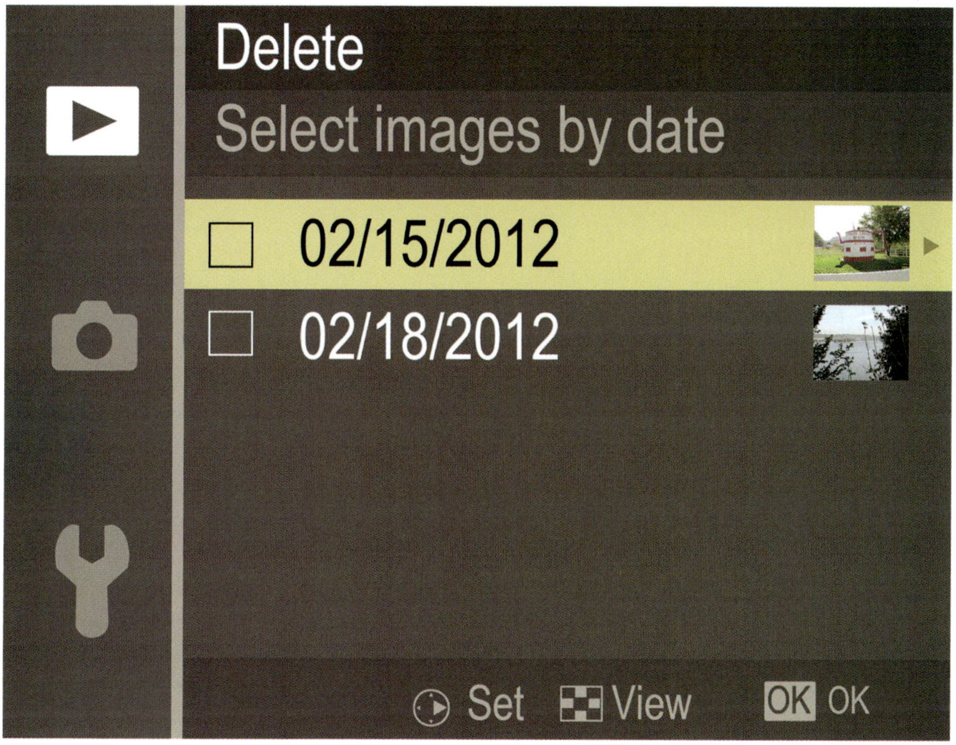

Figure 8.4
Remove only images taken on a certain date.

4. **Return to date selection screen.** When you're satisfied with deleting all the images for that date, press OK to mark them all for deletion. You'll be returned to the date selection screen with a check mark placed next to the thumbnail for that date. You can also press the zoom bar's down button to return to the screen without marking the images.
5. **Mark dates for deletion.** You can review other dates as described in Steps 2-4, or simply mark dates for deletion from this screen by pressing the right multi selector button. Dates scheduled for erasure are indicated with a checked box.
6. **Delete and Confirm.** When you've finished marking dates to delete, press OK. A final screen will appear asking you to confirm the removal of the image(s). Choose Yes to delete the image(s) or No to cancel deletion, and then press OK. If you selected Yes, then you'll return to the Playback menu; if you chose No, you'll be taken back to the selection screen to mark/unmark images.
7. **Exit.** To back out of the selection screen, press the MENU button or tap the shutter release button.

Your final two choices from the main Delete screen are Delete All Images, which removes all the images from your memory card and Discard. Discard removes all images you've marked with the Trash icon rating in the Rating Pictures menu.

Other Ways to Delete

There are other ways to erase images other than from the Playback menu, all discussed elsewhere in this book. To recap, here are your options.

- **Format command.** The Format command, explained in the discussion of the Setup menu later in this chapter, is a much faster way of wiping a whole card than choosing Delete All Images. It's also a safer way of returning your memory card to a fresh, blank state, as it restores the file system to its original pristine state.
- **Delete button.** You can remove whatever image or movie preview is on the screen during playback by pressing the Delete button (with the trash can icon), and then confirming by pressing a second time.
- **Deleting Smart Photo Selector images.** When a Smart Photo is shown on the screen, pressing the Delete button twice removes the images chosen by the Smart Photo Selector. If you're viewing the Best Shot selection dialog, you are shown another screen that asks if you want to delete This Image, or All Except Best Shot. Use the multi selector buttons to choose, and press OK. Or press the playback button to Cancel.

Slide Show

The V1's Slide Show feature is a convenient way to review images one after another, without the need to manually switch between them.

To activate a slide show, just choose Start from this entry in the Playback menu. If you like, you can choose an interval for both still images and movies before commencing the show. During playback, you can press pause, skip back, skip ahead, adjust volume, and exit to playback or shooting mode. The next sections will show you how to set up and run your slide show and use the playback controls.

Setting Up the Show

You can choose what type of images and/or movies will be displayed in your slide show, but, unfortunately, you can't pick and choose exactly which will be shown, except indirectly. Follow these steps to set up your show. First choose what images to view:

1. **Access slide show.** In the Playback menu, navigate to Slide Show and press the right navigational button. The screen shown in Figure 8.5 appears.

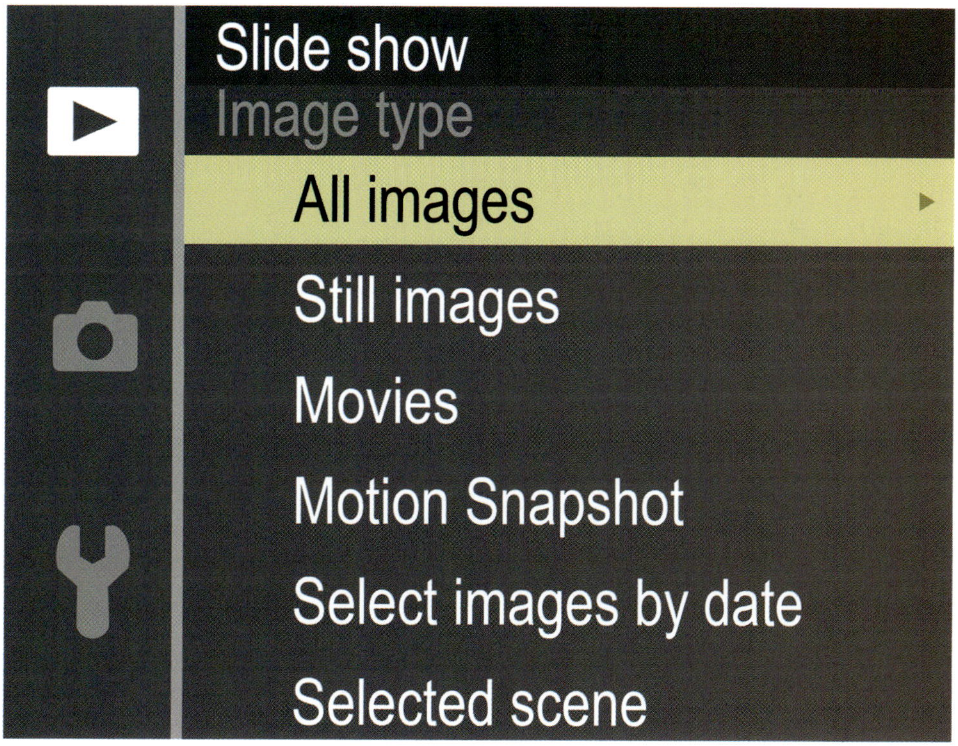

Figure 8.5 Choose which type of stills and movies to include in your slide show.

2. **Select from the eight image/movie types available.** If no images or movies are available of the type you specify, slide show setup will stop until you select an option that has available images. Only the first six are shown on the screen initially; you'll need to scroll down to see the last two, By Rating, and Face Priority. Your choices are:

   - **All Images.** All the movies and still images of any type on your memory card will be included.
   - **Still Images.** Only still photographs are included in the slide show.
   - **Movies.** Your slideshow will display all movie clips.
   - **Motion Snapshot.** The slide show includes only the short movie part of your motion snapshots, and skips the photographs.
   - **Select Images by Date.** A calendar, like the one shown in Figure 8.6, appears. Use the multi selector buttons to highlight a date and press OK. Only the images taken on that date will be included in your slide show.
   - **Selected Scene.** Choose to display only the images that the Auto Scene Selector has selected to take using a particular scene classification. You can select from Auto, Portrait, Landscape, Night Portrait, and Close-ups. Say you've taken a lot of close-up pictures of flowers, or have many landscape-type photos on your memory card; this mode will search through your shots and include the ones the V1 classifies as that type of scene in your slide show. Its selection won't be perfect, but you'll be surprised at how accurate the assessment is.
   - **By Rating.** This is the closest you can come to hand-picking which photos to display in your slide show. Choosing By Rating displays a screen with five rows of stars, from five stars to one star, with a checkbox next to each. Highlight any row and press the right directional button to mark or unmark that rating. You can choose any combination of ratings you like: view only five star pictures, both five star and four star images, or, if you're feeling quirky, choose to see five star *and* one star images for a best shot/worst shot comparison. If you carefully rate your images during playback review you can effectively choose which ones will be included in a slide show. You might, for example, assign five stars to all the photos you want to include in a slide show, even if they aren't necessarily the best ones on the memory card.
   - **Face Priority.** If you hanker to view all your people shots in one sitting, this option will include only shots in which the V1 detected faces (if Face Priority was active during shooting).

3. Advance to setup screen. Once you've selected which images to include, you'll be taken to the setup screen shown in Figure 8.7. The next steps show you how to finish setting up your slide show.

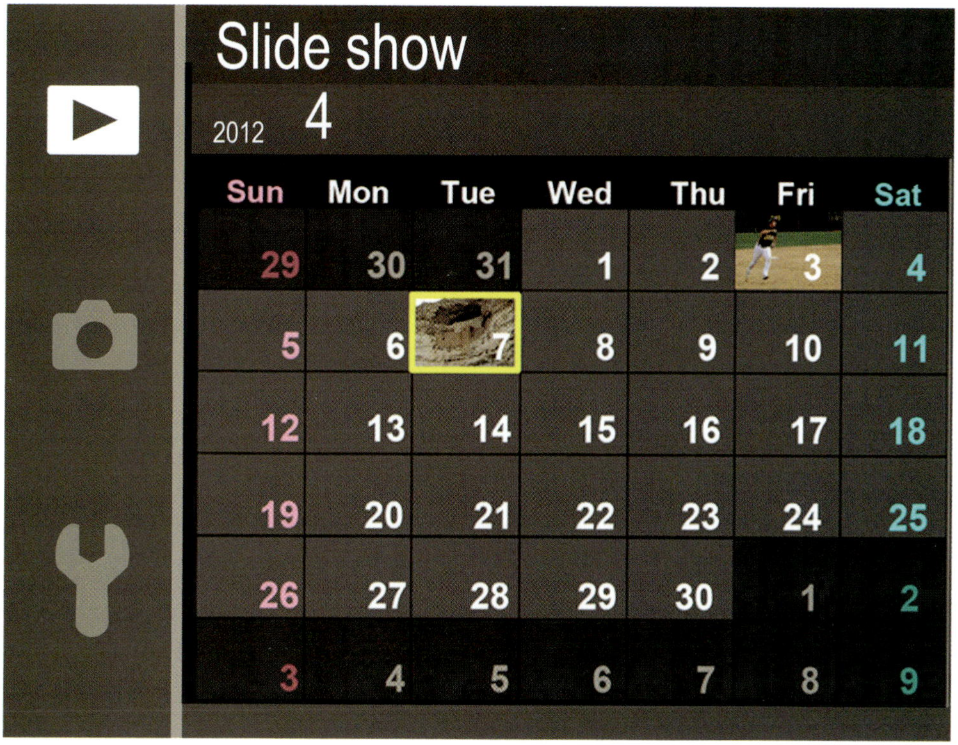

Figure 8.6
You can select only images taken on a particular date.

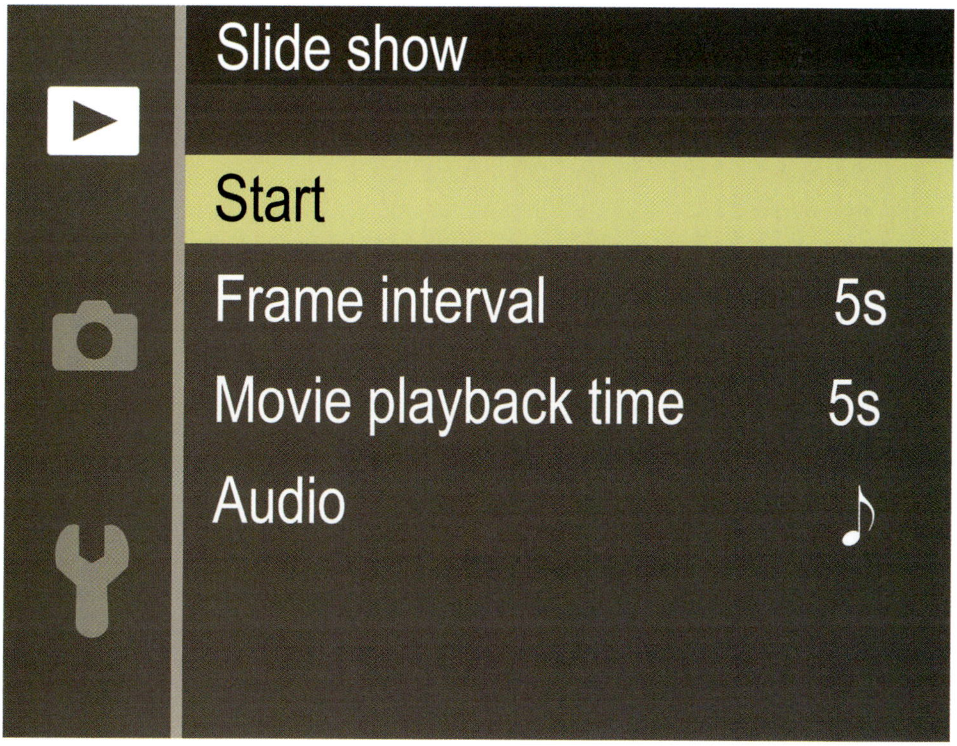

Figure 8.7
Specify the other parameters for your slide show.

After choosing the images/movies to be displayed, follow these steps to specify the other parameters required, and start your show. If the default or displayed values are OK, you can simply skip these steps and select start to begin your extravaganza.

1. **Choose a still frame interval.** Highlight the Frame Interval choice and press the right directional button. Select from 2, 3, 5, or 10 seconds. The V1 will display each image for that amount of time before moving to the next.
2. **Select movie playback time.** When you choose Movie Playback time, you can choose how much of the movie will be displayed before the slide show continues to the next still or movie clip. Your choices are:
   - **Same as Frame Interval.** The slide show will display only the first 2, 3, 5, or 10 seconds of a movie clip, corresponding to the interval you selected for still frames. This option has two effects: it ensures a consistent pace by displaying the still images and movie clips for the same length of time, and it prevents lengthy clips from running so long that they bore your audience. This is a good choice if you want a fast-moving, lively slide show with both stills and movies.
   - **10s/15s.** These two choices display the first 10 seconds or 15 seconds of each movie clip (respectively), regardless of what setting you've selected for the still frame interval. Use this option when you want the ability to let your movie clips run a bit longer than the still frames.
   - **ALL.** This selection tells the V1 to play each movie clip to the bitter end. It's best used when you know that your video segments are not overlong, and won't dominate the still images that are mixed in.
3. **Audio.** This choice controls the sound played with your slide show. The five choices can be a bit confusing for the newcomer, but I'll spell them out for you.
   - **Mute.** No sound is played during the slide show for still images or movies.
   - **Background Track 1/2/3.** Musical background music is played for still images, motion snapshots, and movies.
   - **Movie Sound Tracks.** In this case, the only sounds played back will be the audio that you recorded with your movie clips (if audio was captured). Still images and motion snapshots will be played back with sound muted.
4. **Begin Slide Show.** After all the parameters that you want to specify or change have been entered, highlight Start and press the right directional button to begin your slide show.

Viewing the Slide Show

Once you've started the slide show, you can watch it all the way through to the end, or control how the show is presented on your screen (either the camera's display or an HDTV if linked to the V1 with an optional HDMI cable).

Here are your options (an on-screen display of the available controls isn't shown, as it is for movie playback):

- **Pause.** Press the OK button to pause the show. Press a second time to resume.
- **Forward/Reverse.** Press the left directional button to return to the previous image/movie. Press the right directional button to skip ahead to the next frame.
- **Adjust Volume.** The zoom bar can be pressed up to increase the volume, or down to reduce the playback volume.
- **Exit Show.** Just tap the shutter release to return to shooting mode.
- **Replay.** Once the show is over, a screen pops up giving you the options to restart (select Resume), enter new parameters for playback before restarting, or exit the slide show.

Rotate Tall

When you rotate the V1 to photograph vertical subjects in portrait (tall), rather than landscape (wide) orientation, you probably don't want to view them tilted onto their sides later on, either on the camera display or within your image viewing/editing application on your computer. The V1 is way ahead of you. It has a directional sensor built in that can detect whether the camera was rotated when the photo was taken and hide this information in the image file itself.

The orientation data is applied in two different ways. It can be used by the V1 to automatically rotate images when they are displayed on the camera's LCD monitor, or you can ignore the data and let the images display in non-rotated fashion (so you have to rotate the camera to view them in their proper orientation). Your image-editing application, such as Adobe Photoshop Elements, can also use the embedded file data to automatically rotate images on your computer screen.

Rotation works only if you've set Auto Image Rotation to On in the Setup menu (I'll show you how to do that later in this chapter). Once you've done that, the V1 will embed information about orientation in the image file, and your image editor (such as Adobe Photoshop or Photoshop Elements) will rotate the images for you as the files are loaded.

This menu choice deals only with whether the image should be rotated when displayed on the *camera LCD or electronic viewfinder monitors.* (If you de-activate this option, your image-editing software can still read the embedded rotation data and properly display your images.) When Rotate Tall is turned off, the Nikon V1 does not rotate pictures taken in vertical orientation, displaying them as shown in at left in Figure 8.8. The image is large on your LCD screen, but you must rotate the camera to view it upright.

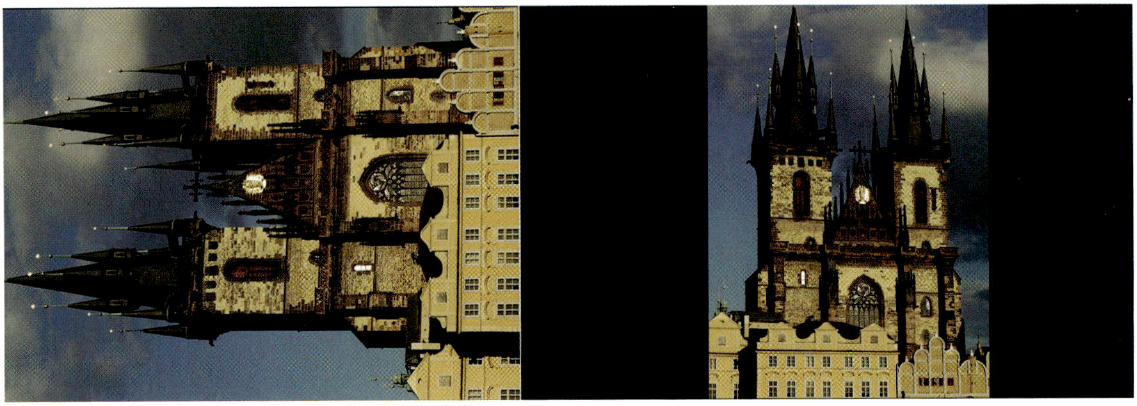

Figure 8.8 With Rotate Tall turned off, vertical images appear large on the LCD, but you must turn the camera to view them upright. With Rotate Tall turned on, vertical images are shown in a smaller size, but oriented for viewing without turning the camera.

When Rotate Tall is turned on, the V1 rotates pictures taken in vertical orientation on the LCD screen so you don't have to turn the camera to view them comfortably. However, this orientation also means that the longest dimension of the image is shown using the shortest dimension of the LCD, so the picture is reduced in size, as you can see at right in Figure 8.8.

So, turn this feature On (as well as Auto Image Rotation in the Setup menu), if you'd rather not turn your camera to view vertical shots in their natural orientation, and don't mind the smaller image. Turn the feature Off if, as I do, you'd rather see a larger image and are willing to rotate the camera to do so.

DPOF Print Order

The Nikon V1 supports the DPOF (Digital Print Order Format) that is now almost universally used by digital cameras to specify which images on your memory card should be printed, and the number of prints desired of each image. This information is recorded on the memory card and can be interpreted by a compatible printer when the camera is linked to the printer using the USB cable, or when the memory card is inserted into a card reader slot on the printer itself. Photo labs are also equipped to read this data and make prints when you supply your memory card to them. You can create a Print Order using this menu entry, or select pictures for printing using the PictBridge menu that pops up when the V1 is connected to a printer.

When you choose this menu item, you're presented with a set of screens that look very much like the Delete photos screens described earlier, only you're selecting pictures for printing rather than deleting them. The button sequences are slightly different, however:

1. **Choose DPOF Print Order.** In the Playback menu, navigate to the DPOF Print Order selection and press the right directional button. You'll see a screen that allows you to select/set the images to be printed, or reset (which unselects any images currently selected).
2. **View images.** Use the multi selector left/right buttons or dial to move among the available images.
3. **Evaluate image.** When you highlight an image you want to print, press the zoom bar upward to temporarily enlarge that image so you can evaluate it further. When you release the button, the selection screen returns.
4. **Set number of prints.** To mark an image for printing, press the multi selector up and down buttons to choose the number of prints you want, up to 99 per image. A printer icon and the number specified will appear overlaid on that image's thumbnail. (See Figure 8.9.)
5. **Reduce prints.** To unmark an image for printing, highlight and press the down button until the number of prints reaches zero. The printer icon will vanish.

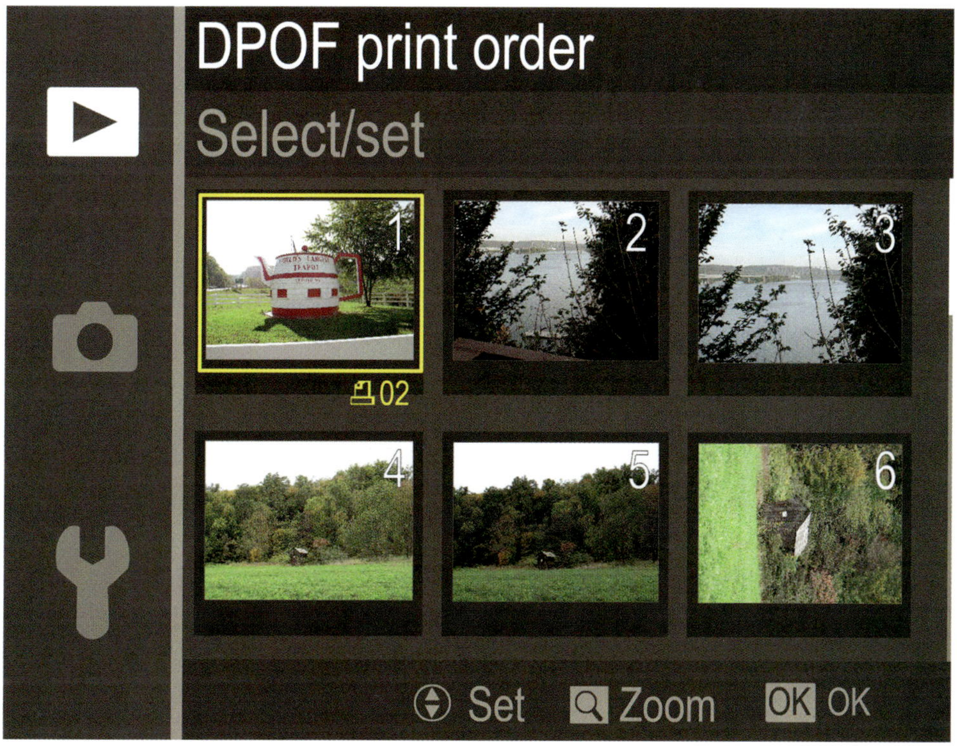

Figure 8.9
Select images for printing.

6. **Confirm.** When you've finished marking images to print, press OK.
7. **Add data.** A final screen will appear in which you can request a shooting data imprint (shutter speed and aperture) or imprint date (the date the photos were taken). Use the up/down buttons to select one or both of these options, if desired, and press the left/right buttons to mark or unmark the check boxes. When a box is marked, the imprint information for that option will be included on *all* prints in the print order.
8. **Finish.** Press OK when done.

Using the PictBridge Menu

The PictBridge menu is not accessible from the Playback menu. It appears when the V1 is connected to a PictBridge-compatible printer. It uses a procedure almost identical to the one described above, but with the following configuration:

- **Select Images for Printing.** This operates the same as the Playback menu's DPOF Print Order entry.
- **Select by Date.** This is an additional option to choose images for printing based on the date, using a screen that's virtually identical to the one shown earlier in Figure 8.4.
- **Print DPOF Print Order.** This selection tells the PictBridge printer to print the order you marked up in the camera using the Playback menu DPOF print order entry.
- **Index Print.** Use this PictBridge option to print a sheet of thumbnail images of the first 256 images on the memory card.
- **Print Options.** When you've told the printer to output the images you've selected, a screen appears that lets you specify additional options, including Page Size, Number of Copies, Print Border, Print Time Stamp, or Crop (available with printers that support cropping; a dialog box appears with a cropping frame that can be changed in size with the zoom bar).

Protect

This choice allows you to view pictures on your memory card and mark them as Protected to keep them from being accidentally deleted. The Protect attribute will not save your images from deletion if you reformat the memory card. The Protect menu has two options: Select/set, which lets you mark pictures using a screen similar to the Delete images and DPOF Print Order selection screens; and Reset, which removes protection from all images on the memory card.

The Protect attribute is also used by other non-Nikon applications. For example, if you have an Eye-Fi card inserted in the V1, that card can be set using the Eye-Fi center software to either upload *all* photos you take, or only those that have been marked with Protect.

Rating

When reviewing pictures during Playback, the F button pops up a scale that allows you to embed a star rating in an image's file, ranging from 0 stars to 5 stars, plus a "trash" (negative) star you can apply to mark an image for deletion. You can also apply ratings manually using this menu entry.

The selection screen for choosing which pictures to rate is virtually identical to the one used for deleting, protecting, and so forth. When the image you want to rate is selected, you can press the zoom bar up to enlarge it temporarily, or press the multi selector up button (if you want to add stars) or down button (to decrease stars, or mark the image with a "negative" star for deletion).

D-Lighting

D-Lighting is a feature that improves the rendition of detail in highlights and shadows when you're photographing high contrast scenes. This option applies the fix to photos that have already been taken. You'll find a setting for Active D-Lighting, which applies while the picture is being taken, described later in this chapter. If you're taking photos in a contrasty environment, D-Lighting can improve the apparent dynamic range of your image as you shoot.

The Playback menu option brightens the shadows of pictures that have already been taken by saving a retouched copy with the changes applied. When you select D-Lighting, you'll see an image selection screen similar to the ones offered by the Protect and other menu entries already discussed in this chapter. The screen works exactly the same way to choose an image, using the left/right directional buttons, the zoom bar up motion to temporarily zoom in, and the OK button to select the highlighted image for application of the effect.

At that point, the screen shown in Figure 8.10 appears. Use the up/down directional buttons to choose from Off and On. Press the OK button to save a retouched copy in JPEG format. I'll explain D-Lighting in more detail and provide some examples in the Shooting Menu section under Active D-Lighting.

Resize

This option creates smaller copies of the selected images. This is a quick way of producing reduced resolution images for e-mailing, posting on web pages, using as thumbnail images, and other applications.

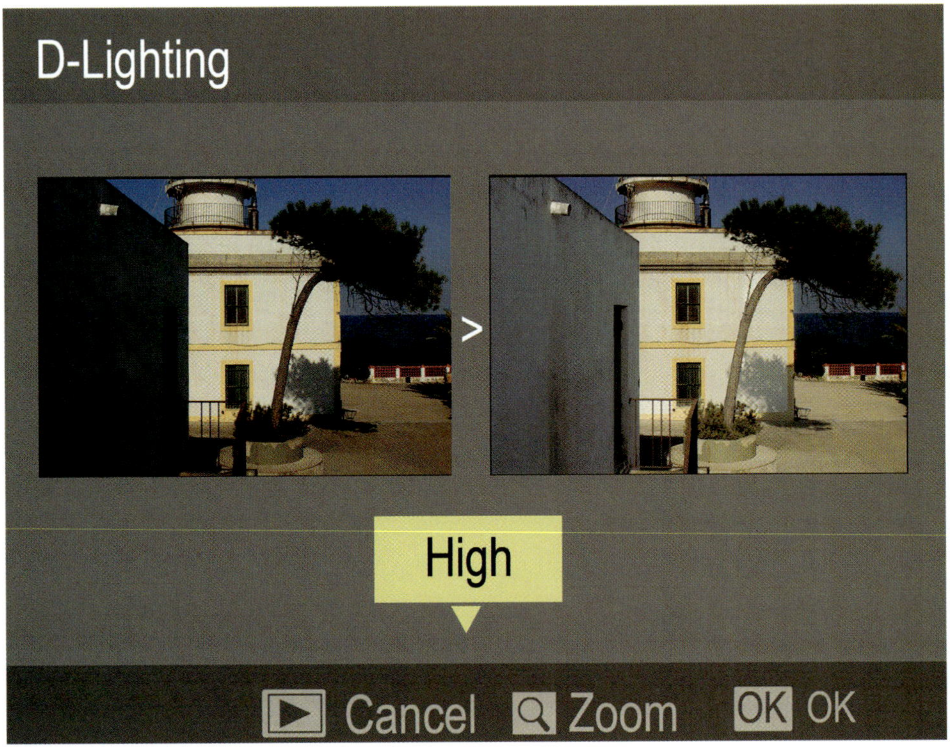

Figure 8.10
Choose the degree of D-Lighting to apply.

There are just four steps to using the feature:

1. **Navigate to Resize.** Press the MENU button, and access Resize from the Playback menu. Press the right directional button and the Resize screen appears.
2. **Select new size.** You can specify a resolution/size for all the copies made. Select Choose Size and opt for 1.1M (1280 × 856 pixels), 0.6M (960 × 640 pixels), or 0.3M (640 × 424 pixels). Press OK to return to the Resize screen.
3. **Select images.** The same image selection screen used previously in this chapter appears. Scroll among the images with the left/right directional buttons or dial and mark still images for reduction using the up button. The down button unmarks any previously specified image.
4. **Confirm.** Press OK when finished marking images. A screen with a message Create Resized Copy/Copies? appears. Choose Yes to confirm, or No to cancel.

It can be applied while viewing a single image in full-frame mode (just press the OK button while viewing a photo), or accessed from the Retouch menu (especially useful if you'd like to select and resize multiple images).

Crop

This option creates copies of still images in specific sizes based on the final size you select, chosen from among 3:2, 4:3, 1:1, and 16:9 aspect ratios (proportions). This is another way to create smaller and trimmed versions of a picture for e-mailing without the need to first transfer the image to your own computer. If you're traveling, create your smaller copy here or with the Resize feature described previously, insert the memory card in a card reader at an Internet café, your library's public computers, or some other computer, and e-mail the reduced-size version. Just follow these steps:

1. **Select your photo.** Choose Trim from the Playback menu. You'll be shown the standard Nikon V1 image selection screen. Scroll among the photos using the multi selector left/right buttons or dial, and press OK when the image you want to trim is highlighted.
2. **Choose your aspect ratio.** Rotate the multi selector dial to change from 3:2, 4:3, 1:1, and 16:9 aspect ratios.
3. **Crop in on your photo.** Press the zoom bar up or down to crop in and out on your picture. The pixel dimensions of the cropped image at the selected proportions will be displayed in the upper-left corner (see Figure 8.11) as you zoom. The current framed size is outlined in yellow.

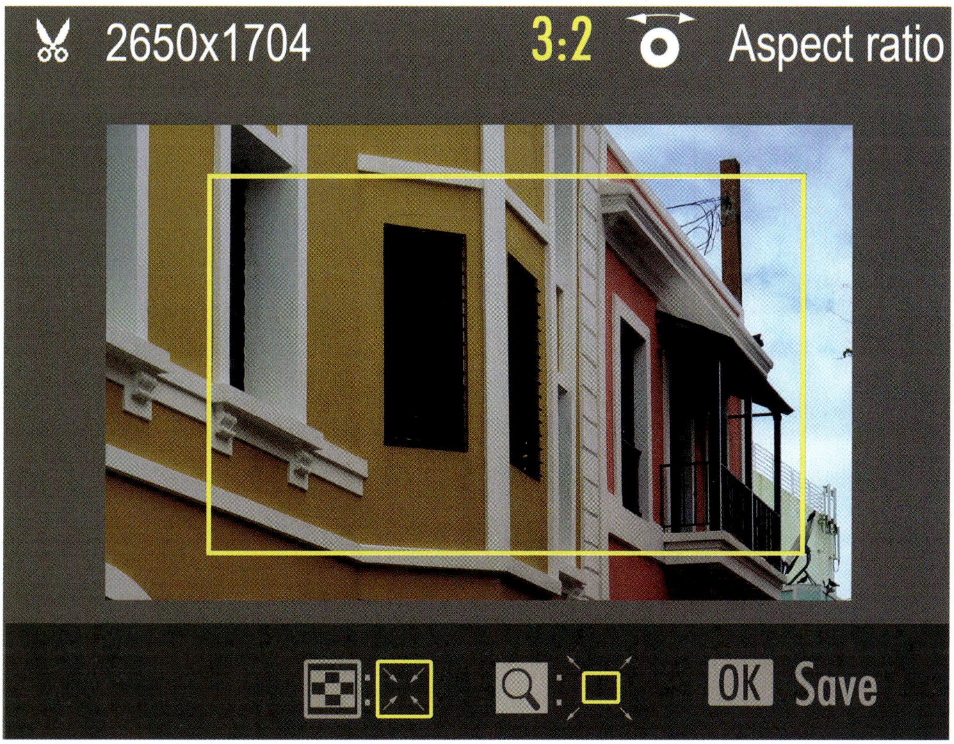

Figure 8.11 The Crop feature allows in-camera cropping.

4. **Move cropped area within the image.** Use the multi selector left/right and up/down buttons to relocate the yellow cropping border within the frame.
5. **Save the cropped image.** Press OK to save a copy of the image using the current crop and size, or press the Playback button to exit without creating a copy. Table 8.1 shows the trim sizes available.

Table 8.1 Trim Sizes

Aspect Ratio	Sizes Available
3:2	3424 × 2280, 2560 × 1704, 1920 × 1280, 1280 × 856, 960 × 640, 640 × 424
4:3	3424 × 2568, 2650 × 1920, 1920 × 1440, 1280 × 960, 960 × 720, 640 × 480
1:1	2560 × 2560, 1920 × 1920, 1440 × 1440, 960 × 960, 720 × 720, 480 × 480
16:9	3424 × 1920, 2560 × 1440, 1920 × 1080, 1280 × 720, 960 × 536, 640 × 360

Edit Movie

You can edit movies as you view them, pausing (using the down directional button) and clipping off portions from the beginning and/or end of the movie to create an edited version. Movie editing can be done from this menu entry. Once you've located and selected a movie clip at least two seconds long in Playback mode, follow these steps for in-camera editing/trimming (a more complete description is in Chapter 7):

1. **View the clip.** Press the OK button to begin playback, using the down button to pause and OK to resume. When you reach the first frame you want to keep, press the down button to pause.
2. **Trim from beginning.** Press the up directional button to delete all the frames that appear before the frame where you paused. Choose Yes from the screen that appears next to save your trimmed movie. An Edit Movie? dialog appears. Choose Yes to confirm, or No to cancel. The V1 will store a copy of the movie on your memory card.
3. **Trim from the end.** To trim video from the end of a clip, watch the movie until you reach the last frame you want to keep and then press the down button to pause. Then press the up button to trim. Choose Yes when the Edit Movie? dialog appears.

Shooting Menu

The Shooting menu differs slightly, depending on whether the mode dial is set for Still Image mode or Movie mode. There are 27 entries in the Still Image mode version, and 15 in the Movie mode version. The three flash entries are available only when you have the optional electronic flash mounted on the V1. The first seven entries in the Shooting menu when in Still Image mode are shown in Figure 8.12.

- Reset Shooting Options
- Exposure Mode
- Frame Rate (High Speed Movie mode only)
- Movie Settings (Movie Mode only)
- Image Quality
- Image Size
- Continuous
- Shutter Type
- Frame Rate
- Movie Settings
- Metering
- White Balance
- ISO Sensitivity
- Picture Control
- Custom Picture Control
- Color Space
- Active D-Lighting
- Long Exposure NR
- High ISO Noise Reduction
- Fade in/Fade Out
- Movie Sound Options
- Interval Timer Shooting
- Vibration Reduction
- AF-Area Mode
- Face-Priority AF
- Built-in AF Assist
- Flash Mode (When flash is mounted.)
- Flash Control (When flash is mounted.)
- Flash Compensation (When flash is mounted.)

Reset Shooting Options

This entry returns the Shooting menu options to their default values, shown in Table 8.2.

Exposure Mode

Use this menu item to specify how the camera chooses shutter speed and aperture, as described in Chapters 2 and 5. Your choices are Scene Auto Selector, Programmed auto (P), Shutter-priority auto (S), Aperture-priority auto (A), and Manual. (See Figure 8.13.)

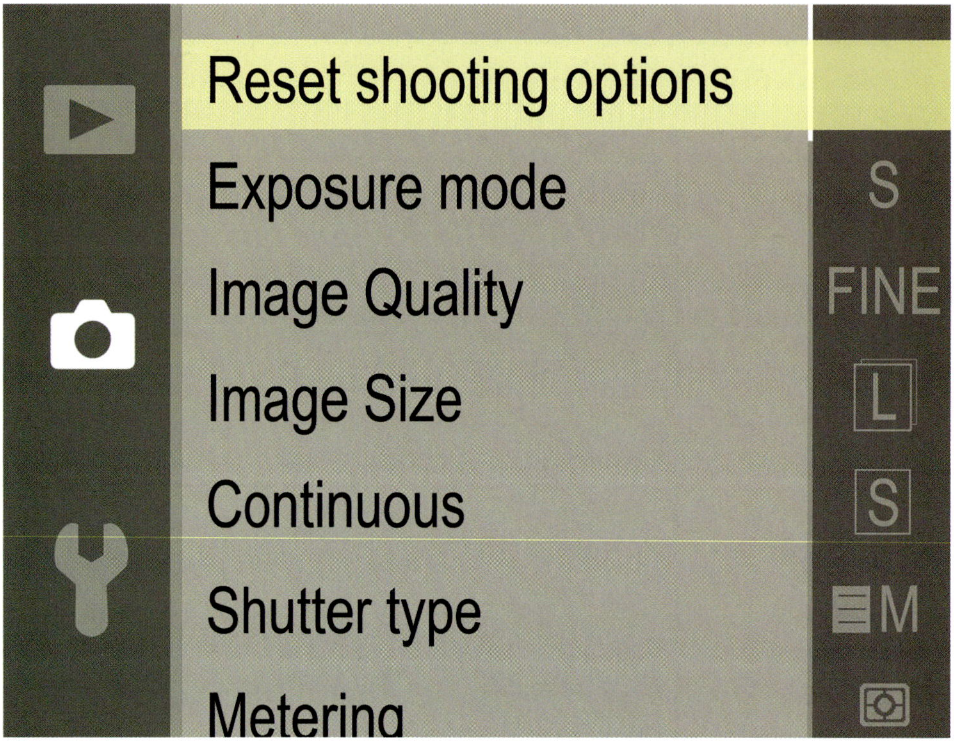

Figure 8.12
The first page of the Shooting menu.

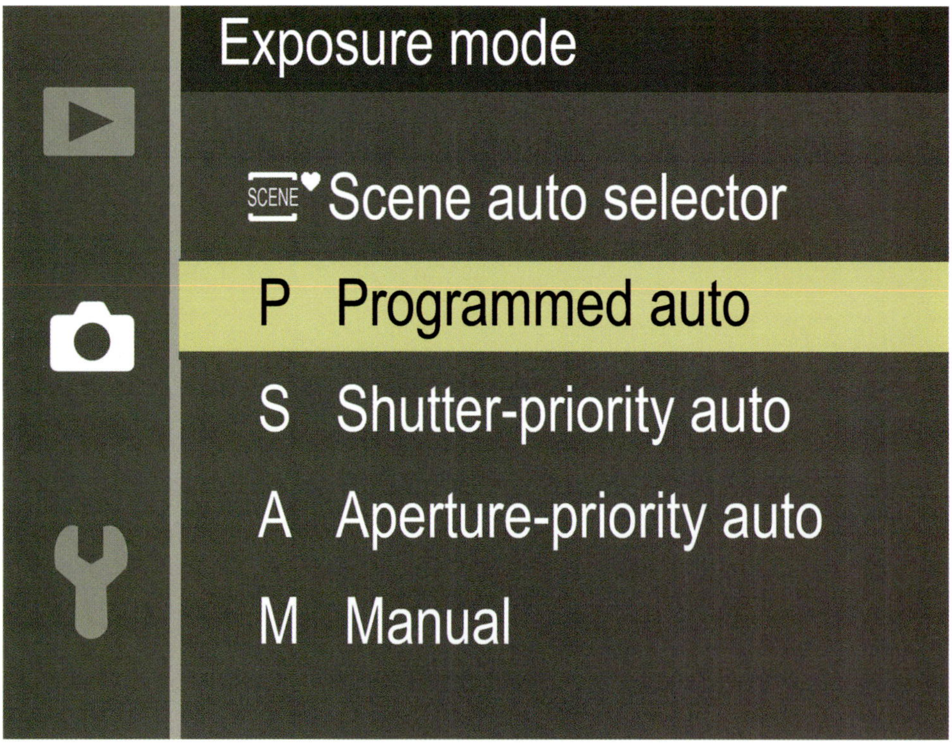

Figure 8.13
Select from Scene Auto Selector, Shutter-priority auto, Aperture-priority auto, and Manual exposure modes.

Table 8.2 Shooting Menu Defaults

Option	Default	Option	Default
Exposure Mode	Scene Auto Selector	Long Exposure NR	On
Image Quality	JPEG Normal	Fade In/Fade Out	None
Image Size	3872 × 2592	Movie Sound Options	
Continuous	Single frame	Microphone	Auto sensitivity (A)
Shutter Type	Mechanical	Wind Noise Reduction	On
Electronic (Hi)	10 fps	Interval Timer Shooting	00:01':00",001
Frame Rate	400 fps	Vibration Reduction	Active/On
Movie Settings	1080/60i	AF-Area Mode	Auto-Area
Metering	Matrix	Face Priority AF	On
White Balance	Auto	Built-in AF Assist	On
ISO Sensitivity	Auto (100-3200)	Flash Mode	Fill Flash
Picture Control	Standard	Flash Control	TTL
Color Space	sRGB	Manual	Full
Active D-Lighting	On	Flash Compensation	0.0
Other Shooting Options		Focus Mode	Varies with shooting mode
Focus Area	Center	Exposure Compensation	0.0
Flexible Program	Off	Movie Mode	HD movie
Autoexposure Lock	Off	Theme	Beauty
Focus Lock	Off	Picture Control	Not changed by reset
Self-timer	Off		

Image Quality

You can choose the image quality settings used by the V1 to store its still image files from this menu entry. You have five choices, NEF (RAW)+JPEG Fine, NEF (RAW), JPEG Fine, JPEG Normal, and JPEG Basic. The RAW/JPEG choices specify the file format used to store your image on your memory card. The JPEG options tell the V1 how much to compress the images. Here's the difference:

- **JPEG, RAW, or both.** You can elect to store only JPEG versions of the images you shoot, or you can save your photos as RAW files, which consume more than twice as much space on your memory card. Or, you can store both at once as you shoot. Many photographers elect to save *both* JPEG and a RAW, so they'll have a JPEG version that might be usable as-is, as well as the original "digital negative" RAW file in case they want to do some processing of the image later. You'll end up with two different versions of the same file: one with a .jpg extension, and one with the .nef extension that signifies a Nikon RAW file.
- **JPEG compression.** To reduce the size of your image files and allow more photos to be stored on a given memory card, the V1 uses JPEG compression to squeeze the non-RAW images down to a smaller size. This compacting reduces the image quality a little, so you're offered your choice of Fine (a 1:4 reduction), Normal (1:8 reduction), and Basic (1:16) compression. You can see an exaggerated version of the effects of JPEG compression in Figure 8.14.

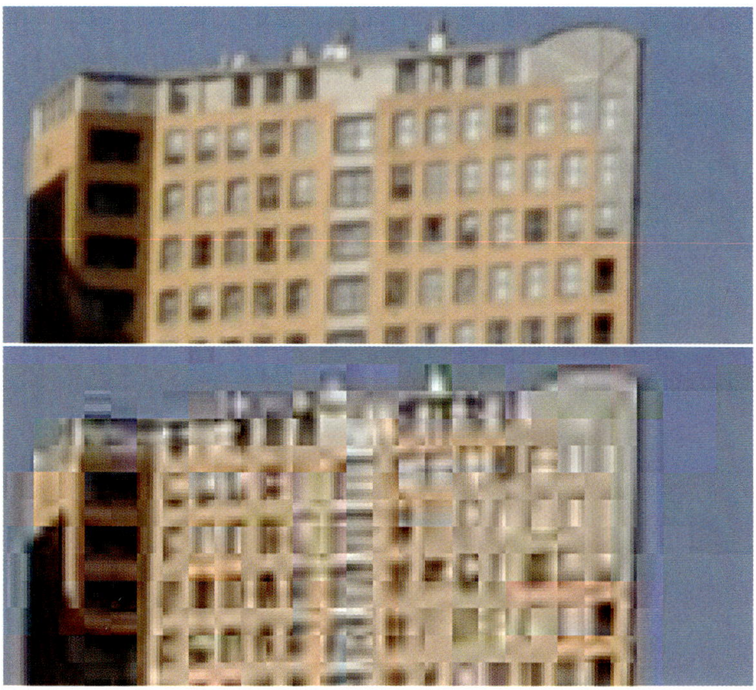

Figure 8.14
At low levels of JPEG compression the image looks sharp even when you enlarge it enough to see the actual pixels (top); when using extreme JPEG compression (bottom), an image obviously loses quality.

To choose the combination you want, access the Shooting menu, scroll to Image Quality, and select it. A screen with the five choices available will appear. Scroll to highlight the setting you want, and either press OK or push the multi selector right button to confirm your selection.

In practice, you'll probably use the JPEG Fine, RAW+JPEG Fine selections most often. Why so many choices, then? There are some limited advantages to using the JPEG Normal and JPEG Basic settings, either at full resolution (Large) or when using the Medium and Small resolution settings. Settings that are less than max allow stretching the capacity of your memory card so you can shoehorn quite a few more pictures onto a single memory card. That can come in useful when on vacation and you're running out of storage, or when you're shooting non-critical work that doesn't require 16 megapixels of resolution (such as photos taken for real estate listings, web page display, photo ID cards, or similar applications). Some photographers like to record RAW+JPEG Normal so they'll have a moderate quality JPEG file for review only and no intention of using for editing purposes, while retaining access to the original RAW file for serious editing.

For most work, using lower resolution and extra compression is false economy. You never know when you might actually need that extra bit of picture detail. Your best bet is to have enough memory cards to handle all the shooting you want to do until you have the chance to transfer your photos to your computer or a personal storage device.

However, reduced image quality can sometimes be beneficial if you're shooting sequences of photos rapidly, as the V1 is able to hold more of them in its internal memory buffer before transferring to the memory card. Still, for most sports and other applications, you'd probably rather have better, sharper pictures than longer periods of continuous shooting. Do you really need 20 or 30 shots of a pass reception in a football game, or a dozen or two slightly different versions of your local basketball star driving in for a lay-up?

JPEG vs. RAW

You'll sometimes be told that RAW files are the "unprocessed" image information your camera produces, before it's been modified. That's nonsense. RAW files are no more unprocessed than your camera film is after it's been through the chemicals to produce a negative or transparency. A lot can happen in the developer that can affect the quality of a film image—positively and negatively—and, similarly, your digital image undergoes a significant amount of processing before it is saved as a RAW file. Nikon even applies a name (EXPEED 3) to the digital image processing (DIP) chip used to perform this magic.

A RAW file is more similar to a film camera's processed negative. It contains all the information, captured in 12-bit channels per color (and stored in a 16-bit space), with no sharpening and no application of any special filters or other settings you might have specified when you took the picture. Those settings are *stored* with the RAW file so they can be applied when the image is converted to a form compatible with your favorite image editor. However, using RAW conversion software such as Adobe Camera Raw or Nikon Capture NX, you can override those settings and apply settings of your own. You can select essentially the same changes there that you might have specified in your camera's picture-taking options.

RAW exists because sometimes we want to have access to all the information captured by the camera, before the camera's internal logic has processed it and converted the image to a standard file format. Even Compressed RAW doesn't save as much space as JPEG. What it does do is preserve all the information captured by your camera after it's been converted from analog to digital form.

So, why don't we always use RAW? Some photographers avoid using Nikon's RAW NEF files on the misguided conviction that they don't want to spend time in post-processing, forgetting that, if the camera settings you would have used for JPEG are correct, each RAW image's default attributes will use those settings and the RAW image will not need much manipulation. Post-processing in such cases is *optional*, and overwhelmingly helpful when an image needs to be fine-tuned.

Although some photographers do save *only* in RAW format, it's more common (and frequently more convenient) to use RAW plus one of the JPEG options, or, if you're confident about your settings, just shoot JPEG and eschew RAW altogether. In some situations, working with a RAW file can slow you down a little. RAW images take longer to store on the memory card, and must be converted from RAW to a format your image editor can handle, whether you elect to go with the default settings in force when the picture was taken, or make minor adjustments to the settings you specified in the camera.

As a result, those who depend on speedy access to images or who shoot large numbers of photos at once may prefer JPEG over RAW. Wedding photographers, for example, might expose several thousand photos during a bridal affair and offer hundreds to clients as electronic proofs for inclusion in an album. Wedding shooters take the time to make sure that their in-camera settings are correct, minimizing the need to post-process photos after the event. Given that their JPEGs are so good, there is little need to get bogged down shooting RAW. Sports photographers also avoid RAW files.

JPEG was invented as a more compact file format that can store most of the information in a digital image, but in a much smaller size. In my case, I shoot virtually everything at RAW+JPEG Fine. Most of the time, I'm not concerned about filling up my memory cards, as I usually have a minimum of five 32GB memory cards with me. If I know I may fill up all those cards, I have a tiny battery-operated personal storage device that can copy 8GB worth of images (a typical day's shooting) in about 15 minutes. Although it's a bit slower, I often copy shots to my Apple iPad because, thanks to its 3G connectivity, I can e-mail them immediately or post them on Facebook or Flickr, no matter where I happen to be.

I also use a netbook with an external 320GB hard drive, and, most recently, a tiny MacBook Air with an 11.6-inch screen (it's not much bigger than my iPad). For short trips, I rely on my V1's capability of copying directly from one memory card to the other in the camera. As I mentioned earlier, when shooting sports I'll shift to JPEG FINE (with no RAW file) to squeeze a little extra speed out of my camera's continuous shooting mode, and to reduce the need to wade through eight-photo bursts taken in RAW format.

Image Size

The next menu command in the Shooting menu lets you select the resolution, or number of pixels captured as you shoot with your Nikon V1. Your choices range from Large (L—3872 × 2592 pixels, 10 megapixels), Medium (M—2896 × 1944 pixels, 5.6 megapixels), and Small (S—1936 × 1296 pixels, 2.5 megapixels). Your best choice is to shoot at full resolution (Large); the other options are useful if you need a lower resolution version for e-mailing or uploading to a website, such as Facebook, and would prefer not to resize the image in an image editor.

Continuous

This menu entry is available in Still Image mode when you haven't selected Electronic (Hi) shutter. Your choices include:

- **Single frame.** In Single frame mode, the V1 takes one picture each time you press the shutter release button down all the way. You can take as many photographs in this mode as you have room for on your memory card.
- **Continuous.** This shooting mode can be set to produce bursts of up to 5 frames per second while the shutter release button is held down. You can take up to 100 pictures in a row in this mode if your memory card has sufficient storage space. (See Figure 8.15.)

Shutter Type

This menu entry essentially duplicates the choices that appear when you press the F button while using Still Image mode. You can select Mechanical, Electronic, or Electronic (Hi) shutter types:

- **Mechanical shutter.** You'll want to use the mechanical shutter for everyday use. It offers shutter speeds from 30 seconds to 1/4000th second. Although the electronic shutter offers higher speeds, this range is sufficient for virtually every scene you might want to photograph. It allows synchronizing the electronic flash at speeds of up to 1/250th second, and continuous shooting at up to 5 fps. One drawback is the audible noise produced by the mechanical shutter.

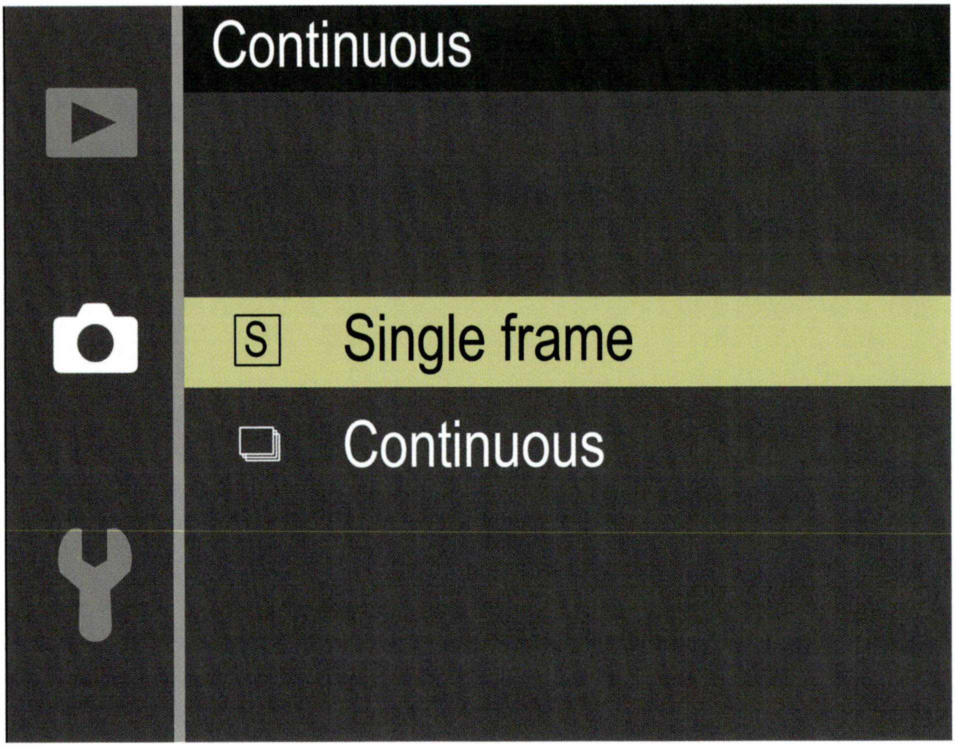

Figure 8.15
Single frame and Continuous shutter modes are available.

- **Electronic shutter.** Because of its higher speeds, the electronic shutter can capture images at faster frame rates, with continuous shooting at 10, 30, or 60 fps. Shutter speeds up to 1/16,000th second are available, but it can sync flash at only 1/60th second, which can produce "ghost" images, as described in Chapter 10. It is subject to an effect called blooming but has the advantage of silent operation.
- **Electronic (Hi) shutter.** The high-speed electronic shutter also provides speeds up to 1/16,000th second, and defaults to 10 fps when shooting continuously. You can also choose 30 fps or 60 fps. The Electronic (Hi) shutter is used for slow-motion movies at reduced resolutions, at 400 fps (640 × 240 pixels) or 1200 fps (320 × 120 pixels). You'll find more about continuous shooting in Chapter 6.

Metering

As you scroll down, Metering appears on the Shooting menu list (see Figure 8.16). Use this setting to choose Matrix, Center-weighted, or Spot metering, as described in Chapters 2 and 5. To recap:

- **Matrix metering.** The standard metering mode; the V1 attempts to intelligently classify your image and choose the best exposure based on readings from a broad span of the sensor area, matched against a database of thousands of patterns.

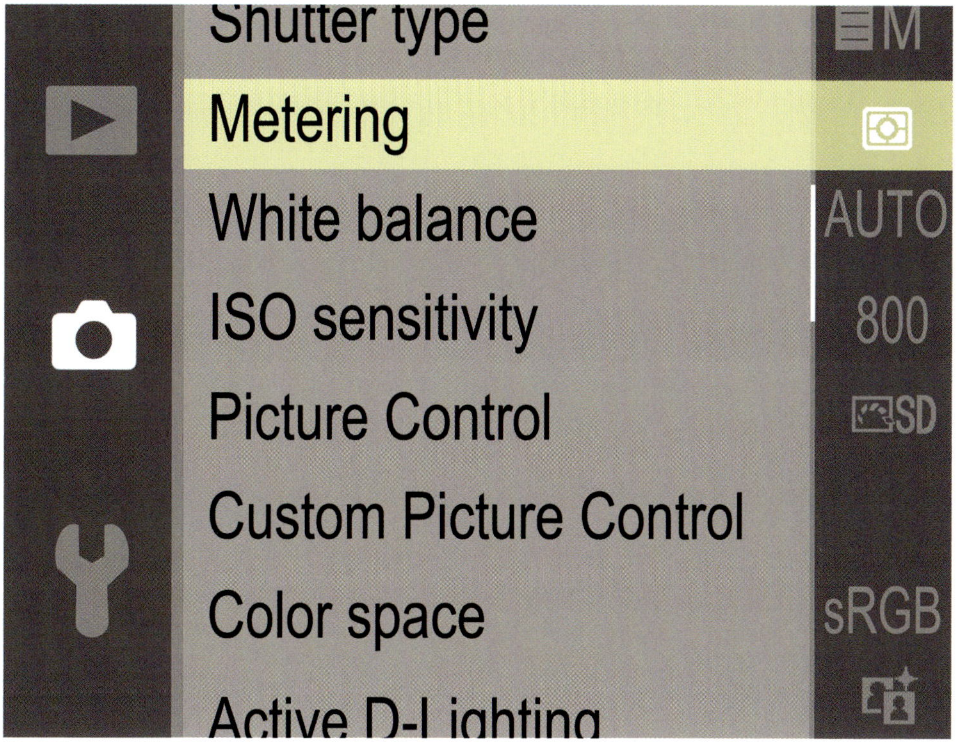

Figure 8.16 Choose the metering method.

- **Center-weighted metering.** The V1 meters the entire scene, but gives the most emphasis to the central area of the frame, measuring about 4.5mm.
- **Spot metering.** Exposure is calculated from a smaller 3mm spot, about 2 percent of the image area, using the center focus area, except when working with Face Priority AF mode, which meters from a focus area spot closest to the center of the selected face.

Frame Rate

This option is available in the Shooting menu when you select Slow Motion as the Movie mode by pressing the F button when the mode dial is set to Movie. You can then choose 400 fps or 1200 fps as the slow-motion movie rate.

As explained in Chapter 7, slow motion movies are silent clips recorded at the reduced aspect ratio of 8:3 at 400 or 1200 frames per second. Played back at 30 fps, one second of 400 fps slow-motion footage requires more than 13 seconds to play out on the screen, and one second of 1200 fps footage takes 40 seconds. At 400 fps, the frame size is just 640 × 240 pixels, and at 1200 fps, a minuscule 320 × 120 pixels. In either case, the maximum shooting length is five seconds, which plays back in 1 minute, 6 seconds from a clip shot at 400 fps to 3 minutes, 20 seconds for a clip recorded at 1200 fps.

Movie Settings

This entry appears when the mode dial is set to Movie mode, and you've selected HD Movie rather than Slow Motion from the F button options. As described in Chapter 7, you have three choices here:

- **1080/60i.** This full HD, 16:9 aspect ratio format provides an interlaced video image at 60 fields per second. (See Chapter 7 for a description of interlaced/non-interlaced.) Use for scenes without a lot of action to get the sharpest image.
- **1080/30p.** This second full-HD format saves storage space and is best for video that has action or motion sequences. You'll find more in Chapter 7 about how and why to choose between these two full HD formats.
- **720p/60 (1280 × 720 pixels).** This 16:9 format is called "standard HD" and for some types of scenes with fast movement can produce a sharper, smoother picture while using even less storage space.

White Balance

This menu entry allows you to choose one of the white balance values applied to JPEG images (and used as the initial setting for RAW images) from among Auto, Incandescent, Fluorescent illumination, Direct Sunlight, Flash, Cloudy, Shade, or a preset value taken from a measurement you make. Your white balance settings can have a significant impact on the color rendition of your images, as you can see in Figure 8.17.

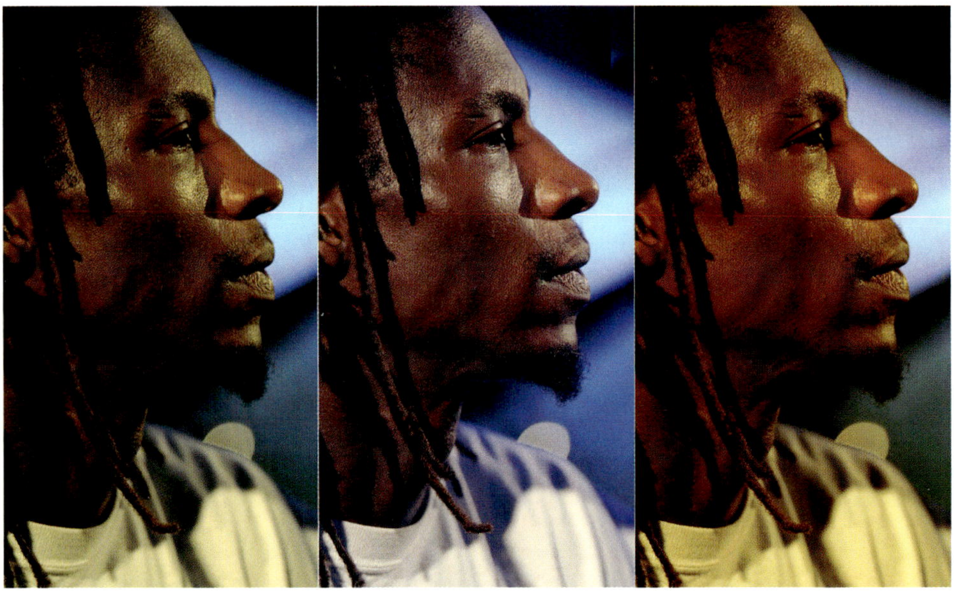

Figure 8.17 Adjusting color temperature can provide different results of the same subject at settings of 3,400K (left), 5,000K (middle), and 2,800K (right).

When you select the White Balance entry on the Shooting menu, you'll see an array of choices, ranging from Auto to Shade, plus Preset. For all settings other than Preset, you can highlight the white balance option you want, then press the multi selector right button (or press OK) to view the fine-tuning screen shown in Figure 8.18 (and which uses the incandescent setting as an example). The screen shows a grid with two axes, a blue/amber axis extending left/right, and a green/magenta axis extending up and down the grid. By default, the grid's cursor is positioned in the middle, and a readout to the right of the grid shows the cursor's coordinates on the A-B axis (yes, I know the display has the end points reversed) and G-M axis at 0,0.

You can use the multi selector's up/down and right/left buttons to move the cursor to any coordinate in the grid, thereby biasing the white balance in the direction(s) you choose. The amber-blue axis makes the image warmer or colder (but not actually yellow or blue). Similarly, the green-magenta axis preserves all the colors in the original image, but gives them a tinge biased toward green or magenta. When you've fine-tuned white balance using the Shooting menu options, an asterisk appears next to the White Balance setting in the Shooting menu and the detailed picture display in playback to remind you that this tweaking has taken place.

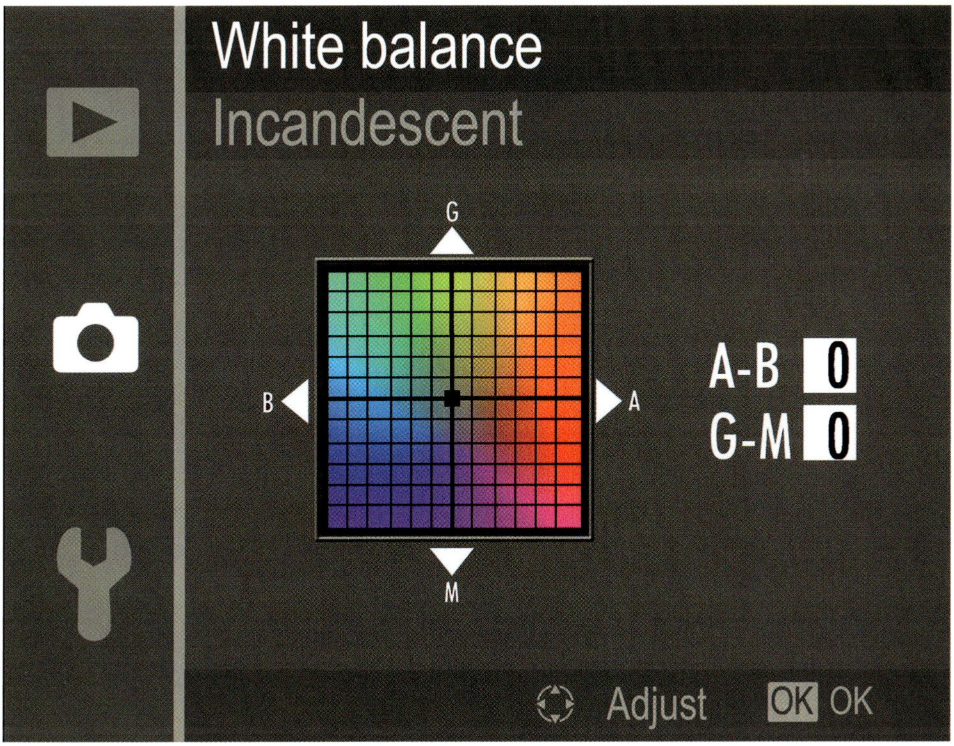

Figure 8.18 Specific white balance settings can be fine-tuned by changing their bias in the amber/blue, magenta/green directions—or along both axes simultaneously.

Using Preset Manual White Balance

If automatic white balance or one of the predefined settings available aren't suitable, you can set a custom white balance using the Preset Manual menu option. You can apply the white balance from a scene by shooting a new picture on the spot and using the resulting white balance. To perform direct measurement from your current scene using a reference object (preferably a neutral gray or white object), follow these steps:

1. **Position reference subject.** Place the neutral reference under the lighting you want to measure.
2. **Change to Preset white balance.** In the Shooting menu, select Preset Manual. A screen appears with the message *Measure a new value for preset manual white balance?* Highlight Yes and press the OK button.
3. **Capture white balance reference.** A message will appear asking you to photograph a white or gray object. After a few seconds, this message disappears, and the monitor will show the standard live view with a flashing PRE in the lower-right corner of the screen. Take the photograph.
4. **Confirm successful capture of white balance.** If the camera successfully measured white balance, a message *White Balance Captured Successfully* will appear. Otherwise, you'll see *Unable to measure present white balance. Please try again.*
5. **Use captured white balance.** You can immediately begin taking pictures using the captured white balance, until you hold down the WB button again and switch to one of the other white balance settings, such as Tungsten or Fluorescent. The next time you switch to Pre, the white balance you just captured will be used again, unless you press the right directional button to activate a new capture.

ISO Sensitivity

This menu entry allows you to specify an exact ISO setting to use, or a range of ISO settings that the V1 will select from automatically, depending on the lighting conditions. Your choices are as follows:

- **A3200 Auto (100-3200).** The V1 will choose an ISO setting from ISO 100 to ISO 3200. Under bright lighting conditions, you'll end up with a relatively low ISO setting and get your best results. However, the camera has the flexibility to go all the way up to ISO 3200 if the illumination is very dim. The drawback of this setting is that the V1 is free to choose a very high setting that will result in a lot of noise. Use this option when your expected lighting conditions will vary widely, and you're willing to accept some visual noise if it means you'll get a picture you might miss otherwise.

- **A800 Auto (100-800).** With this setting, the V1 is limited to ISO 100 to 800. Use this option when you'll be shooting both indoors and outdoors, or in a mixture of bright and dim light conditions, and you're willing to risk a little visual noise.
- **A400 Auto (100-400).** This is the best setting to use when you want to avoid noise, as the camera will limit itself to the range from ISO 100 to 400. You may miss some pictures, or need to make some adjustments on your own (such as mounting the camera on a tripod in low light levels so slower shutter speeds can be used).
- **Specific values.** If you're shooting in relatively constant light levels, you can select an appropriate ISO setting and not be concerned that the V1 will select a drastically different ISO setting without warning. You can select individual settings including ISO 100, 200, 400, 800, 1600, and 3200, plus Hi 1, which is the equivalent of ISO 6400. You can expect to see significant noise in your images at ISO 3200, and at Hi 1, the visual grain may be objectionable. Use higher settings at your own risk.

The auto settings are potentially useful, although experienced photographers tend to shy away from any feature that allows the camera to change basic settings like ISO that have been carefully selected. Fortunately, you can set some boundaries using the A3200 Auto, A800 Auto, and A400 Auto options so the V1 will use this adjustment in a fairly intelligent way.

Picture Control

Nikon's Picture Control styles allow you to choose your own sharpness, contrast, color saturation, and hue settings and apply them to your images as they are taken. There are six predefined styles offered: Standard, Neutral, Vivid, Monochrome, Portrait, and Landscape. The V1 will choose one of these to suit a particular subject if Scene Auto Selector is active. However, you can choose Picture Controls individually and *edit* the settings of any of those styles so they better suit your taste. But that's only the beginning; the V1 also offers *nine* (count 'em) user-definable Picture Control styles, which you can edit to your heart's content and deploy at the press of a few buttons. Even better, you can *copy* these styles to a memory card, save them and edit them on your computer, and reload them into your camera at any time. So, effectively, you can have a lot more than nine custom Picture Control styles available: the nine in your camera, as well as a virtually unlimited library of user-defined styles that you have stored on memory cards.

Moreover, Nikon insists that these styles have been standardized to the extent that if you re-use a style created for one camera (say, your V1) and load it into a different compatible camera, you'll get substantially the same rendition. In a way, Picture Control styles are a bit like using a particular film. Do you want the look of Kodak Ektachrome or Fujifilm Velvia? Load the appropriate style created by you—or anyone else.

Using and managing Picture Control styles is accomplished with two different menu entries. This one, Picture Control, which allows you to choose an existing style and to edit the predefined styles that Nikon provides, and Custom Picture Control, discussed in the next section, which gives you the capability of creating and editing user-defined styles.

Choosing a Picture Control Style

To choose from one of the predefined styles (Standard, Neutral, Vivid, Portrait, Landscape, or Monochrome) or select a user-defined style (numbered C-1 to C-9, available only if you've created a custom style), follow these steps:

1. **Choose Picture Control.** This option is located in the Shooting menu. The screen shown in Figure 8.19 appears. Note that Picture Controls that have been modified from their standard settings have an asterisk next to their name.
2. **Select style.** Scroll down to the Picture Control you'd like to use.
3. **Activate Picture Control.** Press OK to activate the highlighted style. (Although you can usually select a menu item by pressing the multi selector right button; in this case, that button activates editing instead.)
4. **Exit menu.** Press the MENU button or tap the shutter release to exit the menu system.

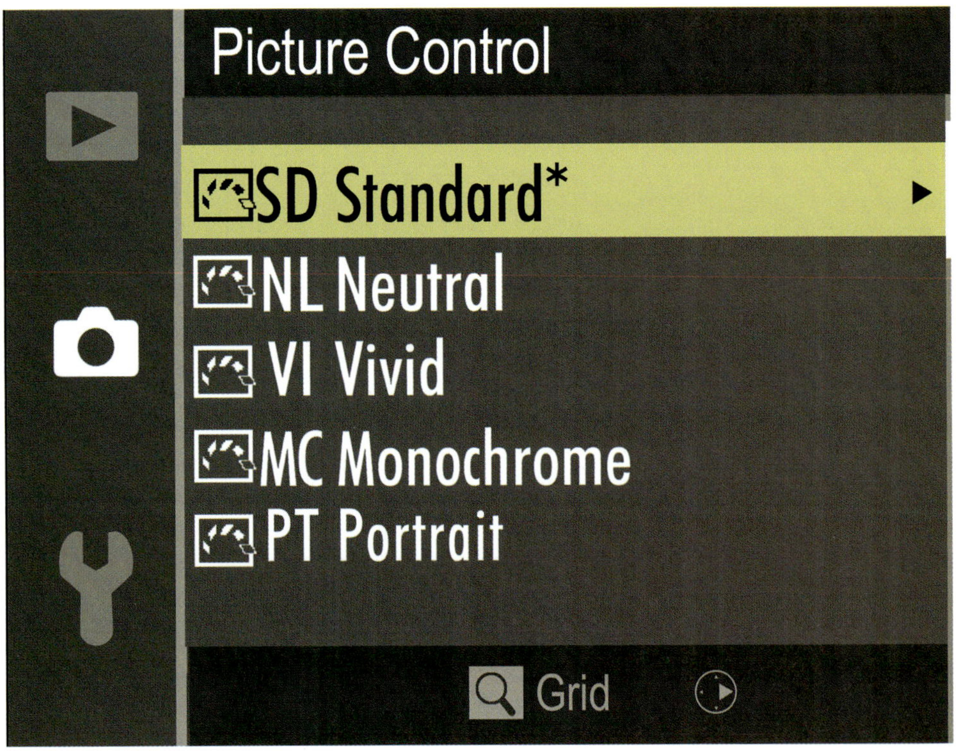

Figure 8.19
You can choose from the predefined Picture Controls, or select a user-defined style.

Editing a Picture Control Style

You can change the parameters of any of Nikon's predefined Picture Controls, or any of the nine user-defined styles you create. You are given the choice of using the quick adjust/fine-tune facility to modify a Picture Control with a few sliders, or to view the relationship of your Picture Controls on a grid. To make quick adjustments to any Picture Control except the Monochrome style, follow these steps:

1. **Access menu.** Choose Picture Control from the Shooting menu.
2. **Select style.** Scroll down to the Picture Control you'd like to edit.
3. **Access adjustment screen.** Press the multi selector right button to produce the adjustment screen shown in Figure 8.20.
4. **Make fast changes.** Use the Quick Adjust slider to exaggerate the attributes of any of the Picture Controls except Neutral and Monochrome.
5. **Change other attributes.** Scroll down to the Sharpening, Contrast, Brightness, Saturation, and Hue sliders with the multi selector up/down buttons, then use the left/right buttons to decrease or increase the effects. A line will appear under the original setting in the slider whenever you've made a change from the defaults. **Note:** You can't adjust contrast and brightness when Active D-Lighting (discussed later in this chapter) is active. Turn it off to make those Picture Control adjustments.

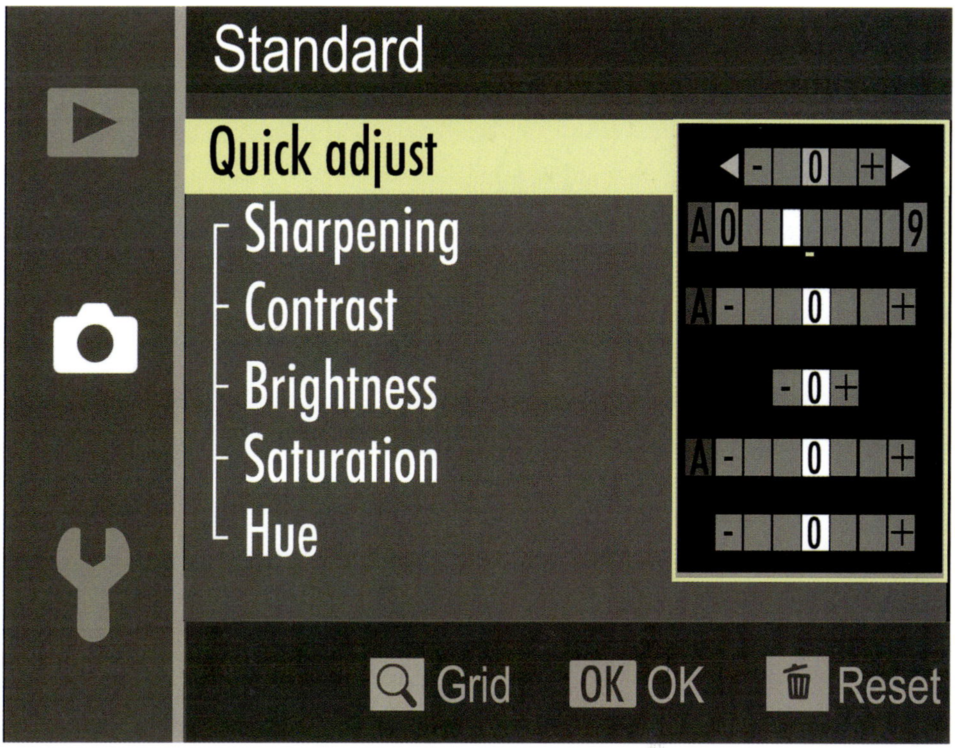

Figure 8.20 Sliders can be used to make quick adjustments to your Picture Control styles.

6. **Or use auto adjustments.** Instead of making changes with the slider's scale, you can move the cursor to the far left and choose A (for auto) instead when working with the Sharpening, Contrast, and Saturation sliders. The V1 will adjust these parameters automatically, depending on the type of scene it detects.
7. **To Reset Values.** Press the Trash button to reset the values to their defaults and confirm by choosing Yes in the screen that appears.
8. **View adjustment grid.** Press the zoom bar up to view an adjustment grid (discussed next).
9. **Confirm changes.** Press OK when you're finished making adjustments.

The changes Picture Controls make to your images are more subtle than you realize, because the values that are applied among the various Picture Controls aren't absolute. Adjustments you make to, say, the Standard or Vivid styles are relative to the base values of those styles themselves. For example, the Standard style is inherently less saturated than the Vivid style, so if you move the Saturation slider two notches to the right, you'll end up with a modified Standard style that is *still* less saturated than the Vivid style's default. You'll want to learn exactly what happens to your images when you adjust each individual Picture Control, and, moreover, use the right Picture Control as your base or "parent" style when creating Picture Controls of your own. If you wanted a very, very saturated Picture Control, you'd start with the Vivid style, then adjust that and save it as Super Vivid (or something along those lines). Figure 8.21 shows pairs of images that compare four of the most frequently adjusted attributes.

Editing the Monochrome style is similar to modifying the other styles, except that the parameters differ slightly. Sharpening, Contrast, and Brightness are available, but, instead of Saturation and Hue, you can choose a filter effect (Yellow, Orange, Red, Green, or none) and a toning effect (black-and-white, plus seven levels of Sepia, Cyanotype, Red, Yellow, Green, Blue Green, Blue, Purple Blue, and Red Purple). (Keep in mind that once you've taken a JPEG photo using a Monochrome style, you can't convert the image back to full color.)

FILTERS VS. TONING

Although some of the color choices seem to overlap, you'll get very different looks when choosing between Filter Effects and Toning. Filter Effects add no color to the monochrome image. Instead, they reproduce the look of black-and-white film that has been shot through a color filter. That is, Yellow will make the sky darker and the clouds will stand out more, while Orange makes the sky even darker and sunsets more full of detail. The Red filter produces the darkest sky of all and darkens green objects, such as leaves. Human skin may appear lighter than normal. The Green filter has the opposite effect on leaves, making them appear lighter in tone. Figure 8.22 shows the same scene shot with no filter, then Yellow, Green, and Red filters.

The Sepia, Blue, Green, and other toning effects, on the other hand, all add a color cast to your monochrome image. Use these when you want an old-time look or a special effect, without bothering to recolor your shots in an image editor. Several toning effects are shown in Figure 8.23.

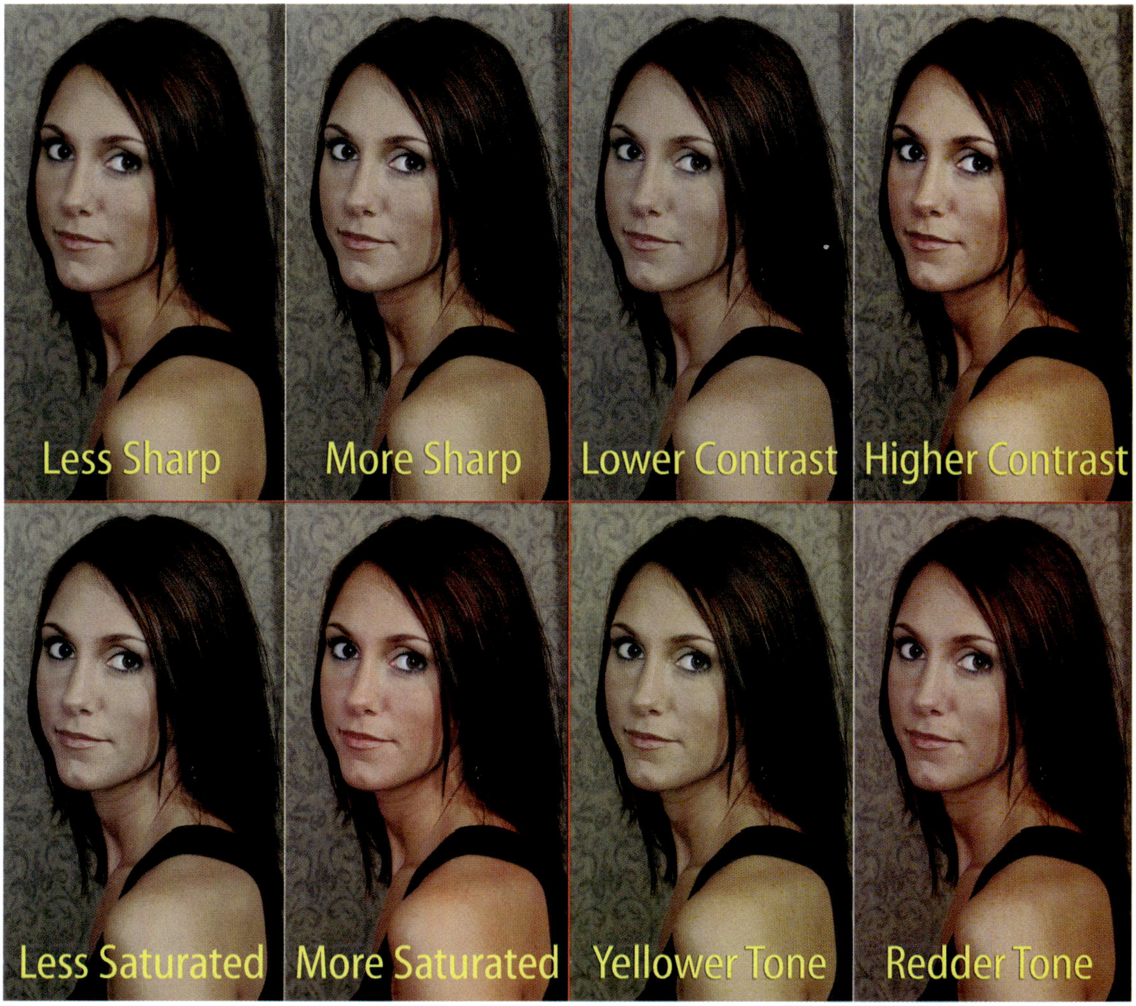

Figure 8.21 Picture Controls allow you to adjust attributes like sharpness (upper-left pair), contrast (upper-right pair), saturation (lower-left pair), and hue (lower-right pair).

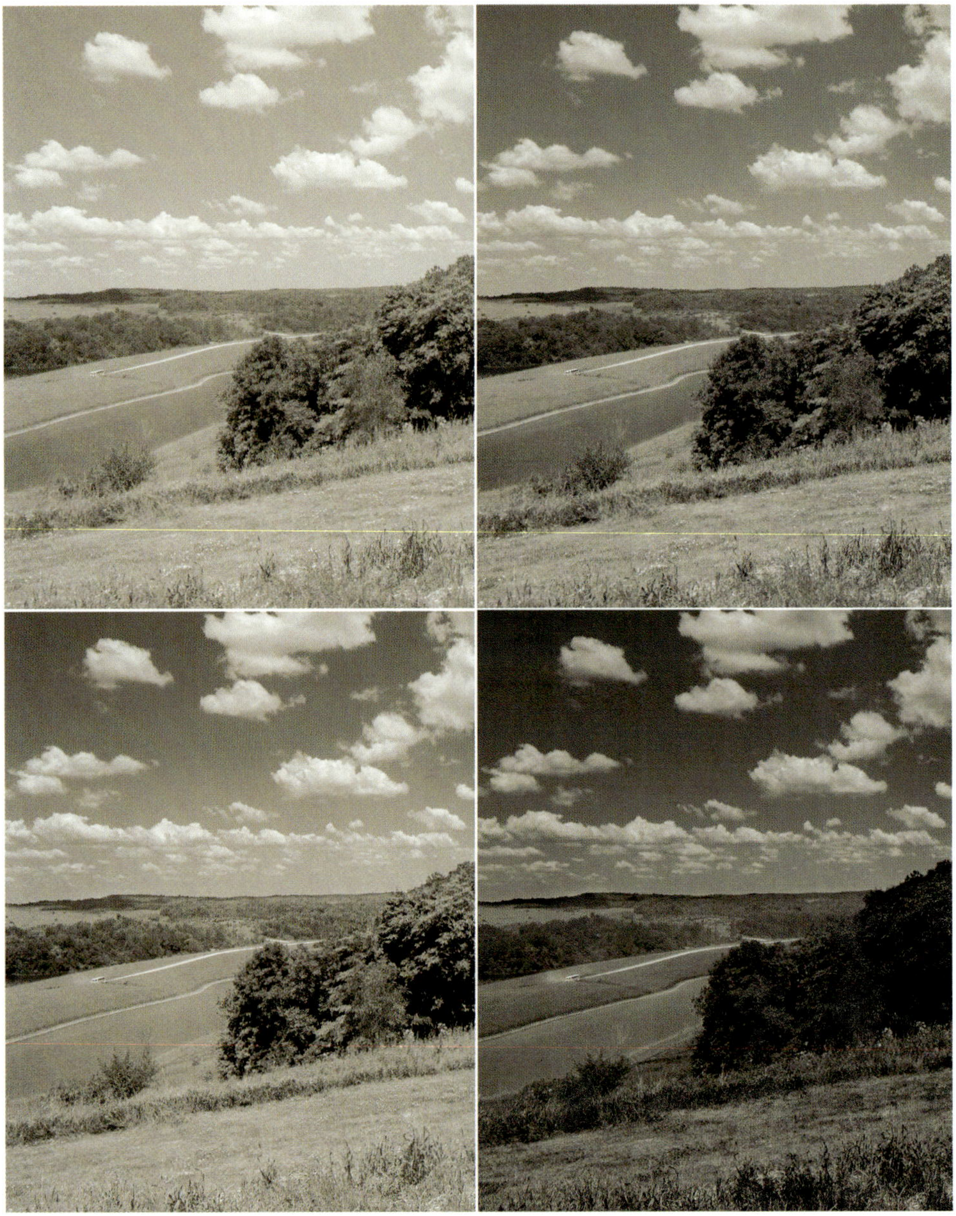

Figure 8.22
No filter (upper left); yellow filter (upper right); green filter (lower left); and red filter (lower right).

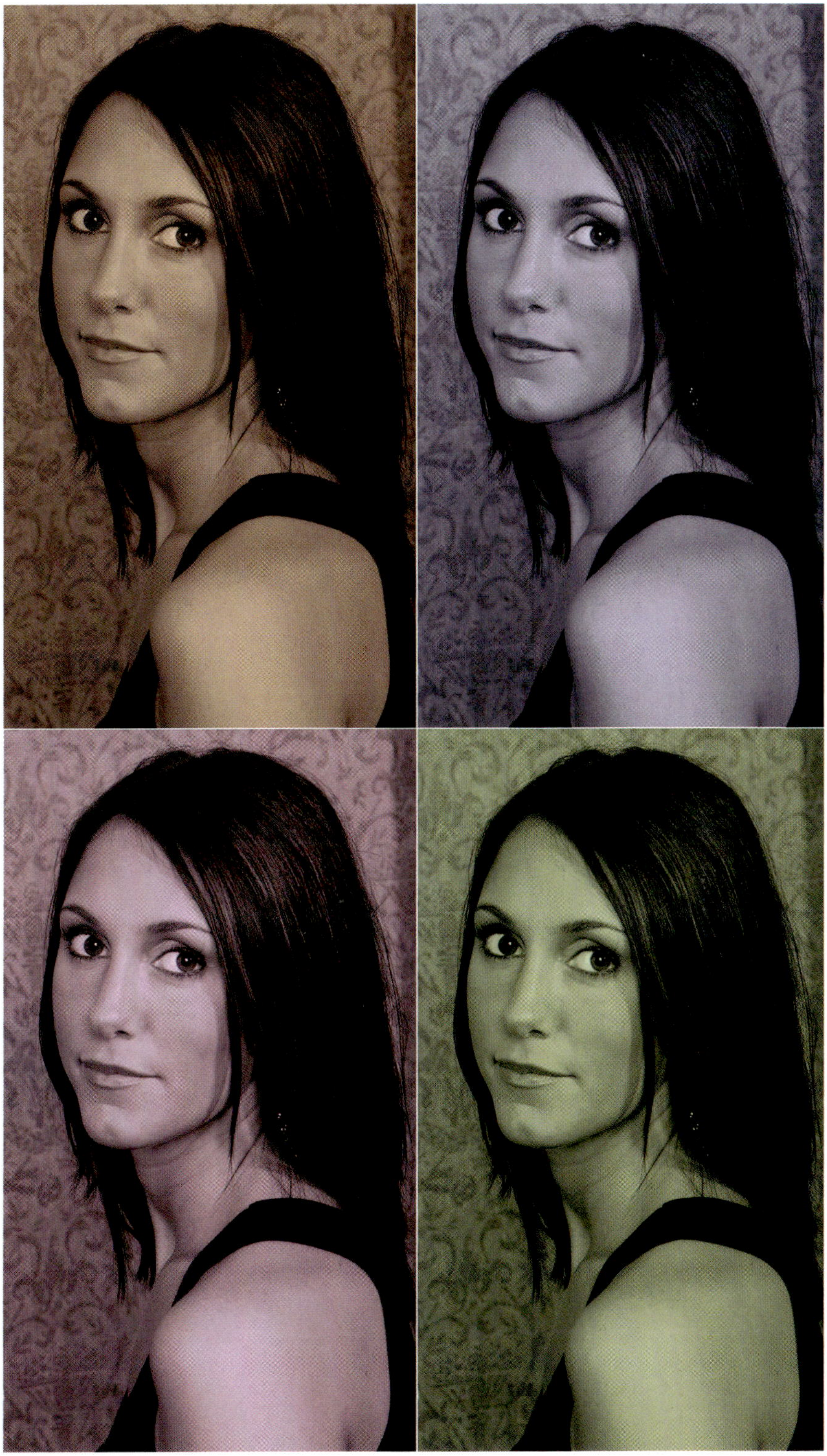

Figure 8.23
Toning effects: Sepia (upper left); Purple Blue (upper right); Red Purple (lower left); and Green (lower right).

When you press the zoom bar up, a grid display, like the one shown in Figure 8.24, appears, showing the relative contrast and saturation of each of the predefined Picture Controls. If you've created your own custom Picture Controls, they will appear on this grid, too, represented by the numbers 1-9. Because the values for autocontrast and autosaturation may vary, the icons for any Picture Control that uses the Auto feature will be shown on the grid in green, with lines extending up and down from the icon to tip you off that the position within the coordinates may vary from the one shown.

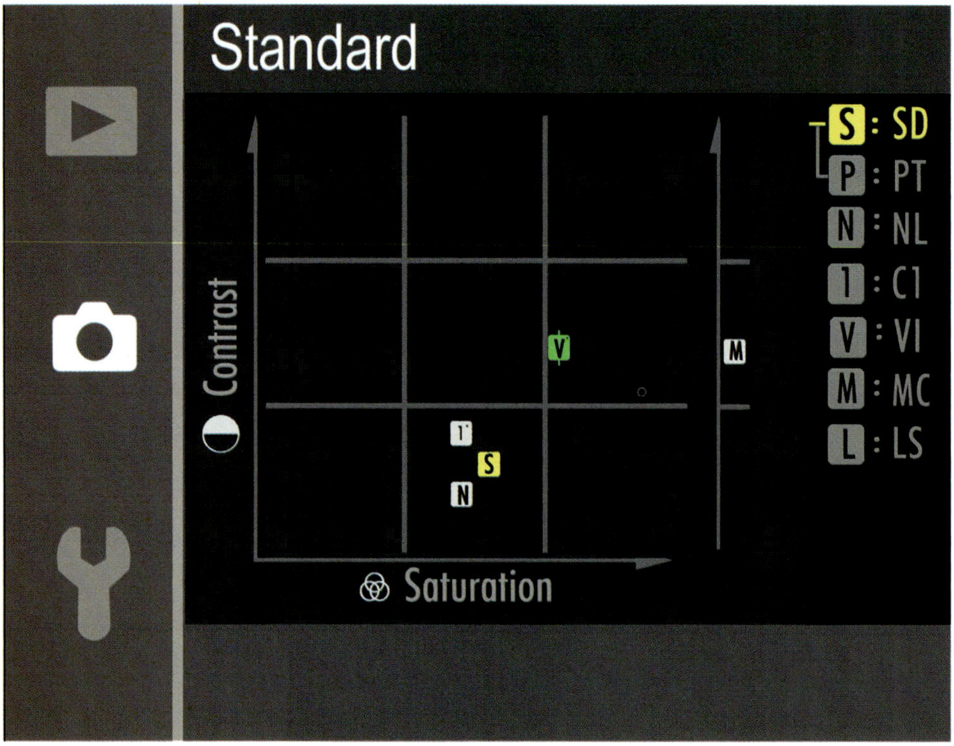

Figure 8.24
This grid shows the relationship of the Picture Controls being used.

Custom Picture Control

The Custom Picture Control menu entry can be used to create new styles, edit existing styles, rename or delete them, and store/retrieve them from the memory card. Here are the basic functions of this menu item, which can be found on the Shooting menu directly below the Picture Control entry:

- **Make a copy.** Choose Edit/Save, select from the list of available Picture Controls, and press OK to store that style in one of the user-defined slots C-1 to C-9.
- **Edit the copy.** In Save Edit, highlight the copy you saved and press the right directional button, and edit the parameters as described in the last section.

- **Save edited copy.** Press OK when finished editing, and then save the modified style in one of the user-defined slots C-1 to C-9.
- **Remove a style.** Select Delete, choose from the list of user-defined Picture Controls (you can't remove one of the default styles), press the multi selector right button, then highlight Yes in the screen that follows, and press OK to remove that Picture Control.
- **Store/retrieve style on card.** Choose Load from/Save to Card, then select Copy to Camera to locate a Picture Control on your Secure Digital card and copy it to the V1; Delete from Card to select a Picture Control on your memory card and remove it; or Copy to Card to duplicate a style currently in your camera onto the Secure Digital card. This last option allows you to create and save Picture Controls in excess of the nine that can be loaded into the camera at one time. Once you've copied a style to your memory card, you can modify the version in the camera, and, in effect, create a whole new Picture Control.

Color Space

The Nikon V1's Color Space option gives you two different color spaces (also called *color gamuts*), named Adobe RGB (because it was developed by Adobe Systems in 1998), and sRGB (supposedly because it is the *standard* RGB color space). These two color gamuts define a specific set of colors that can be applied to the images your V1 captures.

You're probably surprised that the Nikon V1 doesn't automatically capture *all* the colors we see. Unfortunately, that's impossible because of the limitations of the sensor and the filters used to capture the fundamental red, green, and blue colors, as well as that of the phosphors used to display those colors on your camera and computer monitors. Nor is it possible to *print* every color our eyes detect, because the inks or pigments used don't absorb and reflect colors perfectly.

On the other hand, the V1 does capture quite a few more colors than we need. With the V1's 12-bit capture, a RAW image contains a possible 68 *billion* different hues, which are condensed down to a mere 16.8 million possible colors when converted to a 24-bit (eight bits per channel) image. While 16.8 million colors may seem like a lot, it's a small subset of 68 billion captured, and an even smaller subset of all the possible colors we can see.

The set of colors, or gamut, that can be reproduced or captured by a given device (scanner, digital camera, monitor, printer, or some other piece of equipment) is represented as a color space that exists within the larger full range of colors. That full range is represented by the odd-shaped splotch of color shown in Figure 8.25, as defined by scientists at an international organization back in 1931. The colors possible with Adobe

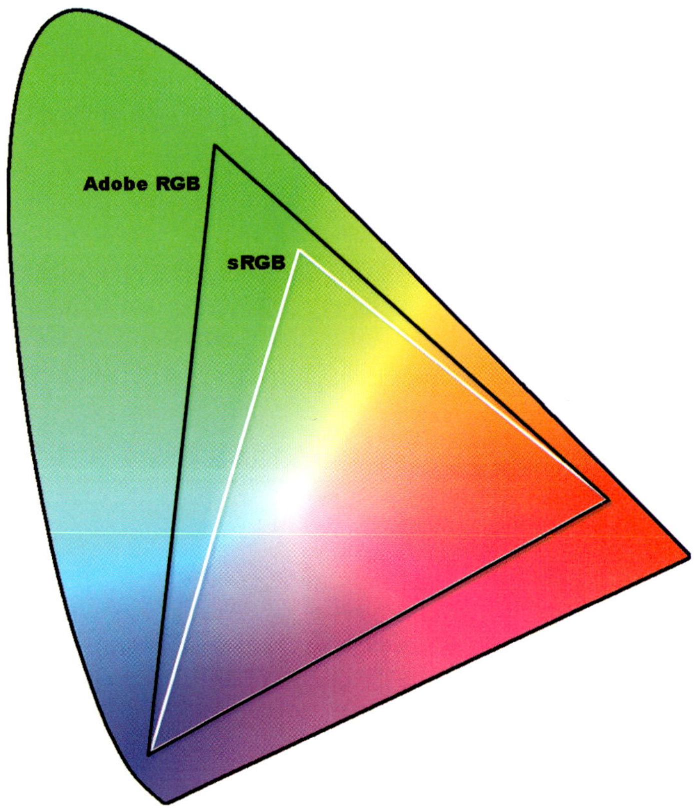

Figure 8.25
The outer figure shows all the colors we can see; the two inner outlines show the boundaries of Adobe RGB (black triangle) and sRGB (white triangle).

RGB are represented by the larger, black triangle in the figure, while the sRGB gamut is represented by the smaller white triangle.

Regardless of which triangle—or color space—is used by the V1, you end up with some combination of 16.8 million different colors that can be used in your photograph. (No one image will contain all 16.8 million! If each and every pixel in a V1's 16-megapixel image were a different color—which is extremely unlikely—you'd need only 16 million different colors.) But, as you can see from the figure, the colors available will be *different.*

Adobe RGB is an expanded color space useful for commercial and professional printing, and it can reproduce a wider range of colors. It can also come in useful if an image is going to be extensively retouched, especially within an advanced image editor, like Adobe Photoshop, which has sophisticated color management capabilities that can be tailored to specific color spaces. As an advanced user, you don't need to automatically "upgrade" your V1 to Adobe RGB, because images tend to look less saturated on your monitor and, it is likely, significantly different from what you will get if you output the photo to your personal inkjet. (You can *profile* your monitor for the Adobe RGB color space to improve your on-screen rendition, as described below.)

While both Adobe RGB and sRGB can reproduce the exact same 16.8 million absolute colors, Adobe RGB spreads those colors over a larger portion of the visible spectrum, as you can see in the figure. Think of a box of crayons (the jumbo 16.8 million crayon variety). Some of the basic crayons from the original sRGB set have been removed and replaced with new hues not contained in the original box. Your "new" box contains colors that can't be reproduced by your computer monitor, but which work just fine with a commercial printing press. For example, Adobe RGB has more "crayons" available in the cyan-green portion of the box, compared to sRGB, which is unlikely to be an advantage unless your image's final destination are the cyan, magenta, yellow, and black inks of a printing press.

The other color space, sRGB, is recommended for images that will be output locally on the user's own printer, as this color space matches that of the typical inkjet printer fairly closely. You might prefer sRGB, which is the default for the Nikon V1 and most other cameras, as it is well suited for the range of colors that can be displayed on a computer screen and viewed over the Internet. If you plan to take your image file to a retailer's kiosk for printing, sRGB is your best choice, because those automated output devices are calibrated for the sRGB color space that consumers use.

BEST OF BOTH WORLDS

If you plan to use RAW+JPEG for most of your photos, go ahead and set sRGB as your color space. You'll end up with JPEGs suitable for output on your own printer, but you can still extract an Adobe RGB version from the RAW file at any time. It's like shooting two different color spaces at once—sRGB and Adobe RGB—and getting the best of both worlds.

Of course, choosing the right color space doesn't solve the problems that result from having each device in the image chain manipulating or producing a slightly different set of colors. To that end, you'll need to investigate the wonderful world of *color management*, which uses hardware and software tools to match or *calibrate* all your devices, as closely as possible, so that what you see more closely resembles what you capture, what you see on your computer display, and what ends up on a printed hardcopy. Entire books have been devoted to color management, and most of what you need to know doesn't directly involve your Nikon V1, so I won't detail the nuts and bolts here.

To manage your color, you'll need, at the bare minimum, some sort of calibration system for your computer display, so that your monitor can be adjusted to show a standardized set of colors that is repeatable over time. (What you see on the screen can vary as the monitor ages, or even when the room light changes.) I use Pantone's Huey monitor color correction system for my computer's main 26-inch wide-screen LCD display, as well as for my matching 26-inch wide-screen secondary display that flanks it. The

Huey checks room light levels every five minutes, and reminds me to recalibrate every week or two, using the small sensor device, which attaches temporarily to the front of screen with tiny suction cups, and interprets test patches that the Huey software displays during calibration. The rest of the time, the Huey sensor sits in the stand, measuring the room illumination and adjusting my monitors for higher or lower ambient light levels.

The Huey (www.pantone.com) is an inexpensive (under $100) system that does a good job of calibrating a single monitor. You can upgrade it, as I did, for use with multiple monitors using a $40 software download. If you're serious about accurate color and making prints, you'll want a more advanced system (up to $500) like the various Spyder products from Datacolor (www.datacolor.com), or Colormunki from X-Rite (www.colormunki.com).

Active D-Lighting

Scroll down the Shooting menu to Active D-Lighting, shown in Figure 8.26. It's a feature that improves the rendition of detail in highlights and shadows when you're photographing high contrast scenes. You'll find the "non-active" D-Lighting feature discussed under the Playback menu earlier in this chapter. Active D-Lighting applies its tonal improvements *while you are actually taking the photo.* That's good news and bad news. It means that if you're taking photos in a contrasty environment, Active D-Lighting can automatically improve the apparent dynamic range of your image as you shoot, without additional effort on your part. However, you'll need to disable the feature once you leave the high contrast lighting behind, and the process does take some time. You wouldn't want to use Active D-Lighting for continuous shooting of sports subjects, for example. There are many situations in which the selective application of D-Lighting using the Playback menu is a better choice. Perhaps you forgot to apply Active D-Lighting and want to use it as a post-shot effect; or, you might want to use the Playback menu so you'll have two versions, one with and one without D-Lighting.

You can turn the Active D-Lighting feature on or off. Note that when this feature is activated, brightness and contrast Picture Control settings cannot be changed. Figure 8.27 shows an example of Active D-Lighting applied. For best results, use your V1's Matrix metering mode, so the Active D-Lighting feature can work with a full range of exposure information from multiple points in the image. Active D-Lighting works its magic by subtly *underexposing* your image so that details in the highlights (which would normally be overexposed and become featureless white pixels) are not lost. At the same time, it adjusts the values of pixels located in midtone and shadow areas so they don't become too dark because of the underexposure. Highlight tones will be preserved, while shadows will eventually be allowed to go dark more readily. Bright beach or snow scenes, especially those with few shadows (think high noon, when the shadows are smaller) can benefit from using Active D-Lighting.

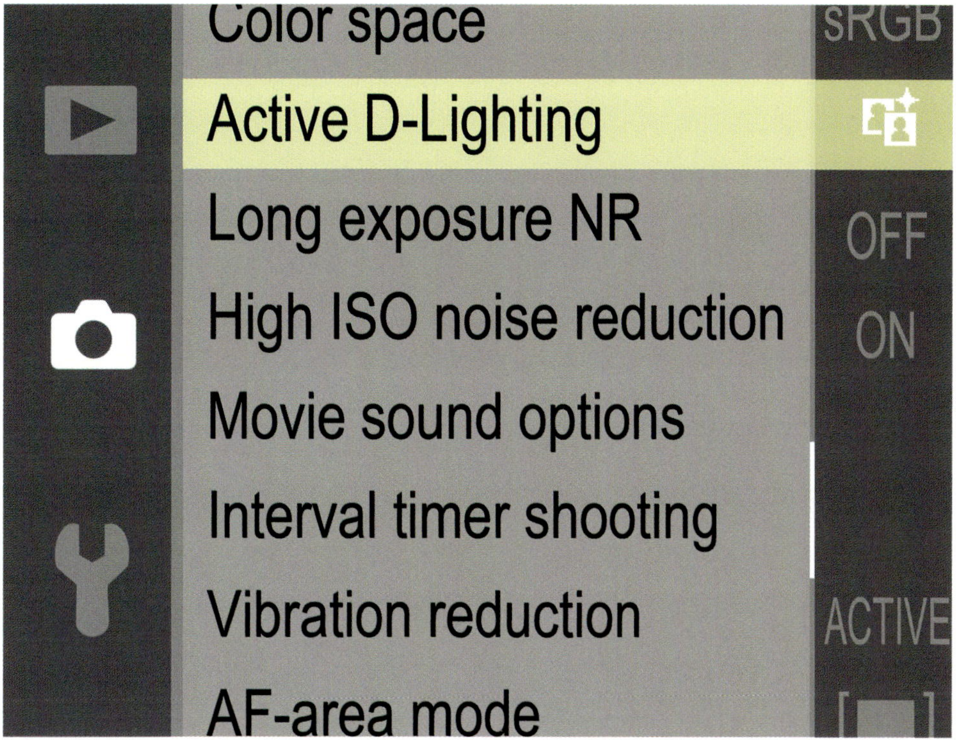

Figure 8.26 The next screen of the Shooting menu.

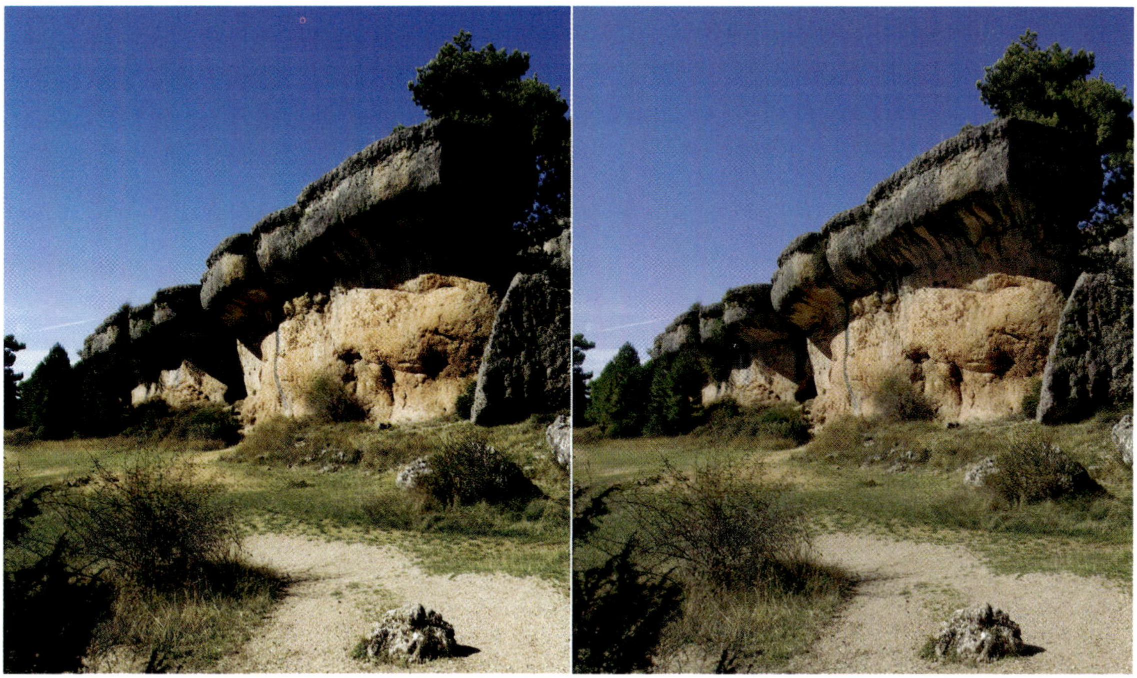

Figure 8.27 No D-Lighting (left); Active D-Lighting (right).

It's important to *always* keep in mind that Active D-Lighting not only adjusts automatically the contrast of your image (that's why you can't adjust the brightness/contrast of a Picture Control when Active D-Lighting is turned on), it modifies exposure for both existing light and flash as well, as I've noted. Exposure for both is reduced from about 1/3 stop to as much as 1 full stop less.

Long Exp. NR

Visual noise is that awful graininess caused by long exposures and high ISO settings, and which shows up as multicolored specks in images. This setting helps you manage the kind of noise caused by lengthy exposure times. In some ways, noise is like the excessive grain found in some high-speed photographic films. However, while photographic grain is sometimes used as a special effect, it's rarely desirable in a digital photograph. There are easier ways to add texture to your photos.

Some noise is created when you're using shutter speeds longer than eight seconds to create a longer exposure. Extended exposure times allow more photons to reach the sensor, but increase the likelihood that some photosites will react randomly even though not struck by a particle of light. Moreover, as the sensor remains switched on for the longer exposure, it heats, and this heat can be mistakenly recorded as if it were a barrage of photons. This menu setting can be used to activate the V1's long exposure noise-canceling operation performed by the EXPEED 3 digital signal processor.

- **Off.** This default setting disables long exposure noise reduction. Use it when you want the maximum amount of detail present in your photograph, even though higher noise levels will result. This setting also eliminates the extra time needed to take a picture caused by the noise reduction process. If you plan to use only lower ISO settings (thereby reducing the noise caused by ISO amplification), the noise levels produced by longer exposures may be acceptable. For example, you might be shooting a waterfall at ISO 100 with the camera mounted on a tripod, using a neutral-density filter and a long exposure to cause the water to blur. (Try exposures of 2 to 16 seconds, depending on the intensity of the light and how much blur you want.) To maximize detail in the non-moving portions of your photos for the exposures that are eight seconds or longer, you can switch off long exposure noise reduction.
- **On.** When exposures are one second or longer, the Nikon V1 takes a second, blank exposure to compare that to the first image. (While the second image is taken, the warning Job nr appears on the monochrome LCD panel and in the viewfinder.) Noise (pixels that are bright in a frame that *should* be completely black) in the "dark frame" image is subtracted from your original picture, and only the noise-corrected image is saved to your memory card. Because the noise-reduction process effectively doubles the time required to take a picture, you won't want to use this setting when you're rushed. Some noise can be removed later on, using tools like the noise reduction features built into Bibble Pro or Nikon Capture NX.

High ISO Noise Reduction

Noise can also be caused by higher ISO sensitivity settings, and the Nikon V1 offers settings up to ISO 3200 (and thence up to the equivalent of ISO 6400 with the Hi 1 setting). Even so, high ISO noise reduction, which can be set with this menu option, may be a good option in many cases. You can choose Off when you want to preserve detail at the cost of some noise graininess. Or you can select On which is applied when ISO sensitivity has been set to ISO 800 or higher.

The effects of high ISO noise are something like listening to a CD in your car, and then rolling down all the windows. You're adding sonic noise to the audio signal, and while increasing the CD player's volume may help a bit, you're still contending with an unfavorable signal to noise ratio that probably mutes tones (especially higher treble notes) that you really want to hear.

The same thing happens when the analog image signal is amplified: You're increasing the image information in the signal, but boosting the background fuzziness at the same time. Tune in a very faint or distant AM radio station on your car stereo. Then turn up the volume. After a certain point, turning up the volume further no longer helps you hear better. There's a similar point of diminishing returns for digital sensor ISO increases and signal amplification as well.

As the captured information is amplified to produce higher ISO sensitivities, some random noise in the signal is amplified along with the photon information. Increasing the ISO setting of your camera raises the threshold of sensitivity so that fewer and fewer photons are needed to register as an exposed pixel. Yet, that also increases the chances of one of those phantom photons being counted among the real-life light particles, too.

Fortunately, the Nikon V1's CMOS sensor and its EXPEED 3 digital processing chip are optimized to produce the low noise levels, so ratings as high as ISO 1600 to ISO 3200 can be used routinely (although there will be some noise, of course), and even ISO 3200 can generate good results. Some kinds of subjects may not require this kind of noise cancellation, particularly with images that have a texture of their own that tends to hide or mask the noise.

Fade In/Fade Out

This movie-only setting has three options: W (white) and B Fade (black), as well as Off. When you choose W or B, each scene will fade to white or black, respectively when you stop capturing. When you resume, the image will start in the faded position (either white or black) and fade into the full scene. Choose Off and no fade in/fade out will take place.

Movie Sound Options

This entry has two adjustments to make: Microphone and Wind Noise Reduction.

- **Microphone.** This setting controls both the V1's built-in microphones as well as the optional Nikon ME-1 mic, or a third-party microphone you have plugged into the mic jack on the side of the camera. Choose to turn the microphone Off if you want to shoot silently (particularly if you are going to add music, voice-over, or other sound later in your movie-editing software). Or, select a sensitivity setting from Automatic, High, Medium, or Low. This is essentially a volume control for your internal microphones, or any external mic you attach.
- **Wind Noise Reduction.** This feature can be switched On or Off, to reduce the effects of air rushing past your microphone. You should also disable the feature on the ME-1 stereo microphone by setting the switch on the back of the ME-1 mic to the Flat position.

Interval Timer Shooting

Nikon V1's built-in time-lapse photography feature allows you to take pictures for up to 999 intervals in bursts of as many as nine shots, with a delay of up to 23 hours and 59 minutes between shots/bursts, and an initial start-up time of as long as 23 hours and 59 minutes from the time you activate the feature. That means that if you want to photograph a rosebud opening and would like to photograph the flower once every two minutes over the next 16 hours, you can do that easily. If you like, you can delay the first photo taken by a couple hours so you don't have to stand there by the V1 waiting for the right moment.

Or, you might want to photograph a particular scene every hour for 24 hours to capture, say, a landscape from sunrise to sunset to the following day's sunrise again. The V1 can do that, too. The Interval Timer Shooting screen is shown in Figure 8.28. The screen shows the current settings, and has an option to Start the shooting. At the very bottom is the setting Interval/Number of Shots. Highlight that and press the right directional button to move to a second screen where you can set the parameters for your time-lapse shooting.

To set up interval timer shooting, just follow these steps.

Before you start:

1. **Set your clock.** The V1 uses its internal World Time clock to activate, so make sure the time has been set accurately in the Setup menu before you begin.
2. **Secure camera.** Mount the camera on a tripod or other secure support.

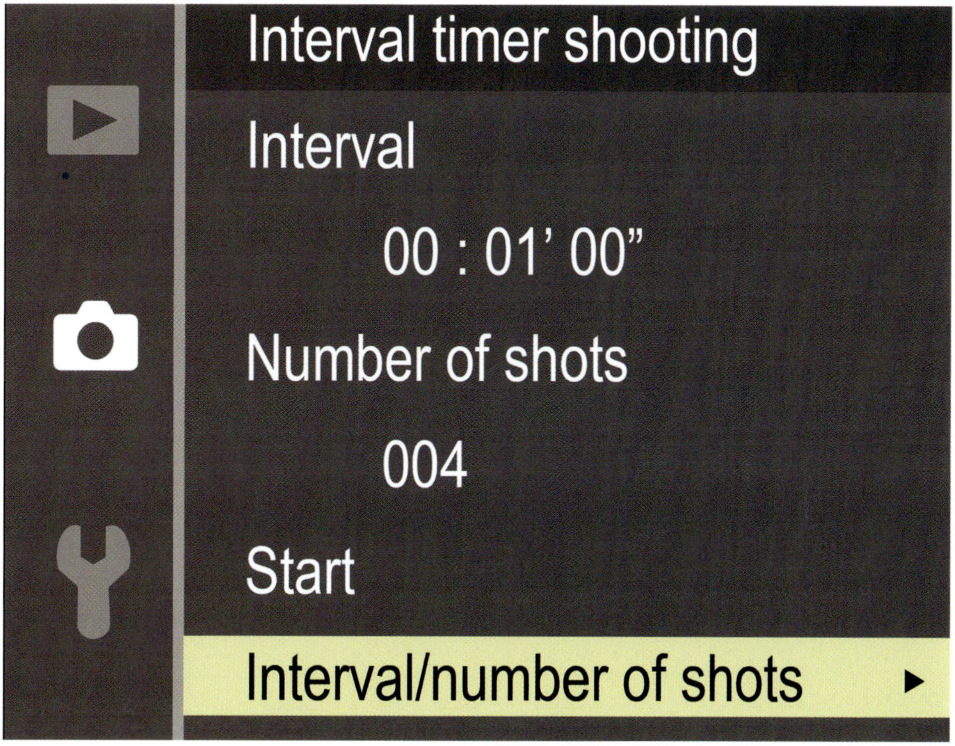

Figure 8.28 The Interval Timer Shooting main screen.

3. **Fully charge the battery.** Although the camera more or less goes to sleep between intervals, some power is drawn, and long sequences with bursts of shots can drain power even when you're not using the interval timer feature.
4. **Protect your camera.** Make sure the camera is shielded from the elements, accidents, and theft.

When you're ready to go, set up the V1 for interval shooting:

1. **Select timer.** Choose Interval Timer Shooting from the Shooting menu; advance to the Interval/Number of Shots screen.
2. **Set the interval between exposures.** You can use the left/right buttons to move among hours, minutes, and seconds, and use the up/down buttons to choose an interval from one second to 24 hours. Press the right button when finished to move down to the number of intervals/shots per interval sub-screen.

Tip

The interval cannot be shorter than the shutter speed; for example, you cannot set one second as the interval if the images will be taken at two seconds or longer.

3. **Set number of total shots.** Highlight the number of shots and select up to 999 intervals.
4. **Confirm.** Press OK to confirm your settings.
5. **Start.** When all the parameters have been entered, you'll be returned to the main Interval Timer Shooting screen. Highlight the Start option and press OK.

PAUSE OR CANCEL INTERVAL SHOOTING

Press the MENU or Playback buttons between intervals (but not when images are still being recorded to the memory card), and the interval shooting will be automatically canceled. A message appears on the LCD to confirm. Shooting will also stop if you turn off the camera, rotate the mode dial to a new setting, the memory card becomes full, or the battery dies.

Vibration Reduction

Certain lenses have built-in anti-shake qualities called *vibration reduction*, which counter the blurring effects of camera movement by shifting lens elements simultaneously to compensate. VR is a "smart" feature, in that it recognizes when the camera is being panned (moved continuously in one direction, generally to follow the motion of a subject), and adjusts *only* for the motion that is not part of the panning action. For example, if you're panning horizontally to follow a running athlete, VR will reduce the effects of virtual shake, while ignoring the side-to-side motion.

VR lenses may offer two types of vibration reduction, *normal* and *active,* and this menu item allows you to choose between them, or switch VR off entirely. Select Normal for most subjects; use Active, if available with your particular lens, under extra challenging conditions, such as shooting when walking or riding in a vehicle. Turn VR Off when the camera is mounted on a tripod or other support and is not needed. Disabling vibration saves power and keeps the camera from hunting for vibration to counter.

AF-Area Mode

The V1 has three different focus area selection modes, which can be selected with this menu entry. I explained how to choose an AF-Area mode fully in Chapter 6, but here's a quick recap:

- **Auto-Area AF.** The V1 always selects the autofocus zone, depending on your subject. In AF-S, AF-A, and AF-C modes, the active focus zones are highlighted in the viewfinder for about one second after focus is achieved. Zones are not used or displayed in manual focus mode.

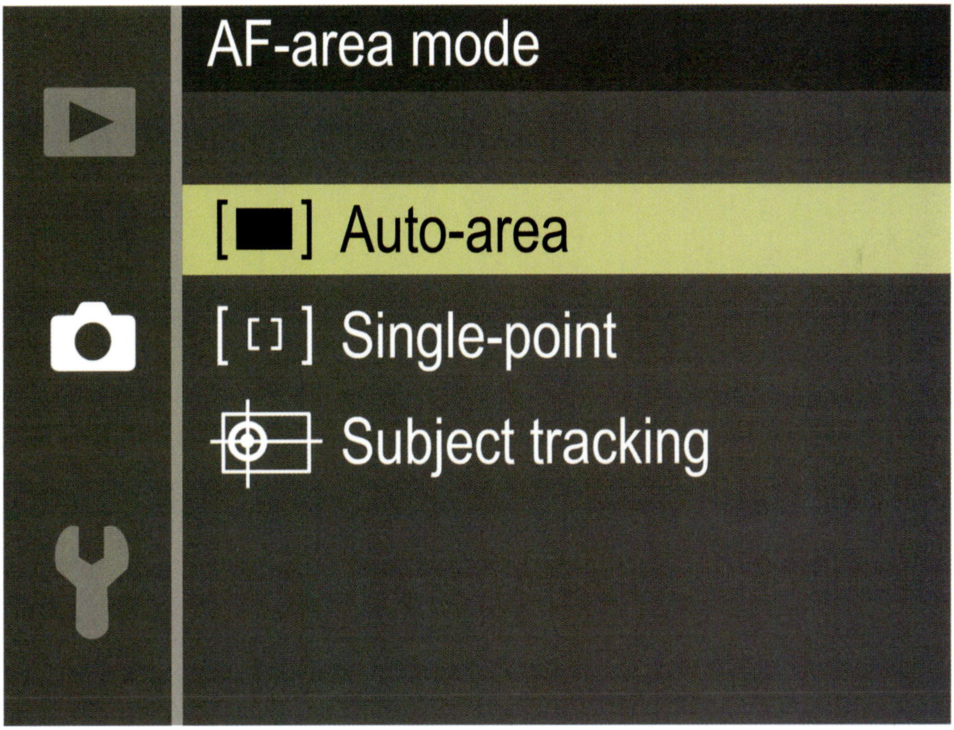

Figure 8.29 Select an autofocus-area mode.

- **Single-Point AF.** You always select the focus zone manually from 135 different areas, using the up/down/left right directional buttons to relocate the active zone. The zones are arrayed 15 across horizontally and 9 vertically. Each zone overlaps the adjoining zone by about one-third, so each time you press the directional button, the zone will jump approximately two-thirds the width or height.
- **Subject Tracking.** As with Single-Point AF, you can select the focus zone used by the V1 to autofocus. However, once you've locked in the initial zone, the camera will relocate the active zone around the screen to track the movement of your subject. While viewing your subject, the OK button activates focus area selection. Use the directional buttons to move the zone around where you want, then press OK to lock it in. The focus zone will move around the screen to track your subject, and when you press the shutter release halfway it will lock.

Face Priority AF

This separate Shooting menu entry is used to enable/disable the AF-Area mode known as Face Priority, which can be used in conjunction with any of the other three AF-Area modes. In Face Priority mode, the Nikon V1 searches for up to five faces and locks in on one of them. Unfortunately, you can't select which face the camera will give priority to, except by re-framing the image. You'll find complete instructions for using Face Priority in Chapter 6. This menu entry has two options On and Off.

Built-in AF Assist

Choose On to activate the AF-assist illuminator lamp on the front of the camera, as described in Chapter 2. The lamp will illuminate as required to help the autofocus system operate in Still Image, Smart Photo Selector, or Motion Snapshot modes when using AF-S. It also will light up as required when AF-A is activated and operating in AF-S mode, using Auto-Area AF mode or when Single-Point AF is used and the center focus area is selected.

Flash Mode

This menu entry and the last two in the Shooting menu appears only when you have the optional SB-N5 electronic flash mounted and turned on. You'll find more about using all the flash options in Chapter 10. It has three options:

- **Fill Flash.** The flash will fire all the time, even in bright lighting conditions, as supplementary illumination to brighten shadows.
- **Red-Eye Correction.** A pre-flash fires, which will cause subjects' pupils to contract (if they are looking at the camera), reducing the effects of red eye in your photographs.
- **Rear-curtain sync/Rear-curtain slow sync.** Causes the flash to fire just before the shutter closes, which can produce a slightly more desirable trailing "ghost" effect under high ambient lighting conditions when using flash. The explanation for this phenomenon is provided in Chapter 10.
- **Slow sync.** Applies longer shutter speeds to allow ambient light to affect the exposure.
- **Red-eye slow sync.** Like slow sync, but with red-eye correction.

Flash Control

You have two choices here, TTL, which activates automatic flash exposure measured through the lens and Manual, which allows choosing full power or 1/2 to 1/32 power. I'll explain use of this control in Chapter 10.

Flash Compensation

If you find your flash exposures are too bright or too dim, you can adjust flash exposure compensation here, selecting up to one full stop more exposure or three stops less exposure, in one-third stop increments. An indicator appears at the lower-right corner of the LCD in shooting mode when you've dialed in flash compensation. Flash compensation is "sticky" and doesn't reset when the V1 is turned off. You'll need to revisit this menu item and zero out flash compensation (change it to +/–0).

Setup Menu

The Setup menu provides options for changing the way your camera operates. You won't change these very often; except for a few settings, like Format Memory Card, these are generally of the "set it, forget it" type—until you're ready to make a specific change. (See Figure 8.30.)

- Reset Setup Options
- Format Memory Card
- Slot Empty Release Lock
- Welcome Screen
- Display Brightness
- Grid Display
- Sound Settings
- Auto Power Off
- Remote on Duration
- Assign AE/AF-L Button
- Shutter Button AE Lock
- Video Mode
- HDMI Device Control
- Flicker Reduction
- Reset File Numbering
- Time Zone and Date
- Language
- Auto Image Rotation
- Battery Info
- GPS
- Firmware Version

Reset Setup Options

This setting returns all the Setup menu options to their factory default value, except for Video mode, Flicker Reduction, Time Zone and Date, and Language (which can only be changed manually). The default values are shown in Table 8.3.

Format Memory Card

I recommend using this menu entry to reformat your memory card after each shoot. While you can move files from the memory card to your computer, leaving behind a blank card, or delete files using the Playback menu's Delete feature, both of those options can leave behind stray files (such as those that have been marked as Protected). Format removes those files completely and beyond retrieval (unless you use a special utility program as described in Chapter 13) and establishes a spanking new fresh file system on the card, including a spanking new DCIM (Digital Camera Images) folder, which will contain subfolders for each model camera that the card happens to be used in. (That's why you can remove a card from your V1, use it in another model camera, and find that the images from each type of camera reside in folders of their own within the main DCIM folder.) Reformatting resets all the file allocation table (FAT) pointers (which tell the camera and your computer's operating system where all the images reside) efficiently pointing where they are supposed to on a blank card.

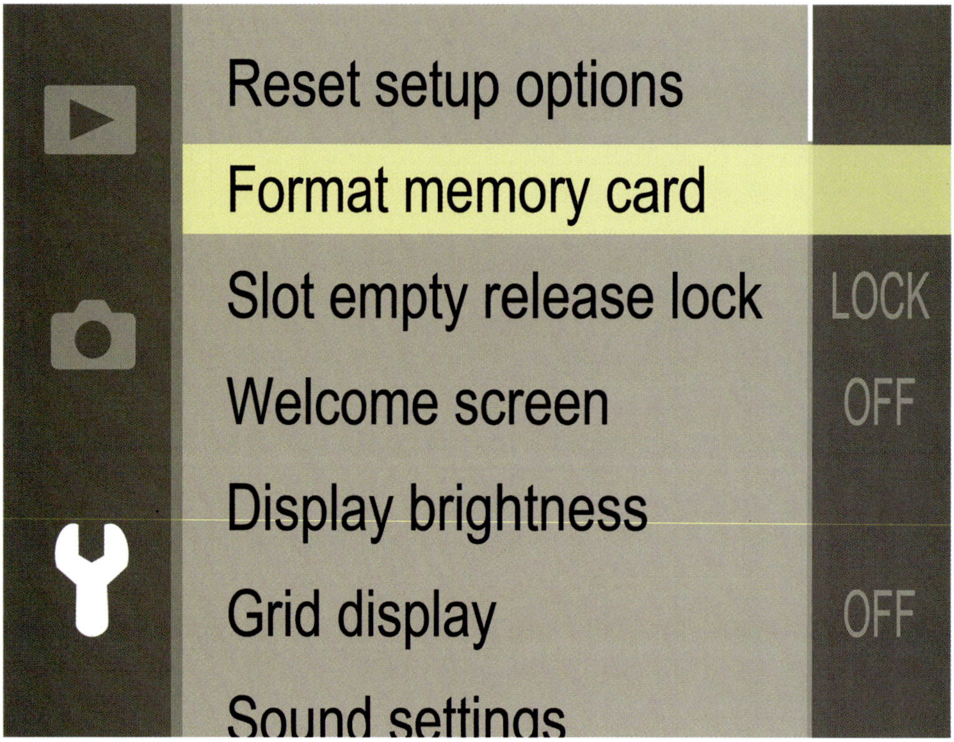

Figure 8.30 The first page of the Setup menu.

Table 8.3 Setup Menu Defaults

Option	Default	Option	Default
Slot Empty Release Lock	Locked	Remote on Duration	5 minutes
Welcome screen	Off	Assign AE/AF-L Button	AE-AF lock
Display Brightness		Shutter Button AE Lock	Off
LCD Brightness	0	HDMI Device Control	Off
EVF Brightness	0	Time Zone and Date	Not changed by reset
Grid Display	Off		
Sound Settings		Daylight Saving Time	Off
Autofocus/Self-timer	On	Auto Image Rotation	On
Electronic shutter	On	GPS	
Auto Power Off	30 seconds	Auto Power Off	Disable
		Use GPS to Set Clock	Yes

Select this menu entry, then select Yes from the screen that appears. Press OK to begin the format process.

Slot Empty Release Lock

This entry gives you the ability to snap off "pictures" without a memory card installed—or, alternatively, to lock the camera shutter release if no card is present. It is sometimes informally called Play mode, because you can experiment with your camera's features or even hand your V1 to a friend to let them fool around, without any danger of pictures actually being taken.

Back in our film days, we'd sometimes finish a roll, rewind the film back into its cassette surreptitiously, and then hand the camera to a child to take a few pictures—without actually wasting any film. It's hard to waste digital film, but "shoot without card" mode is still appreciated by some, especially camera vendors who want to be able to demo a camera at a store or trade show, but don't want to have to equip each and every demonstrator model with a memory card. Choose Enable Release to activate "play" mode or Release Locked to disable it. A red warning indicator appears on the LCD in shooting mode. The pictures you actually "take" are displayed on the LCD during playback with the legend "Demo mode" superimposed on the screen, and they are, of course, not saved.

Welcome Screen

You can select On or Off to show/hide the "Nikon 1" welcome screen that appears when the camera is powered up. If you don't need a reminder of what camera you're using, you can turn this off.

Display Brightness

This menu option allows you to adjust the relative brightness of the LCD display (which Nikon calls the "monitor") and the electronic viewfinder independently. When you access the menu item, a Display Brightness screen appears showing the current settings (+3 to –3) and the option of choosing which of the two you want to adjust. A screen like the one shown in Figure 8.31 appears.

Note that the adjustment screen is shown on whichever display is active, without regard to which one you want to adjust. So, if you see the viewfinder adjustment screen on the back-panel LCD (the "monitor"), bring the camera to your eye and peer through the EVF while making the change. If adjusting the LCD display, do so on the back-panel LCD, and not through the viewfinder.

In either case, you should be able to see all 10 swatches from black to white. If the two end swatches blend together, the brightness has been set too low. If the two whitest

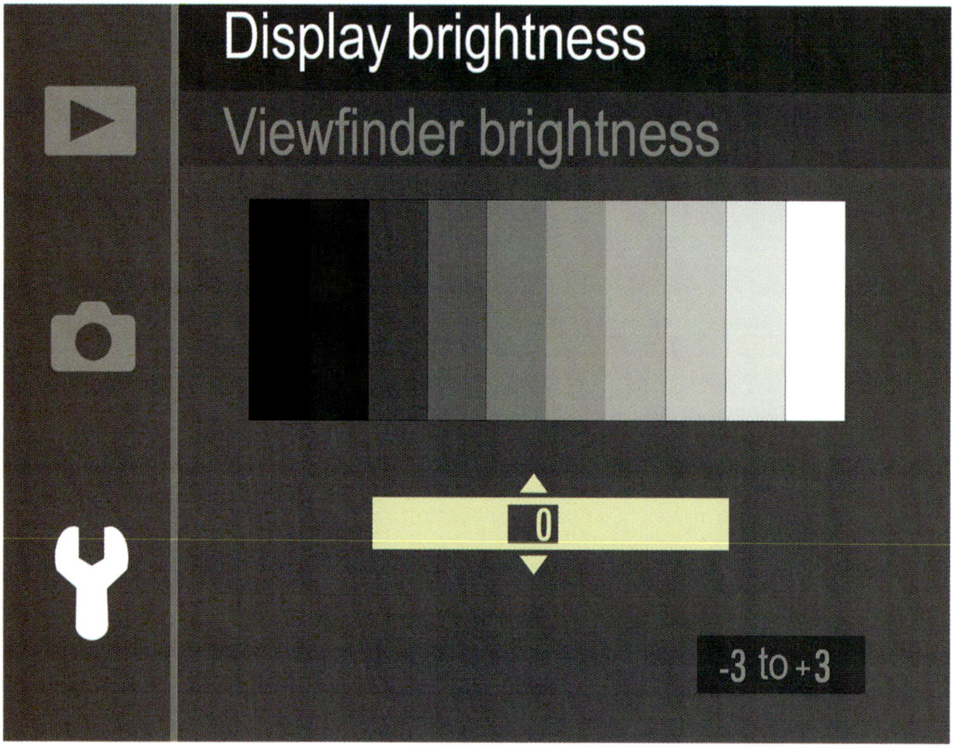

Figure 8.31
Adjust the LCD and EVF brightness so that all the grayscale strips are visible.

swatches on the right end of the strip blend together, the brightness is too high. Brighter settings use more battery power, but can allow you to view an image on the back-panel LCD outdoors in bright sunlight. Use the multi selector up/down buttons or rotate the dial to make the adjustment. When you find the brightness you want, press OK to lock it in and return to the menu. You can cancel and exit the menu system by tapping the shutter release button.

Grid Display

Your On/Off choices in this menu item enable or disable display of the V1's grid overlay, which can be handy for lining up vertical and horizontal components of your image as you shoot. While it's not a "rule of thirds" grid layout, it may still help you in planning your compositions.

Sound Settings

This entry (see Figure 8.33) allows separate enabling/disabling of the V1's sound beeper for two operational components. Highlight the sound feature you want to adjust and press the right directional button to mark/unmark the checkbox next to that feature.

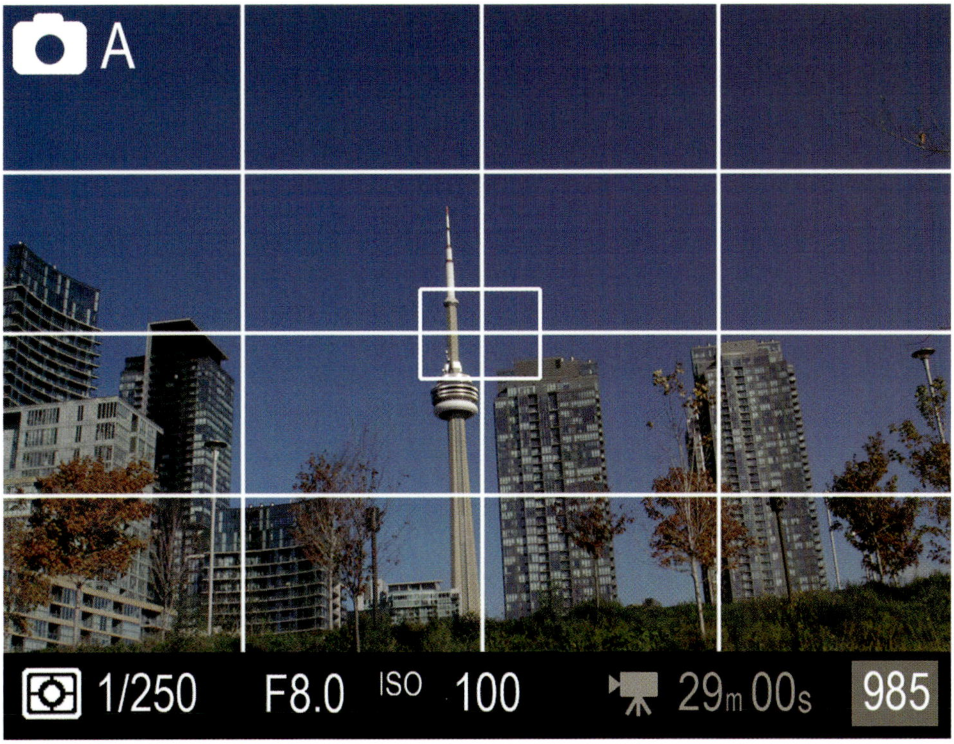

Figure 8.32
The grid display can help you align elements in your composition.

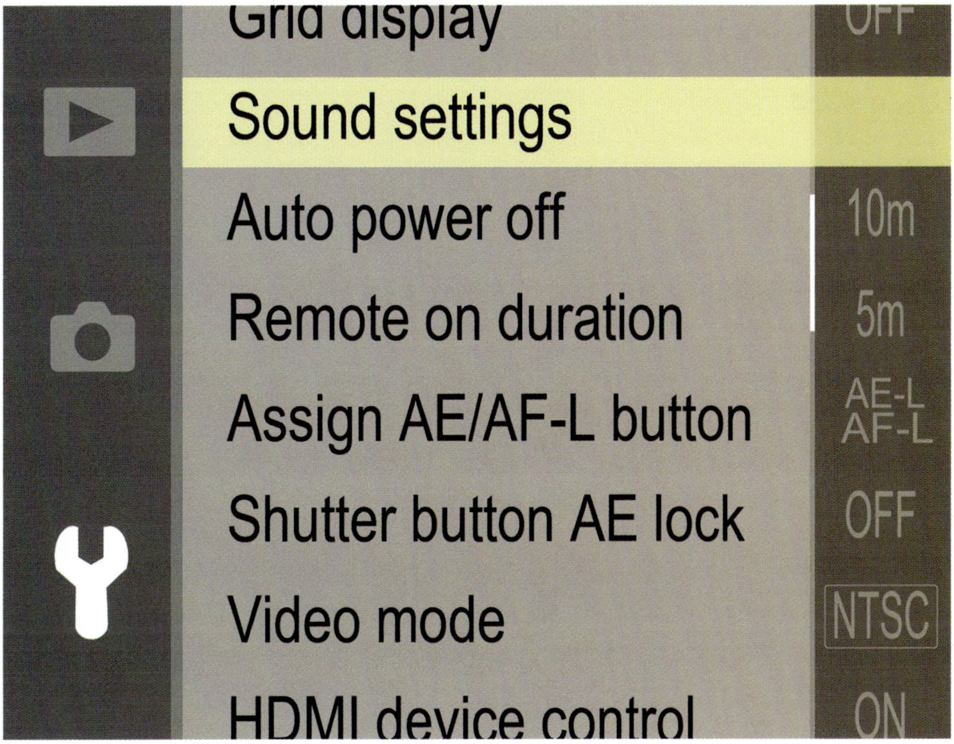

Figure 8.33
Specify sound settings with this entry.

Press the OK button to confirm and go back to the menu, or tap the shutter release button to cancel:

- **Autofocus/Self-timer.** A beep is emitted when the camera finishes focusing, and during the self-timer countdown. If you prefer totally silent operation (say, at a religious ceremony or some other event where you want to be discrete), deactivate this sound.
- **Electronic Shutter.** The silence of the electronic shutter can be great in some circumstances, but if you're not concerned about noise, it can be helpful to hear a clicking sound as confirmation when taking a picture. You can choose either a shutter click or no sound as you prefer.

Auto Power Off

Your Nikon V1 will eventually power down the LCD and EVF displays to save battery power if you perform no operations for a specified period of time. When the displays have turned off, use any control, including a quick tap on the shutter release, to bring them back to life. You can select delays of 15 or 30 seconds, and 1, 5, or 10 minutes.

Remote on Duration

When you use the ML-L3 infrared remote control, the V1 will remain vigilant and look for a signal for a specific period of time. This uses up battery power. So, you can select active remote durations of 1, 5, 10, or 15 minutes. If the specified time expires and you haven't used the remote control, you'll need to reselect the remote control mode to activate it again.

As explained earlier, to activate the remote control, press the self-timer/remote button on the multi selector (the left button), and choose either 2s Delayed Remote or Quick Response Remote.

Assign AE/AF-L Button

This button (the multi selector up directional button) can be programmed by you to provide two different autoexposure/autofocus locking behaviors:

- **AE/AF Lock.** With this default setting, the V1 locks both focus and exposure while the AE-L/AF-L button is pressed. In most shooting situations, when not using Auto-Area autofocus (in which the camera, not you, selects what subject to focus on), this is the best compromise. You can select your focus area in the other two modes (Single Point and Subject Tracking); press the shutter release halfway to achieve both exposure and focus; and then press and hold the up button to lock them at those settings. An indicator appears at the bottom of the EVF/LCD.

While focus and exposure are locked, you can then reframe your picture as desired, without either value changing. If you take a picture *or* remove your finger from the shutter release button, while the AE-L/AF-L button is pressed, the settings remain locked, so you can take several photographs in a row at the same focus and exposure setting.

You'll find the AE-L/AF-L lock button handy when you're shooting subjects that aren't entirely within one of the focus zones. Frame the image and lock focus/exposure for your subject, then re-frame for the final composition you want with both locked using the button.

- **AE Lock Only.** Lock only the exposure while the AE-L/AF-L button is pressed. This option is helpful when you don't want the exposure to change (say, bright or dark, but unimportant objects are wandering in and out of the frame), but want to allow focus to adjust as required.
- **AF Lock Only.** Focus is locked in while the AE-L/AF-L button is held down. In this mode, focus is locked, and you can reframe your image if necessary, but exposure will not be adjusted until you take the picture.

Shutter Button AE Lock

When switched On (the default), exposure is locked when the shutter release button is pressed halfway. If you select Off, then you'll need to press the AE/AF Lock button instead (with AE/AF Lock or AE Lock Only active, as described above) to lock exposure. When Shutter Button AE Lock is deactivated, pressing the shutter release halfway locks *only* the focus, and *only* when you're using AF-S focus mode. The Off mode is most useful when you'd like to use the shutter release to lock focus (say, to fix focus on a particular subject), while allowing the exposure to change as required.

Video Mode

This setting controls the output of the Nikon V1 to a conventional video system through the video cable when you're displaying images on a monitor or connected to a VCR through the external device's yellow video input jack. You can select either NTSC, used in the United States, Canada, Mexico, many Central, South American, and Caribbean countries, much of Asia, and other countries; or PAL, which is used in the UK, much of Europe, Africa, India, China, and parts of the Middle East.

HDMI Device Control

This option, the first on the next page of the Setup menu (see Figure 8.34) controls the Nikon V1's High-Definition Multimedia Interface (HDMI) video connection, used to play back your camera's images on HDTV or HD monitors using a type C cable, which Nikon does not provide to you, but which is readily available from third parties. Before

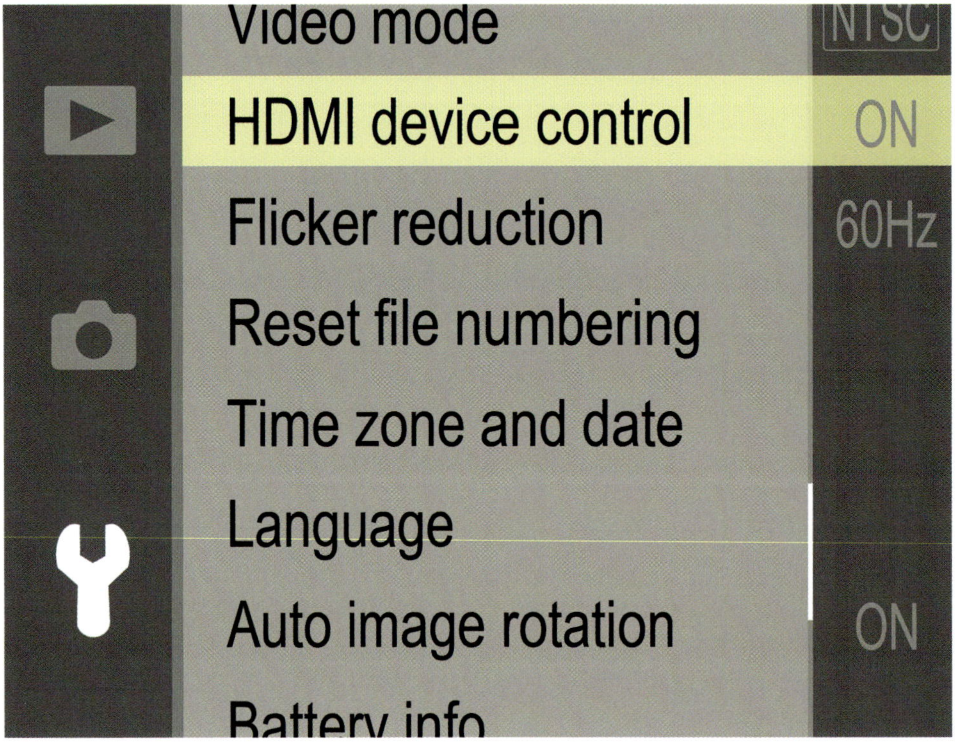

Figure 8.34 HDMI Device Control is the first choice on the next page of the Setup menu.

you link up you'll want to choose the HDMI resolution to be used, from 480p (640 × 480 progressive scan); 576p (720 × 576 progressive scan); 720p (1280 × 720 progressive scan); or 1080i (1920 × 1080 interlaced scan).

You can also choose to turn Device Control on or off. When On is chosen and the camera is connected to a television that supports the HDMI-CEC protocol and both are turned on, you'll see PLAY and SLIDE SHOW messages on the television. You can then use the television's compatible remote control instead of the multi selector and OK buttons to review images and play slide shows. Choose Off, and this capability is disabled.

Flicker Reduction

This option reduces flicker and banding, which can occur when shooting stills or movies under fluorescent and mercury vapor illumination, because the cycling of these light sources interacts with the frame rate of the camera's video system. In the United States, you'd choose the 60Hz frequency; in locations where 50Hz current is the norm, select that option instead.

Reset File Numbering

The V1's file system increments the numbers included in the file names of still photographs or movies by one with each successive capture, up to a maximum of 9999 (as with DSC_9999). Moreover, each image is deposited into a folder on your memory card which can hold up to 999 images. The folders are given a name like 100NC1V1. When 999 images are in the current folder, a new folder with a number one larger (for example 101NC1VI up to 999NC1VI) will be created.

Everything works swimmingly until the V1 runs out of numbers. When you finally get to a folder numbered 999NC1V1, and that folder contains 999 images, the V1 has no place to "put" the next image, as it can't create a higher numbered folder (it doesn't "wrap around" to 100NC1V1, in other words). The same thing happens if that 999NC1V1 folder has an image numbered DSC_9999. The shutter release locks up and you can't take any more pictures until you visit this menu entry, and in the Reset File Numbering screen select Yes. Then, you'll need to insert a new memory card or reformat the current card to continue with the new numbering scheme.

Of course, you can always reset the numbering before the system "tops out." The best reason for doing that would be to ensure that your camera doesn't lock up at an inopportune moment, by resetting a few hundred (or thousand) images before the forced rollover happens.

Time Zone and Date

Use this menu entry to adjust the V1's internal clock. Your options include:

- **Time Zone.** A small map will pop up on the setting screen and you can choose your local time zone. I sometimes forget to change the time zone when I travel (especially when going to Europe), so my pictures are all time-stamped incorrectly. I like to use the time stamp to recall exactly when a photo was taken, so keeping this setting correct is important.
- **Date and Time.** Use this setting to enter the exact year, month, day, hour, minute, and second, using a 24-hour clock.
- **Date Format.** Choose from Y/M/D (year/month/day), M/D/Y (month/day/year), or D/M/Y (day/month/year) formats.
- **Daylight Saving Time.** Use this to turn daylight saving time On or Off. Because the date on which DST goes into effect each year has been changed from time to time, if you turn this feature on you may need to monitor your camera to make sure DST has been implemented correctly.

Language

Choose from these languages for menu display: Czech, Danish, German, English, Spanish, Greek, French, Indonesian, Italian, Dutch, Norwegian, Polish, Portuguese, Russian, Romanian, Finnish, Swedish, Turkish, Ukrainian, Arabic, Simplified Chinese, Traditional Chinese, Japanese, Korean, or Thai.

Auto Image Rotation

Turning this setting On tells the Nikon V1 to include camera orientation information in the still image file (but not in movies or motion snapshots). The orientation can be read by many software applications, including Adobe Photoshop, Nikon ViewNX, and Capture NX, as well as the Rotate Tall setting in the Playback menu. Turn this feature Off, and none of the software applications or Playback's Rotate Tall will be able to determine the correct orientation for the image. Nikon notes that only the first image's orientation is used when shooting continuous bursts; subsequent photos will be assigned the same orientation, even if you rotate the camera during the sequence (which is something I have been known to do myself when shooting sports like basketball).

Battery Info

This screen is purely informational; there are no settings to be made. When invoked, you can see the following information:

- **Charge remaining.** The current battery level, shown as a percentage from 100 to 0 percent.
- **Battery age.** Eventually, a battery will no longer accept a charge as well as it did when it was new, and must be replaced. This indicator shows when a battery is considered new (0); has begun to degrade slightly (1,2,3); or has reached the end of its charging life and is ready for replacement (4). Batteries charged at temperatures lower than 41 degrees F may display an impaired charging life temporarily, but return to their true "health" when recharged above 68 degrees F.

GPS

This menu entry appears only when the optional GP-N100 GPS is attached and functioning. It has three options, none of which turn GPS features on or off, despite the misleading "Enable" and "Disable" nomenclature (what you're enabling and disabling is the automatic exposure meter turn-off). You'll find more about working with GPS in Chapter 11.

Your choices here are:

- **Auto meter-off.** You can choose Enable or Disable. Enabling reduces battery drain by allowing the V1 to turn off exposure meters while using the GP-N100 after the time specified for Auto Power Off in the Setup menu has elapsed. When the meters turn off, the GP-N100 becomes inactive and must reacquire at least three satellite signals before it can begin recording GPS data once more. When you choose Disable, the exposure meters remain activated continuously while using the GP-N100, so that GPS data can be recorded at any time, despite increased battery drain.
- **Position.** This is an information display, rather than a selectable option. It appears when the GP-N100 is connected and receiving satellite positioning data. It shows the latitude, longitude, altitude, and Coordinated Universal Time (UTC) values.
- **Use GPS to set camera clock.** Select Yes or No. When enabled, your V1's internal camera clock will be set using UTC values whenever the GP-N100 is attached to the camera. If you use the device frequently, this will ensure that your camera's clock is always set accurately, and won't require a manual update periodically.

Firmware Version

You can see the current firmware release in use in the menu listing. You can learn how to update firmware in Chapter 13.

9

Working with Lenses

The Nikon 1 cameras were the first interchangeable lens mainstream models introduced by Nikon with an all-new lens mount since 1959. While the latest Nikon digital SLRs can use most of the millions of lenses available for the original F-mount, the Nikon V1 provides full functionality only with lenses designed especially for it. Although Nikon offers an F-mount adapter (which wasn't available for testing when this book was written), and you can bet third-party accessory manufacturers will come up with adapters to allow use of Nikon, Canon, Sony, and other lenses, you're better off with optics created specifically for the CX format. Right now, the number of lenses available is not large, but will be growing in the months and years to come.

The right choice of lenses can give you a wider view, bring distant subjects closer, let you focus closer, shoot under lower light conditions, or provide a more detailed, sharper image for critical work. Other than the sensor itself, the lens you choose for your mirrorless camera is the most important component in determining image quality and perspective of your images. This chapter explains how to select the best lenses for the kinds of photography you want to do.

Sensor Sensibilities

If you had never heard the term *crop factor* until recently, you certainly heard it mentioned when the Nikon 1 line of cameras was introduced. That's because your Nikon V1 has a "crop" factor of 2.7, which is considerably larger than that of any other interchangeable lens camera currently being produced. So, you may be wondering, is that a good thing or a bad thing? And what's a crop factor, anyway? But rather than being a distinct plus or minus, the so-called crop factor, or *lens multiplier factor* has both good effects and bad effects, and is simply something that (perhaps) needs to be understood, and allowed for.

Both crop factor and lens multiplier factor are misleading and inaccurate terms used to describe the same phenomenon: the fact that cameras like the V1 (and most other affordable interchangeable lens cameras) provide a field of view that's smaller and narrower than that produced by the top-end "full-frame" cameras, when fitted with exactly the same lens. Of course, swapping lenses with another camera system is possible only if you happen to have an adapter for your V1 that allows you to mount lenses produced for non-CX format cameras, or you want to compare the perspective of your Nikon 1 lenses with those of other models. If you use only Nikon 1 lenses, and don't care to make comparisons, you can safely ignore the whole crop factor business, because the bottom line is this: *When you look at the electronic viewfinder or LCD monitor, what you see is what you're going to get.* Everything else is just numbers.

Those who do care about crop factors can read on. Figure 9.1 quite clearly shows the phenomenon at work. The outer rectangle, marked 1X, shows the field of view you might expect with a 28mm lens mounted on one of Nikon's "full-frame" FX-format cameras, like the Nikon D3s. The area marked 1.5X shows the field of view you'd get with that 28mm lens installed on a DX-format model like the Nikon D7000. The inner area, marked 2.7X shows the equivalent field of view with that lens (or with your 10-30mm kit lens zoomed in to roughly its maximum focal length). It's easy to see from the illustration that the 1X rendition provides a wider, more expansive wide-angle view, while the inner field of view, in comparison, gives a healthy telephoto effect, because

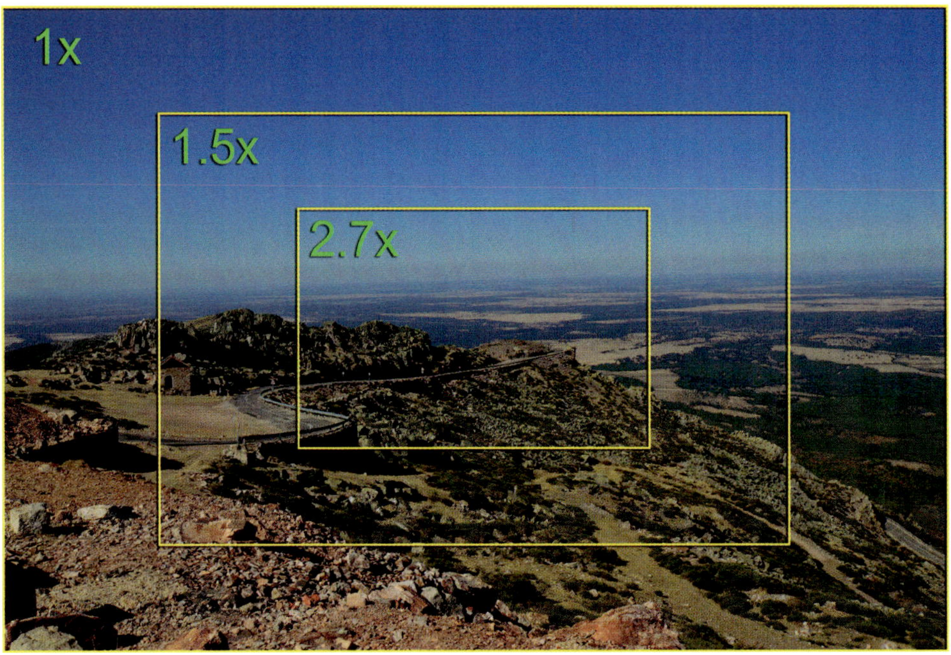

Figure 9.1
Nikon offers interchangeable lens cameras with full-frame (1X) crops, as well as 1.5X and 2.7X.

it's *cropped*. Because of this cropping, a 28mm focal length on an FX camera gives a wide-angle view, while the same focal length on the V1 offers a telephoto image.

The extreme cropping effect is produced because the sensors of CX cameras like the Nikon V1 are smaller than the sensors of the D3s or D7000. In the case of a "full-frame" FX camera, the sensor is the size of the standard 35mm film frame: 24mm × 36mm. Your V1's sensor does *not* measure 24mm × 36mm; instead, it specs out at 8.8 × 13.2mm. The FX sensor is 2.7X times the size of the CX sensor in each direction, producing the 2.7X crop factor.

This translation is generally useful only if you're accustomed to using full-frame cameras (often of the film variety) and want to know how a familiar lens will perform on a digital camera. I strongly prefer *crop factor* over *lens multiplier*, because nothing is being multiplied; your 10-30mm lens doesn't "become" a 27-81mm lens—the depth-of-field and lens aperture remain the same. (I'll explain more about these later in this chapter.) Only the field of view is cropped. But *crop factor* isn't much better, as it implies that the 24 × 36mm frame is "full" and anything else is "less." I get e-mails all the time from photographers who point out that they own full-frame cameras with 36mm × 48mm sensors (like the Mamiya 645ZD or Hasselblad H3D-39 medium format digitals). By their reckoning, the "half-size" sensors found in cameras like the Nikon D700 and D3/D3x are "cropped."

If you're accustomed to using full-frame film cameras, you might find it helpful to use the crop factor "multiplier" to translate a lens's real focal length into the full-frame equivalent, even though, as I said, nothing is actually being multiplied. Throughout most of this book, I've been using actual focal lengths and not equivalents, except when referring to specific wide-angle or telephoto focal length ranges and their fields of view.

Crop or Not?

There's a lot of debate over the "advantages" and "disadvantages" of using a camera like the Nikon 1 series, with 2.7X cropped sensors. The two most important arguments go like these:

- **Dense pixels=more noise.** In order to pack 10 megapixels into the V1's small sensor, each pixel must be much smaller than those found in DX or FX cameras of the same resolution, and will have less light-gathering capabilities. Larger pixels capture light more efficiently, reducing the need to amplify the signal when boosting ISO sensitivity, and, therefore, producing less noise. In an absolute sense, this is true, and cameras like the D3s and D7000 *do* have sensational high-ISO performance. However, the V1's sensor is improved over earlier cameras, so you'll find it performs very well at higher ISOs. You needn't hesitate to use ISO 1600 with the Nikon V1: just don't expect the same low noise results at ISO 3200 as D7000 owners get from their cameras.

- **Lack of wide-angle perspective.** Of course, the 2.7X "crop" factor applies to wide-angle lenses, too, so your V1 needs specially designed extra-wide lenses to provide a wide field of view. To date, the widest lenses available in CX format all have a minimum focal length of 10mm, which, after the 2.7X crop factor is applied, offers the same field of view as a moderate wide angle on an FX model. Ultrawide focal lengths are currently not available for the Nikon 1 cameras.

Your Lens Selections

Currently, it's impossible to purchase any Nikon 1 series camera without a lens. The Nikon V1 is available with the 10-30mm lens, plus various combinations of the other four lenses which make up the initial offerings that debuted with the cameras themselves. Being the Nikon fanatic I am, I purchased all four along with my camera, even though there is some overlap in focal lengths and purpose. (I also bought the Nikon J1, and every accessory available for the Nikon 1 line, including the SB-N5 flash and ME-1 stereo microphone.) The next section is a rundown of the four optics that were available at the time I wrote this book.

1 NIKKOR VR 10-30mm f/3.5-5.6

The kit lens is a must-have, partially because it comes with the camera and there is no easy way to *not* own one of these. (I own two, because I bought both the V1 and J1 models.) Fortunately, it's a handy lens to have, with a combination of compact size, built-in vibration reduction, and a useful, if limited, zoom range. (See Figure 9.2.)

- **Aperture.** The maximum aperture of f/3.5 at the widest 10mm focal length is fast enough for indoor shooting, particularly when you factor in this lens's vibration reduction, which should allow most people to hand-hold the camera at 1/30th second or even slower with no problem. However, at the modest telephoto end of its range, it has a maximum aperture of f/5.6, which is quite slow. You'll want to reduce the aperture one stop for best sharpness, giving you an effective f/8 lens to work with. The smallest aperture available is f/16, which is quite adequate for shooting even under bright lighting conditions, because the V1 has those fast shutter speeds (up to 1/16,000th second with the electronic shutter) to call upon.
- **Zoom range.** This is only a 3X zoom, and its 10-30mm range is good for moderate wide-angle scenes up to short telephoto shots. At 30mm, it's ideal for head and shoulders portraits. But if you want to go longer, say, for sports photography, you'll need to pair this lens with the Nikon 1 30-110mm optic, discussed next.
- **Size.** In use, this lens measures just 2.3 × 1.7 inches, and retracts (manually, by pressing a button on the lens and rotating the barrel) to become even smaller. It's a featherweight 4.1 ounces. This is my walk-around lens, used when I'm toting the

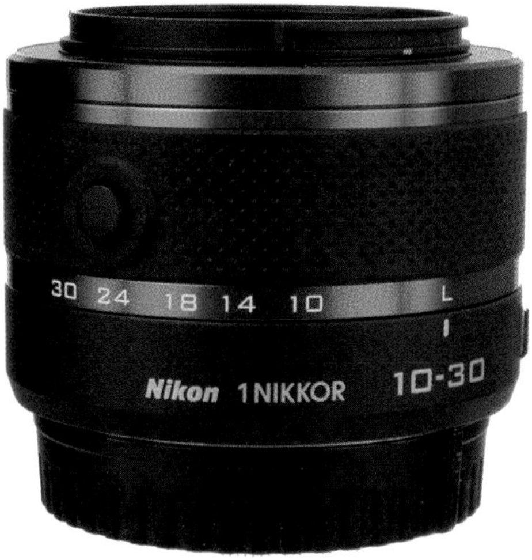

Figure 9.2 The 10-30mm kit lens is a must-have, because there is no way to buy a Nikon V1 without it.

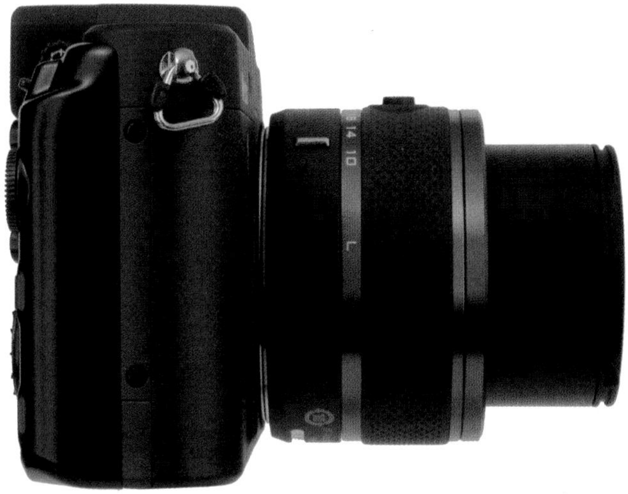

Figure 9.3 The 10-30mm lens and Nikon V1 make a compact package.

V1 around with no special plans to take pictures. I want a compact camera without a lot of weight, and this lens fills the bill nicely. (See Figure 9.3.)

- **Focus distance.** It focuses down to about eight inches, even at 30mm, making it a good choice for simple close-up and macro photography. You can capture great images of flowers and larger insects and other critters. Close focusing adds to its versatility. Because this lens uses internal focusing (the lens elements shift inside the lens barrel as it focuses), it doesn't gain in length when focusing extra close. That means the lens is less likely to cast shadows on your subject when zoomed up close and personal.
- **Other features.** While you need to remember to retract the lens barrel manually, the V1 helpfully reminds you to extend it again when the camera is next powered up. It uses the same 40.5mm screw-on filter size compatible with two of the other three Nikon 1 lenses. These filters are readily available and inexpensive, so you won't have to buy multiple filters unless you own the 10-100mm zoom.

1 NIKKOR VR 30-110mm f/3.8-5.6

Since you, like every other Nikon 1 owner in the universe, already own the 10-30mm zoom, a modest investment of $250 or less will take you from 30mm all the way out to the edges of super-telephoto territory at 110mm. The only hitch? You have to swap this lens for the kit lens to achieve the full 10-110mm zoom range. Even so, this lens is an unbeatable bargain, when you consider the alternative: spending $750 on the massive 10-100mm zoom monster I'll describe later in this section.

- **Aperture.** If you find the kit lens's f/5.6 maximum aperture at 30mm daunting, you'll like the f/3.8 widest f/stop this lens provides at the same focal length. So, if you're shooting sports, concerts, or other more distant subjects, you'll benefit from this lens, faster at its minimum focal length. Of course, at this price you can't expect a constant maximum aperture, like that found in the kit lens; this zoom slows down to f/5.6 by the time it's zoomed to 110mm. But when you consider that, with the crop factor, this lens has the equivalent reach of a near-300mm lens on an FX camera, it's fast enough. It has the same f/16 minimum aperture. Smaller f/stops might be useful for increasing depth-of-field when required, but cameras with small sensors like the V1 tend to be especially vulnerable to a loss of sharpness at tiny apertures, due to a phenomenon down as *diffraction.* Given that the true focal length of this lens at the max zoom position is 110mm, the actual depth-of-field when zoomed is quite adequate.
- **Zoom range.** Zoom range is somewhat limited at 3.7X, but this lens is meant to be paired with the 10-30mm zoom, anyway, and the two lenses together give you a combined zoom range of 11X. This one is suitable for portraits, sports, and other subjects calling for a long reach. Until Nikon introduces an even longer telephoto lens, this one is an inexpensive mate for the kit lens.
- **Size.** This lens is a bit larger than the 10-30mm lens when retracted at 2.4 × 2.4 inches (see Figure 9.4.), but is a *lot* longer when extended and zoomed to its maximum focal length. This one is furnished with a lens hood, which reverses for storage on the lens when the camera is asleep. The lens/hood combination sticks out roughly five inches from the front of the camera, making the V1 a bit front-heavy, and no longer the compact model you envisioned when you purchased it. (Be sure to retract the lens before reversing the lens hood for storage; the retract button is not easily accessible when the hood is de-installed.) Focusing is internal; it's only the zooming that extends the length of this lens. It's not too heavy at 6.2 ounces, so it's easy to store either the 10-30mm or this 30-110mm lens in a pocket while using the other. When I want the most flexibility and the smallest size, I tote my V1 and the 10-30/30-110 combination, and leave my camera bag at home.
- **Focus distance.** This one focuses down to 3.3 feet, so you can use it for some close-up photography, particularly subjects that are best captured from a decent distance away.
- **Other features.** This is another lens that must be retracted manually. It uses the same 40.5mm screw-on filter size as your kit lens, so one set of filters will serve for both. Like all the other Nikon 1 zoom lenses, it has vibration reduction and, if anything, benefits from it more than the kit lens, because camera shake is magnified at longer focal lengths. That makes VR more useful.

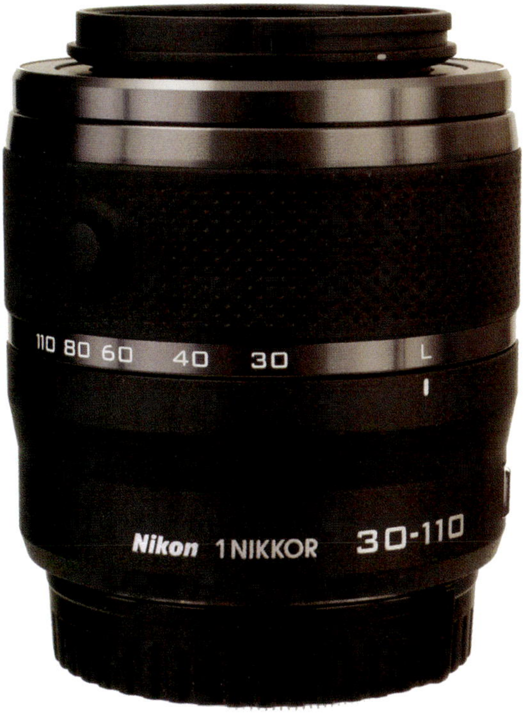

Figure 9.4 The 30-110mm zoom is still fairly compact in size.

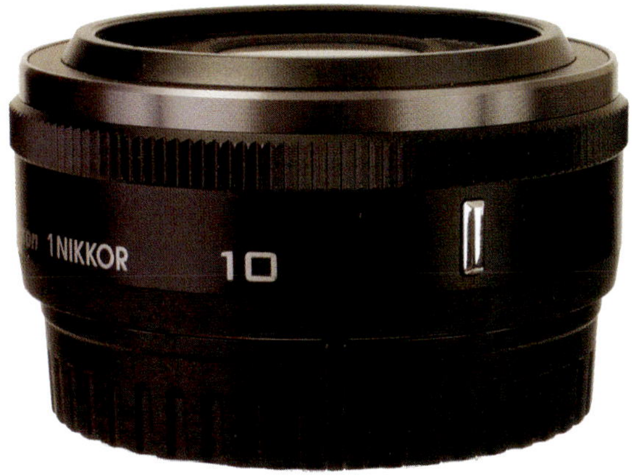

Figure 9.5 The Nikon 1 10mm f/2.8 lens is a compact "pancake" style lens.

1 NIKKOR 10mm f/2.8

I love this lens (see Figure 9.5) as it transforms any Nikon 1 camera into a completely different instrument, a truly compact stealth camera. Many people expected Nikon's mirrorless camera to be smaller than it turned out to be after the very small size of the sensor was revealed. The CX cameras, after all, are not meaningfully smaller than Sony's NEX series cameras, which have a (relatively) huge 1.5X crop sensor virtually identical in size to the one found on the (relatively) huger Nikon D7000. But Nikon redeemed itself with the introduction of this 10mm f/2.8 lens, which is small, fast, and at $250, affordable. It doesn't zoom, and doesn't have VR, but it does what it does very, very well.

- **Aperture.** Of course, at f/2.8, this lens is only 1/3 stop faster than the 10-30mm zoom at 10mm, but it's significantly faster than the Nikon 1 10-100mm optic at that focal length, which is 1.3 stops slower at f/4.5. It's perfect for indoor photography, street photography, and any other low-light work, as this lens is very sharp even wide open. The minimum f/stop is f/11, but given the prodigious depth-of-field this 10mm lens boasts, you won't need a smaller stop to increase the sharpness range, and the V1's very speedy shutter speeds will allow you to get proper exposure under the brightest lighting conditions.

- **Focal length.** No zoom, of course, and this lens is fixed at 10mm. Its field of view is only a moderate wide angle, so if you're looking for any of those freaky apparent distortion effects that ultra-wide lenses provide, you'll be disappointed. Don't hold me to this, but I expect Nikon to introduce a wide-angle attachment for this lens that will broaden its view into the ultra-wide range. (It's already produced such an accessory for the Nikon P7100 compact camera.) This lens is even more suitable for that type of add-on, because it's sharp enough to avoid degradation from a supplementary lens, and, unlike the P7100, it has a filter thread to accept accessories. (The P7100 requires an adapter for its wide-angle attachment.)
- **Size.** At 2.2 × 0.9 inches, this lens is *small.* It doesn't retract for storage, it doesn't get longer as you focus, there is no zoom to extend the lens, and Nikon doesn't provide you with a lens hood. The 10mm f/2.8 lens starts small and stays small. It amounts to just 2.8 ounces, so it won't weigh down your pocket. (I stuff candy bars in my pockets that weigh more than that.) (See Figure 9.6.)
- **Focus distance.** Like the 10-30mm zoom, this lens focuses down to about eight inches, but lacks the focal length to make it suitable for macro photography. I'm hoping Nikon or a third party introduces an automatic extension tube for this lens, because it would be perfect for it.
- **Other features.** It uses the same 40.5mm screw-on filter size as your kit lens and 30-110mm zoom, so one set of filters will fit all three. There's no VR, but with a fixed wide-angle focal length, this lens probably doesn't need it.

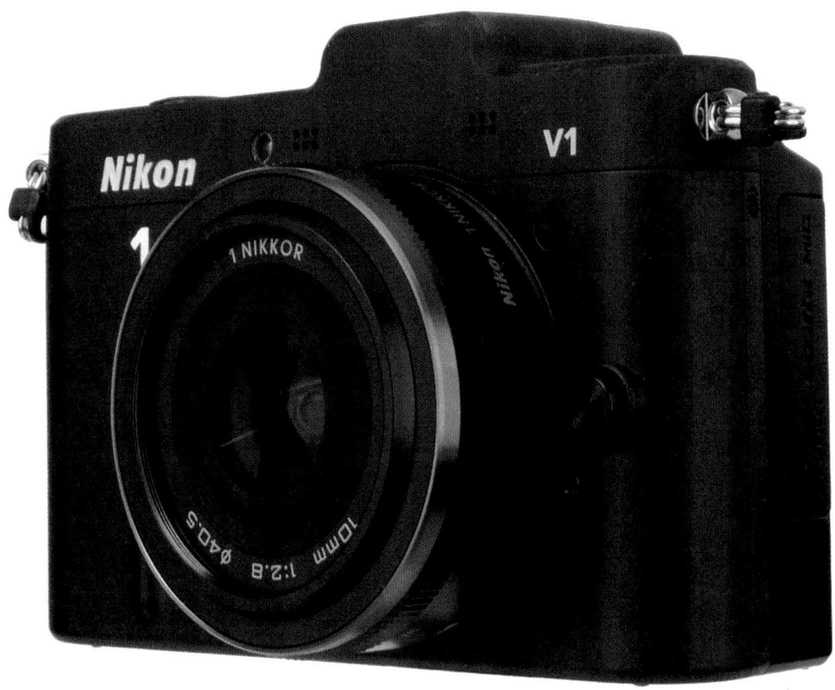

Figure 9.6
The Nikon V1 with the 10mm f/2.8 lens is almost pocket-sized—if you have largish pockets.

VR 10-100mm f/4.5-5.6 PD-ZOOM

What would motivate you to pay $750 for a lens to mount on a camera that costs only a little more than that? In my case, I wanted to push the Nikon 1 system as far as I could while writing this book, so I could share with you exactly what Nikon's mirrorless cameras can and cannot do. In your case, you might want this lens if you planned to shoot movies—it's ideally suited for video production—or if you wanted a single lens that would do (almost) everything, without the need to swap optics. If you do choose this lens, you can forget about stealth mode, or walking around with a compact, lightweight system. The 10-100mm zoom is huge. (See Figure 9.7.) But it's also versatile, and can do some things the other Nikon 1 lenses cannot. Here's a breakdown of the features/benefits you have to look forward to.

- **Aperture.** This is the slowest 10mm lens in the Nikon 1 line. At the widest zoom setting, it has a maximum aperture of f/4.5, which makes it a bit slow for available light shooting, even if the built-in VR does make hand-holding the V1 at slower shutter speeds feasible. At the long end, this lens has an f/5.6 maximum aperture at 100mm, which is actually quite reasonable for the amount of image magnification you get. I suspect that producing a constant aperture 10X zoom with, say, a constant f/4.5 f/stop throughout the zoom range would have made this lens even more expensive, much larger, or, possibly optically impossible. I don't design these things; I just evaluate them. It has an f/16 minimum aperture, which is useful, and expected given the limitations of design for a lens of this type.
- **Zoom range.** The 10X zoom range is great, particularly for shooting movie clips with a continuous zoom shot. This lens covers all the bases, so you don't really need another lens, unless you want something a bit faster for low-light shooting. Because of the overlap, you wouldn't want to buy this lens and the 30-110mm zoom, unless you're a Nikon completist like me. Once you have the 10-100mm zoom, you can use it all the time as a humongous walk-about lens, or alternate between this lens and the 10-30mm kit lens when you want something that takes less of a toll on your neck or shoulders. This range is suitable for everything from moderate wide angle all the way out to super-telephoto shots.
- **Size.** This is a *large* lens, probably larger and heftier than many of the lenses you might own for your digital SLR, if you have one. It measures 3.0 × 3.7 inches (3.5 × 5.5 inches with the lens hood attached) and weighs 18.2 ounces. To put that in perspective, this zoom is heavier than the V1 camera (which tips the scales at 13.5 ounces), and bulkier, too (the camera measures 3.0 × 4.4 × 1.7 inches). (See Figure 9.8.) On the plus side, this road-hugging weight makes the V1 with lens attached fairly stable when the camera is held with the left hand supporting the lens (and left thumb on the zoom button). You'll probably use this lens most often with the

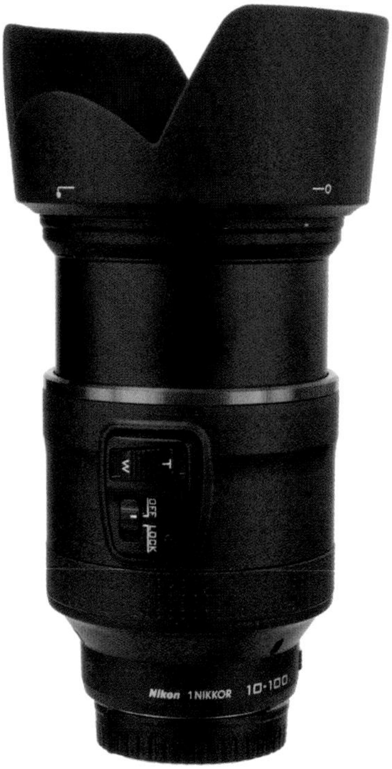

Figure 9.7 The 10-100mm zoom is an expensive lens, with features to match.

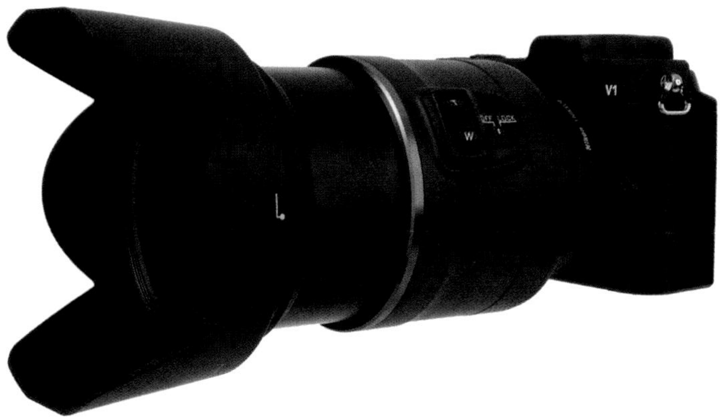

Figure 9.8 With the 10-100mm zoom mounted, the Nikon V1 camera is no longer petite and light in weight.

electronic viewfinder, rather than holding the camera out at arm's length to frame using the LCD monitor. That stance avoids making the lens/camera front-heavy. The built-in VR reduces camera shake.

- **Focus distance.** This one focuses down to 12 inches at the 10mm zoom setting, and 2.8 feet at the 100mm zoom setting. You can use it for some close-up photography, particularly subjects that are best captured from a decent distance away.
- **Other features.** The three-speed power zoom is great for shooting movies, and convenient for changing the focal length when shooting still images, too. This lens automatically retracts when the camera is powered down (you can disable this feature to speed access). Unlike the other three lenses, it uses 72mm filters. I already have a complete set of 77mm filters for my other Nikon lenses, so I purchased a 72mm to 77mm step-up ring and can use any of those filters with this lens.

What Lenses Can Do for You

Though your choice of lenses for your Nikon V1 is currently limited, each of them still provides lots of flexibility and plenty of opportunities for shooting great photos.

This section will reveal some of the things lenses can do for you.

- **Wider perspective.** When your back is up against a wall and you *can't* take a step backwards to take in more subject matter, you'll be thankful for that 10mm setting on your zoom lens. Figure 9.9 was taken using a 10mm focal length from the banks of the Rio Tormes in Salamanca, Spain, showing the "distant" vista of the old city, which really wasn't as far away as it appears in the figure.
- **Bring objects closer.** A long lens brings subjects closer to you, offers better control over depth-of-field, and avoids the perspective distortion that wide-angle lenses provide. They compress the apparent distance between objects in your frame. For Figure 9.10, I stepped a few feet to one side, and photographed this same scene with a 50mm focal length, providing a medium-telephoto look. Then, I zoomed in to 100mm for the ultra-telephoto shot shown in Figure 9.11.
- **Bring your camera closer.** The close focusing capabilities of Nikon 1 lenses (which can focus as close as eight inches) let you grab macro images. At longer focal lengths, you can still maintain a bit of distance from your subject (say, to avoid spooking a skittish creature).
- **Look sharp.** Nikon lenses are prized for their sharpness and overall image quality. While your run-of-the-mill lens available for other cameras is likely to be plenty sharp for most applications, the very best optics are even better over their entire field of view (which means no fuzzy corners), are sharper at a wider range of focal lengths (in the case of zooms), and have better correction for various types of distortion.
- **More speed.** Your 10-100mm f/4.5-5.6 zoom might have the perfect focal length and sharpness for sports photography, but the maximum aperture won't cut it shooting in dark surroundings. You need a faster, if less versatile, lens such as the 10mm f/2.8 pancake optic.
- **Special features.** Some lenses offer special features, such as the power zoom built into the 10-100mm f/3.5-5.6 lens. I expect Nikon will offer other lenses with special features in the future, particularly macro lenses, faster fixed focal-length lenses, and, maybe a fish-eye.

Categories of Lens Focal Lengths

Lenses can be easily categorized by their focal lengths. Different focal lengths have different attributes and can do different things. Here's a description of what each zoom range can do for you.

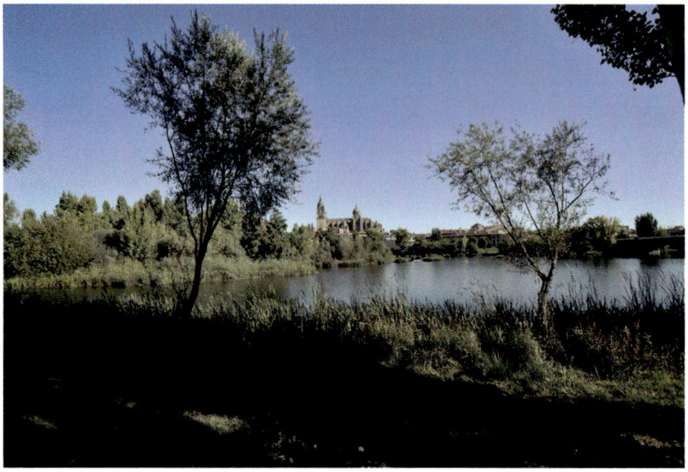

Figure 9.9
A wide-angle lens provided this view of Salamanca, Spain.

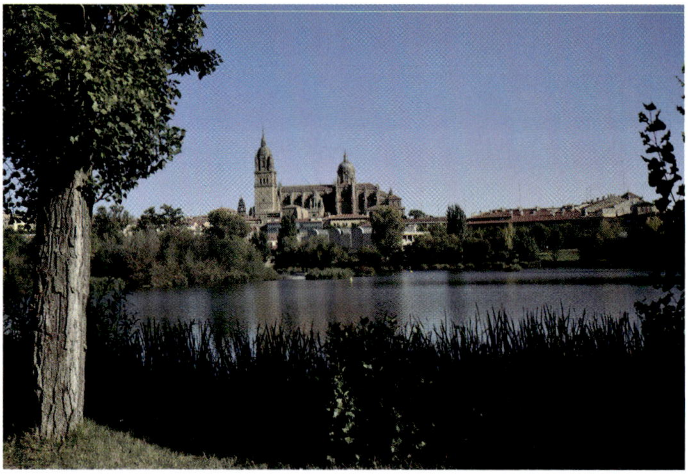

Figure 9.10
This photo, taken from roughly the same distance shows the view using a short telephoto lens.

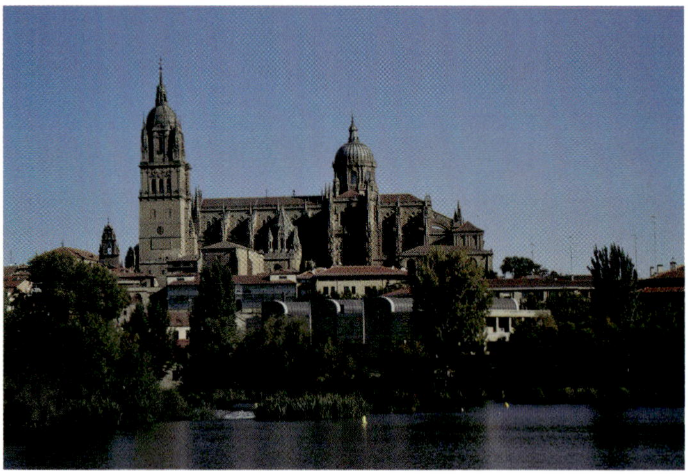

Figure 9.11
The 100mm zoom position captured this close-up view of Salamanca's Old Cathedral and New Cathedral (which are combined in a single edifice).

Using Wide-Angle and Wide-Zoom Lenses

To use wide-angle prime lenses like the 10mm f/2.8 and wide zooms, such as the 10-30mm and 10-100mm Nikon 1 optics, you need to understand how wide-angle perspectives affect your photography. Here's what you need to know.

- **More depth-of-field.** Practically speaking, wide-angle lenses offer more depth-of-field at a particular subject distance and aperture. (But see the sidebar below for an important note.) You'll find that helpful when you want to maximize sharpness of a large zone, but not very useful when you'd rather isolate your subject using selective focus (telephoto lenses are better for that).
- **Stepping back.** Wide-angle lenses have the effect of making it seem that you are standing farther from your subject than you really are. They're helpful when you don't want to back up, or can't because there are impediments in your way.
- **Wider field of view.** While making your subject seem farther away, as implied above, a wide-angle lens also provides a larger field of view, including more of the subject in your photos.
- **More foreground.** As background objects retreat, more of the foreground is brought into view by a wide-angle lens. That gives you extra emphasis on the area that's closest to the camera. Photograph your home with a normal lens/normal zoom setting, and the front yard probably looks fairly conventional in your photo (that's why they're called "normal" lenses). Switch to a wider lens and you'll discover that your lawn now makes up much more of the photo. So, wide-angle lenses are great when you want to emphasize that lake in the foreground, but problematic when your intended subject is located farther in the distance.
- **Super-sized subjects.** The tendency of a wide-angle lens to emphasize objects in the foreground, while de-emphasizing objects in the background can lead to a kind of size distortion that may be more objectionable for some types of subjects than others. Shoot a bed of flowers up close with a wide angle, and you might like the distorted effect of the larger blossoms nearer the lens. Take a photo of a family member with the same lens from the same distance, and you're likely to get some complaints about that gigantic nose in the foreground.
- **Perspective distortion.** When you tilt the camera so the plane of the sensor is no longer perpendicular to the vertical plane of your subject, some parts of the subject are now closer to the sensor than they were before, while other parts are farther away. So, buildings, flagpoles, or NBA players appear to be falling backwards, as you can see in Figure 9.12. While this kind of apparent distortion (it's not caused by a defect in the lens) can happen with any lens, it's most apparent when a wide angle is used.

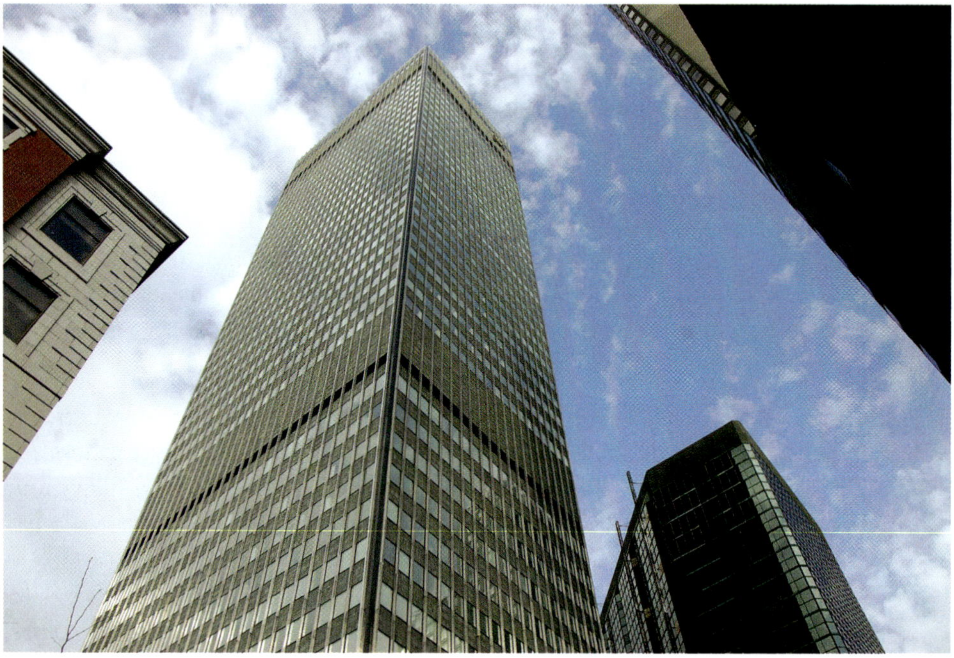

Figure 9.12
Tilting the camera back produces this "falling back" look in architectural photos.

- **Steady cam.** You'll find that you can hand-hold a wide-angle lens at slower shutter speeds, without need for vibration reduction, than you can with a telephoto lens. The reduced magnification of the wide-lens or wide-zoom setting doesn't emphasize camera shake like a telephoto lens does. That's why lack of VR in the 10mm f/2.8 lens isn't much of a handicap, and why its availability in the 10-30mm and 10-100mm lenses is a bonus.
- **Interesting angles.** Many of the factors already listed combine to produce more interesting angles when shooting with wide-angle lenses. Raising or lowering a telephoto lens a few feet probably will have little effect on the appearance of the distant subjects you're shooting. The same change in elevation can produce a dramatic effect for the much closer subjects typically captured with a wide-angle lens or wide-zoom setting.

DOF IN DEPTH

The DOF advantage of wide-angle lenses is diminished when you enlarge your picture; believe it or not, a wide-angle image enlarged and cropped to provide the same subject size as a telephoto shot would have the *same* depth-of-field. Try it: take a wide-angle photo of a friend from a fair distance, and then zoom in to duplicate the picture in a telephoto image. Then, enlarge the wide shot so your friend is the same size in both. The wide photo will have the same depth-of-field (and will have much less detail, too).

Avoiding Potential Wide-Angle Problems

Wide-angle lenses have a few quirks that you'll want to keep in mind when shooting so you can avoid falling into some common traps. Here's a checklist of tips for avoiding common problems:

- **Symptom: converging lines.** Unless you want to use wildly diverging lines as a creative effect, it's a good idea to keep horizontal and vertical lines in landscapes, architecture, and other subjects carefully aligned with the sides, top, and bottom of the frame. That will help you avoid undesired perspective distortion. Sometimes it helps to shoot from a slightly elevated position so you don't have to tilt the camera up or down.
- **Symptom: color fringes around objects.** Lenses are often plagued with fringes of color around backlit objects, produced by *chromatic aberration*, which comes in two forms: *longitudinal/axial*, in which all the colors of light don't focus in the same plane; and *lateral/transverse*, in which the colors are shifted to one side. Axial chromatic aberration can be reduced by stopping down the lens, but transverse CA cannot. Both can be reduced by using lenses with low diffraction index glass (or ED elements, in Nikon nomenclature) and by incorporating elements that cancel the chromatic aberration of other glass in the lens. For example, a strong positive lens made of low dispersion crown glass (made of a soda-lime-silica composite) may be mated with a weaker negative lens made of high-dispersion flint glass, which contains lead.
- **Symptom: lines that bow outward.** Some wide-angle lenses cause straight lines to bow outwards, with the strongest effect at the edges. This is called barrel distortion. You can also minimize this effect simply by framing your photo with some extra space all around, so the edges where the defect is most obvious can be cropped out of the picture. Some image editors, such as Photoshop and Photoshop Elements have a lens distortion correction feature.
- **Symptom: light and dark areas when using a polarizing filter.** If you know that polarizers work best when the camera is pointed 90 degrees away from the sun and have the least effect when the camera is oriented 180 degrees from the sun, you know only half the story. With lenses having a focal length of 10mm, the angle of view is extensive enough to cause visible problems.

Using Telephoto Focal Lengths

Telephoto focal lengths also can have a dramatic effect on your photography. Here are the most important things you need to know. In the next section, I'll concentrate on telephoto considerations that can be problematic—and how to avoid those problems.

- **Selective focus.** Long lenses have reduced depth-of-field within the frame, allowing you to use selective focus to isolate your subject. You can open the lens up wide to create shallow depth-of-field, or close it down a bit to allow more to be in focus. The flip side of the coin is that when you *want* to make a range of objects sharp, you'll need to use a smaller f/stop to get the depth-of-field you need. Like fire, the depth-of-field of a telephoto lens can be friend or foe. Figure 9.13 shows a photo of a statue, photographed at 100mm at f/5.6 to de-emphasize the distracting background.
- **Getting closer.** Telephoto lenses bring you closer to wildlife, sports action, and candid subjects. No one wants to get a reputation as a surreptitious or "sneaky" photographer (except for paparazzi), but when applied to candids in an open and honest way, a long lens can help you capture memorable moments while retaining enough distance to stay out of the way of events as they transpire.
- **Reduced foreground/increased compression.** Telephoto lenses have the opposite effect of wide angles: they reduce the importance of things in the foreground by squeezing everything together. This compression even makes distant objects appear to be closer to subjects in the foreground and middle ranges. You can use this effect as a creative tool to squeeze subjects together.
- **Accentuates camera shakiness.** Telephoto focal lengths hit you with a double-whammy in terms of camera/photographer shake. Lenses like the 10-100mm Nikon 1 zoom are themselves bulkier and more difficult to hold steady unless you cradle the lens in your left hand. Telephotos also magnify any camera shake. It's no wonder that vibration reduction is a must in longer lenses like the 10-100mm and 30-110mm zooms.
- **Interesting angles require creativity.** Telephoto lenses require more imagination in selecting interesting angles, because the "angle" you do get on your subjects is so narrow. Moving from side to side or a bit higher or lower can make a dramatic difference in a wide-angle shot, but raising or lowering a telephoto lens a few feet probably will have little effect on the appearance of the distant subjects you're shooting.

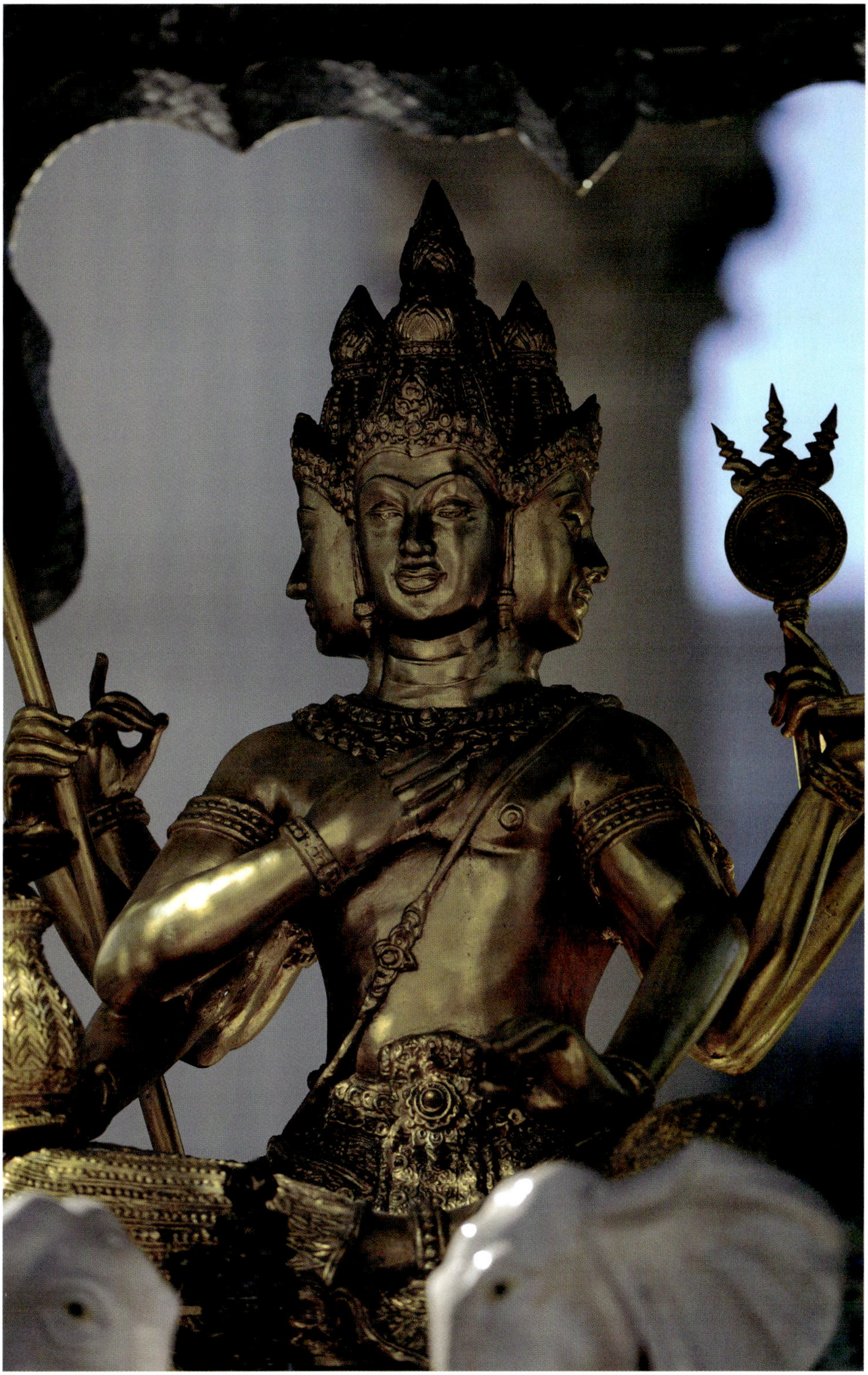

Figure 9.13 A wide f/stop helped isolate the statue from its background.

Avoiding Telephoto Lens Problems

Many of the "problems" that telephoto lenses pose are really just challenges and not that difficult to overcome. Here is a list of the seven most common picture maladies and suggested solutions.

- **Symptom: flat faces in portraits.** Head-and-shoulders portraits of humans tend to be more flattering when a focal length of 25mm to 40mm is used. Longer focal lengths compress the distance between features like noses and ears, making the face look wider and flat. A wide-angle 10mm focal length might make noses look huge and ears tiny when you fill the frame with a face. So stick with 25mm to 40mm focal lengths, going longer only when you're forced to shoot from a greater distance, and wider only when shooting three-quarters/full-length portraits, or group shots.
- **Symptom: blur due to camera shake.** Take advantage of your lens's built-in VR, and, if necessary, use a higher shutter speed (boosting ISO as required). Or, mount your camera on a tripod, monopod, or brace it with some other support. Of those three solutions, only the first will reduce blur caused by *subject* motion; a VR lens or tripod won't help you freeze a race car in mid-lap.
- **Symptom: color fringes.** Chromatic aberration is the most pernicious optical problem found in telephoto lenses. There are others, including spherical aberration, astigmatism, coma, curvature of field, and similarly scary-sounding phenomena. The best solution for any of these is to use a better lens that offers the proper degree of correction, or stop down the lens to minimize the problem. But that's not always possible. Your second best choice may be to correct the fringing in your favorite RAW conversion tool or image editor. Photoshop's Lens Correction filter (found in the Distort menu) offers sliders that minimize both red/cyan and blue/yellow fringing.
- **Symptom: low contrast from haze or fog.** When you're photographing distant objects, a long lens shoots through a lot more atmosphere, which generally is muddied up with extra haze and fog. That dirt or moisture in the atmosphere can reduce contrast and mute colors. Some feel that a skylight or UV filter can help, but this practice is mostly a holdover from the film days. Digital sensors are not sensitive enough to UV light for a UV filter to have much effect. So you should be prepared to boost contrast and color saturation in your Picture Controls menu or image editor if necessary.
- **Symptom: low contrast from flare.** Your 30-110mm and 10-100mm lenses are furnished with lens hoods for a good reason: to reduce flare from bright light sources at the periphery of the picture area, or completely outside it. Because telephoto lenses often create images that are lower in contrast in the first place, you'll want to be especially careful to use a lens hood to prevent further effects on your image (or shade the front of the lens with your hand).

10

Making Light Work for You

Successful photographers and artists have an intimate understanding of the importance of light in shaping an image. Rembrandt was a master of using light to create moods and reveal the character of his subjects. Artist Thomas Kinkade's official tagline is "Painter of Light." The late Dean Collins, co-founder of Finelight Studios, revolutionized how a whole generation of photographers learned and used lighting. Photo guru Ed Pierce conducts seminars called "Captivated by the Light," that reveal his secrets for portrait lighting. It's impossible to underestimate how the use of light adds to—and how misuse can detract from—your photographs.

All forms of visual art use light to shape the finished product. Sculptors don't have control over the light used to illuminate their finished work, so they must create shapes using planes and curved surfaces so that the form envisioned by the artist comes to life from a variety of viewing and lighting angles. Painters, in contrast, have absolute control over both shape and light in their work, as well as the viewing angle, so they can use both the contours of their two-dimensional subjects and the qualities of the "light" they use to illuminate those subjects to evoke the image they want to produce.

Photography is a third form of art. The photographer may have little or no control over the subject (other than posing human subjects) but can often adjust both viewing angle *and* the nature of the light source to create a particular compelling image. The direction and intensity of the light sources create the shapes and textures that we see. The distribution and proportions determine the contrast and tonal values: whether the image is stark or high key, or muted and low in contrast. The colors of the light (because even "white" light has a color balance that the sensor can detect), and how much of those colors the subject reflects or absorbs, paint the hues visible in the image.

As a Nikon V1 photographer, you must learn to be a painter and sculptor of light if you want to move from *taking* a picture to *making* a photograph. This chapter provides an introduction to using the two main types of illumination: *continuous* lighting (such as daylight, incandescent, or fluorescent sources) and the brief, but brilliant snippets of light we call *electronic flash.*

Continuous Illumination versus Electronic Flash

Continuous lighting is exactly what you might think: uninterrupted illumination that is available all the time during a shooting session. Daylight, moonlight, and the artificial lighting encountered both indoors and outdoors count as continuous light sources (although all of them can be "interrupted" by passing clouds, solar eclipses, a blown fuse, or simply by switching a lamp off). Indoor continuous illumination includes both the lights that are there already (such as incandescent lamps or overhead fluorescent lights indoors) and fixtures you supply yourself, including photoflood lamps or reflectors used to bounce existing light onto your subject.

Electronic flash is notable because it can be much more intense than continuous lighting, lasts only a brief moment, and can be much more portable than supplementary incandescent sources. It's a light source you can carry with you and use anywhere. Indeed, although your Nikon V1 does not come with a built-in flash, it can be fitted with a $150 accessory unit like the SB-N5, shown in Figure 10.1. There are advantages and disadvantages to each type of illumination.

Here's a quick checklist of pros and cons:

- **Lighting preview—Pro: continuous lighting.** With continuous lighting, you always know exactly what kind of lighting effect you're going to get and, if multiple lights are used, how they will interact with each other. (See Figure 10.2.)

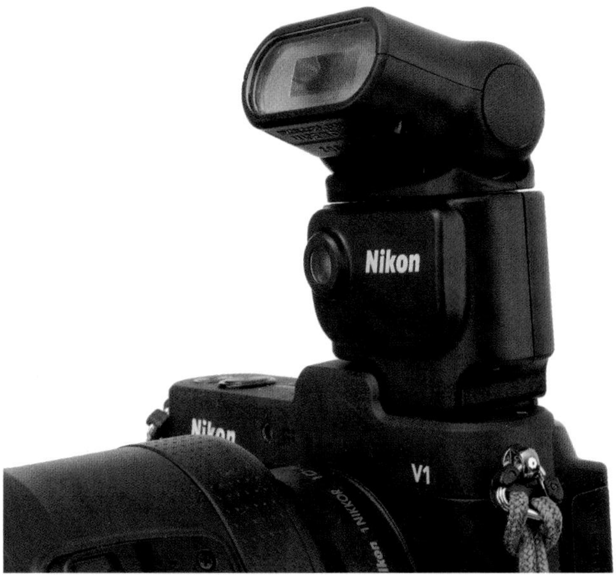

Figure 10.1
One form of supplemental light can be clipped right onto your camera, the optional Nikon SB-N5 Speedlight.

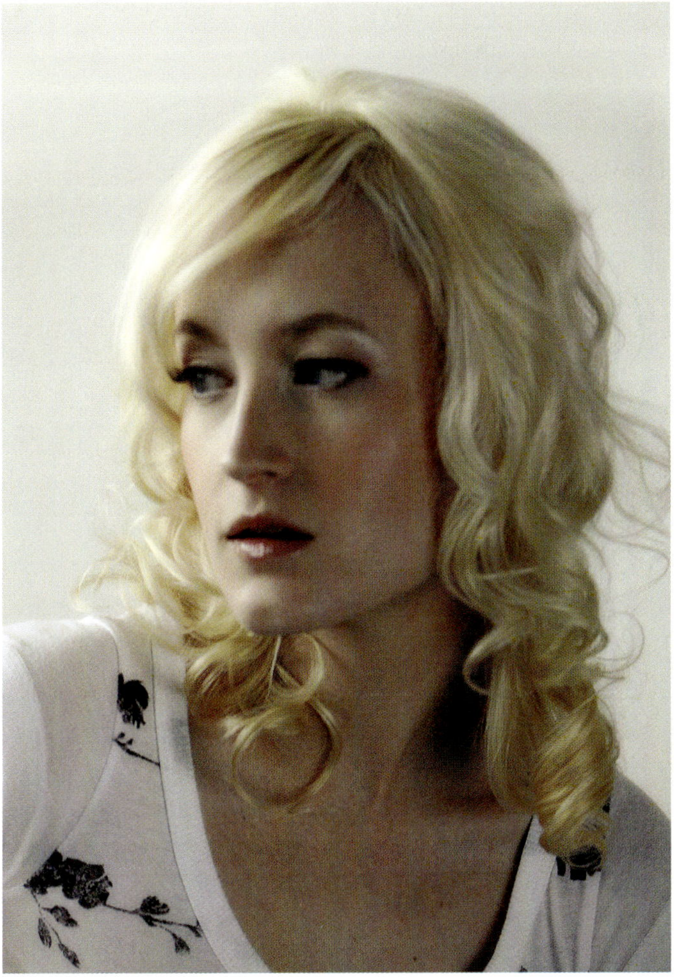

Figure 10.2
You always know how the lighting will look when using continuous illumination.

- **Lighting preview—Con: electronic flash.** With flash, the general effect you're going to see may be a mystery until you've built some experience, and you may need to review a shot on the LCD or EVF, make some adjustments, and then reshoot to get the look you want. (In this sense, a digital camera's review capabilities replace the Polaroid test shots pro photographers relied on in decades past.)
- **Exposure calculation—Pro: continuous lighting.** Your V1 has no problem calculating exposure for continuous lighting, because it remains constant and can be measured right off the imaging sensor. The amount of light available just before the exposure will, in almost all cases, be the same amount of light present when the shutter is released. The V1's Spot metering mode can be used to measure and compare the proportions of light in the highlights and shadows, so you can make an adjustment (such as using more or less fill light) if necessary. You can even use a hand-held light meter to measure the light yourself.

- **Exposure calculation—Con: electronic flash.** Electronic flash illumination doesn't exist until the flash fires, and so can't be measured prior to taking the photo. Instead, the light must be evaluated by metering the intensity of a pre-flash triggered an instant before the main flash, as it is reflected back to the camera and through the lens. If you have a do-it-yourself bent, there are hand-held flash meters, too, including models that measure both flash and continuous light. To use one of these, you need to set the V1 on Manual exposure and use the settings the meter supplies.
- **Evenness of illumination—Pro/con: continuous lighting.** Of continuous light sources, daylight, in particular, provides illumination that tends to fill an image completely, lighting up the foreground, background, and your subject almost equally. Shadows do come into play, of course, so you might need to use reflectors or fill-in light sources to even out the illumination further, but barring objects that block large sections of your image from daylight, the light is spread fairly evenly. Indoors, however, continuous lighting is commonly less evenly distributed. The average living room, for example, has hot spots and dark corners. But on the plus side, you can *see* this uneven illumination and compensate with additional lamps.
- **Evenness of illumination—Con: electronic flash.** Electronic flash units, like continuous light sources such as lamps that don't have the advantage of being located 93 million miles from the subject, suffer from the effects of their proximity. The *inverse square law*, first applied to both gravity and light by Sir Isaac Newton, dictates that as a light source's distance increases from the subject, the amount of light reaching the subject falls off proportionately to the square of the distance. In plain English, that means that a flash or lamp that's eight feet away from a subject provides only one-quarter as much illumination as a source that's four feet away (rather than half as much). (See Figure 10.3.) This translates into relatively shallow "depth-of-light."
- **Action stopping—Con: continuous lighting.** Action stopping with continuous light sources is completely dependent on the shutter speed you've dialed in on the camera. And the speeds available are dependent on the amount of light available and your ISO sensitivity setting. Outdoors in daylight, there will probably be enough sunlight to let you shoot at 1/2,000th second and f/6.3 with a non-grainy sensitivity setting of ISO 400. (See Figure 10.4.) That's a fairly useful combination of settings if you're not using a super-telephoto like the Nikon 1 10-100mm f/3.5-4.5 zoom with a small maximum aperture. But inside, the reduced illumination quickly has you pushing your V1 to its limits. For example, if you're shooting indoor sports, there probably won't be enough available light to allow you to use a 1/2,000th second shutter speed (although I routinely shoot indoor basketball with my V1 at ISO 1600 and 1/500th second at f/4). In many indoor sports situations, you may find yourself limited to 1/500th second or slower, depending on the light available for photography.

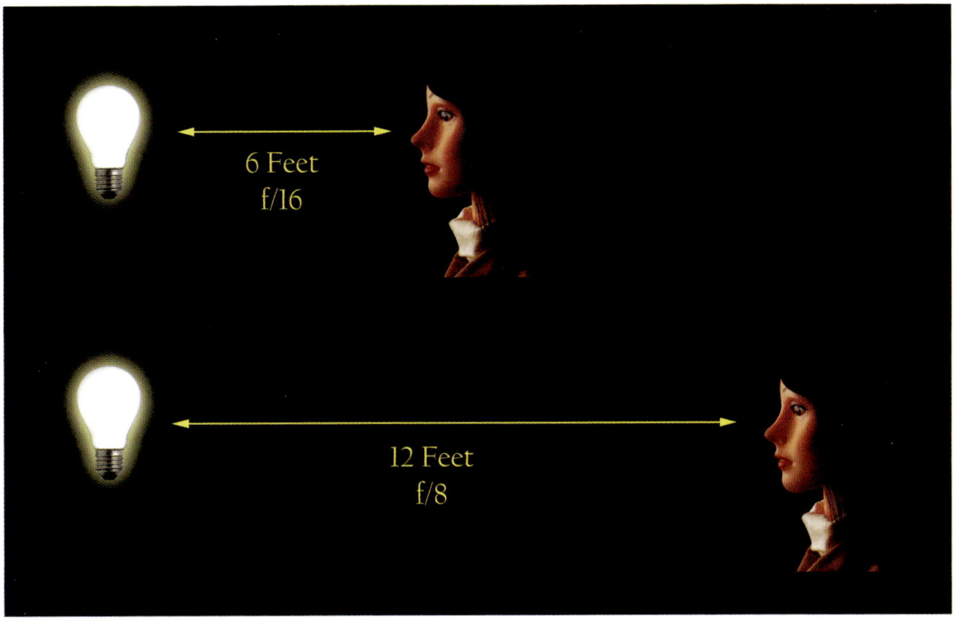

Figure 10.3
A light source that is twice as far away provides only one-quarter as much illumination.

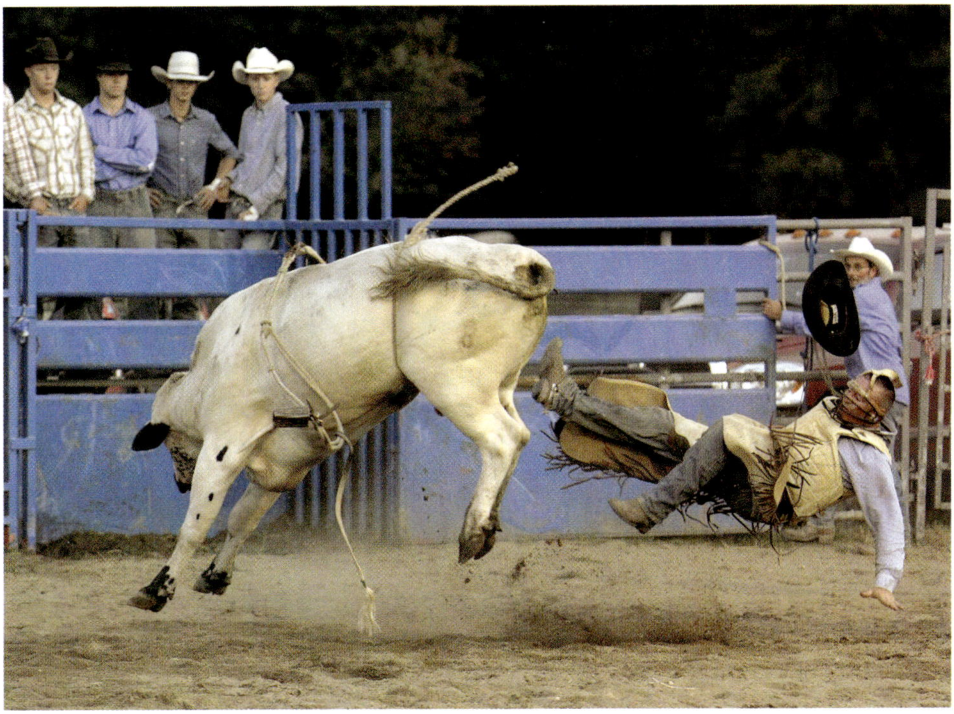

Figure 10.4
A fast shutter speed can freeze almost any action.

- **Action stopping—Pro: electronic flash.** When it comes to the ability to freeze moving objects in their tracks, the advantage goes to electronic flash. The brief duration of electronic flash (1/4000th second when the flash is fired at full power) serves as a very high "shutter speed" when the flash is the main or only source of illumination for the photo. Your V1's shutter speed may be set for 1/250th second during a flash exposure, but if the flash illumination predominates, the *effective* exposure time will be the 1/1,000th to 1/50,000th second or less duration of the flash, because the flash unit reduces the amount of light released by cutting short the duration of the flash. The only fly in the ointment is that, if the ambient light is strong enough, it may produce a secondary, "ghost" exposure, as I'll explain later in this chapter.
- **Cost—Pro: continuous lighting.** Incandescent or fluorescent lamps are generally much less expensive than electronic flash units, which can easily cost several hundred dollars. I've used everything from desktop high-intensity lamps to reflector flood lights for continuous illumination at very little cost. There are lamps made especially for photographic purposes, too. Maintenance is economical, too: many incandescent or fluorescents use bulbs that cost only a few dollars.
- **Cost—Con: electronic flash.** Electronic flash units aren't particularly cheap. The lowest cost (and to date the only) dedicated flash designed specifically for the Nikon mirrorless cameras is the SB-N5, at about $149. The unit is limited in features, however, and intended for those with entry-level cameras.
- **Flexibility—Con: continuous lighting.** Because incandescent and fluorescent lamps are not as bright as electronic flash, the slower shutter speeds required (see Action stopping, above) mean that once you've ventured beyond the anti-shake capabilities of your lens's vibration reduction feature, you may have to use a tripod more often, especially when shooting portraits. The incandescent variety of continuous lighting gets hot, especially in the studio, and the side effects range from discomfort (for your human models) to disintegration (if you happen to be shooting perishable foods like ice cream). The heat also makes it more difficult to add filtration to incandescent sources.
- **Flexibility—Pro: electronic flash.** Electronic flash's action-freezing power allows you to work without a tripod, adding flexibility and speed when choosing angles and positions. Flash units can be easily filtered, and, because the filtration is placed over the light source rather than the lens, you don't need to use high-quality filter material. For example, Roscoe or Lee lighting gels, which may be too flimsy to use in front of the lens, can be mounted or taped in front of your SB-N5 flash with ease.

Continuous Lighting Basics

While continuous lighting and its effects are generally much easier to visualize and use than electronic flash, there are some factors you need to take into account, particularly the color temperature of the light. (Color temperature concerns aren't exclusive to continuous light sources, of course, but the variations tend to be more extreme and less predictable than those of electronic flash, which output relatively consistent daylight-like illumination.)

Color temperature, in practical terms, is how "bluish" or how "reddish" the light appears to be to the digital camera's sensor. Indoor illumination is quite warm, comparatively, and appears reddish to the sensor. Daylight, in contrast, seems much bluer to the sensor. Our eyes (our brains, actually) are quite adaptable to these variations, so white objects don't appear to have an orange tinge when viewed indoors, nor do they seem excessively blue outdoors in full daylight. Yet, these color temperature variations are real and the sensor is not fooled. To capture the most accurate colors, we need to take the color temperature into account in setting the color balance (or *white balance*) of the V1—either automatically using the camera's smarts or manually using our own knowledge and experience.

Daylight

Daylight is produced by the sun, and so is moonlight (which is just reflected sunlight). Daylight is present, of course, even when you can't see the sun. When sunlight is direct, it can be bright and harsh. If daylight is diffused by clouds, softened by bouncing off objects such as walls or your photo reflectors, or filtered by shade, it can be much dimmer and less contrasty.

Daylight's color temperature can vary quite widely. It is highest in temperature (most blue) at noon when the sun is directly overhead, because the light is traveling through a minimum amount of the filtering layer we call the atmosphere. The color temperature at high noon may be 6,000K. At other times of day, the sun is lower in the sky and the particles in the air provide a filtering effect that warms the illumination to about 5,500K for most of the day. Starting an hour before dusk and for an hour after sunrise, the warm appearance of the sunlight is even visible to our eyes when the color temperature may dip to 5,000-4,500K, as shown in Figure 10.5.

Because you'll be taking so many photos in daylight, you'll want to learn how to use or compensate for the brightness and contrast of sunlight, as well as how to deal with its color balance.

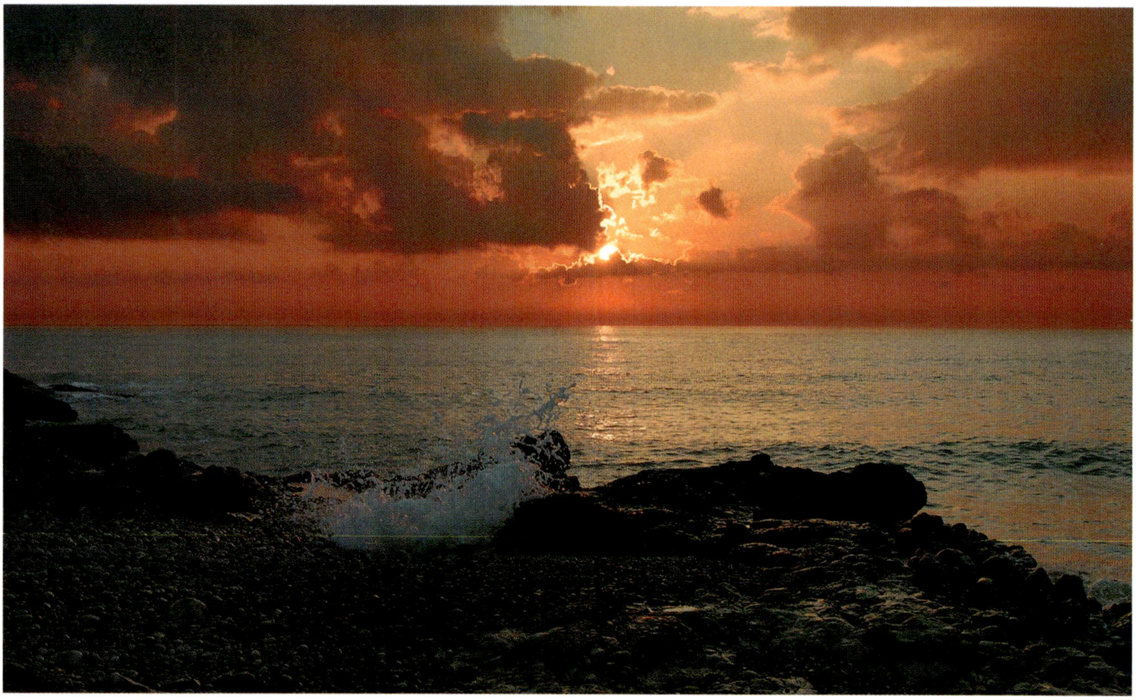

Figure 10.5 At dawn and dusk, the color temperature of daylight may dip as low as 4,500K.

Incandescent/Tungsten Light

The term incandescent or tungsten illumination is usually applied to the direct descendents of Thomas Edison's original electric lamp. Such lights consist of a glass bulb that contains a vacuum, or is filled with a halogen gas, and contains a tungsten filament that is heated by an electrical current, producing photons and heat. Tungsten-halogen lamps are a variation on the basic light bulb, using a more rugged (and longer-lasting) filament that can be heated to a higher temperature, housed in a thicker glass or quartz envelope, and filled with iodine or bromine ("halogen") gases. The higher temperature allows tungsten-halogen (or quartz-halogen/quartz-iodine, depending on their construction) lamps to burn "hotter" and whiter. Although popular for automobile headlamps today, they've also been used for photographic illumination.

Although incandescent illumination isn't a perfect reference source, it's close enough that the color temperature of such lamps can be precisely calculated and used for photography without concerns about color variation (at least, until the very end of the lamp's life).

Of course, old-style tungsten lamps are on the way out, to be replaced either by compact fluorescent lights (CFL) or newer, more energy efficient (and expensive) tungsten lights. Despite government regulations, tungsten lamps can't be phased out completely, because CFLs don't work in all fixtures and for all applications, such as dimmers (even if you purchase special "dimmable" CFLs), electronic timer or "dusk-to-dawn" light controllers, some illuminated wall switches, or with motion sensors. Only certain types of CFLs (cold cathode models) operate outside in cold weather; they emit IR signals that can confuse the remote control of your TV, air-conditioner, etc., and the typical CFL has a Color Rendering Index of 80, compared to the virtually perfect 100 rating of incandescent lights.

The other qualities of this type of lighting, such as contrast, are dependent on the distance of the lamp from the subject, type of reflectors used, and other factors that I'll explain later in this chapter.

Fluorescent Light/Other Light Sources

Fluorescent light has some advantages in terms of illumination, but some disadvantages from a photographic standpoint. This type of lamp generates light through an electrochemical reaction that emits most of its energy as visible light, rather than heat, which is why the bulbs don't get as hot. The type of light produced varies depending on the phosphor coatings and type of gas in the tube. So, the illumination fluorescent bulbs produce can vary widely in its characteristics.

That's not great news for photographers. Different types of lamps have different "color temperatures" that can't be precisely measured in degrees Kelvin, because the light isn't produced by heating. Worse, fluorescent lamps have a discontinuous spectrum of light that can have some colors missing entirely. A particular type of tube can lack certain shades of red or other colors (see Figure 10.6), which is why fluorescent lamps and other alternative technologies such as sodium-vapor illumination can produce ghastly looking human skin tones. Their spectra can lack the reddish tones we associate with healthy skin and emphasize the blues and greens popular in horror movies.

Also gaining in popularity are LED light sources, particularly for movies, in the form of compact units that clip onto the camera and provide a continuous beam of light to fill in shadows indoors or out, and/or to provide the main illumination when shooting video inside. As the Nikon V1 doesn't have an industry standard accessory shoe, if you want to use an LED light source, you'll need to use the optional AS-N1000 multi accessory port adapter or attach a flash bracket to the tripod socket, like the one shown in Figure 7.17 in Chapter 7 (there the bracket was used with the ME-1 microphone).

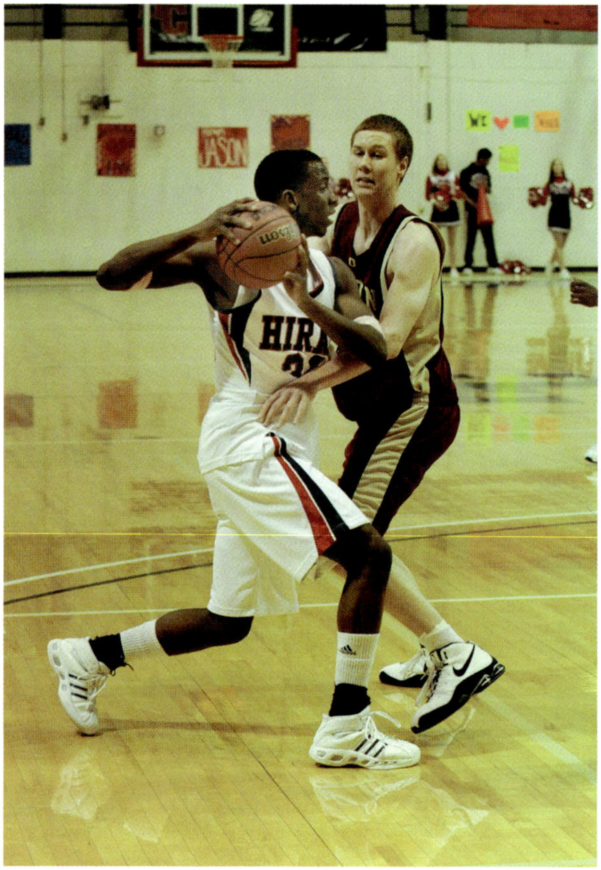

Figure 10.6
The uncorrected fluorescent lighting in the gym added a distinct greenish cast to this image when exposed with a daylight white balance setting.

Electronic Flash Basics

Until you delve into the situation deeply enough, it might appear that serious photographers have a love/hate relationship with electronic flash. You'll often hear that flash photography is less natural looking, and that the built-in flash in most cameras should never be used as the primary source of illumination because it provides a harsh, garish look. Indeed, the most advanced "pro" cameras like the Nikon D2xs and D3 don't have a built-in flash at all. Available ("continuous") lighting is praised, and built-in flash photography seems to be roundly denounced.

In truth, however, the bias is against *bad* flash photography. Indeed, flash has become the studio light source of choice for pro photographers, because it's more intense (and its intensity can be varied to order by the photographer), freezes action, frees you from using a tripod (unless you want to use one to lock down a composition), and has a snappy, consistent light quality that matches daylight. Even experienced photographers will cede that the tiny, optional, and not very powerful SB-N5 flash has some important uses as an adjunct to existing light, particularly to fill in dark shadows.

For the SB-N5, the full burst of light lasts about 1/4,000th second at full power and provides enough illumination to shoot a subject 10 feet away at f/5.6 using the ISO 400 setting. As you can see, the built-in flash is somewhat limited in range. Indeed, at ISO 400, it has a range of about 3.5 feet (at f/16) to 16 feet (at f/3.5). You probably won't be using this Speedlight at ISO 100 or ISO 200 very often, unless you're photographing subjects that are very close.

An electronic flash is triggered at the instant of exposure, during a period when the sensor is fully exposed by an electronic or mechanical shutter. With the electronic shutter, the entire sensor is sensitive to light for a period lasting no more than 1/60th second, so with the electronic shutter the camera must be set to a shutter speed of 1/60th second or slower to allow the full frame to be exposed. As I mentioned earlier in this book, the V1 also has a physical vertically traveling mechanical shutter that consists of two curtains. The first curtain opens and moves to the opposite side of the frame, at which point the shutter is completely open and the sensor is fully exposed. The flash can be triggered at this point (so-called *front-curtain sync*), making the flash exposure. Then, after a delay that can vary from 30 seconds to 1/250th second (with the Nikon V1 using its mechanical shutter), a second curtain begins moving across the sensor plane, covering up the sensor again. If the flash is triggered just before the second curtain starts to close, then *second-curtain sync* is used. (I'll describe these in more detail later in this chapter.) In both cases, though, a shutter speed of 1/250th second is the maximum that can be used to take a photo using the mechanical shutter. If you use a faster shutter speed, you'll expose only the part of the sensor exposed by the gap between the shutter curtains when the flash fires.

Determining Exposure

Calculating the proper exposure for an electronic flash photograph is a bit more complicated than determining the settings for continuous light. The right exposure isn't simply a function of how far away your subject is (which the V1 can figure out based on the autofocus distance that's locked in just prior to taking the picture). Various objects reflect more or less light at the same distance so, obviously, the camera needs to measure the amount of light reflected back and through the lens. Yet, as the flash itself isn't available for measuring until it's triggered, the V1 has nothing to measure.

The solution is to fire the flash twice. The initial shot is a *monitor pre-flash* that can be analyzed whether the light is direct or bounced with the flash rotated, then followed virtually instantaneously by a main flash (to the eye the bursts appear to be a single flash) that's given exactly the calculated intensity needed to provide a correct exposure. As a result, the primary flash may be longer in duration for distant objects and shorter in duration for closer subjects, depending on the required intensity for exposure. This through-the-lens evaluative flash exposure system is called i-TTL (Intelligent Through The Lens), and it operates whenever the SB-N5 is used.

Electronic Flash Nuts & Bolts

The bursts of light we call electronic flash are produced by a flash of photons generated by an electrical charge that is accumulated in a component called a *capacitor* and then directed through a glass tube containing xenon gas, which absorbs the energy and emits the brief flash.

As I mentioned in the previous section, the SB-N5 electronic flash is triggered at the instant of exposure, during a period when the sensor is fully exposed to the incoming light. The V1 has that electronic shutter—which limits flash exposures to no more than 1/60th second. Flash is not possible when using Electronic (Hi). In addition to the electronic shutter, the V1 also has that vertically traveling shutter that consists of two curtains. The first curtain opens and moves to the opposite side of the frame, at which point the shutter is completely open. The flash can be triggered at this point (so-called *front-curtain sync*), making the flash exposure. Then, after a delay that can vary from 30 seconds to 1/250th second (with the V1; other cameras may sync at a faster or slower speed), a second curtain begins moving across the sensor plane, covering up the sensor again. If the flash is triggered just before the second curtain starts to close, then *rear-curtain sync* is used. In both cases, though, a shutter speed of 1/250th second is the maximum that can be used to take a photo.

Figure 10.7 illustrates how this works, with a fanciful illustration of a generic shutter (your V1's mechanical shutter does *not* look like this, and some vertically traveling shutters move bottom to top rather than the top-to-bottom motion shown). Both curtains

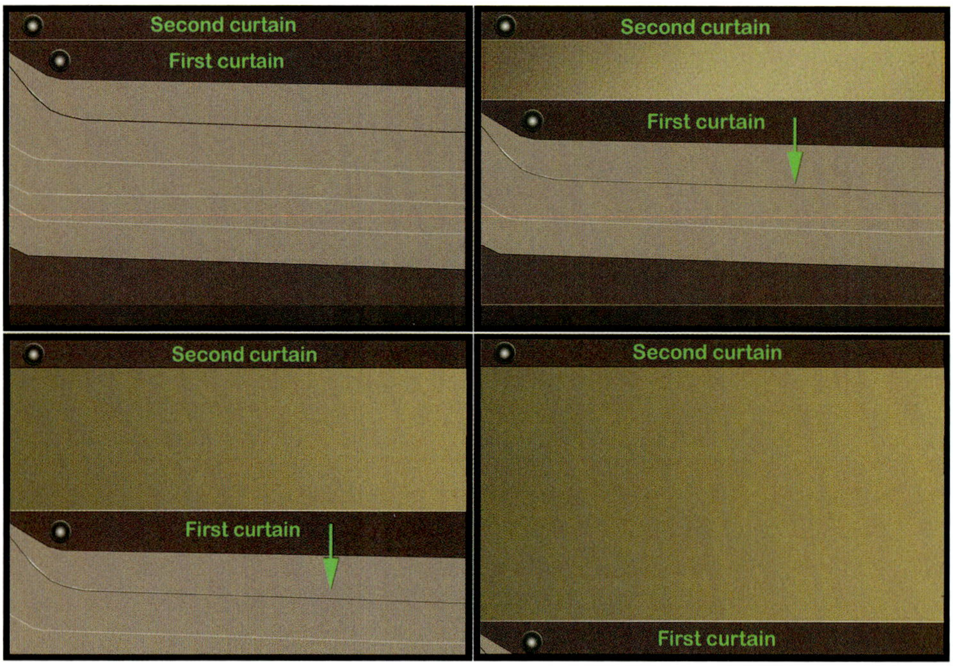

Figure 10.7 A mechanical focal plane shutter has two curtains, the lower, or first curtain, and an upper, second curtain.

are tightly closed at upper left. At upper right, the first curtain begins to move downwards, starting to expose a narrow slit that reveals the sensor behind the shutter. At lower left, the first curtain moves downwards farther until, as you can see at lower right in the figure, the sensor is fully exposed.

When front-curtain sync is used, the flash is triggered at the instant that the sensor is completely exposed. The shutter then remains open for an additional length of time (from 30 seconds to 1/250th second), and the second curtain begins to move downward, covering the sensor once more. When rear-curtain sync is activated, the flash is triggered *after* the main exposure is over, just before the second curtain begins to move downward.

Using the SB-N5 Flash

The Nikon SB-N5 Speedlight, which, as I write this book is the only dedicated flash unit compatible with the Nikon V1, is easy to use. Although you may be able to use the SB-N5 to trigger other flashes when the additional units are set to slave mode, most of us will primarily stick to the official Nikon 1 unit. This next section will explain how to use the flash, and work with its features.

Basics

The SB-N5 uses no batteries, as it's powered by the rechargeable cell in the Nikon V1. So, installation calls for simply sliding the multi accessory port cover off, and slipping the foot of the flash unit into the mount. It locks into place automatically. Store the cover in a safe place where you'll be able to find it easily when you're done using the flash. The components of the SB-N5 are shown in Figure 10.8.

- **Flash lens.** The flash tube resides behind this translucent focusing lens, which directs the beam to provide coverage for focal lengths of 10mm or greater.
- **Swivel head.** The flash head rotates a full 180 degrees left or right, so you could point it behind the camera, to the left or right sides, and any position in between. One conceivable use for the reversing feature would be to turn it around (and probably angle it up slightly) to point the flash at a white card reflector (or even a white shirt) to provide a broad, diffused light source.
- **Tilt angle indicators.** The flash head can also be tilted upwards for bounce flash. There are stops at the 60-, 75-, and 90-degree (straight up) positions. When used with the swivel head in the reversed position, you gain additional angles of 120, 150, and 180 degrees (as well as anything in between the stops), plus equivalent angles to the left and right of the camera when swiveled to one side or the other. That's a lot of flexibility.

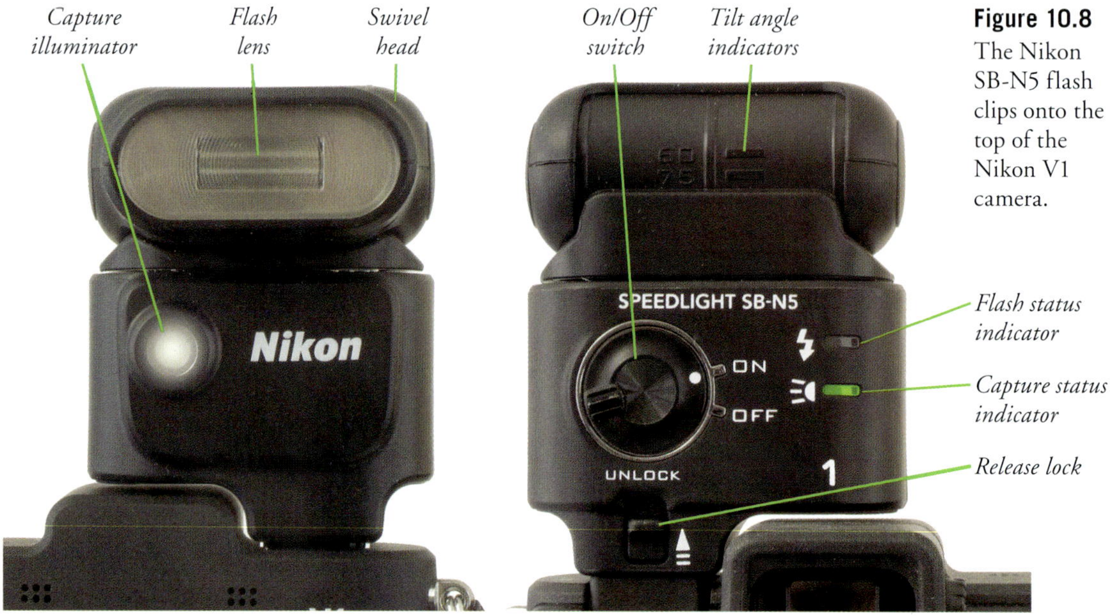

Figure 10.8 The Nikon SB-N5 flash clips onto the top of the Nikon V1 camera.

- **Capture illuminator.** This white LED illuminates in Smart Photo Selector and Motion Snapshot modes for about six seconds while the camera is buffering shots. These modes are described in Chapter 4.
- **Flash Status indicator.** The red top LED lights to show that the flash is charged and ready to shoot. This lamp and the capture status indicator also flash in various ways (described below in Table 10.1) to indicate other status conditions.
- **Capture status indicator.** Glows green when the V1 is set to Smart Photo Selector or Motion Snapshot modes to indicate that the capture illuminator is ready to light up during buffering.
- **On/Off Switch.** Rotate to turn the flash on or off.
- **Release lock.** When you're ready to dismount the flash, press this button upwards to unlock the flash foot.

Choosing a Flash Sync Mode

The Nikon V1 has six flash sync modes, selected by choosing the Flash Mode entry in the Shooting menu, as described in Chapter 8. Not all six modes necessarily appear in the menu at once. When using Programmed auto or Aperture-priority auto exposure modes, only Fill Flash, Red-Eye Reduction, and Rear-Curtain Sync appear. If you're using Shutter-priority auto or Manual exposure, all six are shown. When using Scene Auto Selector mode, you can choose only Fill Flash or Red-Eye Reduction; with Smart Photo Selector, there are no flash choices at all, as the camera makes all the settings. If

Table 10.1 Status Light Indications

Display	Condition
Flash Status Lamp—Steady Red	Flash is charged and ready to go.
Capture Status Lamp—Steady Green	Camera is in Smart Photo Selector or Motion Snapshot modes and flash is ready to provide buffering illumination.
Flash Status Lamp Blinks Red for 3 seconds after photo is taken	Full power flash was insufficient for exposure. Move closer or increase ISO sensitivity.
Either lamp blinks once per second	Flash has overheated from continuous use. Turn flash off to allow it to cool down.
Both lamps blink once every two seconds.	Communication error. Make sure flash is attached to the V1 firmly.
Flash Status Lamp blinks red eight times per second.	Internal error. Turn off camera and remove flash. Remount and try again. If error light returns have the flash serviced.

the SB-N5 flash is not attached, or is attached but not powered on, none of them are available; the Flash Mode, Flash Control, and Flash Compensation menu entries are all removed from the main Shooting menu.

The flash sync modes (which I've listed in logical order, so the explanation will make more sense, rather than the order in which they appear during the selection cycle) are available from the Flash Mode menu (see Figure 10.9) as follows:

- **Front-curtain sync (all exposure modes).** This is the default setting, and does not actually appear in the menu. It operates all the time, and applies to each of the next four sync options. The only time front-curtain sync is not used is when you select either Rear-curtain sync or Rear-curtain sync with Slow sync (described at the end of this list).
- **Fill flash.** The flash will fire all the time, illuminating the shadows of subjects within its range, as in the example shown in Figure 10.10. The only hitch is that you should set the shutter type to mechanical shutter, and must be able to use a shutter speed of 1/250th second or slower for the main exposure, as the V1 locks out faster shutter speeds when the flash is mounted and turned on.
- **Red-eye reduction (all exposure modes).** In this mode, there is a one-second lag after pressing the shutter release before the picture is actually taken, during which the V1's red-eye reduction lamp lights, causing the subject's pupils to contract (assuming they are looking at the camera), and thus reducing potential red-eye effects. Don't use with moving subjects or when you can't abide the delay.

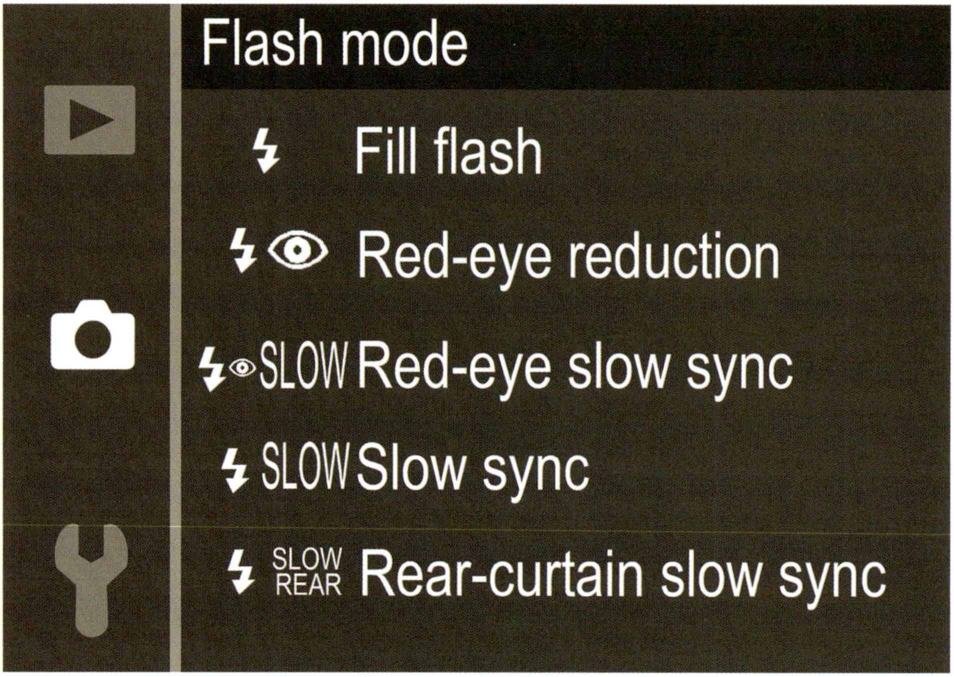

Figure 10.9
Flash sync modes are available from the Flash Mode entry in the Shooting menu.

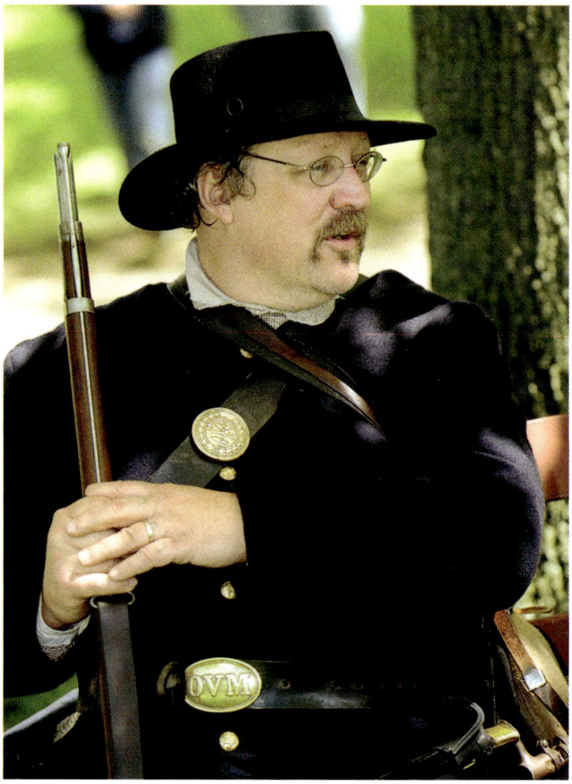

Figure 10.10
Fill flash can brighten inky shadows indoors or out.

- **Slow sync (P and A modes only).** This setting allows the V1 in Program and Aperture-priority modes to use shutter speeds as slow as 30 seconds with the flash to help balance a background illuminated with ambient light with your main subject, which will be lit by the electronic flash. You'll want to use a tripod at slower shutter speeds, of course. As shown in Figure 10.11, it's common that the ambient light will be incandescent illumination that's much warmer than the electronic flash's "daylight" balance, so, if you want the two sources to match, you may want to use a warming filter on the flash. That can be done with a gel. (That's not a convenient approach, and many find the warm/cool mismatch unobjectionable and don't bother with filtration.)
- **Red-eye reduction with slow sync (P and A modes only).** This mode combines slow sync with the V1's red-eye reduction behavior when using Program or Aperture-priority modes.

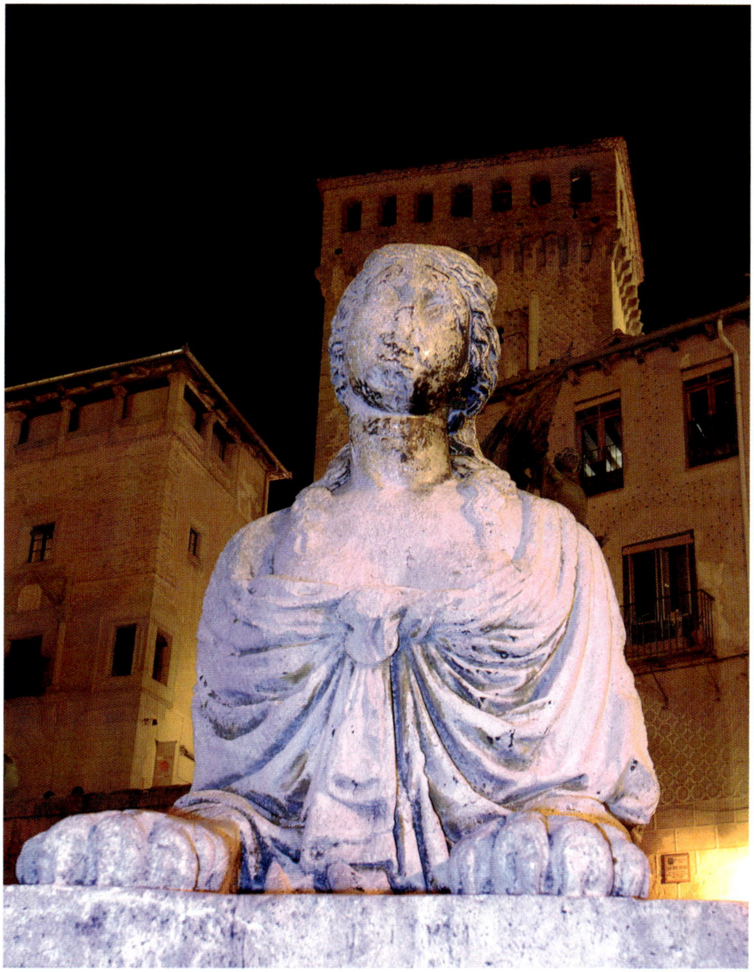

Figure 10.11 I deliberately used flash and slow sync to separate this Roman sphinx sculpture (limned in bluish light from the flash) from the background illuminated by warmer incandescents.

- **Rear-curtain sync (S and M modes only).** With this setting, which can be used with Shutter-priority or Manual exposure modes, the front curtain opens completely and remains open for the duration of the exposure. Then, the flash is fired and the rear curtain closes. If the subject is moving and ambient light levels are high enough, the movement will cause a secondary "ghost" exposure that appears behind the flash exposure (trailing it). You'll find more on "ghost" exposures next.
- **Rear-curtain sync with slow sync (P and A modes only).** With this setting, which can be used with Program and Aperture-priority modes only, the front curtain opens completely and remains open for the duration of the exposure. Then, the flash is fired and the rear curtain closes. If the subject is moving and ambient light levels are high enough, the movement will cause a secondary "ghost" exposure that appears behind the flash exposure (trailing it). You'll find more on "ghost" exposures next. In Program and Aperture-priority modes, the V1 will combine rear-curtain sync with slow shutter speeds to balance ambient light with flash illumination. (It's best to use a tripod to avoid blur at these slow shutter speeds.)

Ghost Images

The difference might not seem like much, but whether you use first-curtain sync (the default setting) or rear-curtain sync (an optional setting) can make a significant difference to your photograph *if the ambient light in your scene also contributes to the image.* That can be a serious problem when using the electronic shutter, which syncs at speeds no faster than 1/60th second. Such a slow shutter speed allows sufficient ambient light that a second exposure is entirely possible.

With the mechanical shutter and faster shutter speeds, particularly the 1/250th second top, there isn't as much time for the ambient light to register, unless it is very bright. If you're within the SB-N5's flash range, it's likely that the Speedlight will provide almost all the illumination, so the choice of first-curtain sync or second-curtain sync isn't very important.

However, at slower shutter speeds, or with very bright ambient light levels, there is a significant difference, particularly if your subject is moving, or the camera isn't steady. In any of those situations, the ambient light will register as a second image accompanying the flash exposure, and if there is movement (camera or subject), that additional image will not be in the same place as the flash exposure. It will show as a ghost image and, if the movement is significant enough, as a blurred ghost image trailing in front of or behind your subject in the direction of the movement.

As I mentioned earlier, when you're using first-curtain sync, the flash goes off the instant the shutter opens, producing an image of the subject on the sensor. Then, the shutter remains open for an additional period (which can be from 30 seconds to 1/250th second). If your subject is moving, say, towards the right side of the frame, the ghost image produced by the ambient light will produce a blur on the right side of the original

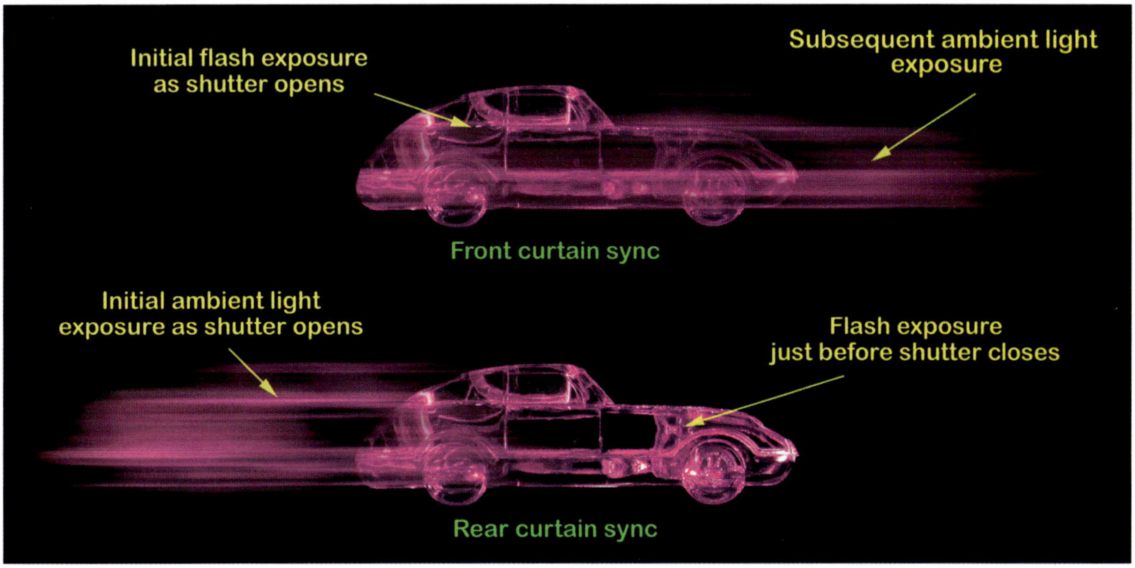

Figure 10.12 Front-curtain sync produces an image that trails in front of the flash exposure (top), while rear-curtain sync creates a more "natural looking" trail behind the flash image (bottom).

subject image, making it look as if your sharp (flash-produced) image is chasing the ghost. (See Figure 10.12, top.) For those of us who grew up with lightning-fast superheroes who always left a ghost trail *behind them*, that looks unnatural (see Figure 10.12, bottom).

So, Nikon provides rear (second) curtain sync to remedy the situation. In that mode, the shutter opens, as before. The shutter remains open for its designated duration, and the ghost image is captured by the sensor. If your subject moves from the left side of the frame to the right side, the ghost will move from left to right, too. *Then*, about 1.5 milliseconds before the second shutter curtain closes, the flash is triggered, producing a nice, sharp flash image *ahead* of the ghost image. Voilà! We have monsieur *le Flash* outrunning his own trailing image.

EVERY WHICH WAY, INCLUDING UP

Note that, although I describe the ghost effect in terms of subject matter that is moving left to right in a horizontally oriented composition, it can occur in any orientation, and with the subject moving in *any* direction. (Try photographing a falling rock, if you can, and you'll see the same effect.) Nor are the ghost images affected by the fact that modern shutters travel vertically rather than horizontally. Secondary images are caused between the time the first curtain fully opens, and the second curtain begins to close. The direction of travel of the shutter curtains, or the direction of your subject, does not matter.

Sync Speed Problems Avoided

Using a shutter speed faster than 1/250th second with the mechanical shutter, or a speed faster than 1/60th second with the electronic shutter could potentially create problems. In either case, because only part of the sensor is exposed/sensitized at one time, you'd end up with only a partial exposure, seen as a narrow band. Fortunately, Nikon has taken care of this problem for us. When you're using the mechanical shutter, any shutter speeds faster than 1/250th second are locked out and unavailable, even if you're shooting in manual mode. If you want to use a faster shutter speed, there's no need to remove the SB-N5; just turn it off and full access to all the speeds will be restored (and the flash will not fire, of course). The same thing happens with the electronic shutter. Speeds faster than 1/60th second are locked out when the flash is mounted and turned on. Not all shutter speeds slower than the sync speed setting are available with particular exposure modes. The usable shutter speeds in each mode are shown in Table 10.2.

Flash Control

The Flash Control entry in the Shooting menu is used to switch between i-TTL (intelligent through the lens) metering, and manual exposure.

- **i-TTL.** This mode, indicated as TTL in the Flash Control menu, tells the Nikon V1 to issue a brief pre-flash just as the shutter opens (or as the electronic shutter becomes active). This pre-flash bounces off your subject and is captured by the sensor, which uses the information to determine the exposure. Because the pre-flash emits just before the main flash burst, it's not noticeable.

Table 10.2 Available Shutter Speeds When Using Flash

Exposure mode	Shutter speeds available
Mechanical Shutter	
Scene Auto Selector	1/250-1 second
Shutter-Priority Auto	1/250-30 seconds
Manual	1/250-30 seconds, Bulb
Programmed Auto	1/250-1/60 second
Aperture-Priority Auto	1/250-1/60 second
Electronic Shutter	
Scene Auto Selector	1/60-1 second
Shutter-Priority Auto	1/60-30 seconds
Manual	1/60-30 seconds, Bulb
Programmed Auto	1/60 second
Aperture-Priority Auto	1/60 second

- **Manual.** If you select this mode, you can press the right directional button and choose a power level for the flash. Select from Full, 1/2, 1/4, 1/8, 1/16, or 1/32 power. No exposure metering is done in manual flash mode, so you'll need to estimate or adjust the exposure yourself. Manual exposure is useful when you want a specific amount of flash, perhaps because you're shooting an extreme close-up photo and i-TTL overexposes the image. Or, you might prefer slightly more or slightly less fill flash and want to use manual adjustments to tailor the power of the SB-N5 to suit. (See also Flash Compensation, described next, for another way to adjust flash exposure.) The flash compensation icon at lower right in the display blinks as a warning when the flash is activated if you've selected Manual flash exposure.

Using Flash Exposure Compensation

You can manually add or subtract exposure to the flash exposure calculated by the V1. Just choose Flash Compensation from the Shooting menu, and select up to +1 more exposure (in one-third stop increments) or –3 stops (in one-third stop increments). The smaller range of plus exposure steps means it's more difficult to boost exposure for flash pictures that are too dark than it is to reduce exposure for overly bright images. That makes sense from a technological standpoint (it's easy to cut the flash burst short) and logical standpoint (as the SB-N5 is a bit underpowered to begin with). Flash compensation will be displayed at the bottom of the LCD/EVF screen, and is "sticky." Turning the camera or flash off does not cancel flash compensation. You must return to the menu and zero it out manually when you no longer need the adjustment.

Part IV

Enhancing Your Experience

What do you do after the shutter clicks and your image has been captured in electrons for posterity? This final part of the book will help you get more from your Nikon V1 as you download and edit the pictures you've taken, and take the steps necessary to keep your camera humming like the finely (non-oiled) machine that it really is.

Chapter 11 discusses some accessories and add-ons that work well with your Nikon V1, including the optional GP-N100 GPS unit, Wi-Fi cards, and smartphone/tablet applications. Chapter 12 details some of your options for downloading and editing your photographs. I'll provide quick introductions to the software bundled with your camera, and describe some of the other applications available to convert RAW files and fine-tune images. The chapter is not a software how-to—this book is virtually 100 percent devoted to photographic shooting techniques. (I want to help you *avoid* having to patch up your pictures in Photoshop where possible, by capturing them correctly in the camera.) Chapter 13 tells you everything you need to know about upgrading your camera's firmware, protecting your LCD and memory card data, and, when necessary, cleaning your sensor manually.

11

Accessories and Add-Ons

Unless you only take pictures, and then immediately print them directly to a PictBridge-compatible printer, somewhere along the line you're going to need to make use of the broad array of software available for the Nikon V1. The picture fixing options in the Retouch menu let you make only modest modifications to your carefully crafted photos. If your needs involve more than fixing red-eye, cropping and trimming, and maybe adjusting tonal values with D-Lighting, you're definitely going to want to use a utility or editor of some sort to perfect your images. After you've captured some great images and have them safely stored on your Nikon V1's memory card, you'll need to transfer them from your camera and memory card to your computer, where they can be organized, fine-tuned in an image editor, and prepared for web display, printing, or some other final destination.

Geotagging with the Nikon GP-N100

The Nikon 1 product line gained a lot of credibility as a tool for serious photographers when Nikon introduced the compact Nikon GP-N100 Global Positioning System device. The unit makes it easy to tag your images with the same kind of longitude, latitude, altitude, and time stamp information that is supplied by the GPS unit you use in your car. (Don't have a GPS? Photographers who get lost in the boonies as easily as I do *must* have one of these!) The geotagging information is stored in the metadata space within your image files, and can be accessed by Nikon ViewNX 2, or by online photo services such as mypicturetown.com and Flickr.

Geotagging can also be done by attaching geographic information to the photo after it's already been taken. This is often done with online sharing services, such as Flickr, which allow you to associate your uploaded photographs with a map, city, street address, or postal code. When properly geotagged and uploaded to sites like Flickr, users can browse through your photos using a map, finding pictures you've taken in a given area, or even searching through photos taken at the same location by other users. Of course, in this day and age it's probably wise not to include GPS information in photos of your home, especially if your photos can be viewed by an unrestricted audience.

Having this information available makes it easier to track where your pictures are taken. That can be essential, as I learned from a trip out West this Spring, where I found the red rocks, canyons, and arroyos of Nevada, Utah, Arizona, and Colorado all pretty much look alike to my untrained eye. Today, I use GPS extensively in my work, for more than just tagging photographs. In addition to the GPS in my automobile, which helps me find the general neighborhood of shooting spots, based on the coordinate information I can get from various mapping applications and utilities installed on my iPad and iPhone, I use a hand-held Garmin Etrex e20 to go to (and mark) exact locations. The e20 lets me download information directly from my computer through a USB cable before I march off in search of a site.

Now we have GPS units especially for cameras, like the GP-N100 for the V1. Like all GPS units, the Nikon unit obtains its data by triangulating signals from satellites orbiting the Earth. At about $150, it's not cheap, but those who need geotagging will find it to be a bargain.

The GP-N100 (see Figure 11.1) slips onto the multi accessory port on top of the Nikon V1. It uses standard GPS—what is called "standalone" or "autonomous" GPS—that operates using radio signals from satellites. It can also use the optional Assisted GPS (A-GPS) services using network data connections to improve accuracy and shorten

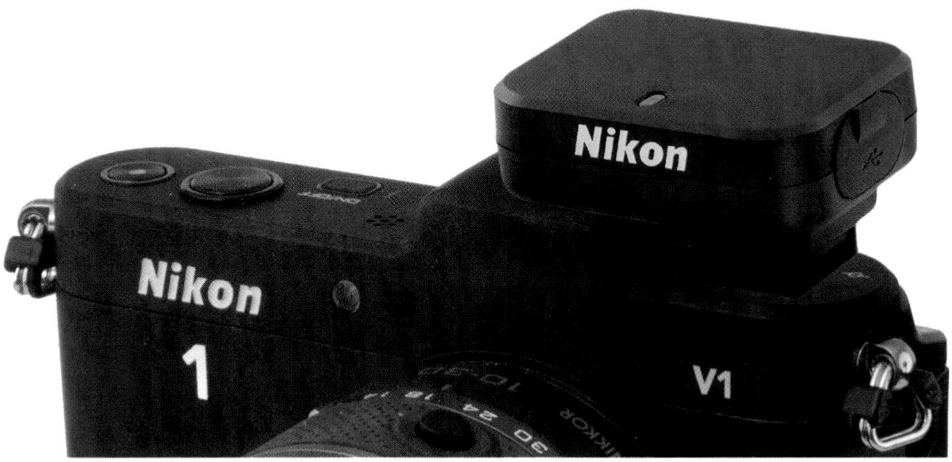

Figure 11.1
Nikon GP-N100 geotagging unit.

what is called "time to first fix" (which can be slow if the unit has difficulty accessing satellite data). In that mode, you need to link the unit (and camera) to an Internet-connected computer (your laptop will do) to use resources provided by Nikon data services. You'll need to download an application called GP-N100 Utility software (in versions for both Windows and Mac OS), which retrieves Assisted GPS files which can be used for up to two weeks before you need to log on again to download an update. Note that you don't need to be connected to the Internet to use A-GPS; once you've downloaded a non-expired data file, GP-N100 will happily work with the data without further fuss until the next update is required.

The unit is easy to use and draws its power from the V1. Accurate to within 33 feet, the 0.7 ounce unit takes about 40 seconds to acquire (under an open sky) positioning data from a cold start, and around three seconds from a hot start after the camera has already been in use.

The first step is to allow the GP-N100 to acquire signals from at least three satellites. If you've used a GPS in your car, you'll know that satellite acquisition works best outdoors under a clear sky and out of the "shadow" of tall buildings, and the Nikon unit is no exception. It takes about 40 seconds for the GP-N100 to "connect." A red blinking LED means that GPS data is not being recorded; a green blinking LED signifies that the unit has acquired three satellites and is recording data. When the LED is solid green, the unit has connected to four or more satellites, and is recording data with optimum accuracy.

Next, set up the camera by selecting the GPS option found under the Setup menu on the Nikon V1, first described in Chapter 8. As I noted, the GPS menu appears only when the GP-N100 device is attached and functioning. You can select:

- **Auto meter-off.** You can choose Enable or Disable. Enabling reduces battery drain by allowing the V1 to turn off exposure meters while using the GP-N100 after the time specified for Auto Power Off in the Setup menu has elapsed. When the meters turn off, the GP-N100 becomes inactive and must reacquire at least three satellite signals before it can begin recording GPS data once more. When you choose Disable, the exposure meters remain on while using the GP-N100, so that GPS data can be recorded at any time, despite increased battery drain.
- **Position.** This is an information display, rather than a selectable option. It appears when the GP-N100 is connected and receiving satellite positioning data. It shows the latitude, longitude, altitude, and Coordinated Universal Time (UTC) values.
- **Use GPS to set camera clock.** Select Yes or No. When enabled, your V1's internal camera clock will be set using UTC values whenever the GP-N100 is attached to the camera. If you use the device frequently, this will ensure that your camera's clock is always set accurately, and won't require a manual update periodically.

Then, if you want to keep the GPS operating for longer periods, select Auto Power Off in the Setup menu and choose a 10-minute period before the camera goes to sleep. That will assure that the camera doesn't power down while you're using the GPS unit. Of course, in this mode the camera will use more power (the meters never go off, and the GPS draws power constantly), but you don't want to go through the 40-60-second satellite acquisition step each time you take a picture. You're all set.

Wi-Fi

These days, GPS and Wi-Fi capabilities work together with your V1 in interesting new ways. Wireless capabilities allow you to upload photos directly from your V1 to your computer at home or in your studio, or, through a hotspot at your hotel or coffee shop back to your home computer or to a photo sharing service like Facebook or Flickr. A special Wi-Fi-enabled memory card that you slip in the SD slot of your camera performs the magic. GPS capabilities—built right into some of those Wi-Fi cards—allow you to mark your photographs with location information, so you don't have to guess where a picture was taken.

Both capabilities are very cool. Wi-Fi uploads can provide instant backup of important shots and sharing. And, as noted in the previous section, geotagging is most important as a way to associate the geographical location where the photographer was when a picture was taken, with the actual photograph itself. It can be done with the location-mapping capabilities of the Wi-Fi card, or through add-on devices that third parties make available for your V1.

A relatively affordable solution is offered by Eye-Fi (www.eye.fi). The Eye-Fi card (see Figure 11.2) is an SDHC memory card with a wireless transmitter built in. You insert it in your camera just as with any ordinary card, and then specify which networks to use. You can add as many as 32 different networks. The next time your camera is on within range of a specified network, your photos and videos can be uploaded to your computer and/or to your favorite sharing site. During setup, you can customize where you want your images uploaded. The Eye-Fi card will only send them to the computer and to the sharing site you choose. Upload to any of 25 popular sharing websites, including Flickr, Facebook, Picasa, Kodak Gallery, MobileMe, Costco, Adorama, Smugmug, YouTube, Shutterfly, or Walmart. Online Sharing is included as a lifetime, unlimited service with all X2 cards.

When uploading to online sites, you can specify not just where your images are sent, but how they are organized, by specifying preset album names, tags, descriptions, and even privacy preferences on certain sharing sites. Some Eye-Fi cards also include geotagging service, which helps you view uploaded photos on a map, and sort them by

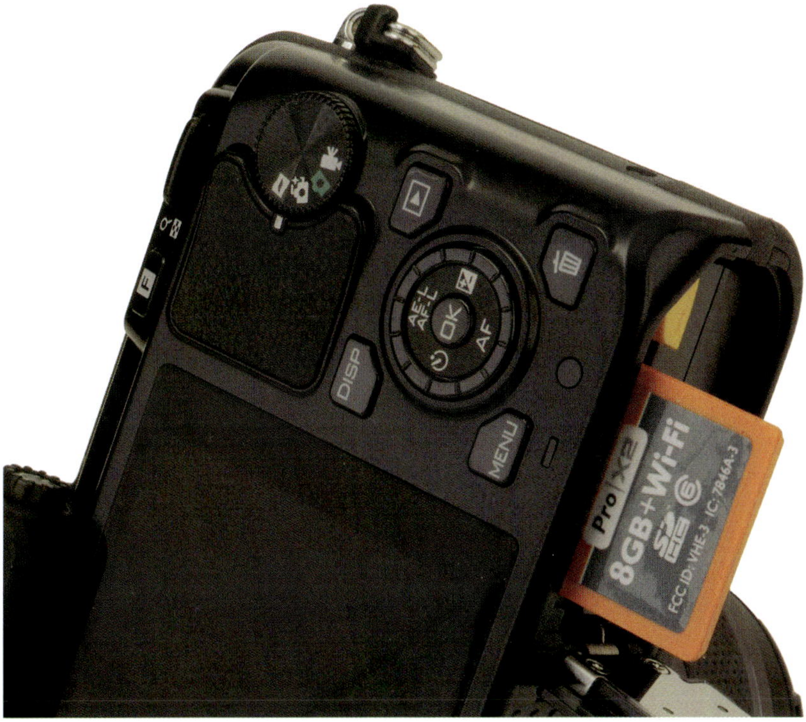

Figure 11.2
The Eye-Fi card is an SD card with built-in Wi-Fi features.

location. Eye-Fi's geotagging uses Wi-Fi Positioning System (WPS) technology. Using built-in Wi-Fi, the Eye-Fi card senses surrounding Wi-Fi networks as you take pictures. When photos are uploaded, the Eye-Fi service then adds the geotags to your photos. You don't need to have the password or a subscription for the Wi-Fi networks the card accesses; it can grab the location information directly without the need to "log in." You don't need to set up or control the Eye-Fi card from your camera. Software on your computer manages all the parameters. (See Figure 11.3.)

Your V1 has an Eye-Fi Upload entry in the Setup menu that allows you to enable or disable this capability. You'll want to turn off Eye-Fi when traveling on an airplane (just as you disable your cell phone, tablet, or laptop's wireless capabilities when required to do so). In addition, use of Wi-Fi cards may be restricted or banned outside the United States, because the telecommunications laws differ in other countries.

If you frequently travel outside the range of your home (or business) Wi-Fi network, an optional service called Hotspot Access is available, allowing you to connect to any AT&T Wi-Fi hotspot in the USA. In addition, you can use your own Wi-Fi accounts from commercial network providers, your city, even organizations you belong to such as your university.

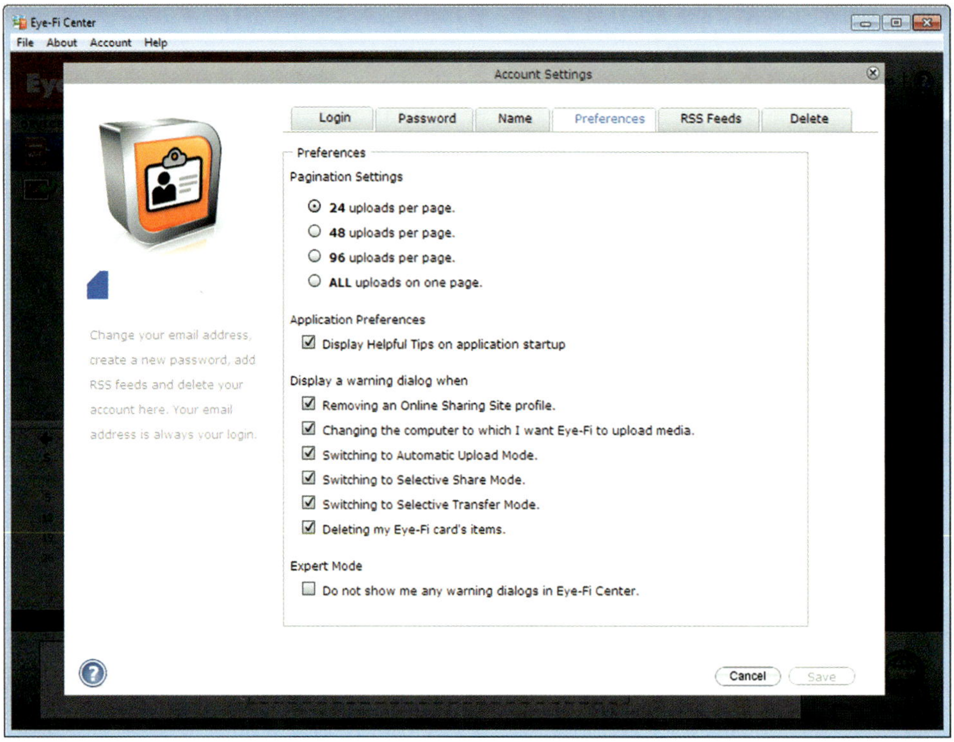

Figure 11.3 Functions of the Eye-Fi card can be controlled from your computer.

The card has another interesting feature called Endless Memory. When pictures have been safely uploaded to an external site, the card can be set to automatically erase the oldest images to free up space for new pictures. You choose the threshold where the card starts zapping your old pictures to make room.

Eye-Fi currently offer four models, including the basic Eye-Fi Home (about $50), which can be used to transmit your photos from the dSLR to a computer on your home network (or any other network you set up somewhere, say, at a family reunion). Eye-Fi Share and Eye-Fi Share Video (about $60 and $80, respectively) are basically exactly the same (Share Video is 4GB instead of 2GB in capacity), but include software to allow you to upload your images from your camera through your computer network directly to websites and digital printing services already mentioned. The most sophisticated option is Eye-Fi Explore, a 4GB SDHC card that adds geographic location labels to your photo (so you'll know where you took it), and frees you from your own computer network by allowing uploads from more than 10,000 Wi-Fi hotspots around the USA. Very cool, and the ultimate in picture backup.

Tablets, Smart Phones, and the Nikon V1

Although tablets and smart phones are still in their infancies, in the future, your iPhone, iPad/tablet computer, iPod Touch/MP3 player, smart phone, or Google Android portable device will be one of the most important accessories you can have for your Nikon V1 (or other) digital camera. We're only now seeing the beginnings of the trend.

The relevant platforms are these:

- **Old-style smart phones.** I include in this category all smart phones that are *not* iPhones or phones based on Google's Android operating system. You can buy lots of interesting apps for these phones, although not many applications specifically for photography. This type of phone should be on its way out, too, with iPhone and Android smart phones dominating, simply because it's easier to write applications for the iPhone's iOS and Android than to create them for multiple "old" smart phone platforms.
- **Android smart phones.** There are already more Android-based smart phones on the market than for all other types, including iOS. Although Apple had a head start, the number of Android applications is rapidly catching up.
- **iPhones.** It might sound strange to say that the skyrocketing sales of iPhones has been held in check, but it's true. The real or imagined shortcomings of AT&T's data network—which only got worse as more users grabbed iPhones—have kept many from switching to the iOS platform. The difficulties may even have contributed to the rapid growth of Android-based phones, which have been offered by Verizon and other suppliers seen as having "better" communications networks. Even so, iOS leads in number of applications, especially for photography apps. When my first app was developed (a camera guide with videos and other non-text features), it appeared for the iOS platform first. With Verizon entering the iOS picture, it's possible that iPhone sales *will* genuinely skyrocket. Or, Android may have picked up enough steam to blunt any dramatic increase in iPhone sales.
- **iPod Touch.** Basically, the latest iPod Touch is an iPhone that can't make phone calls. (Although there are some hacks around that limitation.) Virtually all of the apps that run on the iPhone under iOS also run on the iPod Touch. You need a Wi-Fi connection to access features that use network capabilities, but, these days, Wi-Fi hot spots aren't that difficult to find. Tethering and MiFi (which allow another device to serve as a hot spot for non-connected gadgets like the Touch), and *automobiles* that include built-in Wi-Fi (!) make connectivity almost universal. In my travels through Europe in the last year, I found free Wi-Fi connections in the smallest towns. (Indeed, the only time I was asked to pay for it was when staying in an upscale hotel.) So, for many who are tied to a non-iPhone cell phone, the iPod Touch is a viable alternative.

- **Tablet computers.** I've been welded to my iPad (shown alongside my iPhone in Figure 11.4) since I bought it the first day they became available. I use it to access e-mail, useful apps, and as a portable portfolio. Today, there are alternative tablet computers running Android. I recently picked up an Amazon Kindle Fire, which also does e-mail and a limited number of apps, and which has a Gallery feature (see Figure 11.5) that transforms it into a compact portfolio almost as useful for that purpose as an iPad. (However, only 6 of the Kindle Fire's 8GB of storage are available to the user, so you'll have to limit the size of your portfolio.)

  I use the Kindle Fire and both an iPhone and iPad. (If I'm traveling overseas where my iPhone can't be used, I usually take along the iPod Touch instead.) The iPhone/iPod slips in a pocket and can be used anywhere. I don't even have to think about taking it with me, because I always have one or the other. I have to remember to tote along the iPad or Kindle Fire, and, I do, to an extent you'd probably find surprising. (After the previews end and the featured movie finally starts, I fold them into their cases and use them as a tray for my popcorn bucket.) Tablet computers can do everything a pocket-sized device can do, and are easier to read/view/type on. When I am out shooting, I prefer to have all my apps in a smaller device that I can slip in the camera bag, but if there's room, the iPad goes along instead. Because my iPad (unlike the Kindle Fire) has 3G connectivity, I don't need a Wi-Fi connection to use it almost anywhere. I do have a Wi-Fi hot spot built into my iPhone that I can use to connect the Kindle Fire to the net if I need to.

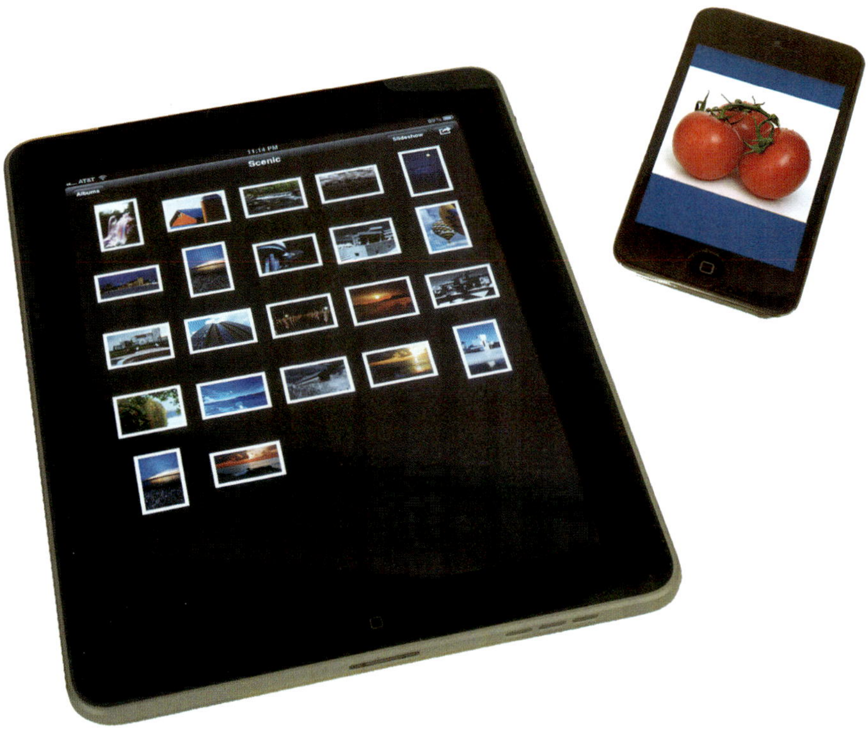

Figure 11.4
The iPad, iPod, and other devices open a whole world of useful apps to the photographer.

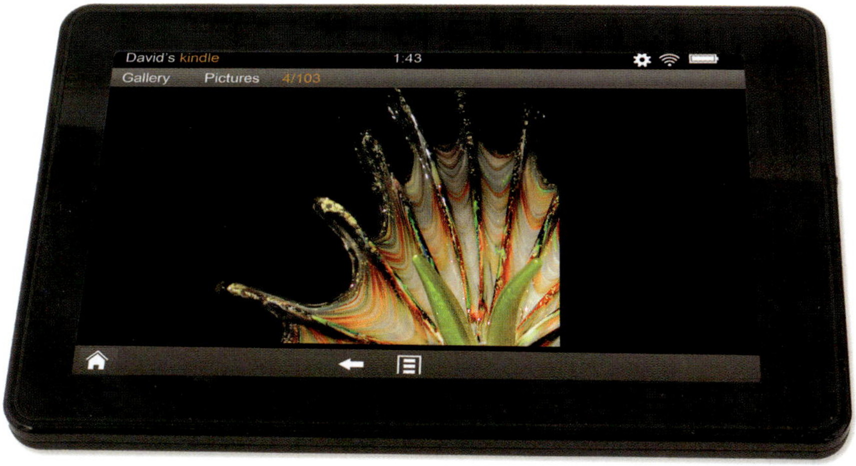

Figure 11.5
The Kindle Fire is a smaller, more affordable alternative to the iPad.

What Else Can You Do with Them?

Many of these devices can serve as a backup for your Nikon V1's memory cards. I've got Apple's camera connection kit, and can offload my pictures to my iPad's 64GB of memory, then upload them to Flickr or Facebook, or send to anyone through e-mail. My iPad also makes a perfect portable portfolio, too. I have hundreds of photos stored on mine, arranged into albums (see Figure 11.4, earlier) ready for instant display, either individually, or in slide shows. I have the same photo library on my iPhone and iPod Touch, and more than a few pictures available for showing on my Kindle Fire.

But the real potential for using these devices comes from specialized apps written specifically to serve photographic needs. Here are some of the kinds of apps you can expect in the future. (I'm developing more than a few of them myself.)

- **Camera guides.** Even the rotten manual that came with your camera is too large to carry around in your camera bag all day. I'm converting many of my own camera-specific guides to app form, while adding interactive elements, including hyperlinks and videos. You can already put a PDF version of your camera manual on your portable device and read it, if you like. In the future, you should be able to read any of the more useful third-party guides anywhere, anytime.
- **Lens selector.** Wonder what's the best lens to use in a specific situation? Enter information about your scene, and your app will advise you.
- **Exposure estimator.** Choose a situation and the estimated exposure will be provided. Useful as a reality check and in difficult situations, such as fireworks, where the camera's meters may falter.

- **Shutter speed advisor.** The correct shutter speed for a scene varies depending on whether you want to freeze action, or add a little blur to express motion. Other variables include whether the subject is crossing the frame, moving diagonally, or headed towards you. The photographer also needs to consider the focal length of the lens, and presence/absence of image stabilization features, tripod, monopod, etc. This app will allow you to tap in all the factors and receive advice about what shutter speed to use.
- **Hyperfocal length calculator.** In any given situation, set the focus point at the distance specified for your lens's current focal length setting, and everything from half that distance to infinity will be in focus. But the right setting differs at various focal lengths. This app tells you, and is a great tool for grab shots.
- **Accessory selector.** Confused about what flash, remote control, battery grip, lens hood, filter, or other accessory to use with your camera or lens? This selector lists the key gadgets, which ones fit which cameras, and explains how to use them.
- **Before and after.** Images showing before/after versions of dozens of situations with and without corrective/in-camera special effects, such as color correction applied.
- **Fill light.** Pesky shadows on faces from overhead lighting indoors? This turns your iPod/iPhone or (best of all) iPad into a bright, diffuse fill light panel. Choose from white fill light, or *colors* for special effects. Makes good illumination for viewing your camera's buttons and dials in dark locations, too.
- **Level.** Set your device on top of your camera and use it to level the camera, with or without a tripod.
- **Gray card.** Turn your i-device into an 18-percent gray card for metering and color balance.
- **Super links.** If you don't find your answer in the Toolkit, you can link to websites, including mine, with more information.
- **How It's Made.** A collection of inspiring photos, with details on how they were taken in camera, or manipulated in Photoshop (if that's your thing).
- **Quickie guides.** Small apps that lead you, step-by-step, through everything you need to photograph lots of different types of scenes. Typical subjects would be sports, landscape photography, macro work, portraits, concerts/performances, flowers, wildlife, and nature.

As you can see, the potential for apps is virtually unlimited. You can expect your smart phone, tablet computer, or other device to be a mainstay in your camera bag within a very short time.

12

Useful Software for the Nikon V1

Unless you only take pictures and then immediately print them directly to a PictBridge-compatible printer, somewhere along the line you're going to need to make use of the broad array of software available for the Nikon V1. If your needs involve more than the in-camera fixes available for red-eye, cropping and trimming, and maybe adjusting tonal values with D-Lighting, you're definitely going to want to use a utility or editor of some sort to perfect your images. After you've captured some great images and have them safely stored on your Nikon V1's memory card, you'll need to transfer them from your camera and memory card to your computer, where they can be organized, fine-tuned in an image editor, and prepared for web display, printing, or some other final destination.

Fortunately, there are lots of software utilities and applications to help you do all these things. This chapter will introduce you to a few of them. Please note that this is *not* a "how-to-do-it" software chapter. I'm going to use every available page to offer advice on how to get the most from your V1. There's no space to explain how to use all the features of Nikon Capture NX 2, nor how to tweak RAW file settings in Adobe Camera Raw. Entire books have been written about both products. This chapter is intended solely to help you get your bearings among the large number of utilities and applications available, to help you better understand what each does, and how you might want to use them. At the very end of the chapter, however, I'm going to make an exception and provide some simple instructions for using Adobe Camera Raw, to help those who have been using Nikon's software exclusively get a feel for what you can do with the Adobe product.

The basic functions found in most of the programs discussed in this chapter include image transfer and management, camera control, and image editing. You'll find that many of the programs overlap several of these capabilities, so it's not always possible to categorize the discussions that follow by function. In fact, I'm going to start off by describing a few of the offerings available from Nikon.

Nikon's Applications and Utilities

If nothing else, Nikon has made sorting through the software for its digital cameras an interesting pursuit. Through the years, we've had various incarnations of programs with names like PictureProject, Nikon View, and Nikon Capture. Some have been compatible with digital SLRs, the new Nikon mirrorless camera and amateur Coolpix product lines. Many of them have been furnished on disc with the cameras. Others, most notoriously Nikon Capture NX 2, have been an extra cost option.

Nikon provides you with just two programs on the disc packaged with the Nikon V1: Nikon ViewNX 2 (a simple viewing/conversion program), and Short Movie Creator (which assembles Motion Snapshots and music of your choice into a brief video compilation). You can find other Nikon software for free on their website, including Nikon Transfer (a tool for moving files from your camera to your computer), and software that you must pay for, like Nikon Capture NX 2.

The next few sections provide some descriptions of the Nikon software you'll want to use with your V1.

Nikon ViewNX 2

This latest incarnation of Nikon's basic file viewer is better than ever, making it easy to browse through images, convert RAW files to JPEG or TIFF, and make corrections to white balance and exposure, either on individual files or on batches of files. It now includes Nikon Transfer and a movie editing tool, and works in tandem with Nikon Capture NX 2, as you can open files inspected in ViewNX in one of the other programs—or within a third-party application you "register."

First and foremost, Nikon ViewNX is a great file viewer. There are three modes for looking at images: a thumbnail grid mode for checking out small previews of your images; an image viewer mode (see Figure 12.1) that shows a group of thumbnails along with an enlarged version of a selected image; and full screen mode, which allows you to examine an image in maximum detail.

If you like to shoot RAW+JPEG, you can review image pairs as if they were a single image (rather than view the RAW and JPEG versions separately), and work with whichever version you need. Should you want to organize your images, there are 10 labels available to classify images by criteria such as images printed, images copied, or images

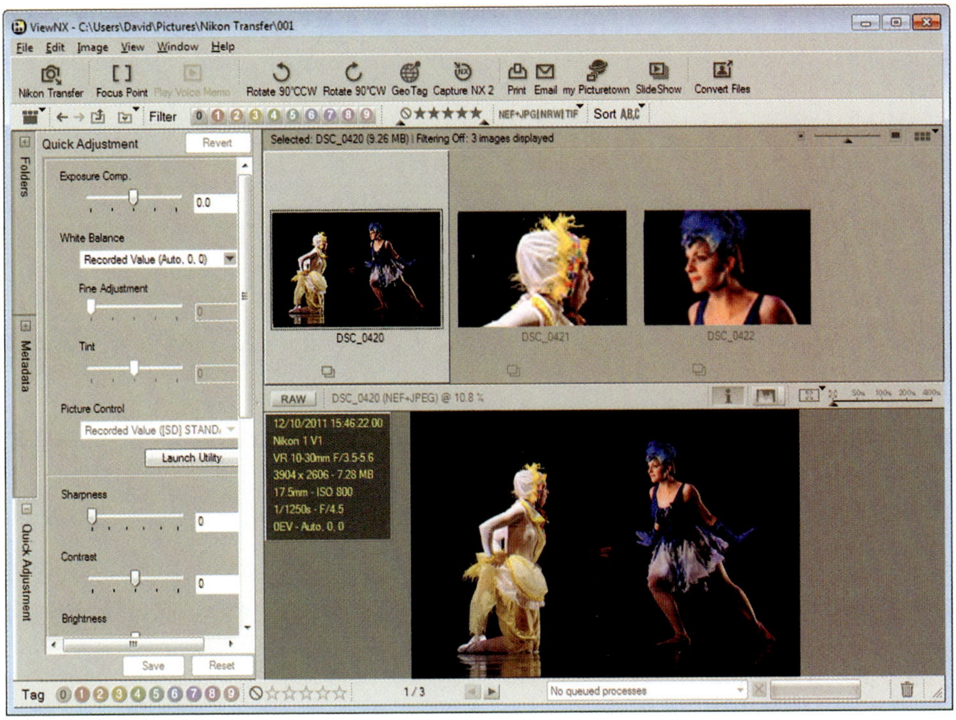

Figure 12.1 Nikon ViewNX is a great basic file viewing utility.

sent as e-mail, and you can mark your best shots for easier retrieval with a rating system of one to five stars. ViewNX also allows you to edit embedded XMP/IPTC information in fields such as Creator, Origin, Image Title, and suitable keywords. The utility can be downloaded from the support/download pages of the Nikon website at www.nikonusa.com.

Short Movie Creator

The other program bundled with the V1 is Nikon's Short Movie Creator. The most interesting application of this program is enhancing your Motion Snapshots (explained in Chapter 4), while making these 2.5 second clips a bit easier to view by combining them—plus music you select—into a compilation. You can choose from four themes or styles: Ultra Plain, Classic Vanilla, Pump it Up, or Scrapbook, search your hard drive for .wav or .mp4 music files, put your clips in any order you like, and then save your short movies to your hard drive.

You can select image and movie files to compile from within ViewNX 2's browser window, and then launch Short Movie Creator directly from ViewNX 2. You're not limited to your Motion Snapshots. You can combine JPEG, TIFF, and RAW still images, and assemble your short movies from Windows video format (AVI) or QuickTime (MOV) files (except for "Motion JPEGs" created with Nikon Coolpix cameras).

Drag and drop image and movie files, change their order, and append up to 20 different music files to use as background tunes. When you're finished, you can save the short movie as a new file that can be viewed on your computer or even saved to a memory card to play back on the Nikon V1. (See Figure 12.2.)

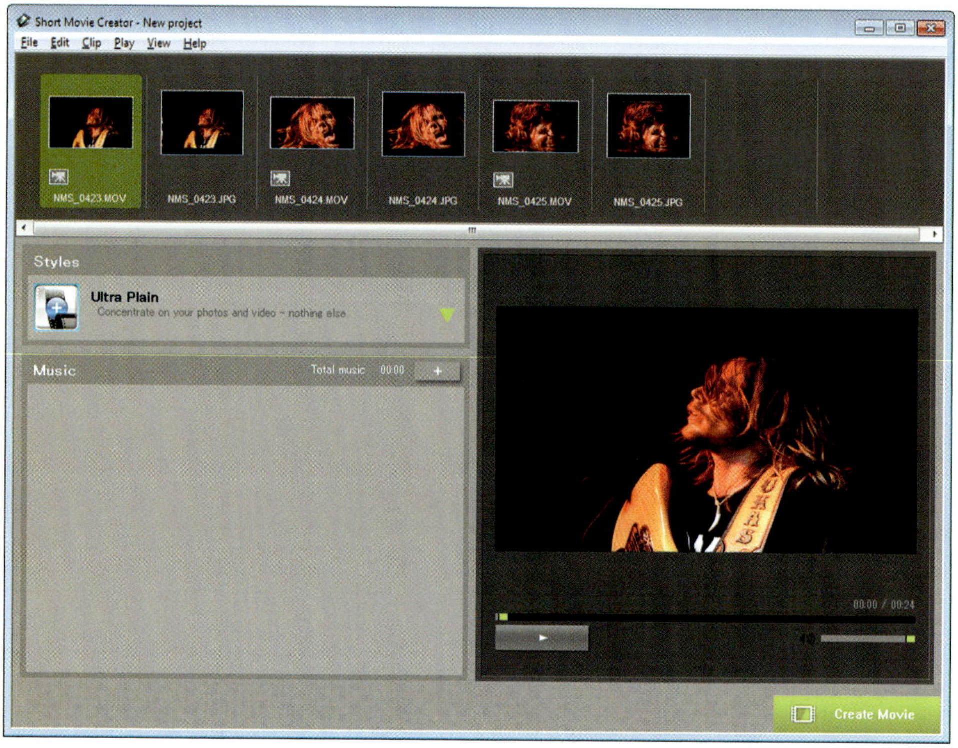

Figure 12.2
Create a simple movie clip with Short Movie Creator.

Nikon Transfer

It seems like everyone offers some sort of image transfer system that automatically recognizes when a memory card is inserted in a reader, or a digital camera like the Nikon V1 is attached to a computer using a USB cable. The most popular operating systems, from Mac OS X to Windows XP, Vista, and Windows 7 have their own built-in transfer programs, and Adobe Photoshop Elements includes one in its suite of utilities.

Nikon Transfer, now included with Nikon ViewNX 2, is particularly well-suited for V1 owners, because it integrates easily with other Nikon software products, including ViewNX and Nikon Capture NX 2. You can download photos to your computer, and then continue to work on them in the Nikon application (or third-party utility) of your choice.

When a memory card is inserted into a card reader, or when the V1 is connected to your computer through a USB cable, Nikon Transfer recognizes the device, searches it for thumbnails, and provides a display like the one shown in Figure 12.3. You can preview the images and mark the ones you want to transfer with checks to create a Transfer Queue.

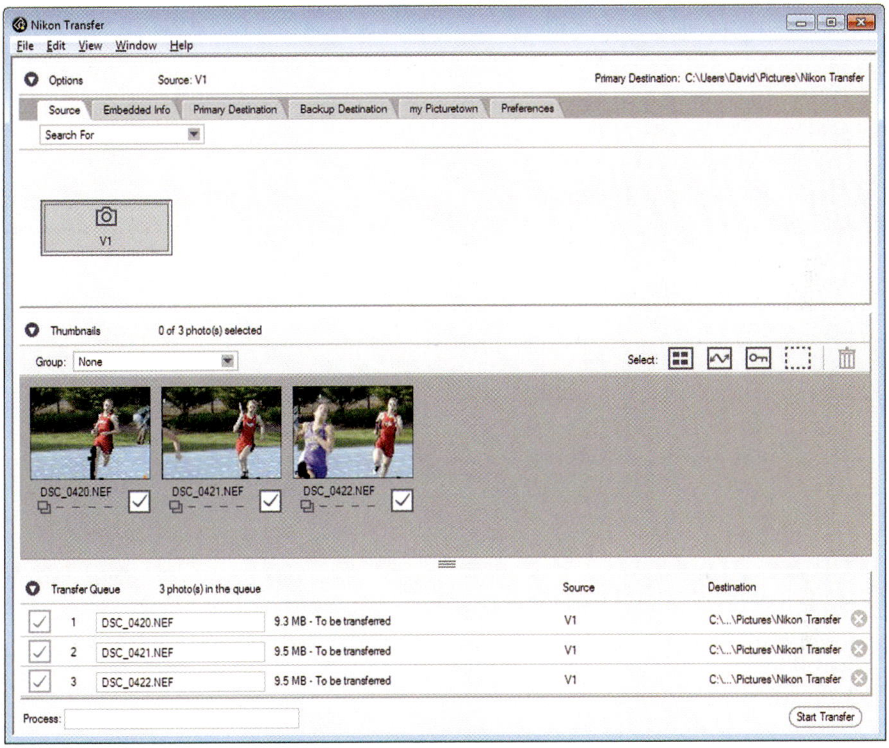

Figure 12.3 After Nikon Transfer displays thumbnails of the images on your memory card or camera, mark the ones you want to transfer.

Then, click on the Primary Destination tab (see Figure 12.4) and choose a location for the photos that will be transferred. Nikon Transfer can create a new folder for each transfer based on a naming convention you set up (click the Edit button next to the box at top center in the figure), or copy to a folder named after the current folder in the V1's memory card. You can keep the current filename as the files are transferred, or assign a new name with a prefix you designate, such as Spain07_ . The program will add a number from 001 to 999 to the filename prefix you specify.

One neat feature is the ability to name a Backup Destination location, so that all transferred pictures can also be copied to a second folder, which can be located on a different hard disk drive or other media. You can embed information such as copyright data, star ratings, and labels in the images as they are transferred. When the file transfer is complete, Nikon Transfer can launch an application of your choice, set with a few clicks in the Preferences tab (see Figure 12.5). Nikon Transfer has a tab and gives you the

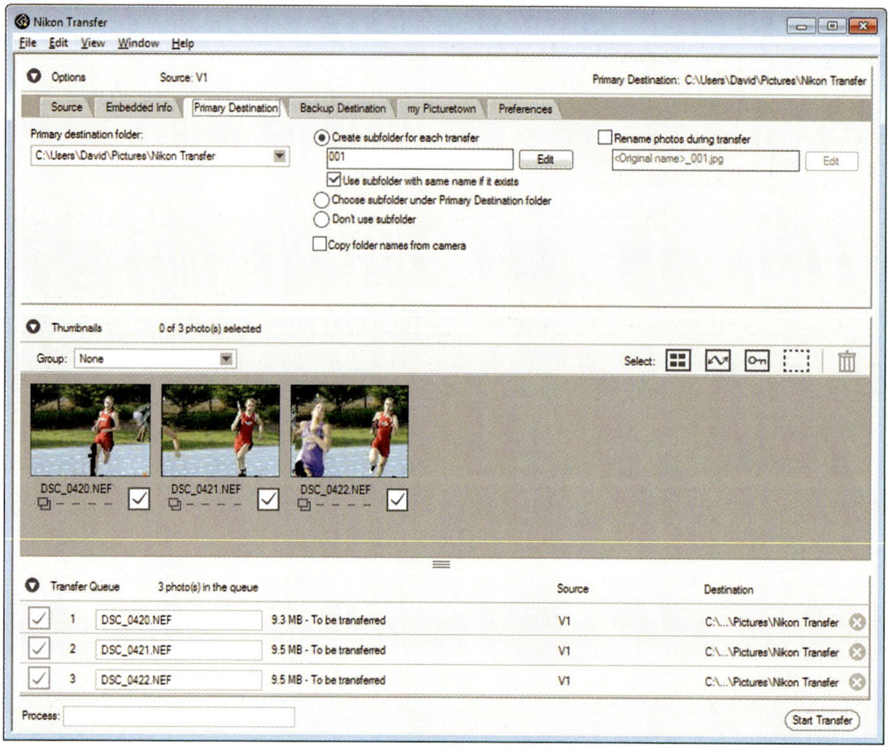

Figure 12.4
Copy files to a destination you specify using an optional file-name template you can define.

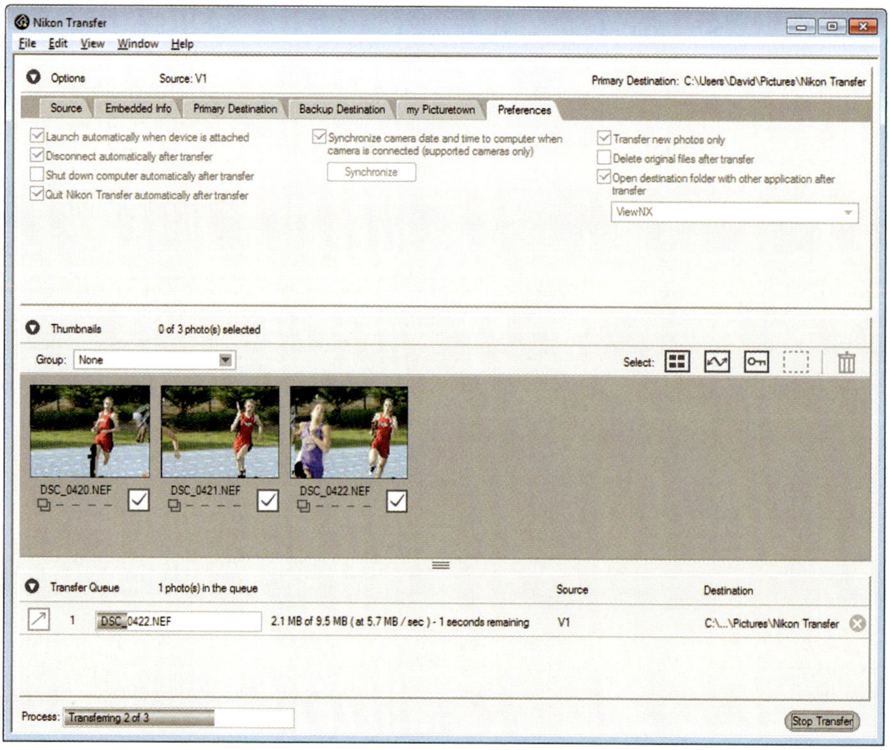

Figure 12.5
You can tell Nikon Transfer what to do after images are transferred in the Preferences tab.

opportunity to sign up for My PictureTown, an online picture sharing site. It allows you to share files, including those made with the Motion Snapshot feature that integrates full HD video and still images made with Nikon 1 cameras like the V1.

Nikon Capture NX 2

Capture NX 2 is a pretty hefty chunk of software for the typical entry-level Nikon owner, but you, as a V1 buyer, should be up to it. However, this program is challenging to master (and is somewhat expensive at about $150), but if you're ambitious and willing to plant your pitons for a steep climb up the learning curve, the program is indeed a powerful image-editing utility. It's designed specifically to process Nikon's NEF-format RAW files (although this edition has added the ability to manipulate JPEG and TIFF images as well). It includes an image browser (with labeling, sorting, and editing) that can be used to make many adjustments directly through the thumbnails. It also has advanced color management tools, impressive noise reduction capabilities, and batch processing features that allow you to apply sets of changes to collections of images. All the tools are arranged in dockable/expandable/collapsible palettes (see Figure 12.6) that tell you everything you need to know about an image, and provide the capabilities to push every pixel in interesting ways.

Photographers tend to love Capture NX or hate it, particularly in the NX 2 version that was current when I wrote this book, and it's easy to separate the fans from the furious. Those who are enamored of the program have invested a great deal of time in learning

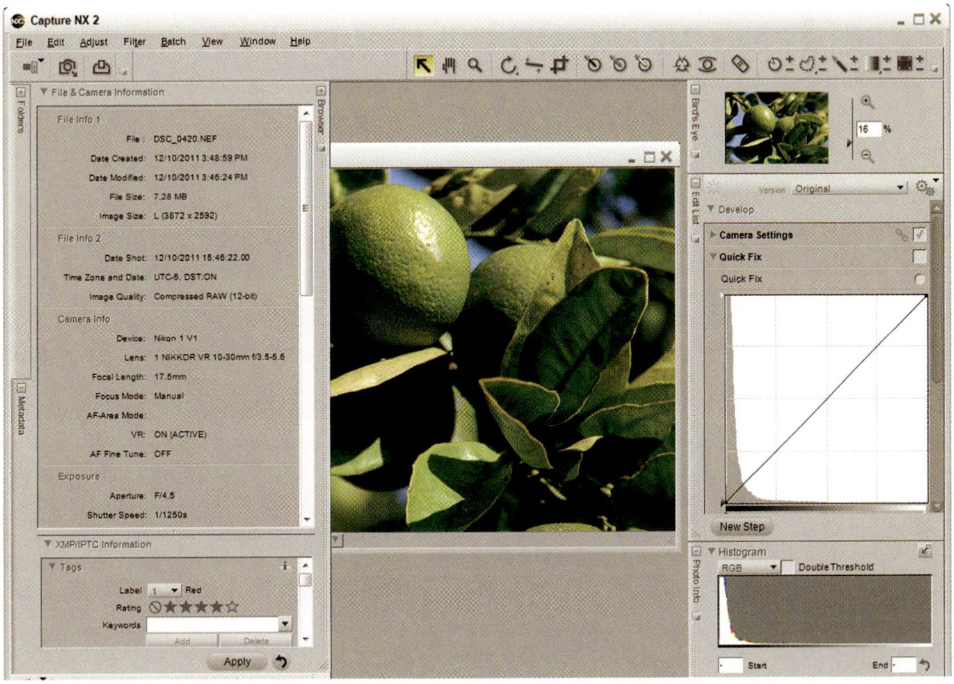

Figure 12.6 Capture NX 2's tools are arranged in dockable palettes.

its quirky paradigm and now appreciate just how powerful Capture NX is. The detractors are usually those who are comfortable with another program, such as Photoshop or even Capture 4, this program's predecessor, and are upset that even the simplest functions can be confoundingly difficult for a new user to figure out. Capture NX's murky Help system isn't a lot of help; there's room for a huge book (or two) to explain how to use this program.

For example, instead of masks, Capture NX 2 uses Nik Software's U Point technology, which applies Control Points to select and isolate parts of an image for manipulation. There are Color Control Points, with up to nine different sliders for each selected area. (See Figure 12.7.) There are also Black and White Control points for setting dynamic range, Neutral Control Points for correcting color casts, and a Red-Eye Reduction Control Point that removes crimson glows from pupils.

The workflow revolves around an Edit List, which contains a list of enhancements, including Camera Adjustments, RAW Adjustments, Light & Color Adjustments, Detail Adjustments, and Lens Adjustments, which can each be controlled separately. You can add steps of your own, cancel adjustments individually, and store steps in the Edit List as Settings that can be applied to individual images or batches.

There are also Color Aberration Controls, D-Lighting, Image Dust Off, Vignette Control, Fisheye-to-Rectilinear Image Transformation ("de-fishing"), and a Distortion Control to reduce pincushion and barrel distortion.

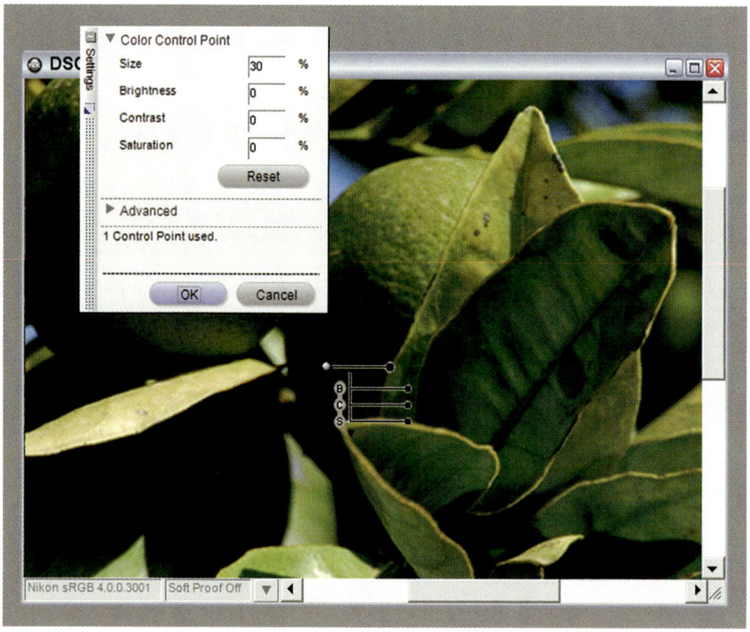

Figure 12.7
Control Points are used to make common adjustments.

Photoshop/Photoshop Elements

Photoshop is the high-end choice for image editing, and Photoshop Elements is a great alternative for those who need some of the features of Photoshop, but can do without the most sophisticated capabilities, including editing CMYK files. Both editors use the latest version of Adobe's Camera Raw plug-in (you'll need Camera Raw 6.6 or later versions to process files from any Nikon 1 camera), which makes it easy to adjust things like image resolution, white balance, exposure, shadows, brightness, sharpness, luminance, and noise reduction. One plus with the Adobe products is that they are available in identical versions for both Windows and Macs.

The latest version of Photoshop includes a built-in RAW plug-in that is compatible with the proprietary formats of a growing number of digital cameras, both new and old, and which can perform a limited number of manipulations on JPEG and TIFF files, too. This plug-in also works with Photoshop Elements, but with fewer features. Here's how easy it is to manipulate a RAW file using the Adobe converter:

1. Transfer the RAW images from your camera to your computer's hard drive.
2. In Photoshop, choose Open from the File menu, or use Organizer or Bridge (depending on the version you have installed).
3. Select a RAW image file. The Adobe Camera Raw plug-in will pop up, showing a preview of the image, like the one shown in Figure 12.8.

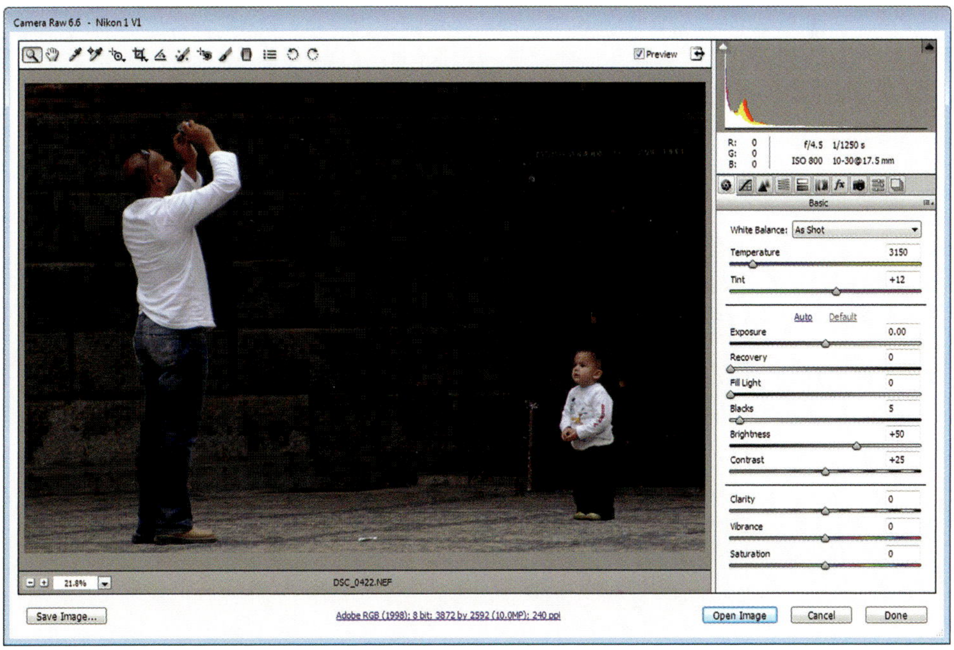

Figure 12.8
The basic ACR dialog box looks like this when processing a single image.

4. If you like, use one of the tools found in the toolbar at the top left of the dialog box. From left to right, they are:
   - **Zoom.** Operates just like the Zoom tool in Photoshop.
   - **Hand.** Use like the Hand tool in Photoshop.
   - **White Balance.** Click an area in the image that should be neutral gray or white to set the white balance quickly.
   - **Color Sampler.** Use to determine the RGB values of areas you click with this eyedropper.
   - **Crop.** Pre-crops the image so that only the portion you specify is imported into Photoshop. This option saves time when you want to work on a section of a large image, and you don't need the entire file.
   - **Straighten.** Drag in the preview image to define what should be a horizontal or vertical line, and ACR will realign the image to straighten it.
   - **Retouch.** Used to heal or clone areas you define.
   - **Red-Eye Removal.** Quickly zap red pupils in your human subjects.
   - **ACR Preferences.** Produces a dialog box of Adobe Camera Raw preferences.
   - **Rotate Counterclockwise.** Rotates counterclockwise in 90-degree increments with a click.
   - **Rotate Clockwise.** Rotates clockwise in 90-degree increments with a click.
5. Using the Basic tab, you can have ACR show you red and blue highlights in the preview that indicate shadow areas that are clipped (too dark to show detail) and light areas that are blown out (too bright). Click the triangles in the upper-left corner of the histogram display (shadow clipping) and upper-right corner (highlight clipping) to toggle these indicators on or off.
6. Also in the Basic tab you can choose white balance, either from the drop-down list or by setting a color temperature and green/magenta color bias (tint) using the sliders.
7. Other sliders are available to control exposure, recovery, fill light, blacks, brightness, contrast, vibrance, and saturation. A checkbox can be marked to convert the image to grayscale.
8. Make other adjustments (described in more detail below).
9. ACR makes automatic adjustments for you. You can click Default and make the changes for yourself, or click the Auto link (located just above the Exposure slider) to reapply the automatic adjustments after you've made your own modifications.

10. If you've marked more than one image to be opened, the additional images appear in a "filmstrip" at the left side of the screen. You can click on each thumbnail in the filmstrip in turn and apply different settings to each.
11. Click Open Image/Open Image(s) into Photoshop using the settings you've made.

The Basic tab is displayed by default when the ACR dialog box opens, and it includes most of the sliders and controls you'll need to fine-tune your image as you import it into Photoshop. These include:

- **White Balance.** Leave it As Shot or change to a value such as Daylight, Cloudy, Shade, Tungsten, Fluorescent, or Flash. If you like, you can set a custom white balance using the Temperature and Tint sliders.
- **Exposure.** This slider adjusts the overall brightness and darkness of the image.
- **Recovery.** Restores detail in the red, green, and blue color channels.
- **Fill Light.** Reconstructs detail in shadows.
- **Blacks.** Increases the number of tones represented as black in the final image, emphasizing tones in the shadow areas of the image.
- **Brightness.** This slider adjusts the brightness and darkness of an image.
- **Contrast.** Manipulates the contrast of the midtones of your image.
- **Clarity.** Use this slider to apply a hybrid type of contrast enhancement to boost midtone contrast.
- **Vibrance.** Prevents over-saturation when enriching the colors of an image.
- **Saturation.** Manipulates the richness of all colors equally, from zero saturation (gray/black, no color) at the –100 setting to double the usual saturation at the +100 setting.

Additional controls are available on the Tone Curve, Detail, HSL/Grayscale, Split Toning, Lens Corrections, Camera Calibration, and Presets tabs, shown in Figure 12.9. The Tone Curve tab can change the tonal values of your image. The Detail tab lets you adjust sharpness, luminance smoothing, and apply color noise reduction. The HSL/Grayscale tab offers controls for adjusting hue, saturation, and lightness and converting an image to black-and-white. Split Toning helps you colorize an image with sepia or cyanotype (blue) shades. The Lens Corrections tab has sliders to adjust for chromatic aberrations and vignetting. The Camera Calibration tab provides a way for calibrating the color corrections made in the Camera Raw plug-in. The Presets tab (not shown) is used to load settings you've stored for reuse.

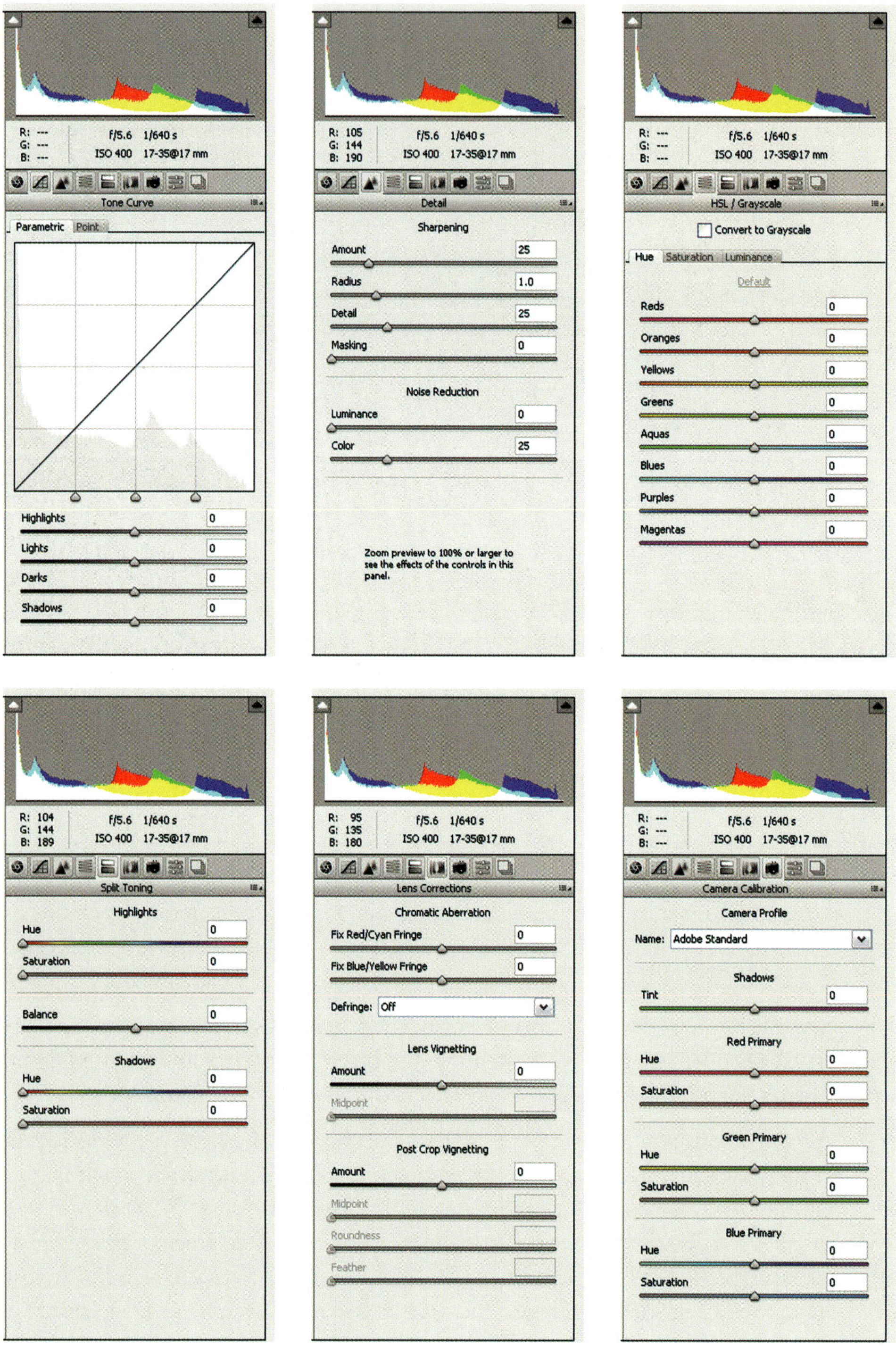

Figure 12.9 More controls are available within the additional tabbed dialog boxes in Adobe Camera Raw.

13

Nikon V1: Troubleshooting and Prevention

One of the nice things about modern electronic cameras like the Nikon V1 is that they have fewer mechanical moving parts to fail, so they are less likely to "wear out." No film transport mechanism, no wind lever or motor drive, no complicated mechanical linkages from camera to lens to physically stop down the lens aperture. Instead, tiny, reliable motors are built into each lens (and you lose the use of only that lens should something fail), and the Nikon 1 series lacks one of the few major moving parts in its dSLR counterparts—the moving mirror. Even the shutter of this camera can function without moving if you choose the electronic version over the mechanical one.

The only other things on the camera that move are switches, dials, buttons, and the door that slides open to allow you to remove and insert the battery and Secure Digital card. There's not a lot that can go wrong mechanically with your Nikon V1.

On the other hand, one of the chief drawbacks of modern electronic cameras is that they are modern *electronic* cameras. Your V1 is fully dependent on two different batteries. Without them, the camera can't be used. There are numerous other electrical and electronic connections in the camera (many connected to those mechanical switches and dials), and components like the color LCD and internal electronic viewfinder that can potentially fail or suffer damage. The camera also relies on its "operating system," or *firmware*, which can be plagued by bugs that cause unexpected behavior. Luckily, electronic components are generally more reliable and trouble-free, especially when compared to their mechanical counterparts from the pre-electronic film camera days.

(Film cameras of the last 10 to 20 years have had almost as many electronic features as digital cameras, but, believe it or not, there were whole generations of film cameras that had *no* electronics or batteries.)

Digital cameras have problems unique to their breed, too; the most troublesome being the need to clean the sensor of dust and grime periodically. This chapter will show you how to diagnose problems, fix some common ills, and, importantly, learn how to avoid some of them in the future.

Battery Powered

I've grown to live with the need for batteries even though I shot for years using all-mechanical Nikon cameras that had no batteries (or even a built-in light meter!). The need for electrical power is the price we pay for modern conveniences like autofocus, autoexposure, LCD image display, backlit menus, and, of course, digital images.

One of the batteries you rely on is the EN-EL15 battery. It's rechargeable, can last for as long as 400 shots, and is user-replaceable if you have a spare. The second power cell in your camera is a so-called *clock battery,* which is also rechargeable, but is tucked away within the innards of the camera and can't be replaced by the user. The clock battery retains the settings of the camera when it's powered down, and, even, when the main battery is removed for charging. If you remove the EN-EL15 for long periods, the clock battery may discharge, but it will be quickly rejuvenated when you replace the main battery. (It's recharged by juice supplied by the EN-EL15.) Although you can't replace this battery yourself, you can expect it to last for the useful life of the camera.

So, your main concern will be to provide a continuous, reliable source of power for your V1. As I noted in Chapter 1, you should always have a spare battery or two so you won't need to stop shooting when your internal battery dies. I recommend buying Nikon-brand batteries: saving $20 or so for an after-market battery may save you a few dollars, but can cost you much more than that if the battery malfunctions and damages your camera.

There are several techniques you can use to stretch the longevity of your V1's battery. To get the most from each charge, consider these steps:

- **Power Off Delay.** In the Setup menu, choose the minimum value, 15 seconds, if you're willing to restart the camera at frequent intervals. As a practical matter, a value of 1 minute might be more convenient and practical. After the specified time, the display will go blank and the green power LED on top of the camera will begin flashing to indicate the camera is about to go to sleep, until the V1 finally powers down completely.
- **Reduce LCD brightness.** In the Setup menu's Display Brightness option, select the lowest of the seven brightness settings that work for you under most conditions. You can set the EVF viewfinder and LCD monitor separately and individually.

- **Turn off the back panel LCD during shooting.** If you generally use the internal EVF for framing your images, press the DISP button until the back panel LCD display turns off completely. The internal EVF will go dark, too, when the camera isn't up to your eye (or resting against your body). That will effectively disable the power-sucking displays except for when you are actually taking a picture.
- **Reduce flash use.** No flash at all or fill flash use less power than a full blast.
- **Cancel VR.** Turn off vibration reduction if your lens has that feature and you feel you don't need it.
- **Use a card reader.** When transferring pictures from your V1 to your computer, use a card reader instead of the USB cable. Linking your camera to your computer and transferring images using the cable takes longer and uses a lot more power.
- **Use the electronic shutter.** The mechanical shutter uses a tiny bit more power. (We're reaching diminishing returns here.)
- **Set minimum Remote On Duration.** Don't let the V1 wait too long for the ML-L3's signal by setting the lowest value in the Setup menu. Of course, unless you use the remote a lot, you won't save all that much power with this option.

KEEPING TRACK OF YOUR BATTERIES AND MEMORY CARDS

Here's a trick I use to keep track of which batteries are fresh/discharged, and which memory cards are blank/exposed. I cut up some small slips of paper and fold them in half, forming a tiny "booklet." Then I write EXPOSED in red on the "inside" pages of the booklet and UNEXPOSED in green on the outside pages. Folded one way, the slips read EXPOSED; folded the other way, the slips read UNEXPOSED. I slip them inside the plastic battery cover, which you should *always* use when the batteries are not in the camera (to avoid shorting out the contacts), folded so the appropriate "state" of the batteries is visible. The same slips are used in the translucent plastic cases I use for my memory cards. (See Figure 13.1.) For my purposes, EXPOSED means the same as DISCHARGED, and UNEXPOSED is the equivalent of CHARGED. The color coding is an additional clue as to which batteries/memory cards are good to go, or not ready for use.

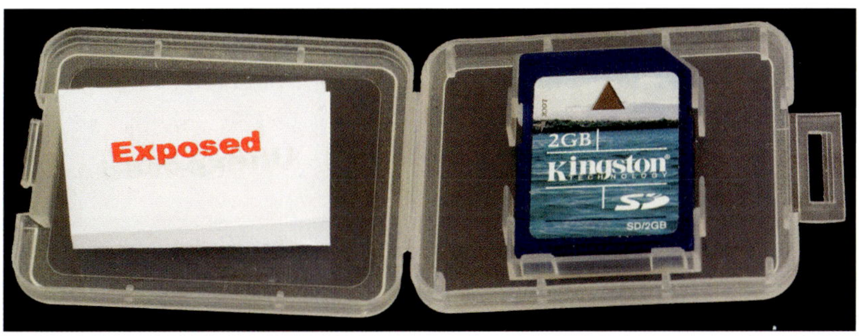

Figure 13.1 Mark your batteries—or memory cards—so you'll know which are ready for use.

Upgrading Your Firmware

The camera relies on its "operating system," or *firmware*, which should be updated in a reasonable fashion as new releases become available. The firmware in your Nikon V1 handles everything from menu display (including fonts, colors, and the actual entries themselves), what languages are available, and even support for specific devices and features, such as the lenses and SB-N5 flash. Upgrading the firmware to a new version makes it possible to add or fine-tune features while fixing some of the bugs that sneak in.

Firmware upgrades are used most frequently to fix bugs in the software, and much less frequently to add or enhance features. The exact changes made to the firmware are generally spelled out in the firmware release announcement. You can examine the remedies provided and decide if a given firmware patch is important to you. If not, you can usually safely wait a while before going through the bother of upgrading your firmware—at least long enough for the early adopters (such as those who haunt the Digital Photography Review forums at www.dpreview.com) to report whether the bug fixes have introduced new bugs of their own. Each new firmware release incorporates the changes from previous releases, so if you skip a minor upgrade you should have no problems.

WHEN TO UPGRADE YOUR FIRMWARE

I *always* recommend waiting at least two weeks after a firmware upgrade is announced before changing the software in your camera. This is often in direct contradiction to the online Nikon "gurus" who breathlessly announce each new firmware release on their web pages, usually with links to where you can download the latest software. *Don't do it!* Yet. Nikon has, in the past, introduced firmware upgrades that were buggy and added problems of their own. If you own a camera affected by a new round of firmware upgrades, I urge you to wait and let a few million over-eager fellow users "beta test" this upgrade for you. Within a few weeks, any problems (although I don't expect there will be any) will surface and you'll know whether the update is safe. Your camera is working fine right now, so why take the chance?

How It Works

If you're computer savvy, you might wonder how your Nikon V1 is able to overwrite its own operating system—that is, how can the existing firmware be used to load the new version on top of itself? It's a little like lifting yourself by reaching down and pulling up on your bootstraps.

Not ironically, that's almost exactly what happens: At your command (when you start the upgrade process), the V1 shifts into a special mode in which it is no longer operating from its firmware but, rather, from a small piece of software called a *bootstrap loader*, a separate, protected software program that functions only at startup or when upgrading firmware. The loader's function is to look for firmware to launch or, when directed, to copy new firmware from a memory card to the internal memory space where the old firmware is located. Once the new firmware has replaced the old, you can "reboot" the camera using the new operating system.

Why Four Firmware Modules?

Your Nikon V1's firmware is divided into four parts; many earlier Nikon models had the firmware in just two sections. Why chop the firmware up in the first place? And what are those third and fourth modules for, anyway?

Previous Nikon cameras had an A and B firmware listing, located in the Firmware Version entry in the Setup menu. There's a good reason why the firmware was previously divided in twain. Each of the two modules was "in charge" of particular parts of the camera's operating system. So, when a bug was found, or a new feature added, it was possible, in many cases, to offer only an upgrade for either Firmware A or Firmware B, depending on which module was affected. Although mistakes in upgrading firmware are rare, you cut the opportunities for user errors in half when only one of the modules needs to be replaced.

But there's a more important reason for having at least two firmware modules. If your camera had just one, and you had the misfortune to munge that firmware during an ill-fated upgrade, it's very likely your camera would be magically transformed into a digital doorstop. Part of the firmware is needed simply to install (or re-install firmware) in the first place. With all Nikon cameras, Firmware A and Firmware B each has the capability of locating and installing replacement firmware. So, if A is ruined, you can use the routines in B to reinstall a new copy of A. And vice versa. We can all agree that this is a wise move on Nikon's part.

So, what are the L and S firmware modules? They control operation of the lenses and any Speedlights (or strobes) that must be attached to the camera. When you visit the Firmware Version entry in the Setup menu, you'll see a display something like the one shown in Figure 13.2.

The information in the display will change depending on what equipment you have attached to the V1. That's because the lower two, the L and S modules, don't report information about the camera itself. Instead, the camera reads the firmware information stored in a solid state module in each lens or in your flash unit, and reports that instead. If you switch lenses, the L firmware status will change to reflect the firmware installed in that particular lens. As I write this, the firmware for the 10mm f/2.8 lens is 1.00; for the 10-30mm and 30-100mm lenses, 1.02; and for the 10-100mm lens, 1.01. Those values will display when each of those lenses are mounted on the V1. The firmware value for the SB-N5 flash is shown only when the flash is mounted. The current version when this book was written was 1.00.

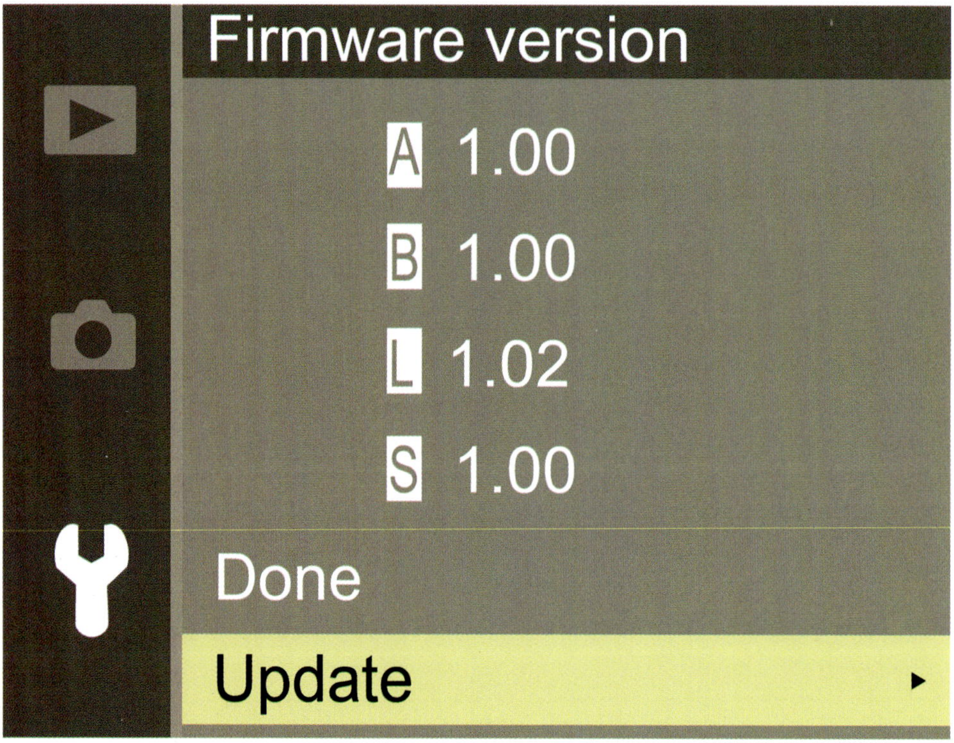

Figure 13.2
The status of your firmware modules is shown in the Setup menu.

> **WARNING**
>
> Use a fully charged EN-EL15 battery to ensure that you'll have enough power to operate the camera for the entire upgrade. Moreover, you should not turn off the camera while your old firmware is being overwritten. Don't open the memory card door or do anything else that might disrupt operation of the V1 while the firmware is being installed.

Getting Ready

The first thing to do is determine whether you need the current firmware update. First, confirm the version number of your Nikon V1's current firmware:

1. Turn on the V1.
2. Press the MENU button and select *Firmware Version* from the Setup menu. The camera's firmware version will be displayed, as shown earlier in Figure 13.2.
3. Write down the Version number for Parts A, B, L, and S.
4. Turn off the V1.

Next, go to the Nikon support site and locate and download the firmware update. In the USA, the place to go is http://support.nikonusa.com/, which will offer a list of choices, including one for current firmware downloads available for Nikon Products. Navigate to the listings for your camera, lens, or electronic flash.

If the version is later than the one you noted in your camera, click the firmware link in either the Windows or Macintosh columns (depending on your computer) to download the file. It will have a name like F-XXXX-V####W.exe" (Windows) or F-XXXX-V####W.dng" (Macintosh), where "XXXX" is the device name and "####" the firmware version. Extract the file to a folder on your computer by double-clicking on it, or using the unzipping or unstuffing software of your choice.

Updating from a Card Reader

To update from a card reader, use a reader connected to your computer with a USB cable. Then, follow these steps:

1. Insert a formatted memory card into the card reader. If you have been using Nikon transfer or the "autoplay" features of your operating system to transfer images from your memory card to the computer, the automated transfer dialog box may appear. Close it.
2. The memory card will appear on your Macintosh desktop, or in the Computer/My Computer folders under Windows 7/Windows Vista/Windows XP.
3. Drag one firmware file to the memory card. Remember to copy the firmware to the *root* (top) directory of the memory card. The V1 will be unable to find it if you place it in a folder.

Updating with a USB Connection

You can also copy the firmware to the V1's memory card using a USB connection. Just follow these steps:

1. With the camera turned off, insert the formatted memory card. Then, turn the camera back on.
2. Press the MENU button and navigate to the Setup menu.
3. Turn the V1 off and connect it to your computer using the UC-E6 USB cable.
4. Turn the camera back on. If you have been using Nikon transfer or the "autoplay" features of your operating system to transfer images from your memory card to the computer, the automated transfer dialog box may appear. Close it.
5. The camera will appear on the Macintosh desktop, or in the Computer/My Computer folders under Windows 7/Windows Vista/Windows XP.

6. Drag one firmware file to the memory card. Remember to copy the firmware to the *root* (top) directory of the memory card. The V1 will be unable to find it if you place it in a folder.
7. Disconnect the camera from the computer.

Starting the Update

To perform the actual update, follow these steps:

1. With the memory card containing the firmware update software in the camera, and the lens or flash unit to be updated mounted (if you're not simply updating the camera itself), turn the camera on.
2. Press the MENU button and select Firmware Version in the Setup menu.
3. Select Update and press the multi selector button to the right.
4. When the firmware update screen appears, highlight Yes and press OK to begin the update. (See Figure 13.3.)
5. The actual process may take a few minutes (from two to five). Be sure not to turn off the camera or perform any other operations while it is underway.

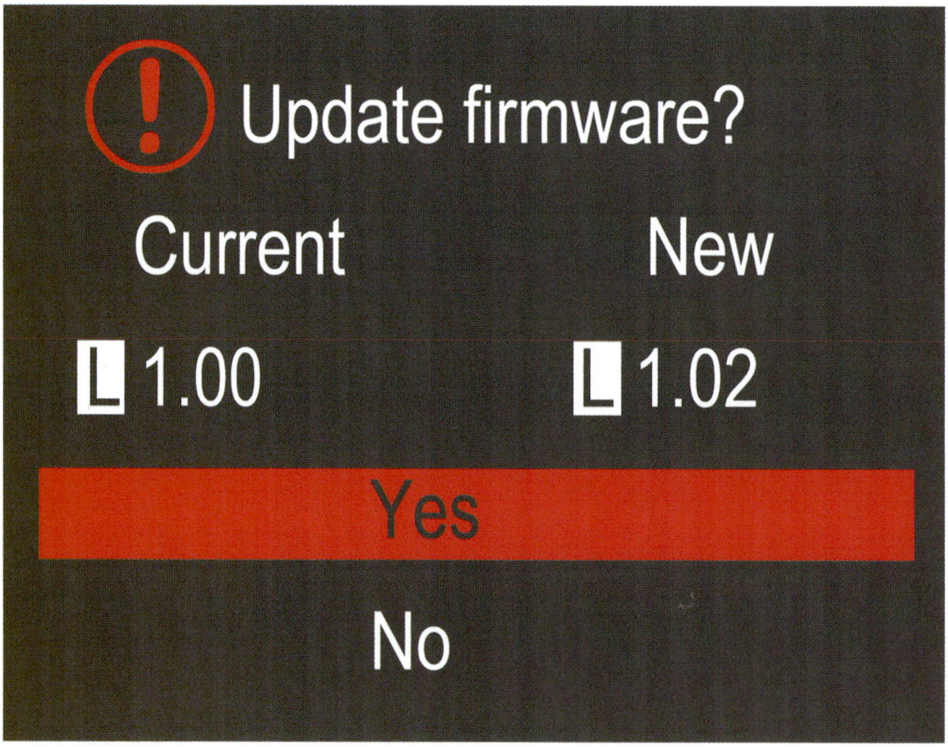

Figure 13.3
Don't turn the camera off while updating is underway.

6. When the update is completed, the warning message will no longer be displayed on the screen. You can turn off the camera when the message disappears.
7. Remove the memory card.
8. Turn the V1 back on to load the updated firmware.
9. Press the MENU button and select Firmware Version in the Setup menu to view the current firmware number. If it matches the update, you've successfully upgraded that portion of the firmware.
10. Reformat the memory card.
11. If there are additional parts to your firmware upgrade, then repeat all the steps for the additional firmware software.
12. Reformat the memory card to return it to a "clean" condition.

Protecting Your LCD

The massive three-inch color LCD on the back of your Nikon V1 almost seems like a target for banging, scratching, and other abuse. The LCD itself is quite rugged, and a few errant knocks are unlikely to shatter the protective cover over the LCD, and scratches won't easily mar its tempered glass surface. However, if you want to be on the safe side, there are a number of protective products you can purchase to keep your LCD safe—and, in some cases, make it a little easier to view. Here's a quick overview of your options.

- **Plastic overlays.** The simplest solution (although not always the cheapest) is to apply a plastic overlay sheet or "skin" cut to fit your LCD. These adhere either by static electricity or through a light adhesive coating that's even less clingy than stick-it notes. You can cut down overlays made for PDAs (although these can be pricey at up to $19.95 for a set of several sheets), or purchase overlays sold specifically for digital cameras. Vendors such as Hoodman (www.hoodmanusa.com) offer overlays of this type. These products will do a good job of shielding your V1's LCD screen from scratches and minor impacts, but will not offer much protection from a good whack.
- **Acrylic shields.** These scratch-resistant acrylic panels, laser cut to fit your camera perfectly, are my choice as the best protection solution, and what I use on my own V1. At about $6 each, they also happen to be the least expensive option. I get mine from a company called 'da Products (www.daproducts.com). They attach using strips of sticky adhesive that hold the panel flush and tight, but which allow the acrylic to be pried off and the adhesive removed easily if you want to remove or replace the shield. They don't attenuate your view of the LCD and are non-reflective enough for use under a variety of lighting conditions. I also like the glass covers from GGS, available from a variety of sources, and shown in Figure 13.4.

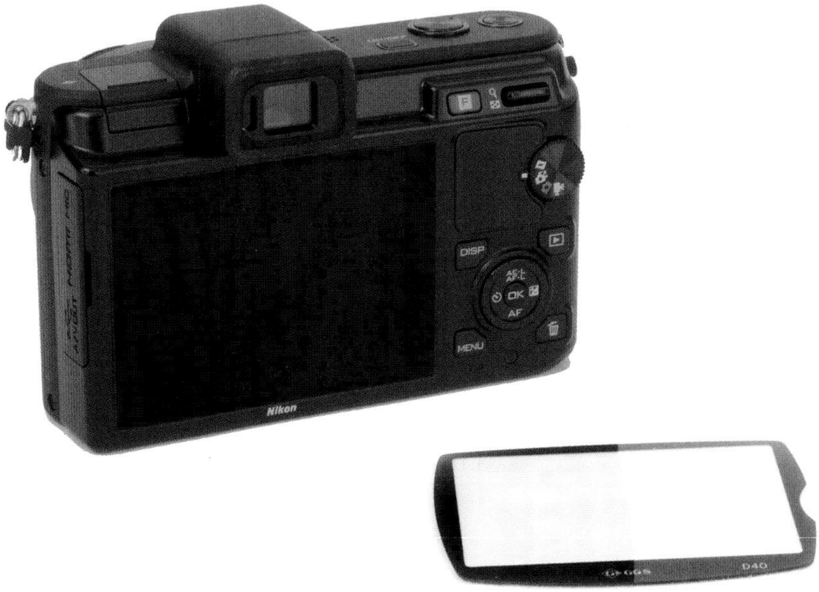

Figure 13.4
A tough glass shield can protect your LCD from scratches.

- **Flip-up hoods.** These protectors clip on and provide a cover that completely shields the LCD, but unfolds to provide a three-sided hood that allows viewing the LCD while minimizing the extraneous light falling on it and reducing contrast. They're sold for about $40 by Delkin (www.delkin.com) and Hoodman. If you want to completely protect your LCD from hard knocks and need to view the screen outdoors in bright sunlight, there is nothing better. However, I have a couple problems with these devices. First, with the cover closed, you can't peek down after taking a shot to see what your image looks like during picture review. You must open the cap each time you want to look at the LCD. Moreover, with the hood unfolded, it's difficult to look through the viewfinder: Don't count on being able to use the viewfinder *and* the LCD at the same time with one of these hoods in place.
- **Magnifiers.** If you look hard enough, you should be able to find an LCD magnifier that fits over the monitor panel and provides a 2X magnification. These often strap on clumsily, and serve better as a way to get an enlarged view of the LCD than as protection. Hoodman and other suppliers offer these specialized devices.

Troubleshooting Memory Cards

Sometimes good memory cards go bad. Sometimes good photographers can treat their memory cards badly. It's possible that a memory card that works fine in one camera won't be recognized when inserted into another. In the worst case, you can have a card full of important photos and find that the card seems to be corrupted and you can't access any of them. Don't panic! If these scenarios sound horrific to you, there are lots of things you can do to prevent them from happening, and a variety of remedies available if they do occur. You'll want to take some time—before disaster strikes—to consider your options.

All Your Eggs in One Basket?

The debate about whether it's better to use one large memory card or several smaller ones has been going on since even before there were memory cards. I can remember when computer users wondered whether it was smarter to install a pair of 200MB (not *gigabyte*) hard drives in their computer, or if they should go for one of those new-fangled 500MB models. By the same token, a few years ago the user groups were full of proponents who insisted that you ought to use 128MB memory cards rather than the huge 512MB versions. Today, most of the arguments involve 16GB cards versus 32GB cards, and I expect that as prices for larger capacity cards continue to drop, they'll find their way into the debate as well.

Why all the fuss? Are 16GB memory cards more likely to fail than 8B cards? Are you risking all your photos if you trust your images to a larger card? Isn't it better to use several smaller cards, so that if one fails you lose only half as many photos? Or, isn't it wiser to put all your photos onto one larger card, because the more cards you use, the better your odds of misplacing or damaging one and losing at least some pictures?

In the end, the "eggs in one basket" argument boils down to statistics, and how you happen to use your V1. The rationales can go both ways. If you have multiple smaller cards, you do increase your chances of something happening to one of them, so, arguably, you might be boosting the odds of losing some pictures. If all your images are important, the fact that you've lost 100 rather than 200 pictures isn't very comforting.

After all, the myth assumes that a damaged card will always be full before it becomes corrupted. Fortunately, memory cards don't magically wait until they are full before they fail. In a typical shooting session, it doesn't matter whether you've shot 3.5GB worth of pictures on a 4GB card or 3.5GB worth of pictures on a 16GB card. If either card fails, you've lost the same number of images. Your risk increases *only* when you start shooting additional photos on the larger card. In the real world, most of us who use larger memory cards don't fill them up very often. We just like having the extra capacity there when we need it.

The myth also says that by using several smaller cards, you're spreading the risk around so that only some pictures will be lost in case of a failure. What is more important to you, your photographs or the members of your family? When going on vacation, do you insist on splitting your kin up and driving several smaller cars?

If you shoot photojournalist-type pictures, you probably change memory cards when they're less than completely full in order to avoid the need to do so at a crucial moment.

(When I shoot sports, my cards rarely reach 80 to 90 percent of capacity before I change them.) Using multiple smaller cards means you have to change them that more often, which can be a real pain when you're taking a lot of photos. As an example, if you use 1GB memory cards with a Nikon V1 and shoot RAW+JPEG FINE, you may get only a few dozen pictures on the card. That's not even twice the capacity of a 36-exposure roll of film (remember those?). In my book, I prefer keeping all my eggs in one basket, and then making very sure that nothing happens to that basket.

Preventive Measures

Here are some options for preventing loss of valuable images:

- **Interleaving.** One option is to *interleave* your shots. Say you don't shoot weddings, but you do go on vacation from time to time. Take 50 or so pictures on one card, or whatever number of images might fill about 25 percent of its capacity. Then, replace it with a different card and shoot about 25 percent of that card's available space. Repeat these steps with diligence (you'd have to be determined to go through this inconvenience), and, if you use four or more memory cards you'll find your pictures from each location scattered among the different memory cards. If you lose or damage one, you'll still have *some* pictures from all the various stops on your trip on the other cards. That's more work than I like to do (I usually tote around a portable hard disk and copy the files to the drive as I go), but it's an option.
- **Transmit your images.** Another option is to transmit your images, as they are shot, over a network to your laptop, assuming a network and a laptop are available. A company called Eye-Fi (www.eye.fi) markets a clever Secure Digital card with wireless capabilities built-in (covered more in Chapter 11), which can be used to transmit your photos from the V1 to a computer on your home network (or any other network you set up somewhere, say, at a family reunion). They include software to allow you to upload your images from your camera through your computer network directly to websites such as Flickr, Facebook, Shutterfly, Nikon's own My Picturetown, and digital printing services that include Walmart Digital Photo Center. Very cool, and the ultimate in picture backup.
- **External backup.** You can purchase external hard disk gadgets called Personal Storage Devices (see Figure 13.5), which can copy files from your memory cards automatically. More expensive models have color LCD screens so you can review your images. I tend to prefer using a netbook, like the one shown in Figure 13.6, or my MacBook Air. I can store images on the netbook or MacBook's internal hard disk, and make an extra backup copy to an external drive as well. Plus, I can access the Internet from Wi-Fi hotspots, all using a very compact device. Lately, I've been backing up many images on my iPad, which has 64GB of storage—enough for short trips.

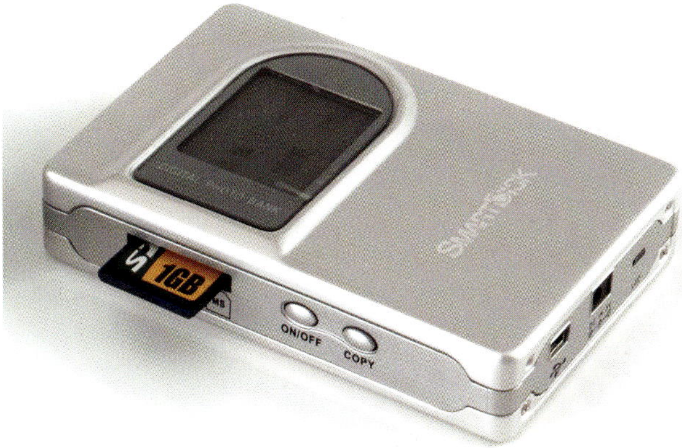

Figure 13.5
Small battery-operated personal storage devices can back up your images.

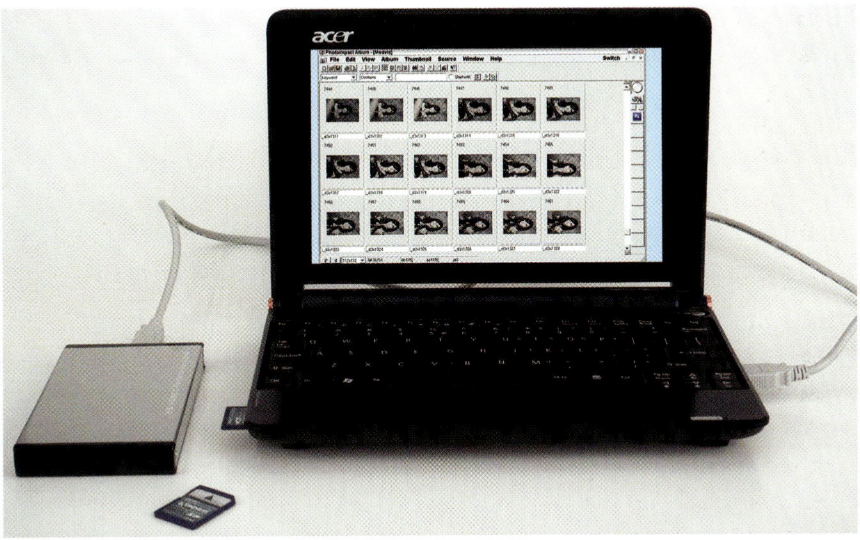

Figure 13.6
A small netbook, with or without an external hard drive, is another backup option.

What Can Go Wrong?

There are lots of things that can go wrong with your memory card, but the ones that aren't caused by human stupidity are statistically very rare. Yes, a memory card's internal bit bin or controller can suddenly fail due to a manufacturing error or some inexplicable event caused by old age. However, if your card works for the first week or two that you own it, it should work forever. There's really not a lot that can wear out.

The typical memory card is rated for a Mean Time Between Failures of 1,000,000 hours of use. That's constant use 24/7 for more than 100 years! According to the manufacturers, they are good for 10,000 insertions in your camera, and should be able to retain their data (and that's without an external power source) for something on the order of 11 years. Of course, with the millions of cards in use, there are bound to be a few lemons here or there.

Given the reliability of solid-state memory compared to magnetic memory, though, it's more likely that your problems will stem from something that you do. Secure Digital cards are small and easy to misplace if you're not careful. For that reason, it's a good idea to keep them in their original cases or a "card safe" offered by Gepe (www.gepe.com), Pelican (www.pelican.com), and others. Always placing your memory card in a case can provide protection from the second-most common mishap that befalls memory cards: the common household laundry. If you slip a card in a pocket, rather than a case or your camera bag often enough, sooner or later it's going to end up in the washing machine and probably the clothes dryer, too. There are plenty of reports of relieved digital camera owners who've laundered their memory cards and found they still worked fine, but it's not uncommon for such mistreatment to do some damage.

Memory cards can also be stomped on, accidentally bent, dropped into the ocean, chewed by pets, and otherwise rendered unusable in myriad ways. It's also possible to force a Secure Digital card into your V1's Secure Digital card slot incorrectly if you're diligent enough, doing little damage to the card itself, but possibly damaging the connectors in the camera, eliminating its ability to read or write to any memory card.

Or, if the card is formatted in your computer with a memory card reader, your V1 may fail to recognize it. Occasionally, I've found that a memory card used in one camera would fail if used in a different camera (until I reformatted it in Windows, and then again in the camera). Every once in awhile, a card goes completely bad and—seemingly—can't be salvaged.

Another way to lose images is to do commonplace things with your card at an inopportune time. If you remove the card from the V1 while the camera is writing images to the card, you'll lose any photos in the buffer and may damage the file structure of the card, making it difficult or impossible to retrieve the other pictures you've taken. The same thing can happen if you remove the memory card from your computer's card reader while the computer is writing to the card (say, to erase files you've already moved to your computer). You can avoid this by *not* using your computer to erase files on a memory card but, instead, always reformatting the card in your V1 before you use it again.

What Can You Do?

Pay attention: If you're having problems, the *first* thing you should do is *stop* using that memory card. Don't take any more pictures. Don't do anything with the card until you've figured out what's wrong. Your second line of defense (your first line is to be sufficiently careful with your cards that you avoid problems in the first place) is to *do no harm* that hasn't already been done. Read the rest of this section and then, if necessary, decide on a course of action (such as using a data recovery service or software described later) before you risk damaging the data on your card further.

Now that you've calmed down, the first thing to check is whether you've actually inserted a card in the camera. If you've set the camera so that shooting without a card has been turned on, it's entirely possible (although not particularly plausible) that you've been snapping away with no memory card to store the pictures to, which can lead to massive disappointment later on. Of course, the no card warning appears on the LCD when the camera is powered up, and the demo message is superimposed on the review image after every shot (assuming you've enabled the V1 to take photos when a card is not inserted), but maybe you're inattentive or aren't using picture review. You can avoid all this by locking the camera when no card is installed, as described in Chapter 8.

Things get more exciting when the card itself is put in jeopardy. If you lose a card, there's not a lot you can do other than take a picture of a similar card and print up some Have You Seen This Lost Flash Memory? flyers to post on utility poles all around town.

If all you care about is reusing the card, and have resigned yourself to losing the pictures, try reformatting the card in your camera. You may find that reformatting removes the corrupted data and restores your card to health. Sometimes I've had success reformatting a card in my computer using a memory card reader (this is normally a no-no because your operating system doesn't understand the needs of your V1), and *then* reformatting again in the camera.

If your memory card is not behaving properly, and you *do* want to recover your images, things get a little more complicated. If your pictures are very valuable, either to you or to others (for example, a wedding), you can always turn to professional data recovery firms. Be prepared to pay hundreds of dollars to get your pictures back, but these pros often do an amazing job. You wouldn't want them working on your memory card on behalf of the police if you'd tried to erase some incriminating pictures. There are many firms of this type, and I've never used them myself, so I can't offer a recommendation. Use a Google search to turn up a ton of them.

THE ULTIMATE IRONY

I recently purchased an 8GB Kingston memory card that was furnished with some nifty OnTrack data recovery software. The first thing I did was format the card to make sure it was okay. Then I hunted around for the free software, only to discover it was preloaded onto the memory card. I was supposed to copy the software to my computer before using the memory card for the first time.

Fortunately, I had the OnTrack software that would reverse my dumb move, so I could retrieve the software. No, wait. I *didn't* have the software I needed to recover the software I erased. I'd reformatted it to oblivion. Chalk this one up as either the ultimate irony or Stupid Photographer Trick #523.

A more reasonable approach is to try special data recovery software you can install on your computer and use to attempt to resurrect your "lost" images yourself. They may not actually be gone completely. Perhaps your card's "table of contents" is jumbled, or only a few pictures are damaged in such a way that your camera and computer can't read some or any of the pictures on the card. Some of the available software was written specifically to reconstruct lost pictures, while other utilities are more general purpose applications that can be used with any media, including floppy disks and hard disk drives. They have names like OnTrack, Photo Rescue 2, Digital Image Recovery, MediaRecover, Image Recall, and the aptly named Recover My Photos. You'll find a comprehensive list and links, as well as some picture recovery tips at www.ultimateslr.com/memory-card-recovery.php. I like the RescuePRO software that SanDisk supplies (see Figure 13.7), especially since it came on a mini-CD that I was totally unable to erase by mistake.

DIMINISHING RETURNS

Usually, once you've recovered any images on a memory card, reformatted it, and returned it to service, it will function reliably for the rest of its useful life. However, if you find a particular card going bad more than once, you'll almost certainly want to stop using it forever. See if you can get it replaced by the manufacturer if you can, but, in the case of Secure Digital card failures, the third time is never the charm.

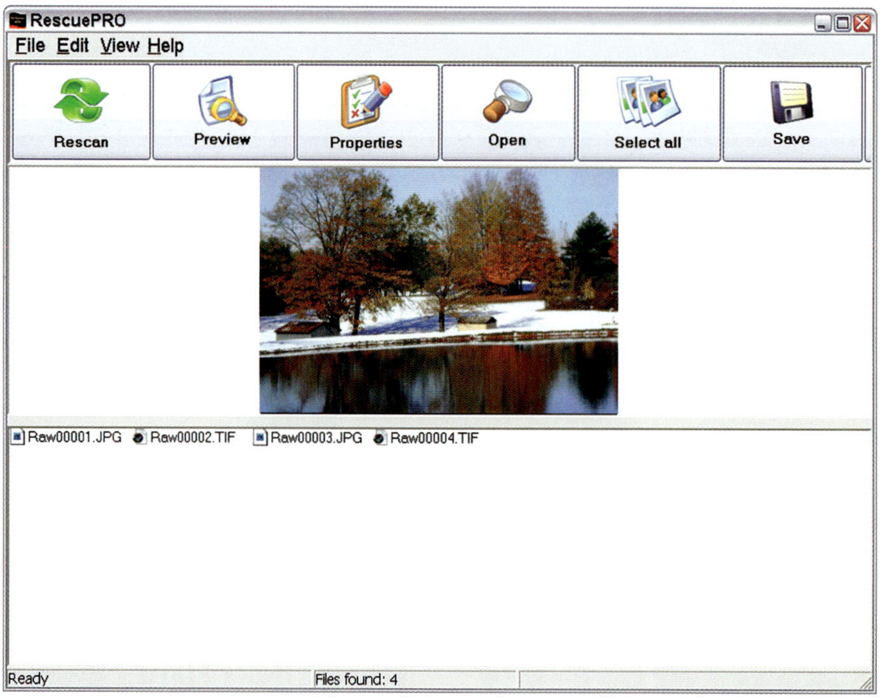

Figure 13.7
SanDisk supplies RescuePRO recovery software with some of its memory cards.

Cleaning Your Sensor

Yes, the Nikon V1 automatically cleans its exposed sensor each time you turn it on or off, using a sensor-shaking cleaning mechanism. But no dust-busting technology is 100-percent effective. Indeed, there's no avoiding dust. No matter how careful you are, some of it is going to settle on your camera and on the mounts of your lenses, eventually making its way inside your camera to settle in the inner chamber. The dust becomes airborne and eventually comes to rest on the anti-aliasing filter atop your sensor. There, dust and particles can show up in every single picture you take at a small enough aperture to bring the foreign matter into sharp focus. No matter how careful you are and how cleanly you work, eventually you will get some of this dust on your camera's sensor. Some say that CMOS sensors, like the one found in the Nikon V1, "attract" less dust than CCD sensors found in cameras from other vendors. But even the cleanest-working photographers using the Nikon V1 are far from immune.

Of course, even with the Nikon V1's automatic sensor cleaning/dust resistance features, you may still be required to manually clean your sensor from time to time. This section explains the phenomenon and provides some tips on minimizing dust and eliminating it when it begins to affect your shots.

Dust the FAQs, Ma'am

Here are some of the most frequently asked questions about sensor dust issues.

Q. I see a bright spot in the same place in all of my photos. Is that sensor dust?

A. You've probably got either a "hot" pixel or one that is permanently "stuck" due to a defect in the sensor. A hot pixel is one that shows up as a bright spot only during long exposures as the sensor warms. A pixel stuck in the "on" position always appears in the image. Both show up as bright red, green, or blue pixels, usually surrounded by a small cluster of other improperly illuminated pixels, caused by the camera's interpolating the hot or stuck pixel into its surroundings, as shown in Figure 13.8. A stuck pixel can also be permanently dark. Either kind is likely to show up when they contrast with plain, evenly colored areas of your image.

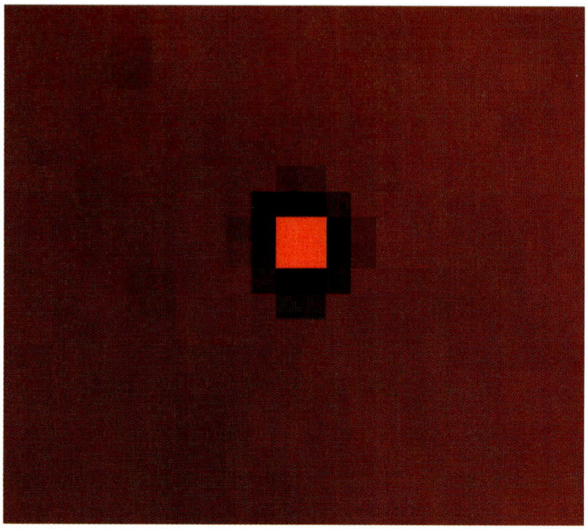

Figure 13.8
A stuck pixel is surrounded by improperly interpolated pixels created by the V1's demosaicing algorithm.

Finding one or two hot or stuck pixels in your sensor is unfortunately fairly common. They can be "removed" by telling the V1 to ignore them through a simple process called *pixel mapping*. If the bad pixels become bothersome, Nikon can remap your sensor's pixels with a quick trip to a service center.

Bad pixels can also show up on your camera's color LCD panel, but, unless they are abundant, the wisest course is to just ignore them.

Q. I see an irregular out-of-focus blob in the same place in my photos. Is that sensor dust?

A. Yes. Sensor contaminants can take the form of tiny spots, larger blobs, or even curvy lines if they are caused by minuscule fibers that have settled on the sensor. They'll appear out of focus because they aren't actually on the sensor surface but, rather, a fraction of a millimeter above it on the filter that covers the sensor. The smaller the f/stop used, the more in-focus the dust becomes. At large apertures, it may not be visible at all.

Q. I never see any dust on my sensor. What's all the fuss about?

A. Those who never have dust problems with their Nikon V1 fall into one of four categories: those for whom the camera's automatic dust removal features are working well; those who seldom change their lenses and have clean working habits that minimize the amount of dust that invades their cameras in the first place; those who simply don't notice the dust (often because they don't shoot many macro photos or other pictures using the small f/stops that makes dust evident in their images); and those who are very, very lucky.

Identifying and Dealing with Dust

Sensor dust is less of a problem than it might be because it shows up only under certain circumstances. Indeed, you might have dust on your sensor right now and not be aware of it. The dust doesn't actually settle on the sensor itself, but, rather, on a protective filter a very tiny distance above the sensor, subjecting it to the phenomenon of *depth-of-focus*. Depth-of-focus is the distance the focal plane can be moved and still render an object in sharp focus. At f/2.8 to f/5.6 or even smaller, sensor dust, particularly if small, is likely to be outside the range of depth-of-focus and blur into an unnoticeable dot.

However, if you're shooting at f/11 to f/16, those dust motes suddenly pop into focus. Forget about trying to spot them by peering directly at your sensor with the shutter open and the lens removed. Dust spots that are even smaller than that can easily show up in your images if you're shooting large, empty areas that are light colored. Dust motes are most likely to show up in the sky, as in Figure 13.9, or in white backgrounds of your seamless product shots and are less likely to be a problem in images that contain lots of dark areas and detail.

To see if you have dust on your sensor, take a few test shots of a plain, blank surface (such as a piece of paper or a cloudless sky) at small f/stops, such as f/16, and a few wide open. Open Photoshop or another image editor, copy several shots into a single document in separate layers, then flip back and forth between layers to see if any spots you see are present in all layers. You may have to boost contrast and sharpness to make the dust easier to spot.

Figure 13.9
Only the dust spots in the sky are apparent in this shot.

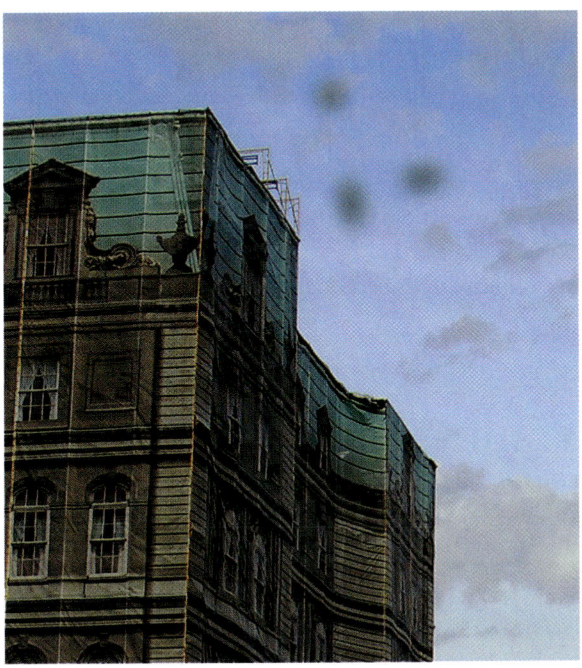

Avoiding Dust

Of course, the easiest way to protect your sensor from dust is to prevent it from settling on the sensor in the first place. Here are my stock tips for eliminating the problem before it begins.

- **Clean environment.** Avoid working in dusty areas if you can do so. Hah! Serious photographers will take this one with a grain of salt, because it usually makes sense to go where the pictures are. Only a few of us are so paranoid about sensor dust (considering that it is so easily removed) that we'll avoid moderately grimy locations just to protect something that is, when you get down to it, just a tool. If you find a great picture opportunity at a raging fire, during a sandstorm, or while surrounded by dust clouds, you might hesitate to take the picture, but, with a little caution (don't remove your lens in these situations, and clean the camera afterwards!) you can still shoot. However, it still makes sense to store your camera in a clean environment. One place cameras and lenses pick up a lot of dust is inside a camera bag. Clean your bag from time to time, and you can avoid problems.
- **Clean lenses.** There are a few paranoid types that avoid swapping lenses in order to minimize the chance of dust getting inside their cameras. It makes more sense just to use a blower or brush to dust off the rear lens mount of the replacement lens first, so you won't be introducing dust into your camera simply by attaching a new, dusty lens. Do this before you remove the current lens from your camera, and then avoid stirring up dust before making the exchange.
- **Work fast.** Minimize the time your camera is lens-less and exposed to dust. That means having your replacement lens ready and dusted off, and a place to set down the old lens as soon as it is removed, so you can quickly attach the new lens.
- **Let gravity help you.** Face the camera downward when the lens is detached so any dust in the mirror box will tend to fall away from the sensor. Turn your back to any breezes, indoor forced air vents, fans, or other sources of dust to minimize infiltration.
- **Protect the lens you just removed.** Once you've attached the new lens, quickly put the end cap on the one you just removed to reduce the dust that might fall on it.
- **Clean out the vestibule.** From time to time, remove the lens while in a relatively dust-free environment and use a blower bulb like the one shown in Figure 13.10 (*not* compressed air or a vacuum hose) to clean out the inner area. A blower bulb is generally safer than a can of compressed air, or a strong positive/negative airflow, which can tend to drive dust further into nooks and crannies.
- **Be prepared.** If you're embarking on an important shooting session, it's a good idea to clean your sensor *now*, rather than come home with hundreds or thousands of images with dust spots caused by flecks that were sitting on your sensor before you even started.

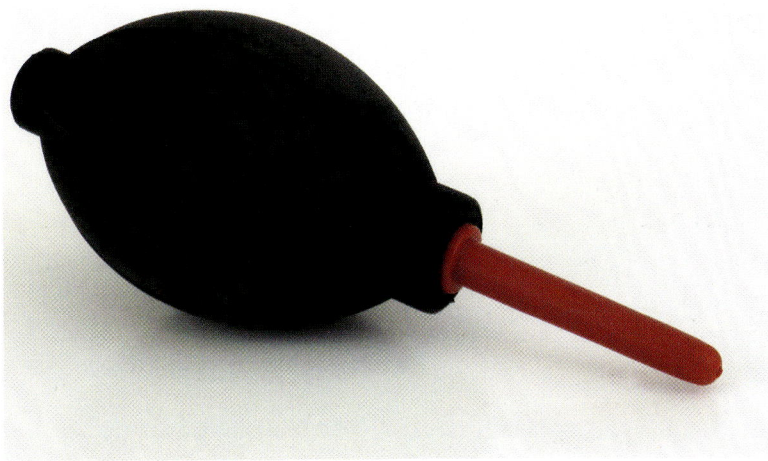

Figure 13.10
Use a robust air bulb for cleaning your sensor.

- **Clone out existing spots in your image editor.** Photoshop and other editors have a clone tool or healing brush you can use to copy pixels from surrounding areas over the dust spot or dead pixel. This process can be tedious, especially if you have lots of dust spots and/or lots of images to be corrected. The advantage is that this sort of manual fix-it probably will do the least damage to the rest of your photo. Only the damaged pixels will be affected.
- **Use filtration in your image editor.** A semi-smart filter like Photoshop's Dust & Scratches filter can remove dust and other artifacts by selectively blurring areas that the plug-in decides represent dust spots. This method can work well if you have many dust spots, because you won't need to patch them manually. However, any automated method like this has the possibility of blurring areas of your image that you didn't intend to soften.

Sensor Cleaning

Those new to the concept of sensor dust actually hesitate before deciding to clean their camera themselves. Isn't it a better idea to pack up your V1 and send it to a Nikon service center so their crack technical staff can do the job for you? Or, at the very least, shouldn't you let the friendly folks at your local camera store do it?

Of course, if you choose to let someone else clean your sensor, they will be using methods that are more or less identical to the techniques you would use yourself. None of these techniques are difficult, and the only difference between their cleaning and your cleaning is that they might have done it dozens or hundreds of times. If you're careful, you can do just as good a job.

Of course vendors like Nikon won't tell you this, but it's not because they don't trust you. It's not that difficult for a real goofball to mess up a camera by hurrying or taking a shortcut. Perhaps someone tries to clean the sensor using masking tape, and ends up with goo all over its surface. If Nikon recommended *any* method that's mildly risky, someone would do it wrong, and then the company would face lawsuits from those who'd contend they did it exactly in the way the vendor suggested, so the ruined camera is not their fault.

You can see that vendors like Nikon tend to be conservative in their recommendations, and, in doing so, make it seem as if sensor cleaning is more daunting and dangerous than it really is. Some vendors recommend only dust-off cleaning, through the use of reasonably gentle blasts of air, while condemning more serious scrubbing with swabs and cleaning fluids. However, these cleaning kits for the exact types of cleaning they recommended against are for sale in Japan only, where, apparently, your average photographer is more dexterous than those of us in the rest of the world. These kits are similar to those used by official repair staff to clean your sensor if you decide to send your camera in for a dust-up.

As I noted, sensors can be affected by dust particles that are much smaller than you might be able to spot visually on the surface of your lens. The filters that cover sensors tend to be fairly hard compared to optical glass. Cleaning the tiny CX sensor in your Nikon V1 within the tight confines of the inner chamber can call for a steady hand and careful touch. If your sensor's filter becomes scratched through inept cleaning, you can't simply remove it yourself and replace it with a new one.

There are four basic kinds of cleaning processes that can be used to remove dusty and sticky stuff that settles on your mirrorless camera's sensor. I'll describe these methods next.

- **Air cleaning.** This process involves squirting blasts of air inside your camera. This works well for dust that's not clinging stubbornly to your sensor.
- **Brushing.** A soft, very fine brush is passed across the surface of the sensor's filter, dislodging mildly persistent dust particles and sweeping them off the imager.
- **Liquid cleaning.** A soft swab dipped in a cleaning solution such as ethanol is used to wipe the sensor filter, removing more obstinate particles.
- **Tape cleaning.** There are some who get good results by applying a special form of tape to the surface of their sensor. When the tape is peeled off, all the dust goes with it. Supposedly. I'd be remiss if I didn't point out right now that this form of cleaning is somewhat controversial; the other three methods are much more widely accepted.

Air Cleaning

Your first attempts at cleaning your sensor should always involve gentle blasts of air. Many times, you'll be able to dislodge dust spots, which will fall off the sensor and, with luck, out of the camera. Attempt one of the other methods only when you've already tried air cleaning and it didn't remove all the dust.

Here are some tips for doing air cleaning:

- **Use a clean, powerful air bulb.** Your best bet is bulb cleaners designed for the job, like the Giottos Rocket. Smaller bulbs, like those air bulbs with a brush attached sometimes sold for lens cleaning or weak nasal aspirators may not provide sufficient air or a strong enough blast to do much good.
- **Hold the camera upside down.** Then look up into the camera as you squirt your air blasts, increasing the odds that gravity will help pull the expelled dust downward, away from the sensor. You may have to use some imagination in positioning yourself. (See Figure 13.11, which illustrates how I clean my Nikon V1.)
- **Never use air canisters.** The propellant inside these cans can permanently coat your sensor if you tilt the can while spraying. It's not worth taking a chance.
- **Avoid air compressors.** Super strong blasts of air are likely to force dust under the sensor filter.

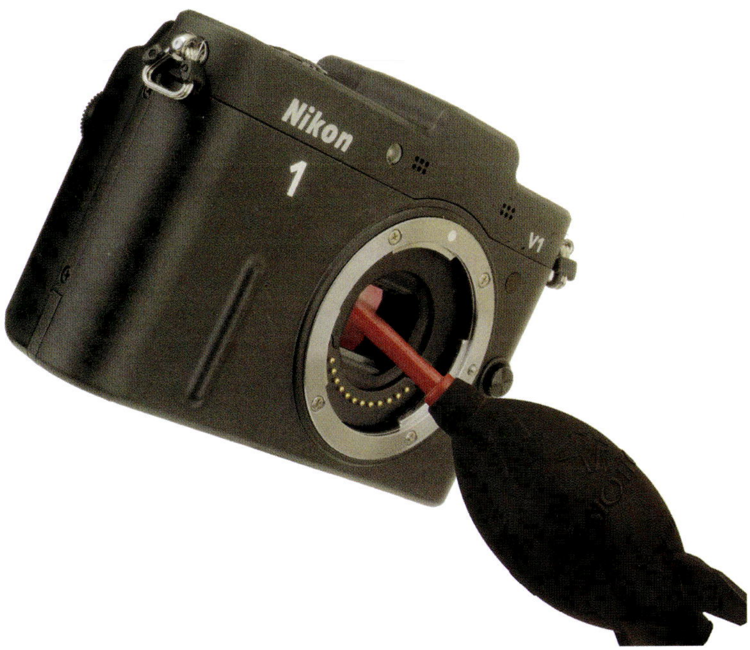

Figure 13.11
Hold the camera upside down and blow the dust off the sensor.

Brush Cleaning

If your dust is a little more stubborn and can't be dislodged by air alone, you may want to try a brush, charged with static electricity, which can pick off dust spots by electrical attraction. You'll need a small one, suited for the tiny CX sensor, and not the common 16mm brushes designed for DX-format cameras. A brush with a grounding strap is shown in Figure 13.12. It can be stroked across the short dimension of your V1's sensor.

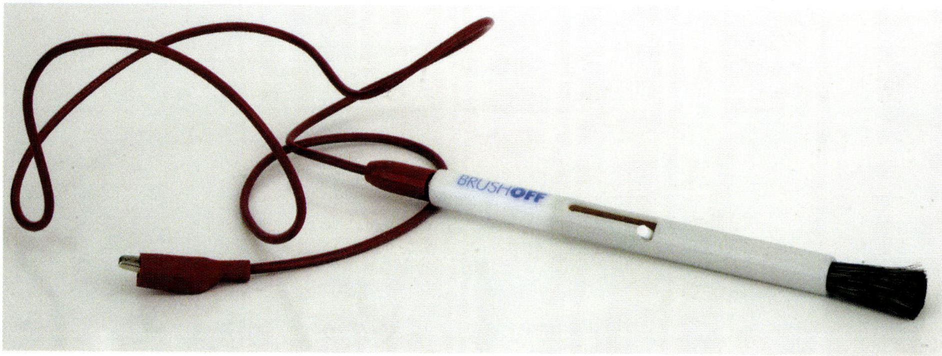

Figure 13.12
A proper brush is required for dusting off your sensor.

Ordinary artist's brushes are much too coarse and stiff and have fibers that are tangled or can come loose and settle on your sensor. A good sensor brush's fibers are resilient and described as "thinner than a human hair." Moreover, the brush has a wooden handle that reduces the risk of static sparks.

Brush cleaning is done with a dry brush by gently swiping the surface of the sensor filter with the tip. The dust particles are attracted to the brush particles and cling to them. You should clean the brush with compressed air before and after each use, and store it in an appropriate air-tight container between applications to keep it clean and dust-free. Although these special brushes are expensive, one should last you a long time.

Liquid Cleaning

Unfortunately, you'll often encounter really stubborn dust spots that can't be removed with a blast of air or flick of a brush. These spots may be combined with some grease or a liquid that causes them to stick to the sensor filter's surface. In such cases, liquid cleaning with a swab may be necessary. During my first clumsy attempts to clean my own sensor, I accidentally got my blower bulb tip too close to the sensor, and some sort of deposit from the tip of the bulb ended up on the sensor. I panicked until I discovered that liquid cleaning did a good job of removing whatever it was that took up residence on my sensor.

You want a sturdy swab that won't bend or break so you can apply gentle pressure to the swab as you wipe the sensor surface. Use the swab with methanol (as pure as you can get it, particularly medical grade; other ingredients can leave a residue), or the Eclipse solution also sold by Photographic Solutions. Eclipse is actually quite a bit purer than even medical-grade methanol. A couple drops of solution should be enough, unless you have a spot that's extremely difficult to remove. In that case, you may need to use extra solution on the swab to help "soak" the dirt off.

You can make your own swabs out of pieces of plastic (some use fast food restaurant knives, with the tip cut at an angle to the proper size to fit the short dimension of the CX sensor) covered with a soft cloth or Pec-Pad, as shown in Figure 13.13. However, if you've got the bucks to spend, you can't go wrong with good quality commercial sensor

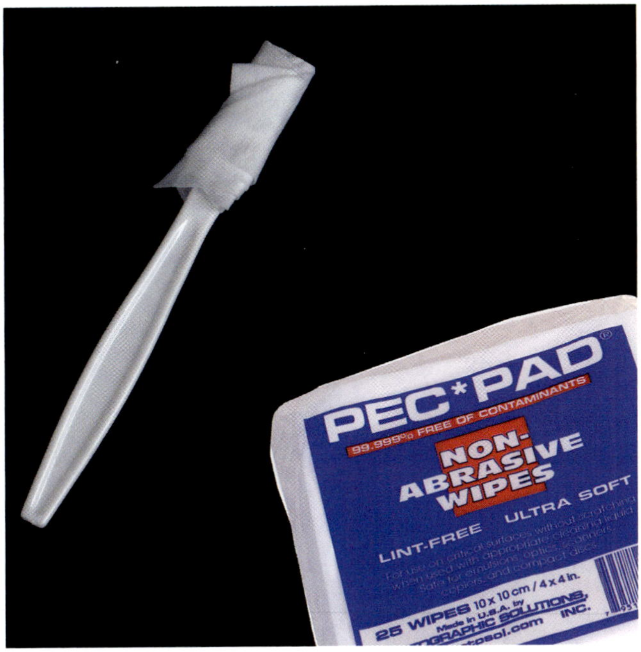

Figure 13.13
Carefully wrap a Pec-Pad around a plastic tool you've trimmed to fit.

cleaning swabs, such as those sold by Photographic Solutions, Inc. (www.photosol.com/swabproduct.htm).

Once you overcome your nervousness at touching your V1's sensor, the process is easy. You'll wipe continuously with the swab in one direction, then flip it over and wipe in the other direction. You need to completely wipe the entire surface; otherwise, you may end up depositing the dust you collect at the far end of your stroke. Wipe; don't rub.

Tape Cleaning

There are people who absolutely swear by the tape method of sensor cleaning. The concept seems totally wacky, and I have never tried it personally, so I can't say with certainty that it either does or does not work. In the interest of completeness, I'm including it here. I can't give you a recommendation, so if you have problems, please don't blame me. The Nikon V1 is still too new to have generated any reports of users accidentally damaging the anti-dust coating on the sensor filter using this method.

Tape cleaning works by applying a layer of Scotch Brand Magic Tape to the sensor. This is a minimally sticky tape that some of the tape cleaning proponents claim contains no adhesive. I did check this out with 3M, and can say that Magic Tape certainly *does* contain an adhesive. The question is whether the adhesive comes off when you peel back the tape, taking any dust spots on your sensor with it. The folks who love this method claim there is no residue. There have been reports from those who don't like the method that residue is left behind. This is all anecdotal evidence, so you're pretty much on your own in making the decision whether to try out the tape cleaning method.

Magnifier Assisted Cleaning

Using a magnifier to view your sensor as you clean it is a good idea. I rely on two types. I have four Carson MiniBrite PO-55 magnifiers (see Figure 13.14), and keep one in each camera bag. So, no matter where I am shooting, I have one of these $8.95 gadgets with me. You can read more about this great tool at my blog (http://www.dslrguides.com/carson/). When I'm not traveling, I use a SensorKlear loupe. It's a magnifier with a built-in LED illuminator. There's an opening on one side that allows you to insert a SensorKlear cleaning wand, a lens pen-like stylus with a surface treated to capture dust particles. (See Figure 13.15.) Both the SensorKlear loupe and the SensorKlear wand are available from www.lenspen.com.

When I'm using the MiniBrite, I locate the dust on the sensor with the magnifier, remembering that the position of the dust will be reversed from what I might have seen on an image on the camera's LCD (because the camera lens flips the image when making the exposure). Then, I use the SensorKlear wand or the blower brush to remove the artifact.

The SensorKlear loupe actually allows you to keep your eye on the prize as you do the cleaning. You can peer through the viewer, rotate the opening to the side opposite the position of the dust, then insert the hinged wand to tap the dust while you're watching. This method allows removing a bunch of dust particles quickly, so it's my preferred procedure when I have the loupe with me.

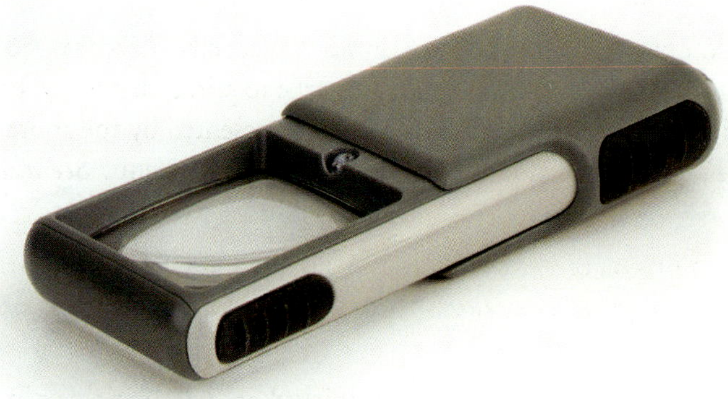

Figure 13.14 The Carson MiniBrite PO-55 is a good value sensor magnifier.

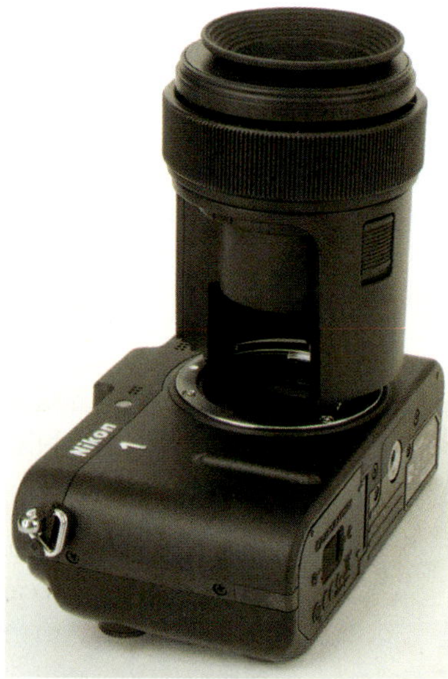

Figure 13.15 The SensorKlear Loupe and wand allow quickly removing multiple dust particles.

Glossary

Here are some terms you might encounter while reading this book or working with your Nikon V1.

additive primary colors The red, green, and blue hues that are used alone or in combinations to create all other colors that you capture with a digital camera, view on a computer monitor, or work with in an image-editing program, such as Photoshop.

ambient lighting Diffuse, non-directional lighting that doesn't appear to come from a specific source but, rather, bounces off walls, ceilings, and other objects in the scene when a picture is taken.

analog/digital converter The EXPEED 3 electronics built into the Nikon V1 that convert the analog information captured by the camera's sensor into digital bits that can be stored as an image bitmap.

angle of view The area of a scene that a lens can capture, determined by the focal length of the lens. Lenses with a shorter focal length have a wider angle of view than lenses with a longer focal length.

anti-alias A process that smoothes the look of rough edges in images (called *jaggies* or *staircasing*) by adding partially transparent pixels along the boundaries of diagonal lines that are merged into a smoother line by our eyes. *See also* jaggies.

Aperture-priority A camera setting, called A, that allows you to specify the lens opening or f/stop that you want to use, with the camera selecting the required shutter speed automatically based on its light meter reading. This setting is represented by the abbreviation A in the Nikon V1's Exposure mode entry in the Shooting menu. *See also* Shutter-priority.

artifact A type of noise in an image, or an unintentional image component produced in error by a digital camera during processing, usually caused by the JPEG compression process in digital cameras.

aspect ratio The proportions of an image as printed, displayed on a monitor, or captured by a digital camera.

autofocus A camera setting that allows the Nikon V1 to choose the correct focus distance for you, based on the contrast of an image (the image will be at maximum contrast when in sharp focus).

backlighting A lighting effect produced when the main light source is located behind the subject. Backlighting can be used to create a silhouette effect, or to illuminate translucent objects. *See also* front lighting and side lighting.

barrel distortion A lens defect that causes straight lines at the top or side edges of an image to bow outward into a barrel shape. *See also* pincushion distortion.

blooming An image distortion caused when a photosite in an image sensor has absorbed all the photons it can handle so that additional photons reaching that pixel overflow to affect surrounding pixels, producing unwanted brightness and overexposure around the edges of objects.

blur To soften an image or part of an image by throwing it out of focus, or by allowing it to become soft due to subject or camera motion. Blur can also be applied in an image-editing program.

bokeh A term derived from the Japanese word for blur, which describes the aesthetic qualities of the out-of-focus parts of an image. Some lenses produce "good" bokeh and others offer "bad" bokeh. Some lenses produce uniformly illuminated out-of-focus discs. Others produce a disc that has a bright edge and a dark center, producing a "doughnut" effect, which is the worst from a bokeh standpoint. Lenses that generate a bright center that fades to a darker edge are favored, because their bokeh allows the circle of confusion to blend more smoothly with the surroundings. The bokeh characteristics of a lens are most important when you're using selective focus (say, when shooting a portrait) to de-emphasize the background, or when shallow depth-of-field is a given because you're working with a macro lens, a long telephoto, or a wide-open aperture. *See also* circle of confusion.

bounce lighting Light bounced off a reflector, including ceiling and walls, to provide a soft, natural-looking light.

bracketing Taking a series of photographs of the same subject at different settings, including exposure and white balance, to help ensure that one setting will be the correct one.

buffer The digital camera's internal memory where an image is stored immediately after it is taken until it can be written to the camera's non-volatile (semi-permanent) memory or a memory card.

bulb The shutter remains open while the shutter release button is held down. This setting is available when the camera is set to Manual mode and the ML-L3 remote control is used.

burst mode Known as continuous shooting mode, burst shooting is the digital camera's equivalent of the film camera's motor drive, used to take multiple shots within a short period of time, with each image stored in a memory buffer temporarily before writing it to the media.

calibration A process used to correct for the differences in the output of a printer or monitor when compared to the original image. Once you've calibrated your scanner, monitor, and/or your image editor, the images you see on the screen more closely represent what you'll get from your printer, even though calibration is never perfect.

Camera Raw A plug-in included with Photoshop and Photoshop Elements that can manipulate the unprocessed images captured by digital cameras. The latest versions of this module can also work with JPEG and TIFF images.

camera shake Movement of the camera, aggravated by slower shutter speeds, which produces a blurred image. You can minimize camera shake by using the V1's image stabilization feature.

Center-weighted metering A light measuring mode that emphasizes the area in the middle of the frame when calculating the correct exposure for an image. *See also* Matrix metering and Spot metering.

chromatic aberration An image defect, often seen as green or purple fringing around the edges of an object, caused by a lens failing to focus all colors of a light source at the same point. *See also* fringing.

circle of confusion A term applied to the fuzzy discs produced when a point of light is out of focus. The circle of confusion is not a fixed size. The viewing distance and amount of enlargement of the image determine whether we see a particular spot on the image as a point or as a disc. *See also* bokeh.

close-up lens A lens add-on accessory that allows you to take pictures at a distance that is less than the closest-focusing distance of the lens alone.

color correction Changing the relative amounts of color in an image to produce a desired effect, typically a more accurate representation of those colors. Color correction can fix faulty color balance in the original image, or compensate for the deficiencies of the inks used to reproduce the image.

compression Reducing the size of a file by encoding using fewer bits of information to represent the original. Some compression schemes, such as JPEG, operate by discarding some image information, while others, such as RAW, preserve all the detail in the original, discarding only redundant data.

contrast The range between the lightest and darkest tones in an image. A high-contrast image is one in which the shades fall at the extremes of the range between white and black. In a low-contrast image, the tones are closer together.

dedicated flash An external electronic flash unit, such as the Nikon SB-N5, designed to work with the automatic exposure features of a specific camera.

depth-of-field A distance range in a photograph in which all included portions of an image are at least acceptably sharp.

diaphragm An adjustable component, similar to the iris in the human eye, that can open and close to provide specific-sized lens openings, or f/stops, and thus control the amount of light reaching the sensor or film.

diffuse lighting Soft, low-contrast lighting.

digital processing chip A solid-state device found in digital cameras, such as the EXPEED 3 chip in the Nikon V1, that's in charge of applying the image algorithms to the raw picture data prior to storage on the memory card.

diopter A value used to represent the magnification power of a lens, calculated as the reciprocal of a lens's focal length (in meters). Diopters are most often used to represent the optical correction used in a viewfinder to adjust for limitations of the photographer's eyesight, and to describe the magnification of a close-up lens attachment.

exchangeable image file format (Exif) Developed to standardize the exchange of image data between hardware devices and software. A variation on JPEG, Exif is used by most digital cameras, and includes information such as the date and time a photo was taken, the camera settings, resolution, amount of compression, and other data.

Exif *See* exchangeable image file format (Exif).

exposure The amount of light allowed to reach the film or sensor, determined by the intensity of the light, the amount admitted by the iris of the lens, the length of time determined by the shutter speed, and the ISO sensitivity setting for the sensor.

exposure values (EV) EV settings are a way of adding or decreasing exposure without the need to reference f/stops or shutter speeds. For example, if you tell your camera to add +1EV, it will provide twice as much exposure by using a larger f/stop, slower shutter speed, or both.

fill lighting In photography, lighting is used to illuminate shadows. Reflectors or additional incandescent lighting or electronic flash can be used to brighten shadows. One common technique for outdoors is to use the camera's flash as a fill.

filter In photography, a device that fits over the lens, changing the light in some way. In image editing, a feature that changes the pixels in an image to produce blurring, sharpening, and other special effects. Photoshop includes several interesting filter effects, including Lens Blur and Photo Filters.

focal length The distance between the film and the optical center of the lens when the lens is focused on infinity, usually measured in millimeters.

format To erase a memory card and prepare it to accept files.

fringing A chromatic aberration that produces fringes of color around the edges of subjects, caused by a lens's inability to focus the various wavelengths of light onto the same spot. Purple fringing is especially troublesome with backlit images.

front lighting Illumination that comes from the direction of the camera. *See also* backlighting and side lighting.

f/stop The relative size of the lens aperture, which helps determine both exposure and depth-of-field. The larger the f/stop number, the smaller the f/stop itself.

gray card A piece of cardboard or other material with a standardized 18-percent reflectance. Gray cards can be used as a reference for determining correct exposure or for setting white balance.

HDMI (High Definition Multimedia Interface) An interface for transmitting audio and video information between a source, such as a digital camera or television tuner, to an output device, such as a high definition television (HDTV) monitor.

high contrast A wide range of density in a print, negative, or other image.

highlights The brightest parts of an image containing detail.

histogram A kind of chart showing the relationship of tones in an image using a series of 256 vertical bars, one for each brightness level. A histogram chart, such as the one the Nikon V1 can display, typically looks like a curve with one or more slopes and peaks, depending on how many highlight, midtone, and shadow tones are present in the image.

hyperfocal distance A point of focus where everything from half that distance to infinity appears to be acceptably sharp. For example, if your lens has a hyperfocal distance of four feet, everything from two feet to infinity would be sharp. The hyperfocal distance varies by the lens and the aperture in use. If you know you'll be making a grab shot without warning, sometimes it is useful to turn off your camera's automatic focus, and set the lens to infinity, or, better yet, the hyperfocal distance. Then, you can snap off a quick picture without having to wait for the lag that occurs with most digital cameras as their autofocus locks in.

image rotation A feature that senses whether a picture was taken in horizontal or vertical orientation. That information is embedded in the picture file so that the camera and compatible software applications can automatically display the image in the correct orientation.

image stabilization A technology that compensates for camera shake, usually by adjusting the position of the camera sensor (with some vendors) or, in the case of the Nikon V1 cameras, lens elements that shift in response to movements of the camera.

incident light Light measured as it falls on a surface, as opposed to light reflected from that surface.

International Organization for Standardization (ISO) A governing body that provides standards used to represent film speed, or the equivalent sensitivity of a digital camera's sensor. Digital camera sensitivity is expressed in ISO settings.

interpolation A technique digital cameras, scanners, and image editors use to create new pixels required whenever you resize or change the resolution of an image based on the values of surrounding pixels. Devices such as scanners and digital cameras can use interpolation to create pixels in addition to those actually captured, thereby increasing the apparent resolution or color information in an image.

ISO *See* International Organization for Standardization (ISO).

jaggies Staircasing effect of lines, most easily seen at large magnifications, that are not perfectly horizontal or vertical, caused by pixels that are too large to represent the line accurately. *See also* anti-alias.

JPEG Short for Joint Photographic Experts Group. A file "lossy" format that supports 24-bit color and reduces file sizes by selectively discarding image data. Digital cameras generally use JPEG compression to pack more images onto memory cards. You can select how much compression is used (and, therefore, how much information is thrown away) by selecting from among the Standard, Fine, Super Fine, or other quality settings offered by your camera. *See also* RAW.

Kelvin (K) A unit of measure based on the absolute temperature scale in which absolute zero is zero; it's used to describe the color of continuous-spectrum light sources and applied when setting white balance. For example, daylight has a color temperature of about 5,500K, and a tungsten lamp has a temperature of about 3,400K.

lag time The interval between when the shutter is pressed and when the picture is actually taken. During that span, the camera may be automatically focusing and calculating exposure. With digital cameras like the Nikon V1, lag time is generally very short.

latitude The range of camera exposure that produces acceptable images with a particular digital sensor or film.

lens flare A feature of conventional photography that is both a bane and a creative outlet. It is an effect produced by the reflection of light internally among elements of an optical lens. Bright light sources within or just outside the field of view cause lens flare. Flare can be reduced by the use of coatings on the lens elements or with the use of lens hoods. Photographers sometimes use the effect as a creative technique, and Photoshop includes a filter that lets you add lens flare at your whim.

lighting ratio The proportional relationship between the amount of light falling on the subject from the main light and other lights, expressed in a ratio, such as 3:1.

lossy compression An image-compression scheme, such as JPEG, that creates smaller files by discarding image information, which can affect image quality.

Matrix metering One system of exposure calculation used by the Nikon V1 that looks at many different segments of an image to determine the brightest and darkest portions. *See also* Center-weighted metering and Spot metering.

maximum burst The number of frames that can be exposed at the current settings until the buffer fills.

midtones Parts of an image with tones of an intermediate value, usually in the 25 to 75 percent brightness range. Many image-editing features allow you to manipulate midtones independently from the highlights and shadows.

neutral color A color in which red, green, and blue are present in equal amounts, producing a gray.

neutral-density filter A gray camera filter that reduces the amount of light entering the camera without affecting the colors.

noise In an image, pixels with randomly distributed color values. Noise in digital photographs tends to be the product of low-light conditions and long exposures, particularly when you've set your camera to an ISO rating higher than about ISO 800.

noise reduction A technology used to cut down on the amount of random information in a digital picture, usually caused by long exposures at increased sensitivity ratings. In the Nikon V1, noise reduction is automatically applied for long exposures. Noise reduction can be switched off if you'd rather not use it.

overexposure A condition in which too much light reaches the film or sensor, producing a dense negative or a very bright/light print, slide, or digital image.

pincushion distortion A type of lens distortion in which lines at the top and side edges of an image are bent inward, producing an effect that looks like a pincushion. *See also* barrel distortion.

RAW An image file format, such as the NEF format in the Nikon V1, which includes all the unprocessed information captured by the camera after conversion to digital form. RAW files are very large compared to JPEG files and must be processed by a special program such as Nikon ViewNX or Adobe's Camera Raw filter after being downloaded from the camera.

saturation The purity of color; the amount by which a pure color is diluted with white or gray.

selective focus Choosing a lens opening that produces a shallow depth-of-field. Usually this is used to isolate a subject in portraits, close-ups, and other types of images, by causing most other elements in the scene to be blurred.

self-timer A mechanism that delays the opening of the shutter for some seconds after the release has been operated.

sensitivity A measure of the degree of response of a film or sensor to light, measured using the ISO setting.

shadow The darkest part of an image, represented on a digital image by pixels with low numeric values.

sharpening Increasing the apparent sharpness of an image by boosting the contrast between adjacent pixels that form an edge, whether done in the camera or in image-editing software.

shutter In a conventional film camera, the shutter is a mechanism consisting of blades, a curtain, a plate, or some other movable cover that controls the time during which light reaches the film. The Nikon V1 has both a mechanical shutter, and an electronic shutter for faster shutter speeds.

Shutter-priority An exposure mode, represented by the letter S in the Exposure entry in the Nikon 1's Shooting menu, in which you set the shutter speed and the camera determines the appropriate f/stop. *See also* Aperture-priority.

side lighting Applying illumination from the left or right sides of the camera. *See also* backlighting and front lighting.

slave unit An accessory flash unit that supplements the main flash, usually triggered electronically when the slave senses the light output by the main unit, through radio waves, or through a pre-burst emitted by the camera's main flash unit.

slow sync An electronic flash synchronizing method that uses a slow shutter speed so that ambient light is recorded by the camera in addition to the electronic flash illumination. This allows the background to receive more exposure for a more realistic effect.

specular highlight Bright spots in an image caused by reflection of light sources, often from shiny surfaces.

Spot metering An exposure measuring method that concentrates on a small area in the image. *See also* Center-weighted metering and Matrix metering.

time exposure A picture taken by leaving the shutter open for a long period, usually more than one second. The camera is generally locked down with a tripod to prevent blur during the long exposure.

tungsten light Light from ordinary room lamps and ceiling fixtures, as opposed to fluorescent illumination.

underexposure A condition in which too little light reaches the film or sensor, producing a thin negative, a dark slide, a muddy looking print, or a dark digital image.

white balance The adjustment of a digital camera to the color temperature of the light source. Interior illumination is relatively red; outdoor light is relatively blue. Digital cameras like the Nikon V1 set correct white balance automatically or let you do it through menus. Image editors can often do some color correction of images that were exposed using the wrong white balance setting, especially when working with RAW files that contain the information originally captured by the camera before white balance was applied.

Index

F

G

H

J

K

L

M

N

O

P

Q

R

S